MW01406947

The Sixteenth Century
in 100 Women

The Sixteenth Century in 100 Women

Amy Licence

PEN & SWORD HISTORY

First published in Great Britain in 2023 by
Pen & Sword History
An imprint of
Pen & Sword Books Ltd
Yorkshire – Philadelphia

Copyright © Amy Licence 2023

ISBN 978 1 39908 382 9

The right of Amy Licence to be identified as Author of this work has been asserted by her in accordance with the Copyright, Designs and Patents Act 1988.

A CIP catalogue record for this book is available from the British Library.

All rights reserved. No part of this book may be reproduced or transmitted in any form or by any means, electronic or mechanical including photocopying, recording or by any information storage and retrieval system, without permission from the Publisher in writing.

Typeset by Mac Style
Printed and bound in the UK by CPI Group (UK) Ltd,
Croydon, CR0 4YY.

MIX
Paper | Supporting responsible forestry
FSC
www.fsc.org FSC® C013604

Pen & Sword Books Limited incorporates the imprints of Atlas, Archaeology, Aviation, Discovery, Family History, Fiction, History, Maritime, Military, Military Classics, Politics, Select, Transport, True Crime, Air World, Frontline Publishing, Leo Cooper, Remember When, Seaforth Publishing, The Praetorian Press, Wharncliffe Local History, Wharncliffe Transport, Wharncliffe True Crime and White Owl.

For a complete list of Pen & Sword titles please contact

PEN & SWORD BOOKS LIMITED
47 Church Street, Barnsley, South Yorkshire, S70 2AS, England
E-mail: enquiries@pen-and-sword.co.uk
Website: www.pen-and-sword.co.uk

Or

PEN AND SWORD BOOKS
1950 Lawrence Rd, Havertown, PA 19083, USA
E-mail: Uspen-and-sword@casematepublishers.com
Website: www.penandswordbooks.com

I would venture to guess that Anon, who wrote so many poems without signing them, was often a woman.

Virginia Woolf

Contents

Introduction xi

1. **Anne of Brittany, Queen of France**, 7 January 1499, Castle of Nantes, Brittany 1
2. **Caterina Sforza**, 12 January 1500, Rocca de Ravaldino, Forli, Italy 4
3. **Unnamed Prostitute**, 31 October 1501, Vatican City, Rome, Italy 7
4. **Catherine of Aragon**, 14 November 1501, St Paul's Cathedral, London, England 10
5. **Margaret Drummond**, 1501, Drummond Castle, Perthshire, Scotland 13
6. **Elizabeth of York, Queen of England**, 11 February 1503, Tower of London, England 16
7. **Lisa del Giocondo, aka Lisa Gherardini**, October 1503, Florence, Italy 19
8. **Isabella, Queen of Castile**, 26 November 1504, Valladolid, Spain 22
9. **Joanna, Queen of Naples**, 23 June 1505, Royal Palace, Valencia, Spain 26
10. **Queen Idia**, 1505, Benin City, Nigeria, Africa 29
11. **Margaret Beaufort, Countess of Richmond**, 29 June 1509, The Deanery, Westminster Abbey, London, England 31
12. **Women of London**, 23 January 1513, London, England 34
13. **Elisabeth van Culemborg, Countess of Hochstrate**, June 1513, Hof van Savoy, Mechelen, Netherlands 36
14. **Margaret Tudor**, 9 September 1513, Linlithgow Palace, West Lothian, Scotland 39
15. **The Money Lender's Wife**, 1514, Antwerp, Netherlands 42
16. **Claude, Queen of France**, 10 May 1517, Paris, France 45
17. **Juana, Queen of Castile and Aragon**, 4 November 1517, Royal Convent, Palace of Tordesillas, Castile, Spain 48
18. **Frau Troffea**, July 1518, City Streets, Strasbourg, Alsace, Holy Roman Empire 52
19. **La Malinche**, 1519, Potonchan, Tabasco, Mexico, New World 54
20. **Elizabeth 'Bessie' Blount**, June 1519, Jericho Priory, Blackmore, Essex, England 57
21. **Roxelana, aka Hurrem Sultan**, September 1520, The Seraglio, Topkapi Palace, Constantinople (modern Istanbul), Turkey 60
22. **'Kindness' (Mary Boleyn)**, 4 March 1522, York Place, London, England 63
23. **Louise of Savoy**, December 1525, Basilica of St Justus, St-Just sur Lyon, Lyon, France 66

24. **Katharina von Bora**, 1526, The Black Cloister, Wittenberg, Germany — 69
25. **Maid of Honour**, 1526, Eltham Palace, England — 72
26. *Lady with a Squirrel and a Starling*, 1527, London, England — 75
27. **Properzia de Rossi**, 24 February 1530, Bologna, Italy — 77
28. **Anne Boleyn**, 31 May 1533, Streets of London, England — 80
29. **Elizabeth Barton**, 20 April 1534, Tyburn Hill, London, England — 84
30. **Margaret Roper**, July 1535, Tower of London, England — 87
31. **Maria de Salinas, Lady Willoughby**, 1 January 1536, Kimbolton Castle, Cambridgeshire, England — 90
32. **Women of the Devonshire Manuscript**, 1530s, the English court, London, England — 93
33. **Margaret Cheney**, 25 May 1537, Smithfield, London, England — 95
34. **Bona Sforza, Queen of Poland**, 1537, Lviv High Castle, Lviv, Poland — 98
35. **Queen Jane Seymour**, 12 October 1537, Hampton Court, Surrey, England — 100
36. **Cecily Bodenham**, 25 March 1539, Wilton Abbey, Wiltshire, England — 103
37. **Anne of Cleves**, 1 January 1540, Rochester Castle, Kent, England — 107
38. **Honor Grenville**, Lady Lisle, May 1540, Calais, English territory in France — 110
39. **Sayyida al Hurra**, 1540, Tétouaen, Morocco, North Africa — 113
40. **Margaret Pole**, Countess of Salisbury, 27 May 1541, Tower of London, England — 115
41. **Jane Boleyn**, Lady Rochford, 13 February 1542, Tower Green, Tower of London, England — 117
42. **Lady Nata, or Otomo-Nata 'Jezebel'**, 1545, Bungo Province, Kyushu, Japan — 120
43. **Mildred Cooke**, December 1545, Gidea Hall, Havering-atte-Bower, Essex, England — 122
44. **Venus**, 1545, Florence, Italy — 125
45. **Anne Askew**, 16 July 1546, Smithfield, London — 127
46. **Ellen Sadler**, 1546, London, England — 130
47. **Levina Teerlinc**, 1546, London, England — 133
48. **Elizabeth 'Bess' Holland**, 14 December 1546, Kenninghall Place, Norfolk, England — 135
49. **Catherine de' Medici**, 31 March 1547, Paris, France — 137
50. **The Four Marys**, 7 August 1548, Dumbarton, Scotland — 140
51. **Katherine 'Kat' Ashley**, January 1549, Hatfield House, Hertfordshire, England — 142
52. **Beatriz de Luna**, aka **Gracia Mendes Nasi**, 1549, Ferrara, Northern Italy — 145
53. **Alice Arden**, 14 February 1551, Canterbury, Kent, England — 148
54. **Anne Seymour, Duchess of Somerset**, June 1552, Tower of London, England — 151
55. **Jane Grey**, 10 July 1553, Tower of London, England — 154

56. **Mary I**, 27 September 1553, Streets of London, England — 157
57. **Louise Labé**, 13 March 1555, Lyon, France — 160
58. **Susan Clarencieux**, July 1555, Hampton Court, Surrey, England — 162
59. **Sofonisba Anguissola**, 1555, Cremona, Lombardy, Italy — 165
60. **Florence Wadham**, 1556, St Decuman's Church, Watchet, Somerset, England — 167
61. **Marian Martyrs**, 10 November 1558, Wincheap, Canterbury, Kent, England — 169
62. **Elizabeth Tudor**, 17 November 1558, Hatfield House, Hertfordshire, England — 171
63. **Anastasia Romanova**, 7 August 1560, Kolomenskoye, near Moscow, Russia — 173
64. **Amye Robsart**, 8 September 1560, Cumnor Place, Oxfordshire, England — 175
65. **Isabella Cortese**, 1561, Venice, Italy — 178
66. **Aura Soltana**, 13 July 1561, London, England — 180
67. **Isabelle de Limeuil**, 1562, Paris, France — 182
68. **Cecilia of Sweden**, 8 September 1565, Dover, England — 184
69. **Weyn Ockers**, 23 August 1566, Oude Kerk, Amsterdam — 187
70. **Elizabeth Talbot 'Bess' of Hardwick**, 2 February 1569, Tutbury Castle, Staffordshire, England — 189
71. **Unknown Woman**, 8 February 1570, Concepcion City, Chile — 192
72. **Suphankanlaya**, 1571, Pegu, Burma — 194
73. **Marguerite of Valois**, 23–24 August 1572, Paris, France — 196
74. **Sophie Brahe**, 11 November 1572, Herrevad Abbey, Scania, Denmark (Modern Sweden) — 199
75. **Margaret Brayne**, 1576, The Theatre, Holywell Street, Shoreditch, London, England — 202
76. **Lettice Knollys**, 21 September 1578, Wanstead Hall, Essex, England — 205
77. **St Teresa of Avila**, 1579, Convent of St Joseph, Toledo, Central Spain — 207
78. **Jury of Matrons**, 3 July 1581, Rochester, Kent, England — 209
79. **Ursula Kemp**, February/March 1582, St Osyth, Essex, England — 211
80. **Anne Hathaway**, November 1582, Stratford-upon-Avon, Warwickshire, England — 214
81. **Penelope Rich**, 1583, the Elizabethan court, London, England — 216
82. **Mary Fillis**, 1583, Smithfield, London, England — 219
83. **Jane Dee**, 1584, Cracow, Poland — 221
84. **Mary, Queen of Scots**, 8 February 1587, Fotheringhay Castle, Northamptonshire, England — 223
85. **Eleanor Dare**, 18 August 1587, Roanoke Colony, Roanoke Island, Dare County, North Carolina, US — 226
86. **Lady Nene**, aka **Kodai-in**, 1588, Osaka Castle, Osaka, Japan — 228
87. **Elena/Eleno de Céspedes**, 1588, Toledo, Spain — 230
88. **Tognina Gonsalvus**, 1588, Fontainebleau, France — 233

89. **'Fair Em, the Miller's Daughter'**, 1590, 'Manchester' in London, England	236
90. **Mistress Minx**, 1592, Streets of London, England	238
91. **Elizabeth 'Bess' Throckmorton**, May 1592, England	239
92. **Margaret Winstar**, August 1592, Dalkeith Castle, Midlothian, Scotland	242
93. **Eleanor Bull**, 30 May 1593, Deptford Strand, Kent, England	245
94. **Grace O'Malley**, September 1593, Greenwich Palace, Kent, England	248
95. **Mathurine de Vallois**, 27 December 1594, Louvre Palace, Paris, France	251
96. **Medusa**, 1597, Rome, Italy	253
97. **Louise Boursier**, 1598, Paris, France	255
98. **Rani Roopmati**, 1599, Madhya Pradesh, India	258
99. **Elizabeth Bathory**, 1600, Cachtice Castle, Slovakia	260
100. **Mary Frith**, 26 August 1600, Middlesex, England	262
101. **Women of the Sixteenth Century**	265

Notes	268
Bibliography	281
Acknowledgements	284

Introduction

Do we recognise the women described in history books?

Do we hear their voices?

See things from their perspectives?

Are we furnished with the context and pressures they experienced, to enable our understanding of their choices?

Do we find them presented with empathy and understanding?

In far too many cases, women have been morphed into one of several recognisable caricatures in historical writing. The beloved consort, the muse, the whore, the witch, the virgin, the victim, the bluestocking, the battleaxe, the mother, the mad woman, the icon. The list goes on. The swing towards a more sympathetic female-oriented narrative began in the nineteenth century under Queen Victoria, with the arrival of women historians such as Agnes and Elizabeth Strickland, Mary Ann Everett Green and Alice Gardner. They asked questions such as that which Julia Kavanagh posed in 1851, the year when patriarchal Victorianism erected its towering glasshouse in Hyde Park: 'What share have women in the history of men?'

'Very little,' we might answer, 'until relatively recently.' Even with the arrival of the 'amateur' lady historian of Victorian times, untutored outside the family circle, denied a university education, dependent upon the indulgence and libraries of their menfolk, the presentation of women tended to draw upon existing research undertaken by those men. Indeed, many of these 'fresh' eyes still peered out from patriarchal goggles, actively critical of past women as bad mothers or daughters, or as guilty of unladylike behaviour. It was not until the 1920s, when Eileen Power shifted the narrative focus onto social rather than political history, that the wider context of women's lives was considered a legitimate area of study. When Joan-Kelly Gadol asked, in 1977, 'Did women have a Renaissance?', she recognised that such a transformative Europe-wide phenomenon could have been experienced differently by half the population. No, Gadol concluded, the Renaissance actively made things worse for women.

Historians are facing considerable difficulties in this process of redefinition. A wall of misogyny and misunderstanding stretches back millennia among the most influential thinkers of Western Europe. Aristotle believed that femininity was reactive and passive. Women were imperfect versions of the active, positive male form, constantly craving male interaction in order to feel complete. While men were driven by the intellect and able to control their emotions, women were changeable, deceitful and untrustworthy, defective or mutilated males, almost monsters of nature. Female psychology was dictated by the Greek belief that the womb (hystera) was able to wander about the body, giving rise to hysterical behaviour. Thomas Aquinas agreed. Christian doctrine added Eve's creation from a portion of Adam's rib, thus defining her inferiority, and laid at her feet the responsibility for original sin. The occasional woman who proved these stereotypes wrong usually did so from within the context of the cloister or the court, but by the arrival of the Renaissance, a select few began to benefit from an education. Even the fashion for texts in praise of female virtue, such as de Bergamo's *Of Illustrious Women* (1497), Goggio's *In Praise of Women* (1487), Equicola's *On Women* (1501), Capra's *On the Excellence and Dignity of Women* (1525) and Agrippa's *On the Nobility and Pre-eminence of the Female Sex* (1529) came out of the patriarchal tradition, from male pens. These found a range of misogynistic answers, ranging from the overt response of John Knox to the reign of Mary I in his 1558 *First Blast of the Trumpet Against the Monstruous Regiment of Women*, to the more subtle denigration of Thomas Nashe's *The Unfortunate Traveller* of 1594.

500 years later, the problem persists. In the twenty-first century, women in some popular history books are still criticised as bad mothers and wives, still judged for their motives, still presented in two-dimensional forms. Recent waves of gender studies have brought increased sensitivity when it comes to the experience of life in the past, finally expanding to include other minority groups, but work remains to be done. Some of this distance is understandable. No historian can be divorced from their historical context. Any study of figures from past centuries is, of necessity, a clash of two different platforms of time, but a recognition of this allows anachronistic judgements to be kept to a minimum. Historically, women are accessible to modern readers in their familiar roles as mothers and wives, lovers and daughters, in the shared emotions of love, bravery and fear that transcend centuries, but we must not be misled into the comforting belief that this always makes them relatable. They were specific to very subtle gradations of time and place, and must be allowed to represent that, even if these are uncomfortable for modern moralities. The answer to this must be a return to primary sources, to seek out women's voices, so that they might speak for themselves. Of course, ironically, this is impossible in most cases due to low levels of female literacy and the consistent undervaluing of their achievements. Virginia Woolf's creation of Judith Shakespeare in 1929 illustrates this gendered obstacle race, further developed by Germaine Greer seventy years later.

This book attempts to create an alternative narrative of the sixteenth century. It seeks to bring together the lives of women worldwide, across class and age, across fame and obscurity; queens and warriors, alongside mothers and prisoners, the high-profile scandals and martyrs who died for their faith, and the anonymous faces captured in paint or glimpsed in the street. Our perception of sixteenth-century women is so often restricted to a small group of elite families, due to the survival of sources, but this sequence of mini-biographies will hopefully allow the reader greater breadth and a global perspective, hitherto lacking, which can allow for the comparison of Margaret Beaufort with Idia, a contemporary African queen. After all, the sixteenth century was a global event, not just restricted to a few privileged bubbles in Europe. By focusing on the lives of women, key events that are usually depicted in terms of male activity, such as the conquest of the New World, the Renaissance and the Reformation, are not bypassed. Instead, they become a little more inclusive. More than anything, I have tried to capture the humanity of all the women selected, and the pivotal roles they played throughout the century. Many more fascinating and significant women existed worldwide outside this carefully considered list, but alas I had not but world enough or time.

Amy Licence
Canterbury, November 2021

1

Anne of Brittany, Queen of France

7 January 1499

Castle of Nantes, Brittany

On a chilly Monday in January, in the chamber of an ancient castle, a young woman stood before a document tied up with silk laces and sealed in green wax. She was fully aware that the words it contained would change her future, and that of her country, and she hoped it would secure the inheritance of the children she would bear one day. On the threshold of a new century, with all the promise of Renaissance and reform that were approaching, Anne of Brittany was one of the few fortunate women with the wealth and status to make her voice heard.

Anne had been a duchess since the age of 11. She was now 22 years old and one of the most wealthy, sought-after heiresses in Europe. Following the early loss of her father, she had already been forced into marriage with one king of France, but, by 1499, she was in a stronger position to negotiate her own terms before she accepted the proposal of another, the new Louis XII. Educated and literate, the agreement Anne made that day was not just a marriage contract, but paradoxically, the blueprint for her own independence.

Carefully, she re-read the final lines:

> These things are granted between the Very Christian King and the said lady, and each have promised to maintain towards each other in good faith and the word of prince and princess, by these present signed of their manual signings, on the seventh day of January, the year 1499. So signed...[1]

Her betrothed stood beside her, a tall, broad figure of 37, with fashionable shoulder-length brown hair and a long face, according to a portrait painted that year. He bent down to the table and signed his name: Louis. Turning, he handed the pen to Anne, who wrote her name beside his.

This was a critical turning point for Anne. So was the location. To confirm that Louis respected her position, the signing took place on her home ground, at the medieval Castle of Nantes, seat of the Dukes of Brittany. Situated on a stretch of the Loire, the castle had immense grey stone walls, huge circular towers and a moat fed by ditches supplied by the passing river, rebuilt by Anne's father as imposing, defensive features. When Louis entered Nantes on that day in 1499, under a blue canopy,[2] he would have been struck by its size and solidity. He crossed the bridge, passed through the massive entrance gate and into the inner courtyard, all reminders of the decades of war between the Bretons and the French. Today, Brittany is a department of modern France, but it had been an independent duchy until the death of Anne's father in 1491. For centuries it had defended itself against invading neighbours.

Anne had been a rich prize on the European marriage market. Several husbands, and potential husbands, had come and gone, their names reading like a catalogue of the royal families of the era and their fluctuating fortunes. At the age of 3, she had been promised to the future Edward V of England, the 'Prince' who disappeared inside the Tower with his brother. Later, the exiled Henry Tudor had also shown an interest in making Anne his wife, before his successful invasion of England and marriage to its Yorkist princess. The English Duke of Buckingham had also been suggested as a possible match, although he was far below Anne in rank, as had two other Breton heirs: Viscount John II of Rohan, whom Anne's father disliked, and Alain of Albret, whom Anne rejected out of personal dislike. At 13, she was married by proxy to the Emperor Maximilian, a union which made a formidable alliance of the countries either side of France, prompting the French king Charles VIII to launch a military campaign against her. This proved so intense, and Maximilian failed to act to protect his wife, so Anne was forced to accept the dissolution of the imperial match and was married to Charles instead. Thus, she exchanged the title of Queen of the Romans for that of Queen of France.

Anne had borne Charles a number of children in the seven years of their marriage, but none of them survived to inherit. In 1498, he had died as the result of a freak accident, when he hit his head upon a door lintel at the royal chateau of Amboise, leaving Anne a desirable widow. The crown of France had passed to his cousin, Louis XII, who declared his intention to have Anne, with whom he was genuinely in love, referring to her as 'so beautiful and well informed that she is pleasing in every sense of the word.'[3] However, Louis was already married. In order to remarry, he claimed that Joan, his childless wife of twenty-two years, was deformed to the extent that consummation of the match had been impossible. Louis had persuaded the Pope to annul the union and the indignant Joan, protesting her innocence, retired to a monastery. She would become an abbess and was later canonised. The way was paved for Anne to become queen of France for the second time.

The 1499 contract opened with the agreement to marry. Louis and Anne 'wanted, consented and promised to take one part by marriage [to] the other... for the good and usefulness' of their lordships. The principality of Brittany was to remain intact, and not abolished or absorbed into France, and the people were to be 'rescued and relieved of their needs and affairs.' While it was assumed that Louis and Anne's first son would inherit the French throne, 'the second male child, or girl in the absence of male... will be and remain prince(ss)... (of Brittany) to enjoy and use as the dukes of his predecessors.'[4] The following day, 8 January, they were married in the castle chapel. Anne made expensive gifts to the local churches and ordered that large quantities of linen be given to the Nantes hospitals.[5]

Anne was one of the lucky ones. Eventually. She was unusual in her marital career and her ability to influence the terms on which she lived. Yet the path to the 1499 contract had not been smooth, and underlined just how much a woman, even a duchess, was at the mercy of patriarchal desire. The stages of her journey are marked by men's misfortunes or failings, starting with her father's death and her first husband Maximilian's inability to protect her, followed by Charles' violent insistence and his subsequent death, then Louis' urgent desire. It was only as a result of the love and respect Louis held her in, that she was enabled to assert her own rights. Ironically, though, this freedom was only made possible at the cost of another woman, Queen Joan.

Anne's experience was far removed from that of the majority of her female peers, who would never experience such power or influence. Nor can she be claimed as a proto-feminist, or even an advocate of women's rights, as she had little choice but to assume a male role in a position that had been left void. What Anne of Brittany did do was fight for her duchy and survive in a man's world, as a figurehead, patron and cultural figure. Her elder daughter would also become a queen, founding a line that continued through the Valois, Navarre, Spanish and Polish royal houses. Anne's influence lies in that signature, placed upon the marital contract of January 1499, as a first step in the emergence of women of influence in the sixteenth century.

2

Caterina Sforza

12 January 1500

Rocca de Ravaldino, Forli,
Emilia-Romagna region, northern Italy

A young woman looks out of the canvas of Lorenzo di Credi's *Lady of the Jasmine*. Her light-brown hair is partially tied back in the Renaissance style, half up, half down. Her facial features are small and regular but fairly unremarkable, and it is difficult to read any specific emotion into their painted passivity. The dark gown she wears is laced and slashed to reveal the white linen shift beneath and her shoulders are long and sloping, conforming to the ideals of the day. Her long white fingers toy with the sprig of jasmine mentioned in the work's title, as she sits before a red curtain and landscape containing a moated castle. The image is reputed to depict Caterina Sforza, Lady of Forli and Imola, but her demure appearance belies a fearsome character who trained her armies in person, fought to the last to defend herself and brutally avenged the murders of two husbands, earning herself the nickname of 'the Tiger'. At the end of her life, she reputedly confessed to a monk that 'if I could write everything that happened, I would shock the world.'[1]

By the end of 1499, Caterina Sforza had dug herself into a hole. At the age of 36, three times widowed and a mother of nine, she shut herself in behind the walls of the Rocca de Ravaldino, her stronghold in the centre of Forli. Her fortress was solid, with imposing towers and walls, surrounded by a wide moat. She would have been grateful that only three years earlier, she had rebuilt and strengthened the structure, supplying it with armaments. The face captured by di Credi, against his bucolic backdrop, now gazed out of heavily fortified windows, across the rooftops of the city, in anticipation of an advancing army sent by the Pope.

Caterina Sforza had been born as the result of a liaison between Galeazzo Sforza, Duke of Milan, and Lucrezia Landriani, the wife of his close friend, and was raised at her mother's home of Pavia and in the cultured Milanese court.[2] She benefited from the humanist curriculum offered to her male peers, but her education was not of the same duration. At the age of 10, she was formally married to Girolamo Riario, Lord of Imola, two decades her senior, although the match would not have been consummated for four years. Riario was the nephew of Pope Sixtus IV, who invited them to live, and serve him, in Rome, a cultured city beset by intrigues. In many ways, Rome was the microcosm of a wider dynastic struggle.

Italy was divided into independent states ruled by families like the Medicis and Borgias, frequently at war with one another, whilst facing the ongoing threat of invasion by the French. Everything changed upon the death of Sixtus, who was replaced by a member of the hostile Borgia clan. In 1488, Girolamo was murdered and Caterina retreated into her Forli fortress. She married a second time, but her unpopular husband, Giacomo Feo, also became the victim of assassination by his rivals in 1495. In response, the widow unleashed her wrath upon the city, executing thirty-eight people and losing the goodwill of her subjects.

Caterina was also to lose the goodwill of important neighbours. Her home states of Forli and Imola were affected by all three husbands of Anne of Brittany. On a map, they appear small, and only 25 miles apart, but they were strategically placed along the route that connected Naples, Venice and the Imperial Empire. In 1494, the Sforzas allied with Charles VIII of France, who was keen to pursue his hereditary claim to Naples, and Caterina allowed him to pass unchallenged and sack the city. However, two years later, the Sforzas changed their minds and invited Charles' rival, the Emperor Maximilian, to invade and oust the French. When the states of Florence and Venice came to blows, Caterina found herself in the middle, and, with the new French king, Louis XII, now backing the emperor, she braced herself for her lands to become a battleground. Her last husband, Giovanni il Popolano, headed an army sent to help defend Florence, but was taken ill on the battlefield and died soon afterwards. This left Caterina alone to face her enemies.

In September 1499, news reached Forli that Louis had crossed the border. As Caterina trained and equipped her militia by hand, she heard that he had taken Piedmont, Genoa and Cremona, before stopping in Milan on 6 October, from whence the remaining Sforzas had fled. By the last week of November, his allies had reached Imola and, three weeks later, were approaching Forli. That autumn, Pope Alexander had become convinced that Caterina was behind an attempt to poison him by the bizarre method of shaking deadly spores from the shroud of a plague victim,[3] and he allied with Louis against her. The joint Franco-Papal forces were led by Cesare Borgia, Alexander's illegitimate son and numbered around 14,000.[4]

Caterina refused to be daunted. Her requests for military assistance from Florence fell upon deaf ears, but this did not prevent her sending her children south to that city for safety. She prepared the ground around Forli by ordering all rural buildings and trees within a quarter of a mile to be destroyed, so that no shelter was offered to the invaders. Lookout posts were created and the citizens were to hoard four months' worth of rations each.[5] Borgia approached the fortress to negotiate, but Caterina refused to capitulate, even attempting to capture him by luring him into the castle and raising the drawbridge.[6] As a result, he put a price of 1,000 ducats upon her head, dead or alive, and from the ramparts, she shouted back that she would give 5,000 for his head.[7]

On 19 December, the siege began. Borgia kept up a constant barrage of artillery all day long, which Caterina returned with cannon fire, spending the night rebuilding what they had destroyed. Her determination, industry and lack of fear were remarked upon by those witnessing her defence, with the Venetian historian Marin Sanudo describing her as a 'generous and virile soul'[8] and Machiavelli referring to her 'magnanimous enterprise'. Songs were composed in honour of her solitary stand. Such compliments highlight the respect and fear in which Caterina was held, not only for the martial masculine role she took, but the degree of success she achieved.

Powerful women of the era, who engaged in military and political campaigns, were often caricatured by their contemporaries as unfeminine, unnatural or even as witches. The fifteenth century witnessed such important figures as Elizabeth Woodville, Queen of England; her mother Jacquetta; the Duchess Eleanor Cobham, and her sister-in-law Jacqueline, Duchess of Gloucester; and the warrior Joan of Arc, all having such accusations levelled against them. The most common way to attack a woman in power, who had exceeded cultural expectations for her sex, was in this kind of personal abuse, but, unusually, in Caterina's case, this is balanced by the comments of her opponents. Thus, she is recalled as an impressive figure, instead of being the recipient of denigration. This may represent a shift in attitude towards women, or a greater chivalric tone in the Italian states, or it may reflect the magnanimity her enemies were capable of, as a consequence of their victory over her. They were no longer threatened by her, so they could afford to be generous.

After almost three weeks, and many changes in tactics, Borgia succeeded in breaching the Ravaldino walls in two places. His forces stormed in, to be met by Caterina herself in hand-to-hand combat. On this occasion, her bravery was not sufficient to overcome the Borgia-French forces and the castle fell. Caterina was captured and imprisoned on 12 January 1500, and taken to Rome to face trial. Whether or not she had tried to poison the Pope, she was released eighteen months later and went to join her children in Florence. Her fortunes changed again with the death of the Borgia Alexander VI in 1503, by which his son Cesare lost his power. Caterina was favoured by his replacement, Julius II, who would have restored her to her lands of Imola and Forli, except that the residents objected. Instead, she remained in Florence with her children until 1509, when she died of pneumonia at the age of 46. She was buried in the chapel of a community of nuns in Florence known as Le Murate, which she had sometimes visited as a spiritual retreat. Her bones were lost when the building was restructured in the 1840s.

As a powerful, martial leader, Caterina commanded the respect of her enemies, in defiance of cultural convention. Legendary for her traditional masculine qualities of ferocity and stamina, the 'Tiger of Forli' showed no fear in meeting opponents face to face, or fighting them with her bare hands. Even the Borgias considered her a rare, formidable opponent and praised her abilities, ensuring the reputation of Caterina Sforza survived. Few women in the sixteenth century had to fight like this, in person, or at the head of troops, but the lives of many women were touched by such conflicts and were shaped by their outcomes.

3

Unnamed Prostitute, Banquet of Chestnuts

31 October 1501

Apostolic Palace, Vatican City, Rome

She might have been anyone. Her name could have been Concetta or Fiora, Bona or Violetta. Fair or dark, tall or short. She was likely to have been humbly born, perhaps the daughter of a farrier or baker who had died or gone bankrupt, but she still had youth on her side and was blessed with good looks. So she dressed herself up and stood plying her trade on the city street earning a few coins, hoping to please a wealthy patron who might offer her a more permanent arrangement. Sometimes she worked alone, sometimes with a friend.

Prostitution was tolerated as a necessary evil in Renaissance Italy, following the various teachings of the Catholic church. St Augustine wrote that it prevented men from corrupting 'good' women and Thomas Aquinas believed that without it, the city would overflow with sin like a sewer and men would turn to the greater sin of sodomy. Prostitution was decriminalised but not respected. Its workers were heavily regulated and required to self-identify by wearing the colour yellow, and gloves, hats or bells on their shoes. When prostitutes appear in contemporary legislation, it is through the eyes and words of the men who controlled them, dictating their place of residence, earnings, clothing and court appearances. The majority of prostitutes in the Italian states, and beyond, would have been illiterate and their voices are entirely absent from official records.

On the last night of October 1501, Concetta and Fiora chose a spot under the bridge, which had been designated acceptable by the city authorities. It was a mild night. Both were in their twenties, and had chosen dresses that featured yellow, painted their lips and eyes, dressed their hair and washed their intimate parts. It was still early, barely dusk, when two men approached them, walking briskly, with purpose in their looks. The women pouted, thrust their chests forwards. Waited.

'You want to work?'

The first man held out a handful of coins, more than they would usually earn in one night. That was when they saw he was wearing livery under his cloak and recognised the badge and colours of the Pope, Alexander VI. The night was looking up.

They were led back into the centre of the city, through formidable gates into the heart of the Vatican itself, usually closed off to visitors, especially women such as them. Inside, it was more a complex of blocky, white buildings than a single palace, but upon entering, they saw frescoes and rich tapestries on the walls, the rooms brightly lit and adorned with expensive furnishings, and gold and silver plate. Their destination was the private apartments built by Alexander VI, Rodrigo de Borgia, Pope since 1492. Upon a dais, the 70-year-old Alexander sat presiding over a banquet, with his children Cesare and Lucrezia, and guests in their finest clothes, arranged around tables lit by candelabra. As musicians began to play, Concetta and Fiora were taken to join a group of other prostitutes waiting by the fire, instructed to remove their clothes and dance.[1] As the party got going, it is unlikely that Cesare gave a second thought to the prisoner he had recently brought to Rome from Forli. Caterina Sforza was currently incarcerated in the Castel Sant'Angelo on the bank of the Tiber, just a ten-minute walk away.

After the meal, servants moved forward to clear the tables and place the candelabra on the floor between them. Then, from silken bags, they took handfuls of chestnuts and scattered them across the floor. Along with the other prostitutes, Concetta and Fiora were told to get to their knees and crawl along the ground to pick them up. Their suggestive movements were intended to entice the male guests to join them, and an orgy upon a grand scale followed. Prizes were given to those who could copulate with the most women, while Concetta and Fiora were given stockings and silk shoes as rewards[2]. Or so the story goes.

The account of the infamous Borgia Banquet of Chestnuts comes from the diary of Alexander's Master of Ceremonies, Johann Burchard,[3] but some of his contemporaries and many later historians have questioned its authenticity. Researchers such as the Victorian Peter de Roo questioned whether a Pope could have participated in 'a scene truly bestial', which appeared inconsistent with the rest of Burchard's account and what is known of Alexander's character, suggesting that it was a smear by enemies of the Borgias. While many acknowledge that Cesare Borgia was entirely capable of such acts, having hosted his own banquet for fifty prostitutes in the palace, the incident of the chestnuts has achieved a more mythical status.[4] It may have happened as Burchard wrote, or it may not. If Concetta and Fiora were not dancing for the Pope that October night, they were entertaining his son, or their friends soon afterwards, their pockets filled with coins and gifts.

With the morning light, the women would steal out of the palace, back through the streets, to the rooms and apartments they shared, to sleep, cook, sew or care for family. And so it continued, until they became too old, or too ill, or they lost their looks, or were infected with one of the debilitating sexually transmitted diseases for which there was no known prevention or cure. Women also ran the risk of pregnancy and the potential for violence, assault and even murder.

Across Rome, across Italy, Europe and worldwide, Concetta and Fiora represent the millions of sixteenth-century women working in the sex industry, whose names, lives and experiences went unrecorded and are, therefore, lost to us. Very few were able to serve members of the aristocracy, with the commensurate rewards this could bring. The majority had little control over their market, or the customers who approached them, exposing themselves not just to disease, but potentially to degradation and violence at the hands of the wrong man. The 'oldest profession in the world' had its risks and its surroundings were rarely as glamorous as the Vatican Palace. Sex might have sold, as it always has, but it paid very little and the costs to prostitutes were often high.

4

Catherine of Aragon

14 November 1501
St Paul's Cathedral, London, England

The bells woke her. For a moment, the 15-year-old princess struggled to recognise the strange, gloomy chamber, so far removed from her native Spain with its scents of spices, incense, olives and oranges. Then it all came flooding back: the long sea voyage amid the storm, being carried ashore, sick with the rocking of the waves, and the journey up through the green fields of Devon and Dorset. She had ridden through the colourful pageants adorning the streets of London amid cheering crowds, and been welcomed here, into these rooms at the Bishop's Palace by St Paul's Cathedral. All for this moment. It was the morning of 14 November 1501, a day that Catherine of Aragon had been preparing for since the age of 3. Today, she was to marry the future king of England, Prince Arthur Tudor.

The Anglo-Spanish union was quite a coup for the king of a new dynasty. Only three years after he had won an unexpected victory at Bosworth, Henry VII had been fortunate to secure an alliance with the daughter of European power couple, Ferdinand and Isabella of Spain. After much delay, and the removal of rivals and threats to the English throne, Catherine left her home, never to return. She believed it was God's chosen destiny for her to be queen of this strange, green island nation, and rose on her wedding day to pray and give thanks for her safe arrival, before her ladies began to dress her. It was the first time that England had seen the farthingale, or vardingale, named for the Spanish word 'verdugos' after the supple green twigs used to create hoops that made the distinctive shape of the skirt. Over it, she wore a long white satin skirt, pleated in folds, creating a hooped effect and her face was covered by a white veil, edged in gold, embroidered with pearls, almost a prototype for what was to become a conventional bridal outfit. Her long hair hung loose, as was traditional for a bride, as a further symbol of her virginity and her long train was carried by ladies in procession behind her.[1]

Henry's choice of location was deliberate. His own wedding had taken place at Westminster, but at this point in London's history, the Palace and Abbey were removed from the main city to the west, a considerable distance outside the walls, far from the mass of citizens whom he had hoped to impress with pageantry and ceremony. Henry wanted news of this wedding to have an international spread and for this, he needed an audience. Geographically, St Paul's sat at the heart of the city, at its middle point and at its peak, on top of the original London Hill. It was large enough to accommodate vast numbers of people, centrally located and sufficiently established to be suitable for the wedding. Henry wanted to employ the tongues of his Londoners to praise the occasion and ensure that it would never be forgotten. It meant maximum exposure for Catherine too.

Even inside the cathedral, Henry intended that the young couple should be seen. A wooden platform was erected along the entire 350 feet from the choir door to the west door, standing 4 feet high and 12 feet wide. Covered in red cloth and approached by a set of steps, it was railed along each side to keep onlookers at bay.[2] Catherine and Arthur were literally to be centre stage, elevated over the heads of Londoners, and because it was their day, King Henry VII, his wife, Elizabeth of York, and mother, Margaret Beaufort, observed the ceremony from behind a screen, so as not to upstage the young pair in terms of precedence. Catherine was led to the cathedral door by an 11-year-old boy, who watched all the proceedings with wide eyes. Also dressed in white, he would one day inherit the throne as Henry VIII, after Arthur's premature death, and become Catherine's second husband.

Arthur was dazzling in matching white satin, taking his place at Catherine's side to repeat their wedding vows before the congregation. The agreement between England and Spain was read aloud, after which the princess was endowed with the titles and lands the king bestowed on her as her settlement. They were formally pronounced man and wife, and the pair turned to acknowledge the crowd, parading along the length of the platform, hand in hand. They were blessed and the Mass was read, before they retired from public gaze back into the Bishop's Palace. The formal part of the proceedings was conducted fairly quickly, but after all the years of waiting, Arthur and Catherine were now officially man and wife, side by side in the flesh.

For all its splendour and theatre, Catherine could not have known that her wedding night would achieve such lasting significance. Thirty years later, exactly what happened between these two inexperienced teenagers behind closed doors would be analysed and dissected to the letter of every nuance. Witnesses were recalled or sought out from retirement in foreign countries, all to establish just how intimate Arthur and Catherine had been when left alone in their chamber, while their attendants slept in the anteroom beyond. Catherine went towards it willingly as a young bride, little fathoming how it would return to haunt her and redefine her life when her second husband sought a reason to annul their match.

The newlyweds slept that night at Baynard's Castle. The bed was inspected and tested, with courtiers sitting on each side to ensure it was comfortable and that no concealed blades had been smuggled into the chamber. Catherine and Arthur travelled from the Bishop's Palace to the Castle, where they were changed and prepared for bed, around eight in the evening. According to protocol, a small crowd gathered to witness the occasion, to offer good wishes and prayers, and to corroborate that the bedding had actually taken place. In the words of *The Receyt of Ladie Kateryn*, 'Lords and ladies accompanied the pair with 'the intent to have the oversight and apparament of the chamber and bedde that the Prince and Princes, aftir the condicion of wedlock, should take in their reste and ease... Aftir the goodly disportes, dancinges with pleasure, mirthe and solace before used, (Arthur) departid to his said arrayed chambre... wheryn the Princess, bifore his comyng was reverently laid and reposid... And thus thise worthy persones concludid and consummated the effecte and compliment of the sacrament of matrimony.'[3]

As the *Receyt* indicates, the princess was brought in first, dressed in her nightgown and laid 'reverently' in bed. Then she had to wait. Arthur stayed up longer, drinking and celebrating with his gentlemen, but finally they carried him in, singing and making merry, possibly reciting some of the many bawdy songs associated with such events. References to sex and fertility would not have been out of place, or too crude, even for a royal wedding. Then, at last, the guests withdrew and the pair were left alone. The following morning, Arthur appeared flushed and thirsty, 'good and sanguine', calling for a drink as he had spent the night 'in the midst of Spain' and that it was a 'good pastime to have a wife'.[4] Thirty years later, those words would return to haunt Catherine, and provide Henry with what he believed to be justification to set her aside and marry Anne Boleyn. Until her death, Catherine maintained that she had remained a virgin throughout her marriage to Arthur and that Henry knew this full well. The controversy and significance of 14 November 1501 would make it the most famous wedding night in history, and Catherine one of the sixteenth century's most famous women.

5

Margaret Drummond

1501

Drummond Castle, Perthshire, Scotland

Drummond Castle is an imposing grey stone edifice sitting on top of a rocky outcrop overlooking the Perthshire countryside in central Scotland. The Drummond family were related to royalty and had gradually acquired greater status, but remained in conflict with other leading clans. Their home reflected their rank, with a new five-storey tower rising above the castle's otherwise modest defences. It is likely to have been in a room within this tower that three sisters sat down to breakfast one morning in 1501. At 26, Margaret was the youngest, with Sybilla still unwed and Eupheme married to Lord Fleming. What they ate is unknown. Breakfast at the time might be anything from a simple meal of bread and cheese or meat, to pottage, broth or hearty meat stew, with ale or wine. Other accounts claim it was a dish of sugared fruit. Within hours, all three were dead.

Food poisoning was not an uncommon occurrence at the time. Poor hygiene and food storage, bacteria, infections, confusion over ingredients and fluctuating temperatures all contributed to symptoms ranging from upset stomachs to days, or weeks, of agony. The Drummond sisters' deaths were seen by their contemporaries as an especially bad case, the result of errors made in the castle kitchens, for which, no doubt, the cook was held accountable. Notably, they did not rush to consider that this was a case of murder, although as the years passed, opinions on this matter shifted. Two centuries on, when a Drummond descendant compiled a family history, it was presented as a deliberate act, politically motivated, to remove the woman that the Scottish king, James IV, was planning to marry. When the women were buried in Dunblane Cathedral, James paid for Masses to be said for Margaret's soul, and his actions were interpreted as confirmation of his affection for her.

Margaret Drummond may have been at the Scottish court as early as 1488, the year of James' accession, when they were both in their mid-teens. It has been suggested[1] that she was an attendant upon James' mother, Margaret of Denmark, but the queen had died two years prior to this. At least one Victorian biographer echoed this, claiming James and Margaret were living together at Linlithgow as early as 1488, but this is based upon a misunderstanding of the records, which list frequent wardrobe payments to a 'Lady Margaret,' who was not Mistress

Drummond, but Margaret Stewart, the king's aunt. The first verifiable entry in the records comes in June 1496, when Margaret was listed as living at Stirling Castle under the care of John and Lady Lindsay until that October. A new bed was purchased for her use, and a Lady Lundie received £10 for various services and offices performed for her.[2] The bed was a highly symbolic item, intended either for her to share with James, or for her lying-in, as it was around this time she bore the king's daughter, who was named after herself. The records show that between October and March 1497, Margaret was staying with Sir David Kingham at Linlithgow, where new clothes were sent to her from Edinburgh, after which she returned briefly to Stirling, then returned home, presumably to Drummond Castle.[3]

Margaret may have been James' favourite mistress, but she was not his only one. By 1497, he was already embroiled in a liaison with Marion Boyd, who bore the first of his two children as early as 1490; he had just met Janet Kennedy, and would later take up with Isabel Fleming, both of whom also presented him with children. Later legend suggested that James was on the verge of fulfilling a promise to Margaret to make her his wife, and this threatened to derail the Anglo-Scottish negotiations that resulted in a Tudor-Stewart marriage in 1503. However, this theory is unlikely for a number of reasons. The negotiations with England were already quite advanced by 1501, and James had no cause to marry Margaret and elevate her to the position of queen. Conversely, he had everything to gain by the proposed Tudor alliance. The significance of the English marriage is even more easy to emphasise with hindsight, in the knowledge that it would eventually unite the two thrones under the Stuart dynasty. It may be that Margaret was not, in fact, the intended victim, a suggestion recorded by James' wife twenty years later.

By 1523, when Margaret was long dead, theories about her demise resurfaced in a letter written by Margaret Tudor. The elder sister of Henry VIII, she had married James as planned in 1503, and had been widowed a decade later after his death at the Battle of Flodden. On 24 November 1523, she wrote to the Earl of Surrey, commander at Flodden, placing the blame for the poisoning at the feet of John Fleming, second Lord Fleming, husband of Margaret's elder sister Eupheme, due to the unhappiness of their marriage. 'Lord Fleming,' she wrote, 'for evil will that he had to his wife, caused poison three sisters, one of them his wife, and this is known as truth throughout all Scotland.'[4] However, Margaret was writing about events that took place before her arrival in the country, so even if her husband had believed this and confided his thoughts to her, these were still at one remove, and unverifiable. Little more is known about Eupheme's marriage other than that she bore John one son and three daughters.[5] The letter's sentiments may also be more suited to the climate of the 1520s. As she admits, Margaret is recording hearsay, which may date more from the period in which Fleming's unpopularity increased, leading to his assassination a year after the letter's composition.

Victorian biographers spun Margaret's death into a myth. Agnes Strickland repeated Margaret Tudor's letter and theory, while, in 1871, the Reverend Morris added the romantic interpretation that James' intention to marry Margaret had 'never been contradicted on evidence; the conduct of the king fully corroborates it… everything in regard to his relationship with Margaret Drummond indicate a tender and devoted love.'[6] Short of disinterring her remains, it is not possible to deduce whether the death of the three sisters was a case of murder or accidental food poisoning. Margaret's royal favour might have made her a target for the king's enemies, but, equally, status was no guarantee against accidents such as poisoning.

Margaret's short life of only twenty-six years reveals the perilous nature of sixteenth-century existence. She is one of an overwhelming number of women of the period, young and old, whose ends are shrouded in mystery, the cause and details unknown. As the king's mistress, Margaret's death drew attention, but if she had not been singled out by James, her poisoning and that of Eupheme and Sybilla would probably not have featured in the history books. The status of a royal mistress was always insecure, based as it was upon personal affection, and liable to change and the enmity of rivals. As the role of a mistress was unofficial, it is also difficult to measure their influence, which could range from companionship through to guidance and the expression of advice concerning policy. Where Margaret stood on this spectrum is unknown, but her life illustrates the dangers of becoming close to the king. She was survived by her daughter, who was raised at Edinburgh Castle and provided with clothes, attendants, lessons and husbands suitable for the daughter of a king.

6

Elizabeth of York, Queen of England

11 February 1503

Tower of London, London, England

In January 1503, Elizabeth, Queen of England, was approaching her thirty-seventh birthday. She was staying in the chilly, foreboding Tower of London, the centuries-old stone bastion sitting on the Thames, symbolic of the city's defensive history, just as Westminster represented its administration. She was heavily pregnant with her seventh child, and intended that she would soon leave her present location, take to the river, and sail down to the newly rebuilt Richmond Palace. There, she would shut herself away in confinement, in rooms hung with tapestries and lit by roaring fires.

Eighteen years had passed since one of the most decisive moments of English history propelled the Tudor dynasty onto the throne. Elizabeth was the firstborn child of the controversial, secret marriage of Edward IV, the first Yorkist king, and Elizabeth Woodville, the widow of a Lancastrian knight. Their daughter inherited the legendary good looks of her parents and an enviable position as the heir to the Yorkist dynasty, following the mysterious deaths of her brothers, the Princes in the Tower. Contemporaries were divided as to the boys' fate, but their disappearance enabled the accession of their uncle, Richard III, who seized the throne in an unexpected coup that summer. Two years later, in August 1485, Richard was defeated on the battlefield by Henry Tudor and, the following January, to cement the alliance between York and Lancaster, Henry made Elizabeth his wife at Westminster Abbey. The Tudor dynasty was born, and personified in the red and white union rose, painted and carved all over their palaces, new and old.

Over the course of the next two decades, Elizabeth had borne six children, of which three remained alive in 1503, tucked away in the bucolic nursery at Eltham Palace. Princess Margaret, aged 13, was shortly to marry James IV, King of Scotland, 11-year-old Henry was Prince of Wales and Princess Mary was just 7. But it was not supposed to be that way. Barely nine months had passed since the terrible news arrived of the death of the couple's eldest son Arthur, the cherished figure of their hopes for England, newly married to the Spanish Princess Catherine of Aragon. The 16-year-old princess, whose arrival had heralded such hope, was now a widow. In dynastic terms, the king and queen comforted themselves with the knowledge that there was another male heir to step into his shoes, but the death left a huge chasm in their lives. And it was this chasm that the new child, conceived soon after Arthur's death, was intended to fill. As she looked out over Tower Green, Elizabeth felt movement in her womb, knowing that her confinement was rapidly approaching.

This had been the queen's most difficult pregnancy of all, even worse than when Arthur came a month early and she suffered from an ague, or fever. Over the last six months, Elizabeth had been attended by a string of nurses; two at the start of her final trimester, then Mistress Harcourt who came out to Westminster, and the French woman just before Christmas.[1] New bedlinen and curtains had been ordered and the special girdle of Our Lady had been brought to her from Westminster, to which she had clung during each one of her deliveries, offering up her prayers to Jesus, Mary and all the saints. She had spent the Christmas season at Richmond with her husband and children, but, a month later, on 26 January, some unknown business brought her to the city, and to lodgings in the Tower.

In the final days of January, Elizabeth was overtaken by sudden pain and went into premature labour. Her midwife, Alice Massey, rushed to her side, and assisted in the delivery of her baby, a daughter who the queen named Catherine and who died shortly after. Soon after the baby's arrival, Elizabeth began to deteriorate, suffering from puerperal fever as the result of bacterial infection. When her attendants realised the severity of her condition, a messenger was dispatched into Kent to fetch a Dr Ayleworth, or Hallysworth,[2] but he did not arrive in time.

Elizabeth slipped away on 11 February, a date which was also her birthday. The English people were grieved to hear of her loss. To them, she was more than a woman, more than a wife, mother and queen. Her popularity is shown in her account books, which list the string of gifts that were brought to her, by local people, whenever she was in residence nearby. Over the years, Elizabeth had become a quasi-religious figure to her subjects, a symbol of peace, prosperity and unity, as well as personifying suffering and mercy, qualities synonymous with those of the Virgin Mary. To some degree, she attracted a following and adoration comparable with that of the most popular religious cult of her day.

By all accounts, Henry VII was devastated at the loss of his wife. For a man unused to showing his feelings, he retreated to Richmond for six weeks, leaving his court in a state of uncertainty. In his absence, Elizabeth was given a magnificent state funeral, borne through the streets of London in a coffin draped with black velvet and gold crosses, its corners hung with white banners. It was topped with a carved wax effigy of the queen herself, life-sized and dressed in robes of estate, jewels, orb, sceptre and crown, with long, free-flowing hair.[3] The upper portion of this torso is still visible in the Abbey collection, with its white-painted face, regular features and rounded eyebrows. Renowned for her beauty, Elizabeth's face is reputed to have been used for the image of the Queen of Hearts on a traditional deck of cards.

More than 1,000 lights burned on the hearse, while thirty-seven virgins in white linen and wreaths of white and green lined Elizabeth's route to Westminster, bearing torches. Eight ladies on white horses followed. The abbey interior was shrouded in black cloth and lit by 273 large tapers, casting their flickering light over the site where work had just begun on what would be the queen's final resting place in the Lady Chapel. On the first anniversary of her death the following year, Henry arranged by indenture that daily Masses were to be said for her soul, and her death day to be marked annually by a requiem Mass, with tapers, bells and alms distributed amongst the poor. Increasingly, he turned to his mother, Margaret Beaufort, as his guide through his final years.

Elizabeth had been a significant queen, but she was essentially a queen of the medieval era. Her royal blood offered her people a connection with the old, popular Yorkist line, uniting that long-standing claim with the new regime of the Tudors. Her qualities of loyalty and regality, together with her piety and grace, epitomised ideals of what a queen should be, as one half of a ruling power couple. As a woman, she was the perfect wife for her times: loyal, faithful and dutiful, loving and supportive, fertile and fecund. Yet it was as a symbol that she transcended her brief life, to represent a universal model of womanhood and motherhood, tinged with suffering. Distant and quasi-divine, she represented the quiet, supportive, Marian figure of pre-Reformation faith, unchallenging, loving and forgiving, but detached from controversy or politics. Like a stone icon in a church alcove, she was worshipped from afar, and appealed to for guidance and mercy.

Yet the world around Elizabeth was changing. This passive ideal was rapidly being superseded by the Renaissance, which encouraged the greater education of women, who were scholars, warriors and politicians. The death of the first Tudor queen marks an historic turning point in the transition of one culture to another. Coming just after the turn of the century, it ended one outmoded form of queenship: the women who subsequently sat on the English throne would bring a new set of aspirations, far more complex than peace and maternity. They would not quietly and submissively accept the decisions of their menfolk, for better or worse, but would espouse reform, speak up for their rights and even challenge the king outright. A new sort of queenship was evolving, which allowed for greater influence but contained considerable risk.

7

Lisa del Giocondo, aka Lisa Gherardini

October 1503

Florence, Italy

Hers is the most famous smile in the whole world. Even more famous than Elizabeth of York's Queen of Hearts with its demure, averted eyes. It is captured in the best-known painting of all time, hanging in the most visited museum, the Louvre in Paris, where over 10 million people a year queue to stare at her. Admitted at timed intervals, they have approximately 30 seconds in her presence before having to make way for the next group. She is tiny, a mere 77 centimetres by 53 and bears the identification number 779. When Lisa del Giocondo, a middle-class cloth merchant's wife of Florence, sat for Leonardo da Vinci in the autumn of 1503, she would have had cause to smile, had she known that her face would capture the world five centuries after it was sketched out on a poplar board.

Mona Lisa is depicted in half-length, visible to the waist, just below her loosely clasped hands. They rest upon a baluster, a supportive railing of wooden pillars, and she is seated in a loggia, allowing for an extensive outside view behind. Perhaps this represents a real Florentine location, with its vineyards and olive groves, or perhaps it is an imaginary landscape, idealised or drawn from memory. Her clothes are plain, black and a darkish gold on the sleeves, a shawl thrown over her left shoulder, but typical of the time. She wears no veil and, perhaps surprisingly for a status-conscious merchant's wife, she wears no jewellery or adornments of any kind. Not in this version, at any rate. Modern high-resolution scans have revealed several other layers of paint beneath the finished picture, in slightly different positions, one of which features the subject with her hair elaborately dressed and hung with jewels.[1] Her pose is reminiscent of contemporary images of the Virgin Mary, with the demure hands, the folded arms and upright posture. Yet there is none of the respectful distance found in those hagiographical works. Da Vinci's painting is remarkable in its intense, close focus upon the sitter, a realistic, flawed, live woman whose presence is palpable.

We know that the *Mona Lisa* depicts Signora Giocondo, because of two sixteenth-century sources. A recently discovered note written in October 1503 by a clerk to the Florentine politician Niccolò Machiavelli states that in that month, da Vinci was working on a painting of Lisa del Giocondo.[2] This confirms the record of the first and most famous of the artist's biographers, Giorgio Vasari in 1550, who wrote that Leonardo 'undertook to paint, for Francesco del Giocondo, the portrait of Mona Lisa, his wife.'[3] Hitherto, despite a furore of speculation arising from her expression, the focus of art history has fallen exclusively on the artist, not the sitter. It may be, though, that Lisa did not even smile for Leonardo. It may be that he deliberately painted in her smile as the calling card of this work.

Each of da Vinci's significant comparable portraits contain symbols. These were a popular Renaissance conceit to leave little clues in the work to identity and allegiance, just as Holbein would do in England later. They were indicative of the 'cunning' of the author, and often coded so as to be deciphered by an elite few. Between 1474–8, da Vinci painted Ginevra de Benci to celebrate her engagement, wreathing her head with a juniper bush, or 'ginepro' in Italian, creating a pun on her name, as well as symbolising female virtue. Likewise, Cecilia Gallerani, the sitter in *Lady with an Ermine*, created in 1488–91, holds exactly that: a larger-than-life ermine, or stoat, an emblem used by her lover, Ludovico Sforza, then Leonardo's employer. Thus, the artist playfully exaggerates visual clues that relate to the identity of the sitter. When it came to Lisa, whose married surname Giocondo translates from the Italian as 'the happy one', it is no surprise that da Vinci depicts her with a wide smile. The centuries of admirers who have speculated exactly what might be the cause of the woman's secret glee may have been misreading the painting entirely.

Lisa was born in Florence on 15 June 1479 into the ancient Gherardini family. She was one of the eight children of Antonmaria di Nolda Gherardini and his third wife Lucrezia del Caccia, and although the Gherardinis had once been part of the aristocracy, they were now solidly mercantile, owning farms that produced livestock, wine, wheat and oil. At the age of 15, Lisa married Francesco di Giocondo, a cloth and silk merchant, bringing him a dowry of 170 florins and a farm, although for the first eight years of their marriage, the couple could not afford accommodation of their own and were forced to share. It may have been to celebrate their purchase of their own house in the Via del Stufa, or the arrival of a son in 1503, that prompted Francesco to approach a painter who had newly returned to the city.[4] In 1502, da Vinci had been employed by Cesare Borgia as his military architect and engineer, even creating for him a map of Imola, recently seized from Caterina Sforza. Yet early in 1503, he returned to Florence where he joined the Guild of St Luke, and accepted commissions to compensate for his lack of a patron.

Little more is known about Lisa. She lived a comfortable, middle-class life and bore six children. Francesco was elected to the Signora, the governing body of Florence in 1512, but he was also a supporter of the feared Medici family, which led to him serving a brief period of imprisonment. He was freed upon the return of the Medici and continued to play a role in local politics. He died in 1538, possibly of the plague, while Lisa survived and lived out her days in a convent, dying in 1542.[5] What is certain is that they never received their commission from da Vinci, who, as a result, was never paid for the work. The *Mona Lisa* never hung on Lisa's wall. When he left Florence for Milan in 1506, the artist took the unfinished painting with him, and then, after receiving an invitation from the French king, Francis I, in 1516, to live at his court, the work arrived at Clos Lucé, the house granted him in the grounds of the Château d'Amboise. It was there that da Vinci died three years later, and the portrait passed into the possession of the French royal family. It was truly a face that spoke of the Renaissance, the rebirth of ancient ideals for a new era.

As she looks back at us, Lisa appears as fresh and enigmatic as the day she first sat for da Vinci in the autumn of 1503. It is difficult to pinpoint exactly what it is about this portrait, this one woman's face, which has entirely captured the world's attention, but apart from the artist's skill, it is tempting to conclude there is something of her character that has been successfully transcribed into paint. Lisa di Giocondo is, without doubt, the most famous woman of the sixteenth century. Perhaps it is because after five centuries, her face is so recognisably human and still invites connection. She is a normal woman, not a queen, or warrior, or infamous mistress, but a merchant's wife, afforded immortality by an accident of timing. We can see our own humanity reflected in her face. And the smile that has enchanted so many may not have been her smile at all.

8

Isabella, Queen of Castile

26 November 1504

Medina del Campo, Valladolid, Spain

Modern visitors to the Royal Palace in Medina del Campo are ushered into the dark, luxurious recreation of a fifteenth-century state bedroom. Amid bare brick walls and a wooden floor, a four-poster bed dominates the room, standing proudly on a dark red carpet against the matching curtains that block out the daylight. The wooden frame is draped in bright, golden hangings, with gold cushions and a black and gold embroidered coverlet, to recreate the kind of bed fit for a queen. This is one of the defining experiences for the tourist: the closest they can get to the deathbed scene of the monarch whose last days are echoed in the palace's new name. Since Queen Isabella of Castile composed her will there, it has become known as the Testamentary Palace, where the parchment pages were signed and sealed with wax.

Well over 500 years have passed since the tiny figure of the queen lay watching the flickering light in the hearth. Born in 1451 and reigning from 1474, Isabella was known for being decisive and divisive. She firmly believed that she was God's chosen instrument, spreading Catholicism through Spain and beyond. Together, she and her husband, Ferdinand of Aragon, had made an unbeatable team, the crusading golden couple of Europe, feared and admired on the international stage. In 1489, at the palace at Medino, draped head to foot in gold, Isabella had received the English ambassadors and signed the treaty of marriage between her youngest daughter, Catherine of Aragon, and Prince Arthur Tudor. She had planned and equipped the military campaigns Ferdinand fronted, reclaimed Muslim territories, expelled heretics from the country, funded Columbus' voyages to the New World and welcomed leading humanist scholars and artists to her court.

The Testamentary Palace is situated in the heart of Medina del Campo, in the south-west of the Valladolid region, in Castile. Central Spain's short, hot summers and long, harsh winters created the perfect conditions for the production of cereal crops and the growth of pine forests. Isabella's life had been peripatetic, constantly spent on the move between the cities, castles and encampments of a vast empire, much of which her marriage had united for the first time. Yet, she had been a frequent visitor to Medina since she was a child, and after she unexpectedly inherited the throne after the deaths of her brothers, and the challenge of a half-sister led to the war of Castilian succession. Isabella's decisive leadership had allowed her to seize the moment, defying her advisors to convene the national court to secure her rights and negotiating directly with rebels. Diminutive and solid in build, with red-gold hair and sombre features set against the ceremonial gold she knew how to wear to best effect, the united Spain's first queen cut a remarkable figure in the latter fifteenth century.

The final years of Isabella's life had been tinged with sadness. The year 1492 had been her defining moment, bringing the conquest of the New World, the fall of Muslim-held Granada and the Expulsion of the Jews, but it was also the start of her personal decline. Her mother died in 1496, then the following year, her eldest son and heir, John, Prince of Asturias, passed away after a short-lived marriage and his young widow, Margaret of Austria, lost her unborn child. In 1498, Isabella's eldest daughter and namesake, Isabella, Queen of Portugal, died in childbirth, and the son she bore, Miguel, only lived for two years. A younger daughter, Maria, married the widowed Portuguese king in 1500 and the remaining children, Joanna and Catherine, had both married and left the country, leaving their mother quite alone. Neither match had been successful. Joanna's husband Philip of Burgundy had made her deeply unhappy and undermined her mental health, while Prince Arthur died prematurely. One of Isabella's final battles, in 1503–4, was writing to the newly widowed Henry VII of England to dissuade him from his ill-advised idea to marry his young, grieving Spanish daughter-in-law.

Catherine's widowhood in England left her destitute and in political limbo, but after a long period of ill health, she was invited to stay at Westminster Palace and accorded the same status as the king's daughter, Princess Mary. Yet the limited news that arrived from her family cast a shadow over her newfound optimism. Her sister Joanna wrote to inform her that both their parents had been ill, and that Isabella experienced 'daily attacks of ague, and the fever which followed'.[1] The king and queen had been at Medina since August, confined to bed, so fearful that they both declared they wanted their remains laid to rest in the chapel at Granada.

But while Ferdinand slowly recovered, Isabella grew worse, struggling to breathe and swelling with dropsy. Pedro Martir, chronicler of the Spanish court, wrote in October that 'the fever has not yet disappeared and seems to be in her very marrow. Day and night she has an insatiable thirst and loathes food. The deadly tumour is between her skin and her flesh.'[2] Her first will was completed on 12 October and issued to her notary and scribe, Gaspar de Gricio, who very likely transcribed it in the small, dark, neat hand of the parchment. On 23 November, as Isabella declined further, codicils were added. One of them specifically exhorted her eldest surviving daughter and heir, Joanna of Castile, and her husband, Philip 'the handsome' of Burgundy, to respect Ferdinand's example and advice, as Joanna's father, but also as an experienced ruler:

> I likewise herewith and very lovingly order the said Princess, my daughter, and the said Prince, her husband – in order to merit and obtain the benediction of God, of the King, her father, and of me – to be always obedient subjects to the King my lord, and never to disobey his orders, but to serve him, treat and

revere him with the greatest respect and obedience, giving and causing to be given him all the honour which good and obedient children owe to their good father, following his orders and carrying out his councils. It is to be hoped that they will comport themselves in such a manner that in all that regards his Highness my absence be not observable, and as though I were alive.

For besides that this honour and reverence is due to his Highness as a father who according to the commandment of God ought to be honoured and revered, they ought to obey his orders and follow his councils, because in addition to these reasons they are bound to do so, as being beneficial and profitable to themselves and to their kingdoms. Also his Highness having so much experience in the government of these kingdoms, they and their kingdoms will greatly profit thereby.

Moreover, his Highness ought to be more obeyed, and revered, and honoured than any other father because he is so excellent a King and Prince, endowed and distinguished by such and so great virtues that by great effort and exertions of his royal person he has conquered these kingdoms, which were so much alienated at the time when I succeeded, and has put an end to the great evils, and losses, and wars caused by all the troubles and risings which then prevailed. With no less danger to his royal person he has gained the kingdom of Granada, and has driven away the enemies of our Holy Catholic Church, who during so long a time had usurped and occupied these kingdoms, to which he has secured the good government administration and justice which by the grace of God they now enjoy.[3]

Isabella's final descent had begun on 25 November, amid a terrible storm that raged around the castle. She lingered as the sun rose, throughout the morning, and passed away at noon. According to the wishes she had expressed that summer, she was buried in the Alhambra Palace at Granada, in the tomb where her husband would later join her. The same day as her death, though, Ferdinand walked out into the marketplace at Medina and renounced his claim to the throne of Castile, in favour of Joanna, who immediately became queen. Then he described his wife's death as 'the greatest affliction that could have befallen him,' which 'pierced his heart' and felt 'boundless'.[4] Catherine wrote to both her parents in concern, from whom she had not heard in months, saying that she could not be 'satisfied or cheerful'[5] until a reply reached her. Her last letter to her mother was dated 26 November. By the time it arrived in Medina, Isabella was already dead. The news would have reached Catherine in England a few days later. The widowed princess had lost her greatest champion.

The loss of a woman such as Isabella had ramifications beyond the grief of her family and subjects. With her exceptional strength and industry, and the single-minded pursuit of her vision, Isabella had been a great crusading queen, propelled into position by her birth, but retaining it through sheer ability. The resulting division of Spain would set her husband against their daughter, and create tensions that would not be fully resolved, even under the accession of her grandson, Charles V. As a woman, she proved herself more than equal to her husband, and other contemporary male rulers, changing the face of Europe and beyond. A contemporary of Elizabeth of York, dying within twenty months of her, Isabella could not have been a more different queen. Her proactive partnership – energetic, visionary and steeped in Renaissance learning – helped redefine the old style of queenship that Elizabeth personified. It was Isabella's example that shaped the concept of female rule that her daughter, Catherine of Aragon, would attempt to fulfil in England.

History has not been kind to Isabella. Today, a more enlightened approach to human rights casts many of her actions in a difficult light and her persecution of Muslims, Jews and other minorities makes for painful reading. Yet Isabella can hardly be judged for not having acted anachronistically, for not having been ahead of her times. She was a complex woman of the late fifteenth century, personifying the paradox of piety and persecution that is found throughout the religious practices of her contemporaries and descendants, and must be seen in that context. Her peers considered her to be the definitive female ruler of their era, a considerable feat in such patriarchal times.

9

Joanna, Queen of Naples

23 June 1505

Royal Palace, Valencia, Spain

On a still, dry summer's day, with the smell of exotic flowers wafting up to the sill, Joanna of Aragon stood at the open window watching the approaching riders. Behind her, looking over her shoulder, was her mother, the widowed Queen of Naples, also Joanna, who signed every letter as 'the sad queen'. Between them, the pair had much to regret, having lost the throne of Naples, both their husbands and their home, and were now living as refugees in the Palace of Valencia as guests of the king of Aragon. The palace was renowned for having 300 rooms, buried among which the women maintained a 'noble sad rule and order' in the privacy of their apartments. Situated on the bank of the River Turia, Valencia was a beautiful cage for the sorrowful widows, with its richly decorated pavilions and gardens planted with fruit trees and flowers brought from the New World. Yet while her mother aged, the daughter had two things on her side. Youth and beauty.

By the summer of 1505, when Joanna was 27, Henry VII of England was considering taking a new wife. Elizabeth of York had been dead for over two years and, although the king himself was approaching 50 and not in the best of health, a younger wife might bring him the spare heirs that might save the Tudor dynasty, should anything happen to his only surviving son. Early in June, he dispatched his ambassadors from London, Francis Marsin, James Braybrooke and John Stile, to Spain,[1] with the very specific mission of reporting back upon the appearance and personal details of Joanna, to see if she met Henry's requirements as a woman and a queen. The instructions he gave them afford an insight into early sixteenth-century ideals of beauty and the perceived correlation between certain physicalities and good health.

Valencia sits on Spain's eastern coast, slightly to the north of the modern resort of Benidorm, overlooking the islands in the Balearic Sea. The direct route for the ambassadors lay overland, through France, a journey of around 1,000 miles. Even if they had sailed along the English Channel and landed on the northern coast, at Santander or Coruna, they would have still faced a considerable trip, bisecting Spain north to east for around 450 miles. However, they arrived safely in the city on 22 June and, the following day, were received in the fortified palace, with newer buildings and towers built around an original Moorish courtyard. Conducted through the splendid grounds with ponds and menagerie, they were taken up to the first-floor reception rooms and received by the two Joannas. They delivered letters from Catherine of Aragon, dowager Princess of Wales, and the queens gave thanks with 'a grave stedfast [sic] countenance'. The elder woman, they recorded, spoke to them 'as a noble wise woman', while the younger spoke little, with a 'sad, noble countenance'.[2]

Their main mission was to report upon the appearance of the younger queen, 'to note well her age, stature and features of her body.' They reported that she was 27 'and not much more', but it was difficult to 'come to any perfect knowledge of her stature' because she was 'wearing slippers after the manner of her country' and her body was hidden under 'a great mantle of cloth'. Henry had asked them 'to mark her visage, whether painted or not, fat or lean, sharp or round, cheerful, frowning or melancholy steadfast, light or blushing,' to which they noted that she was not painted, and her face was 'of a good compass, amiable, round and fat, cheerful not frowning, a demure shame-faced countenance' and that her skin was very clear, her hair brown, eyes greyish-brown, teeth fair, clean and well-set, lips 'somewhat round and full'. Her nose was 'a little rising in the middle and bowed towards the end,' her forehead 'not perfectly to be discerned' because she wore her kerchief low, but her complexion was 'fair, sanguine and clean'.[3]

When it came to Joanna's body, they could observe that her arms were round, 'and not very small' but in proportion, her hands round, full and soft, with small fingers of a 'meetly length and breadth', a full and comely neck, large breasts worn, 'or trussed', somewhat high. Henry asked them to judge whether there was any visible hair growing upon her lips, to which the ambassadors replied they could see none. They were instructed to speak with her when she was fasting, to see if her breath was sweet, and they noted that they 'never felt any savour of spices and believe her to be of a sweet savour.' Upon questioning her physician, a Dr Pastorell, they learned that she had no secret blemishes or deformities, and had always been in good health. Henry also wanted to know about her habits. Watching Joanna at table, the ambassadors noted that she was 'a good feeder and eateth well her meat twice a day, drinketh not often, most commonly water, sometimes cinnamon water and sometimes hippocras.' Ever with an eye to his coffers, Henry requested information about her jointure, which was supplied by one Martyn de Albystur, as being 30,000 ducats of annual rent, while the old queen had 40,000 tied up in confiscated Napolese properties. They received a payment of 15,000 or 16,000 ducats from the king for their expenses.[4]

Henry requested that 'some cunning painter' be commissioned to make a sketch of Joanna, 'to agree as nearly as possible in every point and circumstance with her very semblance' and if the first attempt was not perfect, he was to improve and edit it 'till it be made agreeable in every behalf to her image.'[5] If such a drawing was made, no copies of it survived, but the ambassadors had their pen portraits and descriptions to bring home to Henry. On the return journey, on 17 July, they visited Ferdinand, King of Aragon, widow of Isabella and father of Catherine, to discuss her potential wedding with Henry, Prince of Wales, the future Henry VIII.

Whether it was the details, or the sketch of Joanna that Henry disliked, or something else entirely, he did not pursue her as a bride. In fact, he did not remarry at all, a decision to which the poor state of his health and advancing age may have contributed. In 1506, Joanna and the widowed queen returned to Naples where they lived comfortably. Neither ever remarried, despite the daughter receiving more offers, living instead in her mother's shadow and dying just months after her in 1518. Renowned as a beauty during her lifetime, the instructions issued by Henry VII afford a glimpse not only of Joanna's appearance, but of contemporary ideals of womanhood and good health.

10

Queen Idia

1505

Benin City, Nigeria, Africa

While Henry VII was drawing up his inventory for an ideal wife, a very different kind of beauty and leadership was being celebrated 4,300 miles due south. Far away from the courts of London, Paris, Florence and Naples, in a country of swamps and mangroves, the Edo people of Benin, Nigeria, were carving ivory in praise of their Iyoba, or queen mother. Four masks made of their triumphant Idia survive in museums around the world, looted from the King of the Edos' bedroom during the British expedition of 1897. She is singular for her majesty and imposing features.

Three of the masks are ivory. One is held in room 25 at the British Museum, carved in the form of a naturalistic face, with wide open eyes rimmed in black iron, with iron pupils, wide, defined nostrils and full lips, slightly parted. The hair comprises tiny flat circles, intricately carved, topped with a circlet of European heads, symbolic of the African-Portuguese alliance, inlaid with copper alloy. Following the line of the chin is an intricately carved, pierced ruff, set with more copper, in a plaited design. The ears are flat against the head, with decorated suspension loops above and below. Most striking are the two bars, inlaid with iron, seared upon the forehead above the eyes. The mask stands at just over 24 cm tall, 12 cm wide and 6 cm deep. Such objects, according to the British Museum,[1] were worn on the hip during ceremonies. Very similar masks in the Metropolitan Museum of Art in New York and the Linden Museum, Stuttgart, are also made from elephant ivory, with the latter decorated in coral beads, banded about the temples.[2]

Cast bronze heads reputed to be of Idia also exist, held in museum locations in England, Berlin and Lagos. These are likely to have been commissioned by her son after her death, to be placed upon the entrances to civic buildings in commemoration. She is depicted wearing the ukpe-okhue crown, in the shape of a forward-leaning curving cone, decorated with lattice work and red coral beads, and the same markings on the forehead. Idia was clearly a woman celebrated by her people, but it was at the very pinnacle of her success that she was obliged to step back.

Idia was the wife of the Oba (King) of the Benin people, Ozolua, who reigned from 1483. The Benin Empire had been formed in the eleventh century, initially led by the 'Kings of the Sky', and named Igodomigodo. Ozolua proved himself to be a warlike leader, expanding their territory, conquering neighbouring lands and claiming to have won over 200 battles. He also made an uneasy alliance with European traders, sending an ambassador to Portugal and agreeing to welcome Christian missionaries to Nigeria, and export slaves, in exchange for firearms. A pantheistic system underpinned the Edo people's culture, worshipping gods of death, iron, and other elements, who demanded sacrifices of animals and humans. These were carried out every five days, and in biannual and annual festivities until the eighteenth century.

Ozolua, Idia and their family lived in the city of Benin, which was described in 1500 by one Dutch explorer as about a league long, and 'surrounded by a large moat, very wide and deep, which suffices for its defence'[3] and thick mud ramparts. The surrounding country comprised sandy plains and marshy swamps dotted with lakes, that were fed by the ocean. Inland, there was a mixture of forest, grassland and savanna, fields of mangroves and baobab trees where lions, elephants, hippos, monkeys and antelopes roamed. The climate was hot and humid, with two annual rainy seasons and dry, winter winds that filled the air with reddish dust.

The first decade of the sixteenth century saw the height of Ozolua's power. Upon his death, a bitter dispute erupted between his sons, Esigie, the elder, who held Benin, and Arhuanran, who was based in Udo, a city to the north-west. Idia supported Esigie, offering him military and political advice, and using her medical knowledge and reputed magical powers. He raised an army and defeated his brother to become Oba, upon which Arhuanran drowned himself in a river. According to tradition, now that her son was king, Idia was redundant. She was given the title of Iyoba and installed in the Uselu palace, specially built for her retirement. Here, she continued to practise her skills of advice and magic, to help Esigie conquer the Igala people, but the pair were not allowed to meet again. Idia's death date is unknown, but her son continued to rule over the Edo people until 1550. She was a great warrior queen of a nation far removed from the usual western-centric vision of the sixteenth century, whose existence encompassed what initially appear to be very different values. However, the importance of succession and the ferocity with which she fought for her son's rights, finds a direct parallel with the English monarchy of the 1500s.

11

Margaret Beaufort, Countess of Richmond

29 June 1509

The Deanery, Westminster Abbey, London, England

In comparison with the African ivory mask of Idia, Margaret Beaufort's face stares out of her portrait as a clean, white ellipse with large dark eyes. The work was commissioned shortly after her death in 1509 by her friend and confessor, John Fisher. It was created by the Dutch artist at the court of Henry VII, Meynnart Wewyck, and currently hangs in the Master's Lodge of St John's College, Cambridge.[1]

Margaret is depicted in an exclusively Christian and western cultural context, hands clasped in prayer before an open book, with surrounding iconography. She belongs to a different world entirely to Idia, painted as one of the largest images of her time, a huge 180 by 122 cm, in comparison with the Nigerian masks and statues, which average around 30 cm tall. Yet, for all their differences, there are some surprising visual and character similarities between the Tudor king's mother and the queen of the Edo people. Where Idia wears a ruff, Margaret's portrait has the rumpled white wimple pulled up to her chin. Her head is not adorned with Portuguese victims, but with a gable headdress. White, architectural and symbolic, it makes a statement about character just as much as the heads of Idia's conquests do. Draped from head to foot in folds of material, Margaret's pale face hangs suspended, detached, mask-like and ethereal, but with a fixity of purpose that Idia would have recognised.

No sixteenth-century woman is better known for fighting for the rights of her son, Henry VII, than Margaret Beaufort. Like her counterpart in Nigeria, Margaret guarded her son's inheritance, oversaw his military campaigns, ran his household and gave political advice. However, unlike Idia, she was not required to retire upon his succession to the throne. In contrast, with the birth of the Tudor dynasty, Margaret became the driving force behind the new king, utilising her formidable skills to the utmost. She saw him through the challenges and losses of his reign, advised him, sat on his council, influenced culture at court, organised his family and was at his bedside in April 1509, when Henry VII, King of England, died in his new, extravagant Richmond Palace. The journey of the first Tudor king was over, but Margaret clung on long enough to see the next generation take centre stage. Through the spring and early summer of that year, Margaret ran the royal council to oversee the smooth transition of power to her grandson, the 17-year-old Henry VIII.

Yet the beginning of Margaret's story was far removed from such surroundings. In a wind-swept Welsh castle, on a bitter January day in 1457, she had gone into a long, difficult labour. Only 13 years old, Margaret had been married and impregnated by a man twice her age, in order to gain control of her inheritance. The prospect of giving birth must have been terrifying, but then Margaret's position became even more unstable when she found herself a widow after Edmund Tudor's death from the plague. She fled to the safety of her brother-in-law, Jasper, who sheltered her in Pembroke Castle. It was there that she delivered Henry in January 1457, a process which is likely to have done lasting gynaecological damage, as despite taking two more husbands, Margaret would never bear another child.

Against the unfolding events of the Wars of the Roses, mother and son were frequently separated, with the triumphant York dynasty placing Henry as a ward with the Herbert family. Later, as a teenager, he fled with his uncle Jasper into hiding in France and Brittany, where he received assistance from Duke Francis II, father of Anne of Brittany, as he planned his future. Through spies and secret messengers, Margaret and Henry were able to communicate, and share their plans with important figures who could assist them. It was through Henry's triumphant return in 1485, and his victory at Bosworth, that Margaret's years of effort and suffering were vindicated.

For three months, in the early summer of 1509, Margaret Beaufort steered the Tudor ship safely back to port. Henry VII's death was kept quiet for two days to allow for plans to be laid, and his funeral took place on 10 May, amid much ceremony and court mourning. Henry VIII married Catherine of Aragon in a quiet ceremony at Greenwich on 11 June and their joint coronation took place on 23 June at Westminster Abbey. Both funeral and coronation had been arranged by Margaret, and her grandson took her advice and promoted her suggested men to positions on his council. Less than a week later, as the newlyweds partied with their young court, paid for by wealth amassed in the old king's coffers, Margaret lay dying.

Margaret had made her will that January, suggesting that she was already experiencing poor health. However, when her end came that June, at the age of 66, it was sooner than anticipated. She was staying in Cheneygates, the lodgings of the Abbot of Westminster, when she was taken ill after eating cygnet. Swans were a ceremonial dish, and the timing suggests it may have been consumed at one of the feasts following the coronation. Margaret's physicians brought waters and powders to revive her, but her condition worsened, and she died on the night of 29 June. Her body was moved to the abbey refectory where Masses were said for her soul and candlelit vigils were held. She was buried close to her son in the Lady Chapel, with a bronze-topped tomb designed, like his, by the Italian sculptor Pietro Torrigiano, upon which she lies recumbent in her widow's weeds, surrounded by heraldic devices.

A month after her death, at her 'month's mind', Margaret's chaplain and confessor, Bishop John Fisher, preached a long and eloquent sermon in her memory. Listing her virtues and achievements, outlining her acts of charity and piety, and comparing her to Biblical figures, Fisher's account stands as what the sixteenth century considered to be a paragon of womanhood. In it, Margaret is held remarkable for her nobleness of person, the discipline of her body, the ordering of her soul and in dealing with her neighbours:

> She was also of singular easiness to be spoken unto, and full courtesy answer she would make to all that came unto her. Of marvellous gentleness she was to all folks, but especially unto her own who she trusted and loved right tenderly. Unkind she would not be unto no creature, nor forgetful of any kindness or service done to her before, which is no little part of very nobleness. She was not vengeful not cruel, but ready anon to forget and forgive injuries done unto her, at the least desire or motion made unto her for the same. Merciful also and piteous she was unto such as was grieved and wrongfully troubled, and to them that were in poverty or sickness or any other misery.
>
> Awareness of herself, she had always to eschew every thing that might dishonest any noble woman or disdain her honour in any condition. Trifling things that were little to be regarded, she let them pass by, but the other that were of weight and substance wherein she might profit, she would not let for any pain or labour to take upon hand... She had all in manner that was praisable in a woman, either in soul or in body.[2]

Margaret was a formidable figure who cast a long shadow over the remainder of the Tudor regime. As one of the last survivors of the 'Wars of the Roses', she personified the struggles along the path to the throne, and despite hardship, her life story was ultimately one of great success. More than this, though, she reveals the limitations experienced by women, relegated to the background, during times when men resolved their disputes on the battlefield. Much of her early endeavours took place behind the scenes, writing letters, meeting allies, in patronage and prayer, indicating how women were forced into a life of passivity and reaction, and how she overcame this. After 1485, she proved exactly what a woman could achieve once those constraints were removed. Having been the centralising force of her son's reign, she established the foundations for Henry VIII's rule, trusted and empowered by her male contemporaries who respected her advice. Margaret was also a significant patron, inviting scholars to teach and preach at the colleges she founded, as well as building other schools, chapels and supporting Caxton's first English printing press in Westminster. She also wrote a detailed set of Ordinances setting out the protocol and practicalities for childbirth among royal circles, which set the standard followed by subsequent Tudor queens. Margaret's reach was wide, and her influence long-lasting.

12

Women of London

23 January 1513

London

They come down the cobbled city street, singly, in pairs, or hurrying to meet friends. Mary, Anne, Susan, Catherine and Jane. They are mostly smiling, happy and engaged in chatter and warm greetings, dressed in the fashions of the early decades of the century and enjoying a freedom that was perhaps unknown in other places. Jane meets Margaret, kisses her cheek, shakes her hand, and they head into a local tavern to sit and gossip over a drink, before returning home to prepare the family's dinner.

In January 1513, we catch a glimpse of the women of London through the eyes of a visitor. Little is known about the background of Nicol di Favri, of Treviso in northern Italy, who arrived in the city that month to serve the Venetian embassy. Exploring the streets, he observed English habits and practices, devoting a significant portion of his letter home to describing the appearance and behaviour of women. These were the wives, widows, sisters and daughters of London, unnamed and unknown, glimpsed in passing as they went about their business. The beauty of di Favri's letter is that it provides a snapshot, capturing life in one moment as fully as a photograph, as he stands to watch them walking, going to market and meeting friends:

> In England the women go to market for household provisions; if gentlewomen, they are preceded by two men servants.
>
> Their usual vesture is a cloth petticoat over the shift, lined with grey squirrel's or some other fur; over the petticoat they wear a long gown lined with some choice fur. The gentlewomen carry the train of their gown under the arm; the commonalty pin it behind or before, or at one side. The sleeves of the gowns sit as close as possible; are long, and unslashed throughout, the cuffs being lined with some choice fur.
>
> Their head gear is of various sorts of velvet, cap fashion, with lappets hanging down behind over their shoulders like two hoods; and in front they have two others, lined with some other silk. Their hair is not seen, so is unable to say whether it be light or dark. Others wear on their heads muslins, which are distended, and hang at their backs, but not far down. Some draw their hair from under a kerchief, and wear over the hair a cap, for the most

part white, round, and seemly; others again wear a kerchief in folds on the head: but be the fashion as it may, the hair is never seen.

Their stockings are black and their shoes doubly soled, of various colours, but no one wears choppines, [platformed shoes] as they are not in use in England.

When they meet friends in the street, they shake hands, and kiss on the mouth, and go to some tavern to regale, their relatives not taking this amiss, as such is the custom. The women are very beautiful and good tempered.[1]

As Favri went on his way, about embassy business, the unnamed women of London faded into obscurity, leaving us a brief tableau of daily life in the streets of one of the busiest cities in the world. These unnamed wives, daughters, mothers, sisters, grandmothers and others could represent any one of our ancestors from the past, going about their daily business, unaware that they were being observed, and recorded, and especially that they would be resurrected five decades later. Significantly, we see these women of London through the male gaze, rather from any surviving source of their own making. Female literacy levels were low and the usual business of life was rarely captured in pen and ink, let alone on canvas. No matter how sympathetic those recording the sixteenth century may have been, they were predominantly male, so Jane and Margaret, and the other women in London's streets, are with a few rare exceptions, depicted as 'other', by the opposite sex, with all the misconceptions and biases this may entail. We are told what Jane and Margaret do, how they look and behave, and where they go, but as onlookers at a distance of centuries, we must always be conscious that we are not being told what they think.

13

Elisabeth van Culemborg, Countess of Hochstrate

June 1513

Hof van Savoy, Mechelen, Netherlands

The sunshine bathed the courtyard of the Hof van Savoy in warm summer light. It was a beautiful garden, set out within the confines of the imposing palace in the centre of the Belgian city of Mechelen, then called Malines. The little space was overlooked by four walls of ornate red brickwork, gable roofs, high windows and archways. Below, the footpaths wound between flower beds and ornate bushes, where the scent of roses and herbs were caught on the light breeze.

Waiting under the archway stood an elegant lady in her late thirties, dressed in the most respectable, sober clothes that her exalted rank could buy. For seven years, Elisabeth van Culemborg had been Dame d'Honneur to the owner of this splendid palace: Archduchess Margaret, regent of the Netherlands, daughter of the emperor Maximilian. Since her second marriage, Elisabeth had also been Countess Hochstrate, and her husband Antoine was a member of the Great Council, commanding the Archduchess's bodyguard and household. One of Elisabeth's roles was to oversee the young women Margaret took under her wing, the daughters of important dignitaries and officials from the Netherlands and beyond, who received a good education and polish, using the palace libraries, taking lessons with the many humanist tutors employed there, riding in the surrounding forests and listening as they were instructed in manners and decorum.[1] This morning, the eighteen girls were taking a breath of exercise between their classes. Their French lesson with their favourite Symonet was over and next they would go to Herr Bredemers for instruction on the clavichord.[2] The time was up. Elisabeth clapped her hands and the girls turned obediently, and headed back towards her, into the building.

Without exception, they were good girls. They knew how fortunate they were to receive the opportunity Margaret gave them, and the doors it would open for them. Yet they were still girls, and prone to the upsets and trials of youth. Elisabeth had to remind them to avoid gossiping and foolish conversations, sitting with them during their quiet pursuits of sewing shirts, spinning flax, reading and playing chess with the red and green pieces on the ivory board. At night, she was grateful to hand them over to the care of Anna de Beaumont, who was in charge of their chamber, or for an hour to Marguerite de Poitiers, who was engaged as a tutor, or when they were ill, to be nursed by the Archduchess's own apothecary, the Countess de Horne, with her knowledge of herbs and special preserves.[3] Often, they came together with the Archduchess's own nephew and nieces, the 13-year-old Prince Charles and his sisters, Eleanor, Isabella and Mary, to ride, or eat, to attend jousts, watch dancing bears[4] or attend Mass at the cathedral. Elisabeth especially valued their spiritual welfare, and it was her only regret that her mistress tolerated such figures at her court who were critical of Catholic practices and veered towards heresy, like the Dutchman Erasmus.

Elisabeth herself was an heiress of considerable means. Born in 1475, she was the daughter of Jasper von Culemborg, a member of the lower rungs of aristocracy, and had already been married into the Luxembourg family before making her second, prestigious match. Upon the death of her father, she ruled nominally over the city of Culemborg, just under 100 miles away, mostly whilst being absent, as her service kept her in Mechelen. Her love of art was well served by the extensive collection displayed on the walls of the palace, including the faces of European royalty, and those from further afield, brought as gifts to Margaret by the many travellers who she entertained, from as far-flung places as India, China and even the New World. As Elisabeth watched the girls taking their places in the music room, demure and expectant now, with their clean hands and white linen kerchiefs neatly placed over their hair, she wondered if little Jeanne's cough had cleared up, or if Bonne's nightmares had ceased. And there was the new girl, little Anne Boleyn from England. Twelve years old and a bright, lively soul, just as her father was. She sat up expectantly, fascinated by her surroundings, ready to absorb all she was taught.

It was last year, 1512, when Anne's father, the diplomat Sir Thomas Boleyn, had first arrived at the Mechelen court. Sent by Henry VIII, to negotiate an alliance against the French, he had soon charmed them all with his urbane manners and become a particular favourite of the Archduchess, conversing with her at length on all manner of topics. So when he mentioned that he had two daughters, one already placed at the English court, and another slightly younger, a sparky, intelligent girl hungry for learning and culture, Margaret had suggested that he send Anne to her. The girl had lived up to her proud father's descriptions and her first weeks at court had proved a success. Margaret wrote to Thomas Boleyn, promising to

> ...treat her in such a fashion that you will have reason to be content with it; at least be sure that until your return there need be no other intermediary between you and me than she; and I find her of such good address and so pleasing in her youthful age that I am more beholden to you for having sent her to me than you are to me.[5]

Later that year, the new young King of England, Henry VIII, visited Archduchess Margaret in Lille, whilst engaged on his campaign to claim the French towns of Therouanne and Tournai. Elisabeth may have received instructions to remain behind at Mechelen and continue to oversee her charges, or perhaps she was asked to prepare the girls, and accompany them on the 80-mile journey to Lille. When Margaret dined with Henry, in his gold-hung quarters, she took some of her 'principal damsels' and after some boisterous dancing, the king presented the ladies with a beautiful diamond.[6]

The following year, Anne Boleyn was recalled by her father as the allegiances of international politics shifted. She was sent instead to serve Claude, Queen of France. Elisabeth continued to oversee the Archduchess's finishing school for girls, despairing against the advancing tide of heresy and seeking to repress the writings of Erasmus and encouraging the Catholic order of the Jesuits to thrive in Culemborg. Later, as Margaret's health worsened, Antoine became acting governor of the Netherlands, before her death in 1530. Elisabeth and Antoine remained in Mechelen for a decade after Margaret's niece Mary took over the governorship, but after Antoine's death in 1540, Elisabeth returned to Culemborg. No doubt, from a distance, she would have heard of the incredible rise and fall of her former pupil, Anne Boleyn.

Elisabeth is another of the women in danger of being lost to history. Her story has been remembered largely not for its own merit, but because it impinges upon the lives of her more famous peers. And yet she played a crucial role. She was not an empress, queen or regent, but the position she occupied allowed her to influence key players of the next generation. As a teacher and guardian, her skills and knowledge were instrumental in the young lives of future queens of England (Anne), Portugal and France (Eleanor), Hungary and Bohemia (Mary) and Denmark, Norway and Sweden (Isabella). Elisabeth's influence was controversial, though. Her devout Catholicism extended to the condemnation and burning of books by emerging critical voices, such as Martin Luther, and she welcomed the foundation of a Jesuit community in Culemborg. Thus, she stood in opposition to the values of the Reformation, in a changing world, which some of her pupils would embrace and others reject. Elisabeth must be remembered as a woman fighting for her beliefs in a changing world; only her status and gender placed that battle inside the classroom, rather than the council chamber or field of combat. For better or worse, her standards, ideals and faith influenced the Reformation generation.

14

Margaret Tudor

9 September 1513
Linlithgow Palace, West Lothian, Scotland

Shortly after his visit to Archduchess Margaret at Lille, Henry VIII received important news from home. As he campaigned against the French, a new danger had emerged, or rather an old one had returned. For centuries, the Franco-Scots 'Old Alliance' had threatened English security from north and south, yet, in 1502, Henry and James IV had signed the Treaty of Perpetual Peace, as part of the arrangements by which James had married Henry's elder sister Margaret.

The marriage had been one of great hope, designed to unite two warring neighbours. Its symbolism was celebrated in poetry by William Dunbar as the union of *The Thrissil and the Rois*, with James symbolised by the spiky, warlike thistle and Margaret as the soft, beautiful, fragrant rose to tame him, a combination of red and white:

> Nor hald non udir flour in sic denty
> As the fresche Rois, of cullour reid and quhyt:
> For gife thow dois, hurt is thyne honesty;
> Considring that no flour is so perfyt,
> So full of vertew, plesans, and delyt,
> So full of blisful angeilik bewty,
> Imperiall birth, honour and dignité.[1]

Thus, the two kings were brothers-in-law, a relationship that should have superseded any former alliance. James, though, continued to prepare himself for war. Even the Pope wrote to forbid his actions, and excommunicated him, but James persisted in honouring his former friendship, writing to Henry to cease his campaign. Observing this unfold, and pregnant with her sixth child, Margaret begged her husband not to invade her homeland. For years, she had embodied the union and acted as mediator between the men, but on this occasion, James would not listen.

Before he departed, James entrusted Margaret with his treasure 'in case aught happened other than good to him' and arranged for the last of King Louis of France's subsidies to be paid to his son.[2] He made arrangements for their son to be raised by the Bishop of Aberdeen in the event of his death, with Margaret named as his 'tutrix' or female tutor. James then ordered his wife to remain in the stronghold of Linlithgow Castle. Tradition holds that she sat in a certain window in a small room off the stairs, now called Queen Margaret's Bower, where she prayed and awaited news.

On 9 September 1513, the Scots invaded England and were defeated at the Battle of Flodden, with the loss of around 10,000 men. Among them was King James, whose blood-stained coat was found on the battlefield. This was sent as a trophy to Henry in France by his wife Catherine of Aragon, although she stopped short of sending him James' body, as being too much for English sensibilities. From her base at Woburn Abbey, she wrote to Henry in Tournai:

> Ye shall see at length the great victory that our Lord hath sent your subjects in your absence. Thinks the victory the greatest honour that could be. The King will not forget to thank God for it. Could not, for haste, send by Rouge Cross the piece of the King of Scots coat which John Glyn now bringeth. In this your Grace shall see how I can keep my promyse, sending you for your banners a King's coat. I thought to send himself unto you, but our Englishmen's hearts would not suffer it. It should have been better for him to have been in peace than have this reward.[3]

Catherine's triumphant letter stands in stark contrast to one written on the day of the battle itself, by Margaret, addressed to a lady at the English court, thought to be Lady Dacre:

My good Lady, I pray you remember aupon me in your good prayers. Your loveng frende, Margaret the Qwuen of Scotts.[4]

Margaret continued to wait and pray. Gradually, the survivors returned with their terrible eyewitness accounts of the king being slain in the field, yet rumours still persisted that James had escaped, and there were reputed sightings, including that he was on pilgrimage to the Holy Lands. James, however, was definitely dead. And Margaret, two months' pregnant, had to make a swift decision.

Taking her 17-month-old son, the widowed queen sped to Perth to arrange his coronation, hoping that his blood relationship with her brother would prevent an English invasion. From there, she wrote to Henry, 'deprecating his further hostilities and entreating him not to oppress or harm her little king, his nephew who was, she said, very small and tender.'[5] Henry replied that he regretted James' death as a relative, but as a king, he had 'fallen by his own indiscreet rashness' and that if the Scots wanted peace, they could have it.'[6] Within three weeks, the young boy was crowned at Scone, in what was called 'The Mourning Coronation,' attended by the remnants of the Scottish nobility who had survived the battlefield. Parliament was convened at Stirling Castle that December, and Margaret was recognised as regent, with a committee of lords to assist her. She was just 24. The following April, at Stirling, she gave birth to Alexander, James' posthumous child.

Flodden marked a low point in Margaret's relationship with England, and with her Tudor siblings. Using her familial ties to appeal to her brother, she promised him that she would do all she could to prevent the French candidate for Regency from gaining control. Even a woman as powerful as Margaret, the daughter and sister of English kings, the wife of the Scottish king, could do nothing to prevent disaster unfolding before her eyes. Her usual tools of persuasion, supplication and benevolence were useless against her husband's determination, and her appeals to their family ties, her nationality and even her gut instinct were dismissed. Forced into a passive role, there was little she could do but pray, until news of her husband's death brought her greater freedom and autonomy in deciding how to respond. Once her main identity shifted from that of wife to mother, she was enabled to act decisively in the name of her son. Maternity, especially that of a widow with a son under the age of 12, conferred a certain status upon a woman. In a sense, she fulfilled the masculine role of guidance and direction until he came of age and was able to rule alone.

However, being a lone woman in the cut-throat, factional environment of the Scottish court was very difficult. Margaret's position was complicated by being the sister of an enemy king. In spite of this, she managed to pacify the Scottish factions and be accepted by the council as her son's regent, citing his best interests. Then, though, Margaret made a personal decision that cost her dearly. She sought a protector, but in doing so, she aligned herself with one side, signing over her autonomy and impartiality. Four months after the coronation, in August 1514, she was secretly married to Archibald Douglas, Earl of Angus, believing herself in love. It was an understandable action, but one that weakened her standing as the pro-French, anti-English faction turned against her. By the terms of James' will, this meant she forfeited her Regency and was replaced by the Duke of Albany, with his French affiliations. Upon his arrival in Scotland, Albany claimed custody of Margaret's two sons, and Margaret began to fear for her life. Pregnant by Douglas, she could only travel with permission of the council, to whom she appealed to deliver her child at Linlithgow. Instead of returning to the palace, though, she fled to England, going into labour in Northumberland and delivering a daughter.

Margaret Tudor's life reveals the tension between retaining power and pursuing love. It was no less than the marital dilemmas faced by her brother, Henry VIII, except that her gender made her more open to challenge and more swiftly judged. As a woman, she was considered weak for following her affections, while Henry was able to break with Rome, marry for love and retain his throne. The problem also lay in her choices. No candidate for her hand would have been universally accepted, so Margaret was faced with the stark dilemma of either remaining unmarried as regent, or else pursuing love and affiliation, and accepting the consequences. It was not so much Margaret's choice to be sexually active that was the problem, as a common Tudor trope was that of rampant female desire, but that such activity required a male partner. Her contemporaries considered she had made a poor choice in Douglas, a view that Margaret came to espouse, subsequently divorcing him.

15

The Money Lender's Wife

1514

Antwerp, Netherlands

She sits on her husband's left, the traditional female side. Her arms rest on the green baize counter, indicative of financial transactions, leaning in to watch him at work. Her outer garment is a rich plum red, gathered at the waist with an embroidered belt, and a collar and cuffs of grey fur. Underneath, at the neck, the white line of her shift is visible and at her wrists, the edge of a black sleeve protrudes with a golden decoration. Her head is covered by a white wimple, topped by a flat purple hat with the brim folded back. She is not young, but not old either, perhaps in her late thirties or early forties. Her face is pink and fresh, rounded and devoid of make-up or adornment, and her expression one of concentration, but it is more observation she displays, rather than deep engagement with her husband's work. Her eyes are dark and slightly weary. A single gold band ring sits upon the little finger of her right hand.

The Money Lender and His Wife was painted in 1514, in the financial city of Antwerp, then the richest city in the province of the Netherlands. The artist, Quentin Matsys, had settled there in the 1490s and was well known for producing satirical or moral pieces, founding a new, realistic Antwerp school in the style of the Northern Renaissance. The married pair he depicted in their workshop may well have been a real couple known to him: Gust and Anke, Hans and Marien, or Jan and Sybilla. The Van Eyck-style reflection in the round mirror on the table shows the head of a figure in a red turban, seated off the canvas, which might depict the artist at work. Equally, the pair might be figures drawn from his imagination, inspired by any number of individuals Matsys encountered in the city.

As she watches, the woman's husband is engaged in weighing a coin in a delicate, hand-held pair of scales. He wears a voluminous dark blue coat, belted at the waist by a black band and silver buckle, with brown fur at the chin and wrists. His cuffs beneath it are the same red as his wife's dress and he also wears one ring, on his second finger, set with a black or green stone. He wears a black liripipe, the folded, long-tailed hood, below which his face is clean-shaven with downcast eyes and a cleft chin. He focuses on the task in hand as he prepares to add another coin to the scales. Both couples have long, spindly fingers, almost preternaturally long, symbolic of avarice. Spread before them on the table are coins, weights, rings, pearls and other instruments of their trade. The two shelves behind contain more instruments, books, documents, a candle and more, while the open door to the right shows two people in conversation, perhaps concluding a transaction. It is the kind of detailed workspace portrait that would lead to Holbein's depictions of Steelyard merchants in London and, ultimately, The Ambassadors. Holbein would visit Matsys's home in Shuttershofstraat in 1526, witnessing a number of works in progress, as well as complete pieces. He may well have seen the money lender and his wife, heads bent together in concentration.

Yet while the man's hands are engaged in business, his wife's are in contact with a holy book, lifting her symbolism above the merely mercantile. It is an expensive, decorated item, bound in black leather with carved silver clasps, quite different from the simple brown leather binding of the volume on the shelf behind. The endpages are patterned with a geometric design of diamonds. With her left hand she holds down a page of text with an illuminated capital letter, whilst her right is caught midway through turning the next to reveal an illustration of the Virgin and child, whose colouring echoes the dark red and blue of the couple's clothing, suggesting affinity.

In the early sixteenth century, Antwerp was experiencing an influx of immigrant 'heretics' from Spain, fleeing the Catholic Inquisition established by Isabella and Ferdinand. This expanded the existing market for borrowing and exchanging money, although this was in direct conflict with the traditional church doctrine against usury. The picture's juxtaposition of avarice and prayer may be the key to understanding its purpose. While some critics hold that it is satirical, making a moral comment about the greed of the couple, it is equally likely that Matsys intended to show that economic activity was acceptable, and reconciles doctrine with a new naturalism.[1] The fruit and snuffed candle on the back shelf represent the brevity of life, subtle memento mori that remind the viewer that material wealth cannot be taken into the kingdom of heaven, while devotion can.

It is significant that the instrument of the religious message is the money lender's wife. With her demure downcast face, her middle-class clothes and her fingers laced between the pages of a devotional book, she is a complex figure, straddling different worlds. She represents the point where the mercantile meets avarice, but she is a woman in that world, stereotypically bringing a feminine softness to the question of fairness in the transaction, but also attracted by the shiny baubles laid out on the table. She is both demure and modest, but with a glowing pink earthiness, a far greater physicality than the husband who pales beside her. There is something immediate about her, that draws the viewer and invites questions. Looking up from her text, she might be neglecting her devotions in favour of profit, or bringing the wisdom of the book to the transaction.

Whoever she may be, the money lender's wife is a knot of paradoxes that historians have yet to satisfactorily untie. The faces of women from paintings in the sixteenth century present a fascinating false reality as representations of contemporary life, but filtered through the artist's vision. Like the Mona Lisa, this Antwerp woman is satisfyingly real, yet is also symbolic of all women of her class and profession, and even of perceived female qualities beyond them. However, in spite of all this, we must never lose sight of the fact that this representation of a woman has been created by a male artist, portrayed through the male gaze, according to patriarchal values of the day. However sympathetic the artist may have been, *The Money Lender and his Wife* is still a construct of femininity, rather than a woman expressing or depicting herself.

16

Claude, Queen of France

10 May 1517

Paris, France

The marriage treaty signed at Nantes back in January 1499 had swiftly borne fruit. To return to the first woman of this collection, Anne of Brittany had fallen pregnant swiftly after her marriage to Louis XII of France. After losing all the children from her first marriage, Anne feared that history would repeat itself, so she undertook a pilgrimage to pray for the baby's safe delivery. Her daughter Claude arrived in October, at Romorantin-Lanthenay, but proved to be a tiny, sickly child, with a strabismus in her eye and scoliosis curving her spine, and it was doubted whether she would survive. Yet Claude was stronger than she looked. She made it through the difficult years of infancy and grew to be good-natured and pious. The chronicler Brantôme described her as 'very good and very charitable, and very sweet to everyone and never showed displeasure to anybody in her court or of her domains. She was deeply loved by the King Louis and the Queen Anne, her father and mother, and she was always a good daughter to them.'[1]

As the child of such significant parents, Claude was expected to marry young. In 1505, when Louis was ill and despaired of fathering a son, he betrothed his infant daughter to his cousin Francis. Anne of Brittany and Francis' mother, Louise of Savoy, had never been friends, and the queen actively opposed this new match. However, after Anne's death in January 1514, Claude inherited her title of Duchess of Brittany and, three months later, married Francis, to whom she signed over her Breton inheritance. In a *Commémoration* book dedicated to her that year, Claude is pictured as a tiny figure seated in a large throne, with her feet resting on a cushion of black and gold. A posthumous illustration in the *Book of Hours* of her daughter-in-law, Catherine de' Medici, shows Claude with a devout expression, her dark hair pulled back under a plain white hood, hands together in prayer, surrounded by her female relatives. After six months of marriage, she became pregnant, soon after her fifteenth birthday. Just two months later, with the death of Louis XII at the end of 1514, she succeeded as queen of France and bore her first child, a daughter named Louise, in August 1515. Soon after Christmas, she was pregnant again, bearing Princess Charlotte the following October. Her birth, and her family circumstances, propelled Claude into adulthood, and parenthood, at a very young age.

In May 1517, over two years since Claude had become queen, she was finally given a full coronation. This had been delayed in order to accommodate her pregnancies, but the occasion was most certainly not an after-thought, as Francis organised an ostentatious display in her honour. The day before, Claude prayed in memory of her parents at the Church of St Denis, 'in great devotion and contemplation over the tomb and statue of her father and mother, and not without tears and lamentations.'[2] Her ladies helped her into her overgarment and bodice trimmed with the Breton symbol of the ermine, from her coat of arms, as a reminder that she was simultaneously queen and duchess. Before her death, Claude's mother had given her a cape to wear for the occasion, 'sewn with little leaves of gold onto silver cloth, filled with beautifully fashioned ermines in the form of raised animals, all completely covered with raised pearls,' with a huge ruby set into the clasp.[3] Among those helping Claude prepare was the 16-year-old Anne Boleyn, who had arrived three years earlier from the court of Archduchess Margaret in Mechelen. The two young women were close in age, which may have led to an intimacy between them.

The city of Paris was decorated in honour of its queen. Seven sites of pageantry had been created along Claude's route, colourful with ornamentation, actors and musicians. The crowds pushed in on all sides to see them, as well as to catch a glimpse of the young woman being carried in the litter. Francis had hired Pierre Gringore to provide the entertainment, the most famous Parisian poet, actor and playwright of his day, who had recently composed a mystery play about Louis XII but was also known for his satires on the papacy.[4] The first display was staged at the Châtelet, the Parisian seat of justice, and featured the genealogy of Brittany, as designed and related by Gringore; 'the aforementioned lady arrived at the Châtelet of Paris, where she found a tree with many branches, like a Tree of Jesse, on a large scaffolding. In the upper branches were a crowned king and queen… and on each side of these branches were several princes, princesses, kings and dukes of Brittany, demonstrating the line and genealogy from which the aforementioned lady arose.'[5]

At St Denis, an actor playing the queen stood surrounded by six Biblical women, each symbolising one of the desirable qualities of a French queen: fertility (Leah), modesty (Esther), loyalty (Sarah), prudence (Rebecca), amiability (Rachel) and education (Deborah). At the site of Saint Innocents, three large open hearts contained female figures representing Divine Love, Conjugal Love and Natural Love. The depiction of women in civic pageantry was usually aspirational, with local or guild women, or young boys, posing in suitable costumes, holding up or reciting verses, or singing. On that May day in 1517, a number of Parisian women had the honour of speaking directly to their queen as representatives of the city. They would have been selected for their status, as the wives, sisters or daughters of leading guild members, and possibly for their good name, or their beauty.

Claude was carried into Notre Dame Cathedral on a litter draped in cloth of silver, head to toe in jewels. With Francis observing from behind the customary grille so as not to upstage her, the Duke of Alençon held the heavy crown of Charlemagne above her head, the Constable of Bourbon knelt to hold her train, the Comte de Guise held the hand of justice and the Prince de la Roche-sur-Yon held the sceptre. Under Notre Dame's Gothic vaulting and great rose window, Claude was anointed and made her promises. She was crowned by Cardinal Philippe de Luxembourg, then an old man of 72, who had ruled on her father's divorce from his first wife in 1498.[6]

At the banquet held afterwards in her honour at the Palais du Justice, food was served on gold and silver plates, set on cloth of gold, covering marble tables. The following day a tournament was held, at which the Knights of the Day, dressed in white and led by Francis, competed against the Comte de St Pol and his black-clad Knights of the Night.[7] Following the Parisian festivities, the French royal family set off on progress. They followed the route of the Seine through Picardy, almost 90 miles to Rouen, where Francis made an official entry into the city on 2 August, dressed in cloth of gold, riding a horse decked out in the same material. The following day, Claude made her entry, second to her husband according to protocol, but ensuring that she received the limelight in her own right. Conceiving another child around the time of her coronation, the years ahead would be dominated by pregnancies and lying-in for Claude. Heavily pregnant, she would preside over the Anglo-French festivities at the Field of Cloth of Gold in June 1520, and deliver her fifth child on 10 August. Anne Boleyn would serve her, observing the importance of producing healthy male sons, until the end of 1521 or early 1522 when she was recalled to England.

Claude died in July 1524 at the age of 24, having worn herself out delivering seven children in eight years. Her death may have occurred during or after labour, bearing a child that did not survive, or her history may have created a complication in her already delicate health. It was also rumoured that her licentious husband Francis had infected her with syphilis, although this cannot be proven. She was buried in a huge marble tomb, which she later shared with Francis in the Basilica St Denis in northern Paris, a popular site of pilgrimage. Her son Henri would become king of France and her daughter Madeleine, briefly Queen of Scotland. As queen of France, her tenure had been brief, but sufficient to establish her character as one of piety, morality, majesty and endurance – almost saintliness in the face of great physical suffering.

17

Juana, Queen of Castile and Aragon

4 November 1517

Royal Convent, Palace of Tordesillas, Castile, Spain

By 1517, the Royal Palace at Tordesillas was wrapped in a mood of isolation and sadness. With its once-majestic courtyards planted with vegetables, crumbling Mudejar architecture and rooms hung with dusty tapestries, it was in need of constant repair. The once imposing view across the vineyards was encroached upon all sides by poor, ugly houses.[1] For the 38-year-old Castilian queen inside, who was not permitted to linger by the window, it had become a prison.

Traditionally referred to as 'Juana, or Joanna, the mad', modern interpretations of Queen Juana of Castile have been more sympathetic. Recent historians have concluded that those behaviours her contemporaries considered to be evidence of insanity could be the result of depression or schizophrenia, or were the justifiable responses to manipulation by her husband and father as a way of wresting power from her control.[2] Because she was considered a heretic, and difficult, her family conspired to prevent Juana from claiming the throne. Although she inherited Castile upon the death of Isabella in 1504, her father continued to rule in her place and, after his death in January 1516, her rights passed to her 16-year-old son.

Juana was the third child of Isabella of Castile and Ferdinand of Aragon, the all-powerful, most Catholic monarchs. Upon the deaths of her elder sister and brother, she became her parents' heir, but her childhood had not been easy. A letter written by Mosen Ferrer, one of Ferdinand's gentlemen of the bedchamber in March 1516, refers to times when Juana had been disciplined as a young woman, suggesting that she had been anorexic and had been subjected to corporal punishment: 'the King her father could never do more until, to prevent her from destroying herself by abstinence from food, as often as her will was not done, he had to order that she was to be put to the rope (cuerda) to preserve her life.'[3] The use of the rope stemmed more from Juana's heretical beliefs, or her refusal to conform to her parents' strict practices. It was a method of torture used by the Inquisition to extract confession, by which a victim was suspended from the ceiling by a rope and weights were attached to their feet. When Acua, Bishop of Zamora, was subjected to this method, he was warned that 'he was in danger of having his limbs broken or dislocated, and even of losing his life.'[4] Juana's parents had caused thousands of heretics to be burned at the stake for minor transgressions, and they were not prepared to tolerate the slightest insurrection in their daughter, their heir and the future Queen of Spain.

After her mother's death in 1504, Juana intended to rule Castile jointly with her husband Philip, while Ferdinand retired to his native Aragon. The marriage was tempestuous, as a result of Philip's repeated infidelities and attempts to undermine his wife in order to use her power. They left their marital home in the Netherlands for Spain in 1506, but Philip died shortly after arriving in September, possibly as the result of poison. Juana was pregnant at the time and, despite his cruelty, her grief was intense with rumours circulating that she carried her husband's body about with her. Famine, plague and public disorder created a climate over which it was very difficult for Juana alone to regain control, especially as she was not granted the necessary funds required to act by her council. Ferdinand remained in Aragon, deliberately not offering any assistance or guidance. During this time, Juana was also in the final trimester of her sixth pregnancy, delivering her daughter Catherine on 14 January. As an inexperienced ruler, denied support in a full-scale crisis, and undergoing childbirth, these few short months were considered sufficient to judge her incapable.

Ferdinand returned to Castile the following spring. His arrival happened to coincide with the plague and famine abating, for which he was given credit. Juana was forced to sign over power to him, protesting that it was against her will, and becoming queen in name only. Shortly afterwards, Ferdinand dismissed all Juana's servants and imprisoned her in the Royal Palace, which comprised one large room and a number of small ones, ill-lit and poorly ventilated.[5] Juana was confined to certain rooms, sharing the space with her jailer, the Marquis of Denia and his family, and she was constantly watched by twelve women, also in residence. Her windows overlooked the river, but she was not allowed to remain there, looking out, in case she called for assistance to a passer-by. Often, she was kept in a back room lit only by candles.[6] In the meantime, Ferdinand remarried in the hope of fathering a son who might have a superior claim to the crown from Juana, by virtue of his gender.

By the time of her father's death in January 1516, Juana had been at the palace for almost seven years. Ferdinand's will stipulated that rule should pass to Juana's sons, either the eldest, Charles, who had been raised in the Netherlands, or the younger, Ferdinand, his grandfather's personal choice, who had been born and raised in Castile. As the months advanced, Juana could only sit tight in the palace as her young co-monarch approached. In October the following year, Charles and his sister Eleanor, whom Juana had not seen since they were small children, sailed into the Bay of Biscay. On 4 November 1517, they visited their mother and sister Catherine at Tordesillas.

It must have been a strange reunion for all those involved. Among the Burgundian delegation was historian Laurent Vital, who recorded how he accompanied Charles to the door of his mother's chamber, but was forbidden from taking a light into the room.[7] In the darkness, the hopeful mother met her children. She was a prisoner who had not been permitted outside or to enjoy the daylight, whose reputation for instability preceded her. However, Juana was no longer at the mercy of her father and was prepared to make any concessions her son requested, granting him permission to be her co-ruler of Castile and Aragon. She may have entertained hopes of finding Charles sympathetic to her plight, of regaining some measure of influence, or at the very least, her liberty. After the meeting, Charles and Eleanor made their entry into Valladolid, where Charles took part in the tournaments and jousts, carrying a shield bearing the device *Nondum*, or 'not yet'.[8]

Nothing changed for Juana as a result of the meeting. She had no political power, no concession to allow any sort of co-rule and no greater freedoms were permitted her during her confinement. If she had hoped that her son would set her free, Juana was bitterly disappointed. Whether Charles simply accepted the status quo as necessary to facilitate his rule, or if he saw Juana with his own eyes as unfit to rule, her confinement in the Royal Palace would continue. The only change was that Catherine, the young daughter who had shared her imprisonment, was given her own household and permitted greater mobility, and would eventually be allowed to leave in order to marry. Juana would not see Charles or Eleanor again, but perhaps she heard about the latter's marriage to Francis I in 1530.

Within a few months, Juana's guardian, the Marquis of Denia wrote to Charles about his mother's longing to go outside:

> The Queen our lady has spoken with me oftentimes, and told me that she desired to go out, and that I was to accompany her. Every time that she spoke to me on this subject, I answered that the weather was bad for her health, and her Highness ought not, therefore, to go out; but as soon as the weather should be good, I would let her know, and then she could go out. Every time that she speaks to me about her going out, and that is often, she insists on it very much, but hitherto I have prevented it, making use of the best words possible. Her Highness has likewise told me to call some grandees into her presence, because she intends to complain of the manner in which she is treated, and wishes to know about her affairs. I replied to her Highness that the grandees would do nothing in this affair, because the Catholic King and they, together with the whole kingdom, have settled the manner in which her Highness was to be treated.[9]

Denia's response to Juana reveals the continuing agreement to deny her freedom, assistance and the exercise of her wishes. In response to her repeated requests, the queen was misled and given false hope, and her attempts to exert her will and call upon the support of grandees were denied. Her avenues for complaint were shut down and her incarceration represented as final, or settled, as a joint agreement with the 'whole kingdom'. Even had Juana been exhibiting the behaviour her contemporaries considered to be madness, such treatment can only have worsened any existing mental health condition. To the modern eye, it appears a barbaric and oppressive patriarchal conspiracy to limit female power behind the convenient term of instability.

G.A. Bergenroth, editor of the State Spanish Papers, believes that a conspiracy was hatched to prevent Juana exercising power on account of her heretical views, which would have undermined the work of her parents:

> Under these circumstances it was decided to prevent Juana from becoming Queen. The plan seems to have been ripe in the year 1501, and was communicated to the Cortes, who held their sittings, in the years 1502 and 1503, first in Toledo, then in Madrid, and finally in Alcala de Henares. To make the true reasons public would have been a humiliation, and perhaps not without danger, considering the great unpopularity of the Inquisition. Some pretext was, therefore, absolutely necessary. In the Rolls of the Cortes it is only stated that King Ferdinand, after the death of Queen Isabel, should continue to carry on the government, in case Juana should be 'absent, or unable, or unwilling' to exercise her royal prerogative. In an additional clause to her testament, the Queen ordered, once again, and more explicitly, that her husband Ferdinand should be her immediate successor, without mentioning the conditions of her daughter's 'absence, unwillingness, or incapacity'.[10]

Whatever the truth of Juana's situation may have been, the forces ranged against her were too powerful, too overwhelming, for a single woman to fight, even when that woman had inherited the throne. She remained incarcerated in the Royal Palace of Tordesillas for a total of forty-six years until her death in April 1555. Charles only outlived her by three years.

18

Frau Troffea

July 1518

City Streets, Strasbourg, Alsace, Holy Roman Empire

By the early 1500s, Strasbourg was a major city, with busy marketplaces and narrow medieval streets centred around the Romanesque Cathedral of Our Lady. The pioneer Johannes Gutenberg had perfected his moveable-type printing press there in the 1440s and his workshop had been producing pamphlets and early books, called incunabula, for decades since. Other world firsts included the production of the first printed advertisement and the opening of the first spectacle shop. Located in territory that continually changed allegiance, the city had been under the rule of the Holy Roman Empire since 1469, but in recent years it had rejected the empire's intense Catholicism in favour of the Protestant reforms that were sweeping Europe.

However, in 1518, Strasbourg's residents were suffering. A recent epidemic of smallpox had swept through the city and the harvests had failed miserably, driving up prices to the highest in living memory. Hospitals and charities were overwhelmed by the numbers of poor and needy, asking daily for shelter and alms.[1] It was amid these conditions, on a summer's day in the middle of July, that a lone woman walked out into the streets and began to dance. Only one source records her name, and that was eight years after the event. When Swedish physician Paracelsus arrived in the city in 1526, the story of Frau Troffea's exertions was still being told. He related how the local people were initially sceptical, believing that the incident occurred after her husband thwarted her will, and she danced publicly to irritate him and have her revenge.[2] But Frau Troffea's performance lasted all day and drew a crowd. It was not just choreomania, as Paracelsus called it, but chorea lascivia, or sensual desire.[3] She eventually dropped, exhausted, but rose up the next morning and began again, continuing for several days and attracting other young women to join her. Soon the streets were overwhelmed with dancers and the city council sent musicians,[4] in the hope of wearing the participants out. This tactic failed.

As news spread, Strasbourg was filled with a strange carnivalesque mood, underpinned with desperation. People turned out to watch the strange spectacle, to speak with the dancers, either to encourage or dissuade them from continuing. Some felt compelled to join them, as if the phenomena was catching. However, the dancers seemed to take no pleasure in the act, often collapsing or crying out for help, with bleeding feet and sores, but were unable to stop until sleep overcame them. When they were roused from their stupor, they begged to be delivered from their torments. Within a week, thirty-four people had joined the ongoing dance, and by the end of July, there were between 100 and 400, depending upon the chroniclers.[5] The strange event drew mixed responses. Some believed it was a message from heaven, while, conversely, it was also seen as evidence of demonic possession. Local physicians claimed it was the result of overheated blood. Paracelsus prescribed fasting, or a plain diet, solitary confinement, immersion in cold water or corporal punishment.[6]

Although the outbreak was a surprise, it was not without precedent, even in Strasbourg. Former occurrences of dance mania had been recorded in an area of northern Europe centred upon the Netherlands, the German States and the Holy Roman Empire. Strasbourg was one of the locations of the largest of these, in 1347, also affecting Cologne, Ghent, Maastricht, Liege, Trier, Metz, Aachen and Utrecht. More recently, choreomania struck Zurich in 1418 and 1452, Schaffenhausen in 1442 and Eberhardsklausen in 1463. Cases had also been recorded in Italy, especially in fifteenth-century Perugia, where it was called tarantism, from the belief that it was caused by the bite of the tarantula.

In 1518, the city officials of Strasbourg concluded that the dance was a punishment sent by St Vitus, traditionally the patron saint of those who had epilepsy or the falling sickness, who was known to be vengeful. After four or six days of dancing, depending upon the chronicler, Frau Troffea was loaded onto a wagon and taken the 30 miles out of the city to Saverne, to the small, rural shrine of St Vitus. No contemporary chronicles record deaths resulting from the persistent dancing, but later versions do. As a form of 'madness', its manifestation was vastly different from that believed to have taken hold of Queen Juana of Castile. As 'madness in great ones must not unwatched go,'[7] Juana's mental health was kept behind closed doors, a construct of patriarchal interpretation. For the lower-class women of Strasbourg, their public displays of mania required a public response within the patriarchal, Catholic structure. Thus, the male officials took the disruptive woman to be cured by the saint.

Modern interpretations of the event tend to explain it as either ergot poisoning, caused by a fungus that grows on the grains used in bread making, with psychoactive ingredients, or the collective outpouring of stress by the lower classes in response to the dire socio-economic conditions and societal oppression.[8] The phenomenon now known as 'St Vitus' Dance' has also been identified as Sydenham's chorea, an autoimmune disease arising from childhood infection that causes jerking movements in the face and hands. It affects more women than men, but adult-onset cases are rare.[9] While it might explain Frau Troffea's action, it cannot offer an explanation for the collective response it provoked.

There is no account of what happened to Frau Troffea. Presumably she was 'cured' and returned home to her husband: had she been struck by the strange phenomenon of choreomania for a second time, no doubt Paracelsus would have recorded it. This was not the final case of dancing mania. It took over the city of Basel in 1536 and possessed one man in Anhalt in 1551, continuing into the seventeenth century when it seems to have died out.

19

La Malinche

1519

Potonchan, Tabasco, Mexico, New World

Over 5,500 miles west of Strasbourg, another young woman waited anxiously to learn her fate. Her life was as different from that of Frau Troffea or Juana of Castile as it could be, unfolding on the Mexican coast, yet the gender dynamics that affected the Old and New Worlds were universal. Navigating the patriarchal structures, and defying expectations of femininity, were challenges women worldwide met with varying degrees of success. Still considered a controversial symbol for her response to the conquistadors, La Malinche proved herself to be a pragmatist and a survivor through her use of her talents and the choices she made.

For the indigenous communities in the state of Tabasco in 1518, tribal warfare had long been the main threat to peace and stability. Now, the arrival of Spanish and Portuguese explorers, seeking wealth and glory, brought new challenges. The first to appear in La Malinche's world was Hernán Cortés, who had been secretary to the Governor of Cuba, before he struck out independently to explore Mexico. Sailing west, he encountered the people of Potonchan, who resisted his arrival and met him in battle. But the Spanish had two key advantages: firearms, capable of killing at a distance beyond traditional weapons, coupled with the terrifying sight of men mounted on horses, creatures never before seen in the New World. This combination forced the Potonchans to submit. The Spanish occupied the city and sent Cortés a number of gifts, including gold, jade, turquoise, jewellery, food, clothing, animal skins and twenty women.[1] Waiting among them, a young slave girl called Malina or Malintzin was sanguine about the need for her people to ally with their conquerors.

Contrary to the western dogma that America was 'discovered' by Christopher Columbus in 1492, the indigenous Mayan civilisation stretched back at least as far as 2,000 bc. Initially a collection of villages dependent upon agriculture, it evolved into a sophisticated culture with cities full of palaces, temples and flat-topped pyramids, as well as observatories and homes, municipal buildings and public ballparks. Theirs was a distinctive architecture, ornamented with carvings of kings, gods, animals, the natural world and heads, and featuring around 1,000 distinct hieroglyphs. Their days were governed by a complex system of calendars, informed by an accurate understanding of astrology and mathematics. Like the Edo people of Benin, ruled over by Queen Idia, they also engaged in human sacrifice. Some of the first European invaders, arriving in the second decade of the sixteenth century had become victim to this practice, although others managed to escape whilst reputedly being 'fattened' in captivity.[2]

After Columbus' arrival, several more private adventurers had tried their luck in the New World, seeking as their rewards items they could steal, or land they claimed by conquest. The first regimes maintained their order based on torture, public humiliation and corporal punishment. The city of Potonchan had first been glimpsed by western eyes in 1518, with Juan de Grijalva using local translators to reassure the inhabitants, before talking and trading amicably with them and then departing. When Hernán Cortés arrived at the mouth of the River Tabasco the following March, he was the latest in a line of men whose approach was inconsistent, and the sight of 'the river, the river banks and the mangrove thickets... swarming with Indians' in addition to 'more than ten thousand warriors all prepared to make war on us'[3] assembled in the town, provoked him to attack. Now, with the people of Potonchan defeated, Cortés founded a new city on the hill outside, taking his spoils with him. Among them was Malina.

Even her name is uncertain. As a figure of national myth and a literary symbol, she has been called Malina, Malintzin and La Malinche, which was Mexican for 'twisted grass'. She was born around 1500, a member of the Nahua people, the largest indigenous tribe, perhaps in Paynala[4] or Olutla, as her daughter later claimed. Sources agree that she was of noble blood, either related to, or descended from, the tribe leader, and was referred to in Spanish as 'Dona' or Lady, implying status. The chronicler Diaz described her as being 'of good appearance, a busybody and forward'.[5] One account has her being sold into slavery by her mother, after the death of her father and the woman's remarriage, but she was certainly enslaved as a child, and ended up among the chosen delegation of women to be offered to the Spanish in 1519.[6] As commodities, along with gold and food, they were granted to the men as gifts. La Malinche was initially given to Captain Alonso Hernandez Puertocarrero, but soon her superior language skills came to the attention of Cortés, who claimed her for his own. She was christened Dona Marina by the Spaniards: a new name for a new identity.

Cortés' success derived, in part, from his method of dividing the indigenous tribes. By befriending one against another, he exploited existing structures to make progress in conquest and trade. La Malinche played a significant role in this process, bringing her local knowledge, enabling communication and winning the trust of her people. As a result, she has been cast in a range of historical roles: as instrumental to the conquest of Mexico, as a national heroine, a traitor, an Eve-like figure of temptation and rebirth, or as a victim.[7] She is a key symbol in Mexican literature, a symbolic cultural figure, whose presence and purpose were documented by the chroniclers, although her voice is never heard. She bore Cortés a son, Martin, in 1522, who was the first of the mestizo population of combined Mexican-European descent. Later, she married and had a daughter, dying in her late twenties.

Many of the events in La Malinche's life remain a mystery, but as a key player in the conquest of the New World and a woman of influence in the narrative of the sixteenth century, her story deserves to be set alongside those of her contemporaries. She does not initially appear to be a figure who can be claimed for feminism, as a facilitator of an oppressive, patriarchal regime, but as a woman and a survivor, she displayed ability, adaptability and a pragmatism that enabled her to succeed, even to prosper. Some critics might dispute her success, and her name is sometime invoked as an insult,[8] although she was one small aspect of a well-oiled conquistador machine whose success was inevitable. However controversial, her life impacted the course of history in an unprecedented way, representing the collision of two different worlds.

20

Elizabeth 'Bessie' Blount

June 1519

Jericho Priory, Blackmore, Essex, England

In the summer of 1519, three months after Hernán Cortés arrived in the New World, one of the queen's ladies disappeared from the English court. Her name was Elizabeth Blount, affectionately known as Bessie, and she was the daughter of Sir Thomas Blount of Kinlet in Shropshire, a minor court official who accompanied Henry VIII on his French campaign in 1513. Bessie was renowned for her beauty, and for the last five years, she had been a frequent presence in the household of Catherine of Aragon, tending to her mistress's needs, reading to her, dressing her hair, riding with her and dancing at court entertainments. During this time, the vivacious teenager also found her way into the king's bed. Thousands of miles across the ocean to the west, La Malinche bore Cortés an illegitimate son whose significance transcended his person, just as Bessie bore Henry's son out of wedlock, a son whose very existence seemed to vindicate the king and symbolise a potential future.

The village of Blackmore in Essex was small, quiet and distanced enough from court as to be discreet. Close to the large town of Chelmsford and the royal palaces of Havering and Beaulieu, it was a well-chosen location for Bessie to deliver her child. Not that she had had any choice in the matter: all the arrangements had been made by Henry's chief minister Thomas Wolsey. Bessie's expanding belly had prompted a flurry of behind-the-scenes arrangements, particularly as her pregnancy overlapped with the queen's sixth and final delivery, which resulted in a stillborn daughter. At the age of 33, considerably older in Tudor times than today, Catherine would not conceive again; at 19, Bessie was ready to present the king with a son.

Bessie Blount first appeared in Catherine's household in 1512, when she was aged around 12, and in May 1513, she received the not inconsiderable sum of 100 shillings for a year's wages.[1] In May 1515, Bessie is likely to have been one of the queen's women who rode with her and Henry to Shooter's Hill 'to take the ayr' and came across a group of huntsmen dressed in green, like Robin Hood, inspiring the king to dress that way in the field.[2] She would have been with Catherine that Christmas at Eltham, witnessing the Twelfth Night pageant of a castle on wheels, and perhaps she was one of the ladies who emerged from the structure, 'ryche and straungely disguised' in clothes of gold braid, with silver and gilt spangles set on crimson satin, in the Dutch fashion. No doubt she was present at the banquet that followed, which comprised fifty dishes.[3] Bessie would have attended Catherine in February 1516 when the queen delivered her only surviving daughter, and fulfilled some official role at Mary's christening. Two years later, Cardinal Wolsey held an entertainment at his home, York Place, for the French ambassadors, where 'Elizabeth Blont [sic]' danced in a masque, along with the king, in red satin gowns, carrying cups of gold.[4] There was also an impressive supper, which the Venetian ambassador stated that 'the like of which, I fancy, was never given either by Cleopatra or Caligula: the whole banqueting hall being so decorated with huge vases of gold and silver, that I fancied myself in the tower of Chosroes, [sic] where that monarch caused divine honours to be paid him.'[5] It was shortly after this masque that Elizabeth showed the first signs of pregnancy, and disappeared from court soon afterwards.

Exactly when Henry and Bessie became lovers is uncertain. It may have been a one-night encounter, but it is more likely to have been a long-standing relationship. Bessie was in a position to have made a good marriage, at a time when aristocratic women were often betrothed in their mid-teens, and the lack of potential husbands on the horizon may have been the result of the king's interest in her. Henry was discreet when it came to his lovers, and Bessie's position in the queen's household necessitated sensitivity. Assuming Bessie experienced an average nine-month pregnancy, she would have conceived in mid-September 1518, while Catherine was well into her final trimester, and contemporary medical science placed her out of her husband's reach for sexual activity, which was thought to be harmful to the unborn child. Henry was careful to ensure that no other evidence survived concerning his relations with Bessie, and that none of his ushers and gentlemen of the bedchamber spoke out: literally, the only reason we know that he slept with Bessie is because she fell pregnant.

It was Cardinal Wolsey who took care of the arrangements, to distance the process from the king. Soon afterwards, Bessie undertook the journey, about 30 miles north-east from York Place, passing out of the city walls, through the suburbs of London, the open fields, forest and villages into the green Essex countryside. She would have found a small settlement, with a few lanes overlooked by half-timbered buildings close by the twelfth-century Augustinian priory, and wooden-spired church of St Laurence. The place was then under the rule of Thomas Goodwyn, who had been appointed prior in 1513, and a later plan indicated the presence of a cloister court on the southern side of the church, surrounded by a chapter house, parlour, refectory, kitchen and cellarers' rooms, with guest houses above. However, it was to the prior's own lodgings, the moated medieval Jericho House where Bessie was taken. It was a location known to be used by the king as a house of pleasure, prompting the courtly epithet that when he was absent wooing women, he had 'gone to Jericho'. Also known as Jericho Priory, the original building was demolished and replaced in 1712, situated behind the wall beside the church. The moat was fed by a stream called the Jordan. Here, away from prying eyes, Bessie bore a son, named Henry Fitzroy. Wolsey was absent from court from

19 to 29 June, suggesting that the boy's arrival took place on, or slightly before these dates, and that Wolsey departed in order to fulfil his role as godparent for the christening service.

After the birth of her son, Bessie took a back seat. Henry was not interested in her beyond the service her womb had provided, although she was cared for and favoured at court, as a mark of respect, as the boy's mother. The king did not even consider marriage to her, to legitimise young Fitzroy, when he believed his succession was in crisis in the late 1520s, by which point she was already married to Gilbert Tailboys, bearing him three children.

The priory at Blackmore was dissolved on 10 February 1525 by an agent of Thomas Wolsey. It had dwindled in size and purpose, with only three canons resident, its spiritual commodities valued at £41 13s 4d and its earthly ones at £43 11s 3d.[6] When Henry turned six, four months later, he left his mother and was given his own establishment at Bridewell Palace. He received a princely education, status and titles, and was frequently at court with his father, featuring in illustrations in the court rolls. Fitzroy was married in 1533, to Mary, a daughter of the Duke of Norfolk, aligning him to the rising Boleyn faction, but died prematurely three years later, possibly from tuberculosis. Bessie was widowed, and remarried, bearing three more children. She returned to court as a lady-in-waiting in 1540, but soon retired due to ill health.

Had she not borne Henry's son, Bessie Blount might have been remembered as a footnote to the Tudor court; one of its brightest ornaments who danced, sang, banqueted and faded away. She would have always remained a marginal figure, as many of her female contemporaries, save for that one moment of chance, when circumstances favoured her encounter with the king, leading to conception and a safe delivery. Fitzroy's survival is more remarkable for all the other children the king lost, through miscarriage or stillbirth, or whose gender was female, and his existence helped convince the king that he was able to father healthy sons so his marital failures in that respect must be the responsibility of his wife Catherine. It also raises the question of the king's sexual exploits, and the other potential lovers he enjoyed, whose identities were lost to history, who did not conceive or lost their pregnancies, about whom Henry maintained his cordon of silence.

For a while, when Fitzroy looked like the most viable heir, Bessie could glimpse a future as a potential king's mother, but that glory was snatched away before it could materialise. Elizabeth Blount represents a Tudor woman for whom sex was definitive, whose bodily functions permanently altered her status and won her a place in the history books. Her life has literally been given meaning, in biographical terms, as the result of the 'magic touch' of a man. The act of the king giving her a child, impregnating her with a life, had the result of creating a new life for Bessie during her lifetime, and a reputational afterlife following her demise.

21

Roxelana, aka Hurrem Sultan

September 1520

The Seraglio, Topkapi Palace, Constantinople (modern Istanbul), Turkey

As Bessie Blount discovered at the court of Henry VIII, youth, beauty and accomplishment could serve as a passport to royal favour. At the time when her affair with Henry was at its height, another woman like her was finding favour with one of the king's most significant enemies. To the Christian world, the Ottoman Empire was a huge ominous presence to the east, centring its barbaric practices in the capital of Constantinople but spreading into Asia, Africa and threatening Europe. Under its new young leader, Suleiman the Magnificent, who succeeded in 1520, the Turks would reach the height of their powers.

Suleiman's favourite mistress was painted by Titian, as a voluptuous, pale-skinned figure with pouting lips, straight nose and dark, seductive eyes. She was born in Rohatyn, in Ruthenia, today part of Poland, but in 1502, or thereabouts, it had been incorporated into the expanding empire. The daughter of an Orthodox priest, she was captured by the Tartars on one of their raids across the border and sold into slavery. She may have been named Anastasia or Aleksandra Lisowska[1] but by the time she had reached the Turkish capital, and was waiting to be admitted to the Sultan's harem, she was known as Roxelana, 'the Ruthenian one'.

In September 1520, Roxelana was about to enter, for the first time, the most magnificent palace she had ever seen, which was to become her home for life. Set on a promontory overlooking the Sea of Marmaris, the Topkapi Palace contained a Sergalio of hundreds of rooms, begun in 1459, six years after the Turks had conquered the city. According to an old plan of the site, visitors entered through the carriage gate, passing under the dome, through courtyards peopled by black eunuchs to the main harem door and into the golden way. Deep inside the warren of rooms were the corridors of consorts, apartments for the Sultan's first and second favourites, reception rooms, mirrored rooms, treasuries, secret staircases, pools, fountains and courtyards, bedrooms, bathrooms, sitting rooms, dining rooms, prayer rooms, fruit rooms and an elephant house. These were all highly decorated with tiles, mosaics, archways, coloured glass, domes, intricately carved stone and woodwork, picked out in white, blue, red, ochre and gold in floral and geometric designs. Here, Roxelana would join the many women gathered to satisfy the Sultan's appetites.

While Henry VIII discreetly stowed his mistress away at a rural priory, his contemporary rulers were far less coy about their sexual encounters. Some, such as Francis I of France, offered their lovers official titles and celebrated their multiple affairs openly, with a wife, an official mistress and many other casual relationships. Francis' antics occasionally raised tolerant eyebrows at court, but outside the Christian tradition, the ritualised practice of rulers with multiple sexual partners was seen by the west as further evidence of heathen wickedness. Suleiman the Magnificent would have a total of seventeen women in his harem, and Roxelana would rise to be the most powerful of all, eclipsing all rivals. The exact date when she came to his attention is unknown, but she is likely to have been bought by a member of the Sultan's household in a slave market in the city, with an eye to entering the palace in service of some form. Some sources claim she was brought there by Suleiman's sister, but most suggest that it was by his favourite male advisor, Ibrahim. She found herself in a strictly hierarchical establishment, where daily life was ritualised and men were not permitted, save for the many eunuchs.

Suleiman was reported to be 'very lustful' and frequently visited 'the palace of the women'.[2] He quickly became infatuated with Roxelana, promoting her through the ranks of the harem to become his favourite. Within months, she was pregnant, bearing him a son just over a year after Suleiman's enthronement, followed by four more children. He addressed her in poetry, using his pen name Muhibbi:

Throne of my lonely niche, my wealth, my love, my moonlight.
My most sincere friend, my confidant, my very existence, my Sultan, my one and only love.
The most beautiful among the beautiful…
My springtime, my merry faced love, my daytime, my sweetheart, laughing leaf…
My plants, my sweet, my rose, the one only who does not distress me in this world…
My Constantinople, my Caraman, the earth of my Anatolia
My Badakhshan, my Baghdad and Khorasan
My woman of the beautiful hair, my love of the slanted brow, my love of eyes full of mischief…
I'll sing your praises always
I, lover of the tormented heart, Muhibbi of the eyes full of tears, I am happy.[3]

Breaking with the tradition of marriage to only noble women, Suleiman made Roxelana his official wife, and she was known as Hurrem Sultan, 'the cheerful one', or Haseki Sultan, moving out of the harem into the Old Topkapi Palace. Increasingly, she involved herself in political decision-making, offering advice and guidance, and writing to foreign heads of state. She was also a patron to many establishments in the city, especially those who cared for the poor. Her active role initiated the meritocracy of the Sultanate of Women, a period of over a century that saw low-born women rising to political influence due to their looks and abilities. Yet rivalry in the harem had been intense and in order to achieve her position,

Roxelana had come into conflict with Suleiman's former favourite, his minister Ibrahim and his mother emerging triumphant.

Roxelana died in April 1558 and was buried in the white, domed Suleymaniye Mosque, built earlier that decade, on the third hill outside Constantinople. Her tomb, or turbe, lies inside a carved wooden grille, in a domed chamber ornamented with blue and white tiles. Her name, like that of La Malinche, has taken on a cultural significance, appearing in works of art, literature, music and in Turkish and Ukrainian folklore. Unlike La Malinche's complex legacy, though, Roxelana is celebrated as a national figure of historical importance and power. Across Europe, the Renaissance initiated greater social mobility which was increasingly celebrating the rise of low-born figures due to merit, rather than the traditional accident of birth. Roxelana's life shows that this was also happening in the Ottoman court. She contributed to an increasing respect for female ability that empowered women at the side of Sultans, albeit balanced with the task of embodying masculine ideals of femininity. However, she still owed her power to the affections of the Sultan, rather than wielding it independently of him. She had influence by permission, by indulgence. With a few exceptions, at this point in the sixteenth century, female power was more usually a gift given by men to women of their choice.

Again, this was not feminism, or a form of proto-feminism, or even female solidarity; such labels would be not only anachronistic but incorrect. Like the other female survivors of her era, circumstances placed Roxelana in competition with other women and she succeeded by becoming adept at playing the patriarchal game. These women were survivors within perimeters they had not defined, but still excelled in. Through their personal charms, careful observations and subtle influence, they demonstrate that women were not merely passive receptacles of male rule, but could be capable, active players, shaping their own destinies. This makes them signposts along the journey of collective effort that would, eventually, reach the threshold of modern feminism.

22

'Kindness' (Mary Boleyn)

4 March 1522
York Place, London, England

The effect was exotic, intoxicating. They appeared inside the castle, one by one, in time to the music: eight young women dressed in Milanese white gowns, with golden bonnets upon their heads, set with jewels. The great hall at York Place was hung with arras and dozens of wax branches illuminated the pageant's central tower and two smaller ones at the sides, called the Château Vert. From each tower flew a banner representing different stages of love: one depicted three torn hearts, the next showed a woman's hand gripping a man's heart, while the third was the same hand turning the heart.[1] Their symbolism suggested that a woman had the king's heart in her power.

At a distance waited King Henry VIII, enjoying Cardinal Wolsey's hospitality along with his guests, the Imperial Ambassadors. Already that evening they had partaken of a rich supper, before their host conducted them to their places, to the scene of the pageant. As the women came closer, dancing towards the audience, the flickering light illuminated their dresses, showing their characters' names embroidered in gold. The king recognised his own sister Mary leading them, with the name of Beauty. Then came Gertrude Blount, Countess of Devonshire, as Honour, followed by a pair of sisters known to the king through the service of their father, the diplomat Sir Thomas Boleyn. The younger came first, as Perseverance, a dark-haired girl named Anne, recently returned from years spent across the Channel at the court of Francis I, but it was her sister Mary who followed, in the role of Kindness, who Henry sought with his eyes.

Described by Francis as 'a very great whore, the most infamous of all', his 'English mare' and 'hackney', Mary Boleyn had also spent time in France where she was rumoured to have had a string of lovers. Like all such rumours relating to her family, though, these are likely to have been exaggerated, and certainly did not affect her standing, as she returned to England and took a prestigious position in the household of Catherine of Aragon. In February 1520, she had married William Carey, a Gentleman of the Privy Chamber and close associate of the king, who attended the wedding and made an offering of 6s 8d.[2] Around this time, Mary became Henry's mistress, replacing Bessie Blount. This is most likely to have occurred before they attended the Field of Cloth of Gold that summer, where the English and French courts met for a month of entertainments. Just like with Bessie, the duration of their relationship is unknown, and its existence only acknowledged by default, when Henry later wished to marry Mary's sister Anne. Even Mary's appearance had remained a mystery until 2020, when the portrait of an 'unknown woman' at Holyrood Palace, known as the *Jordaens Van Dyck Panel Painting* was identified as being Mary, and one of a series of fourteen beauties who adorned the walls of Anne's former bathing room at Windsor Castle. Mary is dressed in ermine and black, with orange trim, pearls and a brooch adorned with drooping red flowers, possibly roses, possibly carnations. Her face and neck are full and rounded, the eyes bright, almost golden, the cheeks rosy and a playful smile about the lips. From what can be gleaned despite the headdress, her colouring appears to be fair.

However, on Shrovetide evening, 1520, it was Mary, not Anne, who drew the king's attention. Leaving his guests, he crept away to dress himself in crimson satin covered in burning flames of gold, returning in the role of Ardent Desire to lead eight gentlemen in storming the castle, and freeing the ladies. The women were defended by figures such as Disdain and Scorn, Jealousy and Unkindness, who threw bows and balls, while the weapons of those inside were the daintier comfits and rose water. The men responded by launching oranges and dates to the sound of guns firing, until they had driven away the enemy. Then, triumphantly, they led the ladies out by the hand and danced with them 'very pleasantly', removing their masks, before all partook of a banquet. The choice of Mary's role as 'Kindness' may have been a random allocation, or it may have reflected a personal quality she was known for at court. In this context, her kindness might have been taking pity on a king whose heart was represented as being gripped in her hand, or even her susceptibility to male advances in general. Was her kindness genuinely that, or a euphemism for amorousness? Was she named in the hope that she would look kindly upon the king, or to reflect the fact that she already had? Was the entire pageant a metaphor for Henry's pursuit of Mary and her capitulation? It is impossible to know now, but her prominent role, and the timing of the event, could imply its connection to their developing relationship.

Mary bore two children: Catherine in 1524 and Henry in 1526, whom various historians have tried to claim were sired by the king. However, there is no proof of his paternity. Henry never attempted to identify them as his own, even his namesake, the son, when he was in desperate need of a male heir. Legally, all children borne by a married woman were considered to be fathered by her husband, unless a scandal proved otherwise, by which Henry would have been forced to admit he had committed adultery. By 1526, his attention had moved to Anne, and soon after, Mary was widowed when William Carey died from the dreaded sweating sickness. She remained at her sister's side as Anne rose to power, and later remarried for love, to a man lower in status, of whom her family disapproved. Her historical significance would have been far less if Henry had not feared their relationship may have compromised his marriage to Anne. To avoid the same legal impediment arising that had blighted his union with his former sister-in-law, Catherine, he admitted that he had slept with Mary, but never their mother, and proceeded to marry again. Thus, Mary is remembered as the Boleyn sister who shared the king's bed, but not his throne. She was also a survivor of the family scandal, who lived out her final days in the countryside, far from the court that had defined, and then broken, her family. Seeking to rise due to the king's favour, the Boleyns would fly, Icarus-like, too close to the flames.

On the night of 4 March 1522, though, the tempestuous future still lay ahead. Before it unfolds, in its full devastation, let us allow the lens of history to rest briefly upon an innocent, happy Mary, who could dance and bask in the affection of her royal lover's gaze.

23

Louise of Savoy

December 1525

Basilica of St Justus, St-Just sur Lyon, Lyon, France

Kneeling before the altar, surrounded by the flickering lights of candles, the anxious mother waited for news of her son. Head bent in prayer, she was no longer a young woman, being in her fiftieth year, and her habitual black clothing and severe coif and hood gave her the air of devotion and severity. They were equally suited to her surroundings.

The monastic site at St Just sur Lyon contained a large central church and a collection of outbuildings, surrounded by high walls. Situated 280 miles south-east of Paris, and 250 miles east of the king of France's favourite retreat of Amboise, it was used to hosting royalty and had formerly been chosen as a location for the coronation of Popes. Now it sheltered Louise of Savoy, mother of Francis I, far from home, amid the worst national crisis the country had experienced in years. In December 1525, it was ten months since the reckless, fun-loving Francis had been taken prisoner by the emperor, held in a series of remote castles, unable to rule his kingdom. Louise felt powerless to assist him in the face of the stream of messages reporting his illness and suffering. First, she turned to God for help, and then she set about doing what she had always done best: building diplomatic alliances.

The path to the throne had not been easy for Francis and Louise. Widowed at 19, with two young children, the young woman left behind their home in Cognac and moved to the Parisian court of Louis XII, her husband's cousin. Despite the many advantages this brought, Louise was not welcomed by Louis' wife, Anne of Brittany, who vehemently opposed suggestions for a marriage between Francis and their daughter. Proving himself to be a bright, energetic child, Francis was the closest thing the Valois family could produce to a royal heir, given the lack of royal male children, and soon became the king's favourite. Louise was convinced that he was destined to rule, described as one contemporary as 'the most serious trait in her character'.[1] She steered him as best she could, teaching him herself from her love of books and the art of the Italian Renaissance. It was only after the death of Anne that the marriage was permitted and, on 1 January 1515, the young couple, Francis and Claude, inherited the French throne. With Francis bent on pleasure and military glory, and Claude frequently pregnant or ill, it was Louise who represented the real power behind the throne.

This was recognised by her appointment as regent during Francis' absence in the Italian wars, and as hostess to the English at the 1520 Field of Cloth of Gold. Louise had maintained good relations with its architect, Cardinal Wolsey, in particular, continuing to work with him towards peace in Europe, culminating in the Treaty of the More.

However, in February 1525, Francis' run of luck came to an abrupt end. Leading an aggressive campaign to recapture lands he had lost in Lombardy, he was caught out at Pavia by the fall of night, the woodland location and the skill of the imperial troops, who slaughtered his men and took him prisoner after the battle. Such a significant international prize was a feather in the cap of the emperor, who intended to fully utilise his new asset. Francis was taken first to the nearby castle of Pizzighettoni, where he was allowed to write to Louise. Hot on the heels of the news of his ignominious defeat, came his letter, informing his mother that 'all is lost to me save honour and life, which is safe'.[2] The outlook for France was bleak, with no way of knowing when, or if, their king would return, and his eldest son was only 7. Louise embraced the role of regent again, but voices were raised on the royal council in objection to her gender. For the brief duration of Francis' campaign in 1515, Louise had been an acceptable figurehead, due to the king's imminent return, but now, with such uncertainty hanging over the kingdom, appeals were made to Francis' closest male relative, Charles de Bourbon, Duc de Vendome. However, Charles refused the post, being unwilling to divide the country in times of emergency. Instead, he joined Louise's advisors.[3]

At once, Louise set to work. She saw that the only way to pressure the emperor into releasing Francis was to enlist the support of powerful European leaders. She sent letters to England and Scotland, to the Pope and Italian states, asking them to support Francis' release, but in an unprecedented move, she also went further in her desperation, reaching out to the traditional enemies of the Christian world: the infidel Turks. Sultan Suleiman the Magnificent headed the expanding Turkish empire from his base in Istanbul, a new young player on the international stage, the same age as Francis. Emperor Charles was so powerful, with the combined Netherlands and Spain under his control, that the might of an equally significant empire was required. It was a risky, controversial move, and reveals the depths of a mother's desperation. In the summer of 1525, Louise sent an initial embassy to Constantinople, carrying letters from her and Francis, but her servants were lost on the way, possibly murdered.[4]

In September, terrible news reached the basilica near Lyon. Francis had been taken ill in confinement at Toledo, with an undiagnosed abscess in the head. His life was in danger and Louise could do little more than pray for his recovery as he lay in a coma. Louise's daughter, Marguerite, travelled to Spain to be with him, but her offers of a huge ransom were declined. Louise offered to concede a portion of Burgundy in exchange for his release, but this was also refused. However, Francis' abscess burst, he regained consciousness and began to return to health.

This inspired Louise to redouble her efforts, sending a new negotiator, John Frangipani, to ask Suleiman for a joint attack against the empire. Arriving successfully in Constantinople, Frangipani warned the Sultan that otherwise Francis would have to come to terms with Charles, making him the 'master of the world'.[5] The following February, Frangipani returned with a warm and encouraging but fairly non-committal response from Suleiman:

> You have informed me that the enemy has overrun your country and that you are at present in prison and a captive, and you have asked aid and succours for your deliverance. All this your saying having been set forth at the foot of my throne, which controls the world. Your situation has gained my imperial understanding in every detail, and I have considered all of it. There is nothing astonishing in emperors being defeated and made captive. Take courage then, and be not dismayed. Our glorious predecessors and our illustrious ancestors (may God light up their tombs!) have never ceased to make war to repel the foe and conquer his lands. We ourselves have followed in their footsteps, and have at all times conquered provinces and citadels of great strength and difficult of approach. Night and day our horse is saddled and our sabre is girt. May the God on High promote righteousness! May whatsoever He will be accomplished! For the rest, question your ambassador and be informed. Know that it will be as said.[6]

However, the reply came too late. On 14 January, Francis had been forced to sign the humiliating Treaty of Madrid, ceding much land to the emperor, whose sister Francis was to wed, and whose liberty was bought only after he promised to substitute his sons for himself in captivity. Prior to signing, Francis made a private declaration not to honour such punitive terms. He did, though, marry the emperor's sister, Eleanor, and sent Princes Francis and Henri into captivity. Suleiman did not send direct aid, but he did assist indirectly by resuming his conquest of Hungary, putting pressure on the emperor.[7]

Louise's role in this process was innovative. By reaching out to Suleiman, she broke taboos about Christian-Muslim alliances and laid the foundation for future relations. A contemporary manuscript illumination by Jean Bellemare depicts Louise 'taking over the rudder' of rule in France. Dressed in her widow's black, she sits under a green cloth of state, with bright blue and pink angelic wings. In both hands, she holds a disembodied rudder, the end of which sits in a small square tank at her feet, full of choppy waters. On the floor beside it, lies the prostrate figure of Suleiman, remarkably western-looking, but with a cloth wound about his head, in a loose semblance of a turban. It is a projection of wishful thinking, rather than being reflective of their relationship, but shows the respect in which Louise was held. Francis returned home, sobered, in 1526 and Louise continued to exert her considerable influence for the next five years, before her death in 1531. There is no doubt that her powerful actions and bravery helped steer France through an unprecedented crisis.

24

Katharina von Bora

1526

The Black Cloister, Wittenberg, Germany

The nuns waited with bated breath. A group of eight young women, in their late teens and early twenties, they were conspicuous in their black and white habits, watching the monastery gate. Their leader was the eldest, Katharina, a dark-haired woman from Saxony with slanting eyes, who had written the letters herself and hatched the plan for freedom. They shivered with excitement as the gates opened and a cart rolled in, heading round to the refectory with its delivery of herring. This was their chance.

> The merchant cast a look around before approaching them.
> 'Fraulein von Bora?'
> 'Yes, I am Katharina von Bora.'
> 'My name is Leonhard Koppe, you can trust me. Climb into the back of the cart.'
> He saw the hesitation in her eyes.
> 'It's alright, Luther sent me. Be quick.'

By the 1520s, the Catholic church was in turmoil. With the arrival of the Reformation in northern Europe, traditional methods of worship were being called into question, including the monastic way of life. The outspoken scholar and priest, Martin Luther, had preached in favour of clerical marriage, one of the big proposed changes to centuries-old ways of life. He argued that it was acceptable to breach the vows of chastity on this occasion, because marriage was a civil affair, not a religious one, and far better than the existing hypocrisy of clerical concubinage. Luther was a controversial figure in other respects, having nailed his ninety-five theses to the door of Wittenberg church and been summoned to answer to the emperor as a result. Even excommunication by the Pope failed to deter him, and he continued to assist monks and nuns to escape their vows, helping arrange their subsequent marriages. It was for that reason that Katharina had written to him, and he had promised to help her and her sisters find suitable husbands.

Katharina von Bora had always been intended for a religious life. Born into a noble family in January 1499 in the rural village of Lippendorf,[1] Saxony, she had been sent to a Benedictine cloister at Brehna at the age of 3 or 4, and then to join her aunt at the Cistercian abbey of Marienthron at Nimbschen. The ruins of the building remain, in solid pink-grey stones, with the empty space for windows, tall archways and gable ends. New trees overhang the broken walls, filtering down light into the place where Katharina and her sisters once slept and prayed. Yet, having spent most of their life following a strict regime, they became part of an exodus of women who wanted to experience what the secular world could offer. Once they broke free, in Leonhard Koppe's herring cart on the night of 4 April 1523, the nuns were taken 50 miles north to the city of Wittenberg. Katharine was lodged first with Philipp Reichenbach, the city's clerk, then with the family of the artist Lucas Cranach, the elder, and his wife Barbara.

Initially, Luther had no success in trying to arrange a marriage for Katharina. With the other sisters provided for, he offered her potential husbands, whom she rejected, saying she would only marry Luther himself or a close friend of his. At the age of 41, Luther was an unlikely bridegroom, but he was convinced by his father's approval of the match. Writing that it would 'please his father, rile the Pope, cause the angels to laugh and the devils to weep,' he rejected opposition voices from his contemporaries, like Philipp Melanchthon, who preached that clerical marriage would damage the Reformation. He wrote that he felt neither passionate love, nor 'burning' for her, perhaps to evade allegations of lust, but that he 'cherished' her.[2] On 13 June 1525, Martin Luther married Katharina, who was then around 26, with Melanchthon, Lucas and Barbara Cranach among the witnesses. An elaborate breakfast and bedding celebrations followed. Two weeks later, they had a more formal, official ceremony. Frederick, Elector of Saxony gave them the Black Cloister in Wittenberg, the former dormitory for Augustinian friars where Luther had once lived as a novice. There, they raised six children and Katharina opened a guest house, provisioning it with vegetables from their gardens, rearing cows and pigs, and running a brewery. Proving herself more than a competent manager, she also acted as agent for Luther with his publishers.

In 1526, probably to mark the occasion of their marriage, Lucas Cranach painted dual portraits of Luther and Katharina. On separate panels, against an olive-green background, Luther faces right, while his new wife faces left, conforming to the traditional marital composition. Doctora Lutherin, as he called her, out of respect for her intellect, is depicted in striking black and white, with her hands folded in front, showing her gold rings. She is tight-laced across the waist, with a white shirt open at the throat and an embroidered orange-brown panel across her breasts, matching the band on her headdress. Her face is distinctive, with high cheekbones and square chin; her lips curve on one side, with the suggestion of a smile, and her eyes stare out directly with a knowledgeable air. The picture bears out the confidence Luther had in his 'Lord Katie', his 'morning star', his 'boss', to whom he gave 'complete control' over their household, and who could convince him of anything she wished. Most touchingly, Luther wrote that he was 'woven into my girl's plaits.'[3]

The Luthers were significant in being one of the first examples of clerical marriage, especially given Martin's status and role in the Reformation. His actions were controversial, revolutionary, proving that taking a wife did not damage the cause of reform, but helped him in his work. Theirs was also a successful partnership, acknowledging and facilitating female ability. Luther gave his wife respect, control and a voice, redefining marital relations in the sixteenth century and raising the status of women. As one of the first clerical wives, and a former nun herself, Katharina was a role model for others seeking to shift the direction of their lives.

25

Maid of Honour

1526

Eltham Palace, England

In 1526, she would have been in her mid- to late teens, a young woman grateful for her good fortune, dressed in the best clothing her family could afford. She might have been named Catherine, after the queen, or Elizabeth or Margaret, after the king's grandmothers, shortened to Cat, Bessie or Meg. The position of maid of honour to Catherine of Aragon, Queen of England, was highly sought after. However, for all the glamour and influence of the Tudor court, it was frequently a dirty job as she was expected to wait upon the queen's bodily needs. It would have been her hands that shook out the bedsheets, replaced them with new ones, or scattered lavender on the mattress. She would have been required to bathe her mistress in water scented by rose petals, fetch the fresh clothing, dressing her in layers, lacing her tight. When Catherine needed to visit the close stool, or toilet, her maid of honour needed to be on hand to wipe her clean afterwards with sponges and cloths. They would have known all the secret, intimate details of her life and the hidden, private places of all the royal palaces.

Henry VIII's court could be a riotous place. While the king was still relatively young, he prioritised enjoyment, spectacle and the cult of love. No one could keep the wealthy, play-boy king in check, and by the mid-1520s, the outrageous behaviour of his close band of male friends, his 'minions', was causing concern, and bringing his name into disrepute. Cardinal Wolsey was trusted to make the necessary reforms. In January 1526, he presented his Eltham Ordinances, named after the palace of their conception, expelling the minions and strictly defining the roles and protocol, boundaries and entitlements of all those who served the king and queen. This extraordinary document allows us to glimpse into the world of those working behind the scenes, who witnessed the daily life of the Tudor court and the bodily functions of its king and queen, but so frequently went unrecorded. Thanks to the Eltham Ordinances, the Cats, Bessies and Megs of Catherine of Aragon's court can be seen going about their duties, fetching, carrying and keeping secrets.

A number of women were permitted inside the queen's ornate apartments, according to a strict hierarchy. The inner circle comprised ladies-in-waiting, also known as ladies of honour, high-born women whose husbands were employed in Henry VIII's privy chamber, of whom there were eight in 1526. This was an honorary role, and included the king's sister Mary, Duchess of Suffolk; Catherine's close friend from Spain, Maria de Salinas, now Lady Willoughby; and Lady Guildford, whose husband was charged with implementing the new rules. Next, there were around thirty maids-in-waiting, usually unmarried daughters of the nobility, appointed in their late teens and selected for their beauty and accomplishments. Their primary function was to keep the queen company and attract a suitable husband. Following them, it was the maids of honour who did all the hard work. They performed such practical tasks as making the bed, dressing the queen, washing and bathing her, as well as fetching and carrying, serving at table and seeing to any other needs that arose.

The maids of honour would have taken turns, in pairs, to sleep on a 'pallet' in the queen's chamber, or in an anteroom outside, to attend to her needs throughout the night. Otherwise, they were ready at eight, or earlier if Catherine wished to rise earlier for chapel or hunting. Pages would make up the fire as the maids met the yeomen of the wardrobe at the door to receive the queen's garments, some of which were already warmed before a fire. Then, they helped dress the queen 'in reverent, discreet and sober manner',[1] and attend her in her private dining chamber and chapel, before she emerged to the world. They were charged to be 'friendly to each other, and keep secret all things done there; not to enquire about the king's absence where he is going, or talk about his pastimes,' and to immediately report any individuals using 'unfitting language of the King' or queen.[2]

While they were entitled to be fed, the maids only ate after serving the queen. Unless it was a holy day, dinner was served at ten, and supper at four, but when Catherine dined in her chamber, attended by her maids, the hours shifted back to eleven and six. After dinner, Catherine read to her ladies from religious texts and, in the evenings, they sewed garments for the poor.[3] Moderate games of chess and cards were permitted, as were singing, dancing and playing musical instruments. Cat, Bessie and Meg should be ready in case Catherine required bread or drink to be brought up from the kitchens, sending ushers to fetch it, and receiving it at the door.

In return, they received salaries, were accommodated and fed at court, and given stabling for horses. Twice a year, at Whitsun and Christmas, as well as on important occasions, they were given new clothing, and received gifts at New Year. In January 1528, thirty-three women were given gifts of gold items ranging in weight from 10oz to 22 oz.[4] Faithful servants were also rewarded with annuities, often of £10 or £20, or pensions once they had reached a certain age. The quantities of privilege descended with rank: a countess was allocated fourteen horses and five beds; a baroness, ten horses and three beds; a knight's wife, eight horses and three beds; the queen's gentlewomen, six horses and two beds; and the queen's maids, between them, shared six horses and three spare beds. The ladies were granted an exception to the rule that none save those with permission could own dogs, being allowed to own a spaniel or two.[5] Many of them married well, finding husbands from within the court who could offer them status and security, after which they left the role of maids of honour, possibly to return as ladies, companions or guests within the wider household. It was also a pool from which Henry drew his lovers and future wives: Bessie Blount, Mary and Anne Boleyn, Jane Seymour and Catherine Howard.

The queen's maids of honour were in a privileged position. They witnessed not only the daily intimacies of Catherine's life, but also the unfolding drama at the heart of the court, as Henry fell out of his love with his wife and sought to part from her in order to marry Anne Boleyn. The maids must have witnessed trysts, tears and quarrels, but their formalised roles, governed by tight codes of conduct, meant they were forbidden from recording or sharing their secrets. So the Cats, Bessies and Megs of the Tudor court are known to us through the Eltham Ordinances, going about their important duties, but their voices are never heard.

26

Lady with a Squirrel and a Starling

1527

London, England

Her gaze is off to the left. Her expression is serious, focused, even a little severe. She seems not to notice the bushy red squirrel seated in her lap, gnawing down on a nut, or the glossy starling on the branch just over her shoulder, looking as if it was about to burst into song. Instead, she sits calmly, hands loosely together, dressed in demure black and white, her hair covered by a thick, plain hood with no adornment. Two small branches rise from behind her, scantily clad with a few olive-green leaves that appear to be catching the light. The background is a dazzling bright blue, made from azurite mixed with white, like a jewel or enamelled colour. She is a young woman, her face unlined and her chin and neck a little rounded. The eyes look slightly downwards and, below the straight nose, her mouth is drawn out at both sides, but not in a smile, and her chin is heavy. It is not a beautiful face, but it is pleasant and regular, apparently mild in temperament.

It is easy to imagine the sitter of this 1526 picture rising to her feet after long hours of posing for the artist, stepping away from the azure backdrop and setting down the squirrel and starling as she stretches out her limbs. However, it is far more likely that she was seated in the corner of some hall, with servants sweeping the floor about her, or in a quiet antechamber, with no branches, animals or birds in sight. When she rose, stepped away and nodded to the painter seated a few metres away on his wooden stool, it was from a black and white sketch, drawn on paper, unfinished, unimagined. She returned to a world of routine and chores, balancing the books, ordering the servants, teaching the children to read; a world far removed from the colourful symbolism the portrait would become. The painter rolled up his sketch and carried it away to his studio where he would transfer it onto a wood panel, before adding the background details and colour. He was a young man, newly arrived from Germany, keen to impress potential patrons with his court portraits. His name was Hans Holbein.

The sitter for the 1526 portrait *Lady with a Squirrel and a Starling* is thought to be Anne Lovell, the new wife of Sir Francis Lovell of Barton Bendish, an esquire to the body of Henry VIII. Two years earlier, Francis had inherited the manor at East Harling, Norfolk, from his childless uncle Thomas. It was built around 1490 on the site of a medieval manor, with a large central tower and accommodation with huge windows and a partially crenellated roof. Anne was the daughter of George Ashby of Hertfordshire. She became Thomas's wife at the age of 28 and probably bore their son Thomas at East Harling soon after. The picture may have been commissioned in celebration of all these elements, marking the new family's position, explaining the presence of the animals. While squirrels and starlings were common household pets of the time, Holbein's playful symbolism is suggestive of his sitter's pedigree: the starlings are a pun on Harling and the gnawing squirrel features on the Lovell family arms.[1]

Anne was a Tudor woman who happened to be in the right place at the right time, to be captured in paint, her face presented to us as fresh as the day she sat for Holbein, before returning to her life. Again, this is a male artist, but whose skill and empathy captures a realism that brings his sitters to life, to a level of almost photographic detail. Due to his ability, the years between 1526 and the present day melt away and we are brought face to face with a real woman of the sixteenth century.

27

Properzia de Rossi

24 February 1530
Bologna, Italy

Writing about Properzia de Rossi in the fourth volume of his *Lives of the Artists*, Giorgio Vasari took the opportunity to comment upon female artists in general. They had not feared, he wrote, reducing them to a sculptural detail, 'to place themselves, with their tender white and lily-white hands, in the mechanical arts between the roughness of marble and the harshness of iron, in order to attain their desire and to earn renown.' Including only four women in total in his six-volume work, Vasari conceded that Rossi was exceptional among her sex because she was not only 'skilful in household duties like other women, but in countless fields of knowledge, so that not only the women but all the men were envious of her.'[1] And yet, renowned for her skill and beauty, Properzia was dogged by scandal and died, bankrupt and alone, on the very day that Pope Clement VII was hoping to meet the woman described to him as a 'noble and elevated genius'.

Properzia was born in the city of Bologna in northern Italy in 1490. One source claims her father was a notary, while another has him condemned to the galleys for eighteen years for manslaughter.[2] The family appears to have been wealthy and Properzia received an enlightened Renaissance education, learning painting, poetry and classical literature, as well as the more traditional accomplishments of dancing and singing. Many female artists of the time entered the profession under the supervision of a male relative, usually a father or husband working in the field, but Properzia had no such family connection. Instead, she sought role models in Bologna. She took additional lessons with the engraver and artist Marcantonio Raimondi, who was influenced by Dürer and collaborated with Raphael, and possibly also studied at the university in the city. In the 1520s, she entered a competition to decorate the altar of the Sanctuary of Madonna del Baraccano but her degree of success is not recorded.

According to Vasari, Properzia's talents were recognised as she practised carving upon fruit stones, a suitably domestic means of transition to the art world. Using peach, apricot and even tiny cherry stones, she created miniature religious works, including a crucifixion scene, which was an entire Passion of Christ carved as an intaglio. Still, Vasari had to frame this accomplishment within the context of feminine qualities and beauty. The artist was admired not only for her patience and precision, 'but for the slender figures she carved on them and her most truly delicate style of arranging them.'[3] It was through the recognition of men that she received her first commission, using an intermediary with the trustees of the Church of San Petronio, to carve marble friezes upon the western doors. Properzia's first commissioned portrait in marble was of Count Guido de Pepoli, and had been judged 'extremely pleasing' but the marble frieze was 'graceful' to the amazement of all Bologna. Her subject matter was Joseph and Potiphar's wife, which Vasari believed was inspired by her 'burning passion' for a handsome young man who did not return her feelings.[4] The carving was solid, but fluid, with the rippling fabric and hair of the characters suggesting movement, echoed in the material of the bed behind. The woman's hands are powerful; one clutches the shawl of the escaping Joseph while the other anchors her firmly to the bed. She also executed a Solomon and the Queen of Sheba, various angels and portraits, and may have been influenced by the Florentine Niccolo Tribolo, who visited Bologna with Cellini.

Properzia appears to have had a rivalry with another Bolognese artist, Amico Aspertini, who came from an artistic family and had travelled to Rome. Vasari described him as eccentric and 'half-insane', being able to paint separately with his two hands at the same time, and his work featured on the ceilings, walls and doors of local churches, placing Properzia in direct competition with him. According to their biographer, Amico always 'discouraged her out of envy' and 'always spoke badly of her to the trustees' and was 'so malicious' that he ensured she was paid poorly for her work.[5] Without an artistic family to back her, or a father, husband or brother, with a reputation among the guilds, it was difficult for a lone woman to counter such attacks, even after the quality of her work had spoken for itself. The Renaissance had seen a flourishing of support for artists, but this did not extend to women and ideas of artistic equality published in Castiglione's *Book of the Courtier*[6] had yet to have a universal impact. Women's powers of invention were considered inferior, and it was thought they were suited to more routine tasks, leaving the big commissions to men. This might have contributed to Properzia's decision to stop sculpting and take up copper engraving, moving into another field to escape such pressure. She did this, according to Vasari, 'faultlessly and to great praise'.[7]

Properzia's private life was controversial. One source suggests she inherited the same hot temper as her father[8] but this cannot be corroborated. In 1520, she was accused of destroying a private garden in the city, and in 1525, of assaulting Amico, in the context of his campaign of bullying against her. Her notorious infatuation with the young nobleman on whom she modelled Joseph – Antonio Galeazzo Malvasia de Bottigari – proved a driving factor in her life; some sources claim her feelings were unrequited, while others believe them to have been lovers. There are records of payments she made in 1529 to a local plague hospital, suggesting that she may have been suffering from the disease. This would also explain why her artistic output declined and she was living in penury the following year. The plague was particularly virulent in Italy following the Sack of Rome in 1527. 100 kilometres to the south, Florence lost a quarter of its inhabitants and the city ground to a halt with businesses closed. Lorenzo de Filippo Strozzi wrote:

If by chance relations meet, a brother, a sister, a husband, a wife, they carefully avoid each other. What further words are needed? Fathers and mothers avoid their own children and forsake them.... A few provision stores are still open, where bread is distributed, but where in the crush plague boils are also spread. Instead of conversation... one hears now only pitiful, mournful tidings – such a one is dead, such a one is sick, such a one has fled, such a one is interned in his house, such a one is in hospital, such a one has nurses, another is without aid.[9]

By 1530, Florence had 600 temporary structures built outside the walls to accommodate the sick. It is likely that similar buildings appeared around Bologna.

Despite her rival's best efforts, Properzia's fame as an artist had spread, with the people of Bologna considering her nothing less than 'one of the greatest miracles of nature' of their time. Her talents reached the ears of Pope Clement VII, who resolved to meet the woman described to him as a 'noble and elevated genius'. On 24 February 1530, Clement was in Bologna to crown Charles V Emperor, and made enquiries about visiting Properzia, only to be told she had just died. Vasari claims he was 'very distressed at the news.' Aged 40, or just before, she passed away, alone, in penury. Her death may have been accelerated by plague, and Strozzi's words could explain its lonely nature.

Properzia had been aware of her approaching death, giving credence to the plague theory. She had already drawn up her last will and testament, in which she specified her wish to be buried in the Ospedale della Morte, founded in the fifteenth century. It was a traditional burial site for plague sufferers, recently expanded, and likely to have been the recipient of Properzia's earlier payments. The location of her burial is unknown, and after expansion, only the apse remains of the original site.

Properzia had chosen an unconventional life, followed her extraordinary talent and won acclaim, but the costs had been high. Being a 'miracle of nature' did not pay the bills. Instead, it heightened the rivalry and intimidation she had experienced from male artists in defence of their traditional hegemony. No known self-portrait of Properzia survives, although Vasari believed Potiphar's wife to bear her features. It is a fitting metaphor for the female artist, trying to cling to a contemptuous male figure who rejects her, echoing Properzia's journey. Women entering the art world were vulnerable, even when they came from established families or studios; raw talent alone was insufficient. It is remarkable that Properzia chose to dedicate her life to art against such odds and suggests a real calling. Had she found influential patrons, such as the Pope, earlier on, her life may have turned out differently. However, as Clement discovered in 1530, by then it was too late. The struggle for equality in the arts had barely begun.

28

Anne Boleyn

31 May 1533

Streets of London, England

Anne Boleyn. Her name resonates down the years like no other. Her story, of feminine allure, love against the odds, her meteoric rise, volatile marriage and brutal demise, continues to capture the popular imagination, while her face appears on mugs and Christmas decorations, soft furnishings and postcards. She inspires a devoted cult following all across the globe, from people of all ages, nationalities and races, who are touched by her story, or feel some affinity with her, five centuries after her death. Something about Anne still feels relevant, fresh in the modern world, as new generations continue to succumb to the romance of her tragic life.

Of all the days in Anne's journey, 31 May 1533 marks the pinnacle of her success. This was her coronation procession in which she rode, clad in finery, through the streets, showing herself to the crowds. She had been waiting for this day for years, and after it, as she delivered a daughter, not the promised son, and her marriage unravelled, nothing could rival the hope and excitement of that May day. Anne was born into the English aristocracy, in around 1501. Her mother Elizabeth came from the prestigious Howard family while her father Thomas, the grandson of a former Lord Mayor of London, had already proved himself to be a skilled diplomat, fluent in languages and good with people. Anne had spent a year in the court of the Netherlands as a girl and six more years in the service of Claude, Queen of France. Returning to England with her French accent, sophistication and accomplishments, she represented a new style, lively and flirtatious, outstripping the English women who demurely followed their devout Spanish mistress.

Anne's rise had been meteoric in its height, from a knight's daughter to a queen, but it had not been as swift as that adjective might suggest. She had secured Henry VIII's affections in 1526, received his proposal of marriage in 1527, and spent the next five years waiting as the king sought legal and religious loopholes, his ministers convened courts and appealed to the Pope, and every excuse was found to marginalise Catherine of Aragon, England's queen since 1509. Nor did Catherine go quietly, asserting her status, refusing to leave and protesting her innocence. Henry had finally deserted her at Windsor in the summer of 1531, separated her from her daughter and confined her to country houses. Anne became Marquess of Pembroke in 1532, accompanying the king to Calais for an audience with Francis I, whose approval gave Henry the final push to bed and then marry his paramour. Anne fell swiftly pregnant, her belly growing with the son she had promised to bear. Finally, the years of waiting were over and the long-desired prize was in sight. What had once seemed impossible was about to come true. Yet Anne's position had attracted controversy from those loyal to Catherine and the old religion, or those who resented her rise or had been at the sharp end of her tongue. Cases of libel and slander had been dealt with harshly in the city, and the mood was uncertain.

On Saturday 31 May, Anne prepared herself in the Tower, from where she would process through the London streets to Westminster. She wore silver tissue, with her hair loose over her shoulders and a coronet upon her head, and sat in a chair of cloth of gold under a silver canopy. Venetian Capello described how she was accompanied by 'the greater part of the nobility of this kingdom, with the utmost order and tranquillity' through the decorated streets where the houses were 'crowded with persons of every condition, in number truly marvellous.'[1] Women featured prominently in Anne's procession. Behind her were twenty-eight ladies of the highest estate, in crimson velvet, borne along in four gold chariots, containing her relatives and gentlewomen; her mother, step-grandmother, sister Mary, sister-in-law Jane, aunts, cousins and others. Then came thirty gentlewomen, in velvet and silk, bearing the liveries of their ladies, followed by more women on horseback, in black velvet.

Six pageants had been spread through the city, to designs by the leading guilds. The details of each were carefully chosen to reflect Anne's identity and hopes for her future. Children sang songs of welcome in English and French, dressed as merchants, as a reminder of the city's wealth and her roots. Fountains ran with wine, and she was greeted by classical gods and goddesses, the Nine Muses and the Three Graces. Towers and triumphal arches, some designed by Holbein, were festooned with roses and Anne's motif of the falcon, with angels, children and poetry, and she was showered with wafers and presented with prophecies and a purse of gold.[2]

Anne's detractors were quick to dispatch their accounts to those who were hostile to Anne, such as the Pope or the Emperor Charles V. The imperial ambassador wrote that it had been a 'cold, meagre, and uncomfortable thing, to the great dissatisfaction, not only of the common people, but also of the rest.'[3] Another, anonymous, manuscript asserted that even though it was 'customary to kneel, uncover and cry "God save the King, God save the Queen", whenever they appeared in public, no one in London or the suburbs, not even women and children did so on this occasion.'[4] The source continues with as much vitriol as it can muster whilst remaining plausible, and includes some blatant errors:

> One of the Queen's servants told the mayor to command the people to make the customary shouts, and was answered that he could not command people's hearts, and that even the King could not make them do so.... Her dress was covered with tongues pierced with nails, to show the treatment which those

who spoke against her might expect. Her car was so low that the ears of the last mule appeared to those who stood behind to belong to her. The letters H. A. were painted in several places, for Henry and Anne, but were laughed at by many. The crown became her very ill, and a wart disfigured her very much. She wore a violet velvet mantle, with a high ruff of gold thread and pearls, which concealed a swelling she has, resembling goitre.[5]

It is extremely unlikely that any form of dissent was tolerated in the streets on 31 May. Anne rode among the people, hearing their cheers and applause, seeing upturned faces of the crowds that lined the streets. Her greatest triumph of all was her pregnancy, visible for all to see as she approached her final trimester, a sign of hope and her undeniable success. On 31 May 1533, Anne had won. This was her moment of triumph. The following day, she was crowned queen of England.

1 June 1533 was a Sunday. Between eight and nine in the morning, Anne processed from Westminster Hall to the Abbey dressed in purple velvet, with a jewelled circlet on her loose hair. The lords and ladies following were all clad in scarlet, with their fur collars powdered according to their degrees. When the Mass was concluded, Anne mounted a specially constructed platform and sat on an elevated seat, covered in tapestry, for the duration of the service. Then, she was invited forward by Archbishop Cranmer and prostrated herself at the High Altar. He anointed her on the head and breast and placed the crown of St Edward briefly upon her head, before being substituted for a lighter one of her own. She made an offering at the shrine of Edward the Confessor, before being led out to the sound of trumpets.[6] Henry himself watched the proceedings from a little closet, accessed by the cloisters, so as not to upstage Anne with his presence.

The details of Anne's fall are already well known. That September, she delivered a daughter, Elizabeth, not the son the king had hoped for, and in the coming years she suffered a miscarriage and, probably, a stillbirth. After Henry had tired of her, and her enemies at court had gained the upper hand, she was indicted on fabricated charges of treason and adultery, confined to the Tower and executed. Modern historians are almost unanimous in their belief in her innocence underpinned by Henry's volte-face of emotion.[7] Anne's dramatic trajectory still has the power to move and shock us, for its opposites of romance and tragedy. As a study in gender relations, it exposes the superficiality of the power that Anne was granted by her royal lover while she had his affection. Yet titles, wealth, and even a crown were not enough to save her life once Henry had decided to move on.

The dynamic between Anne and Henry was complicated by his royal status. During the game of courtly love, he gave her power over him, acting the role of devoted suitor, but it was only ever an illusion as his position as king always gave him the ultimate control. The swiftness and completeness by which this gift was snatched away from Anne in April 1536 is a reminder, just as Henry warned her, that he could cast her as low as he had raised her. It is chilling to consider how a man could reject and condemn to death a woman he had once loved deeply, but Henry and Anne can never be considered merely on gender terms; they were always king and subject.

Anne's fate underlines a constant theme in this book: the illusion of power with which the patriarchal society could indulge its favoured women, and just how deadly that could prove once those women started to feel secure in that position. As a tragic wife and as a representative of the changing culture of the 1520s and 1530s, Anne Boleyn is a poignant example of sixteenth-century womanhood. She embodied many women's experiences of gender power play but the location for her drama, centred upon the throne, lifts her story into the stuff of legends. It is difficult to underestimate just how shocking the execution of an English queen was in 1536. Such an act was unprecedented. It makes Anne as famous for her shocking death as she is for her extraordinary life.

29

Elizabeth Barton

20 April 1534
Tyburn Hill, London, England

In the East Kent village of Court-at-Street, just off the present B2067 between Aldington and Lympne, stand the crumbling walls of the Bellirica Chapel, built in the twelfth century to serve a local manor house. Open to the elements today, with few surviving features, they once provided the location for one of the most significant events in the life of a local sixteenth-century woman. Elizabeth Barton would rise from obscurity to become notorious, basking in the king's favour before losing his goodwill and suffering a traitor's death.

Barton was born in 1506 into a poor family living in the village of Aldington, 2 miles to the west of the chapel. Despite being a tiny place, it was a favourite of the last two Archbishops of Canterbury, John Morton and William Warham, who frequently visited their palace beside the church. In 1511, it gained further religious significance when the Dutch scholar Desiderius Erasmus, then visiting England, was appointed by Warham as rector of Aldingham and lived in the parsonage for a year. Erasmus was already being vocal in favour of church reforms and his influence may have had an impact upon the village community, who certainly would have been aware of him. However, they would not have understood him, and it is unlikely that he preached in the church as he spoke no English.

When she was in her teens, Elizabeth entered service as a maid at the village inn, then she joined the family of Thomas Cobb, Warham's estate steward, who lived at the newly built Cobb's Hall. It appears that she suffered from 'fits and trances', and the detailed description left by William Lambarde in his *A Perambulation of Kent* suggests this was due to epilepsy. Born two years after Barton's death, Lambarde never saw her but is likely to have drawn upon local memory and legend. He states that during these episodes, 'she told wonderous things done in other places, while she herself was neither present, nor had heard report thereof.'[1] Soon, people were gathering to witness her trances in Aldington church.

In November 1525, she announced that the Virgin had commanded her to visit the Chapel of Our Lady at Court-at-Street, in which dwelt a hermit. There, Mary had promised that Elizabeth would be cured. The Aldington rector reported this to Warham, who set up a commission to investigate Barton and her claims, so that when she actually visited the tiny chapel, it was in the company of a church committee, 'ladies and gentlemen of the best sort' and around 3,000 commoners.

Thus, a large audience was present when she fell into a passionate swoon before a figure of the Virgin.[2] An eyewitness account related that 'her face was wonderfully disfigured, her tongue hanging out, and her eyes being in a manner plucked out, and laid upon her cheeks, and so greatly disordered. Then was there heard a voice speaking within her belly as it had been in a tun. This continued three hours, the voice speaking sweetly of heaven and terribly of hell. After a long time, she came to herself, and was perfectly whole. The miracle was solemnly rung, and a book of it was afterwards printed and sold.'[3] This likely refers to the pamphlet printed by Robert Redman, of which 700 copies were made, although possession of it was swiftly made illegal. One copy survived long enough for Lambarde to see, but all others were destroyed. Shortly after, at the recommendation of the committee, Elizabeth was found a place in the Convent of St Sepulchre at Canterbury, aged around 18.

Barton's role as a prophetess continued for several years, until the death of her patron Warham in 1532 and the king's reform of the English church. She had previously met leading courtiers such Thomas More, John Fisher and Thomas Cranmer, and twice, Henry VIII himself when he visited Canterbury. Yet her devout Catholicism would not let Barton accept the king's proposed marriage to Anne Boleyn. She prophesized that if he did so, Henry would be dead within weeks, and when later questioned about why this had not taken place, she replied that he was no longer king. This was sufficient to launch an investigation into charges of treason. The imperial ambassador went further and claimed that she had experienced a revelation of Henry's impending damnation and had 'seen the place and seat prepared for him in Hell.'[4] By July 1533, Thomas Cromwell was calling her 'the hypocrite nun', and under his questioning, she confessed 'many mad follies' and that she had 'feigned' them all.[5] She and her friends were brought before the Star Chamber and then committed to the Tower. Five were condemned with her, and even Thomas More was implicated, although he was able to produce letters proving he had attempted to dissuade her, so he escaped punishment for now.

What prompted Elizabeth's confession is clear. The pressure exerted by a determined Cromwell would be enough to make anyone crack, but her admission of 'follies' and 'heresies' raises the question of her genuine faith. Either she had always been a charlatan, or else she truly believed in her visions, as did many around her, and was intimidated into denying them. Perhaps she was manipulated by those around her who saw an opportunity to censure the king's chosen path from an apparently divine source. Perhaps others convinced her that they were inspired by a diabolical connection. Elizabeth was popular with the people, and so was Catherine of Aragon; Henry's imminent reforms and marriage were not. Cromwell, and Henry, needed to publicly correct her narrative and make an example of those who opposed the king. She was exhibited on a scaffold outside St Paul's Cathedral, and also in Canterbury, where her guilt was publicly proclaimed as heresy and treason, and she read aloud a confession that had been written for her.[6]

One sad aspect of Barton's fall arises in a letter written by Gertrude, Marchioness of Exeter, in November 1532. Having previously experienced miscarriages and stillbirths, Gertrude had appealed to Barton to pray for her, for the safe delivery of her next child. After Barton was disgraced, she rushed to defend herself in a letter to Henry. In doing so, she drew upon gender stereotypes to appeal for pity, presenting her weakness and her susceptibility when it came to the influence of another woman. Gertrude was keen to assert that she had listened to no male opinion, which had greater credence, and asked Henry to intercede in her unhappy marriage; the subtext of this was that, without a husband's guidance, she had been led astray:

> Has received his gracious letter… concerning her abuse, lightness, and indiscreet offences committed in frequenting the conversation and company of that most unworthy, subtle, and deceivable woman called the Holy Maid of Kent, and in giving too much credence to the malicious and detestable proceedings of her and her adherents, which are now manifest to all the world to have been abominably compassed by sedition and malice against the King; and also containing his gracious remission of her offences.
>
> Reminds the King that she is a woman, whose fragility and brittleness is easily seduced and brought to abusion and light belief. Is now the most sorrowful and heavy creature alive, that she has been so unfortunate as to offend the King and his laws, or be in danger of his indignation or displeasure. Cannot excuse her offences in listening to the seditious tales, blasphemies, and execrable and false prophecies set forth by the said most unworthy person and her adherents. Her lightness proceeded rather from not revealing them than from any credence she gave to the false revelations. Thought them so full of folly and untruth as to be unworthy to be revealed or believed.
>
> Protests that she never acted from any 'male opinion', malice, or grudge against the King, the Queen, or their posterity. Begs the King to require her husband, who is much displeased, to forgive her. Thanks the King for his goodness, and expresses her obligations to him.[7]

Elizabeth Barton was 28 years old when she died. On 20 April 1534, she was tied to a hurdle at the Tower and drawn through the streets to Tyburn, a journey of about 4 miles, which took her across the city from east to west and outside the walls. On the scaffold, she addressed the crowd with the statement that she was responsible for her own fate, as 'a poor wench without learning' who had been 'puffed up with the praise' of clever men who encouraged her 'because the things which fell from me were profitable to them.' This led her into a 'certain pride and foolish fantasy, which had brought me to this.'[8] She was hanged and then beheaded, with her head being displayed upon Tower Bridge; the only woman to have ever suffered this fate. Five male supporters died with her.

Elizabeth Barton's death was a shocking preliminary for the trajectory Henry's reign was about to take. She may have acted with genuine conviction that Henry had sinned, out of a sense of duty, or a belief that she was divinely inspired, or she may simply have been naïve and manipulated by men in power. Yet her popularity, her holy orders and her gender made her brutal demise shocking and give her story a poignancy that still brings pilgrims to the chapel in Court-at-Street today.

30

Margaret Roper

July 1535

Tower of London, England

On a summer's day in 1535, a young woman hurried away from the grey stone walls of London's notorious Tower. She was aged around 30, her clothes and bearing suggested she was not aristocratic, but certainly well-born. Over the previous year, she had become a frequent visitor, known to the guards, who now simply waved her through the gates. Today, though, was different, as she blinked away the tears of frustration that threatened to spill. Under her cloak, she carried the last letters written by her father, warm from his hands, with his instructions to distribute them among his friends. Her final pleas and persuasions had gone unheeded and, as she looked back at the forbidding Bell Tower,[1] Margaret knew that nothing could halt the inevitable now. Her father, Sir Thomas More, recently the king's close advisor and friend, would be executed for treason.

Margaret was More's eldest daughter, born to his first wife in 1505. Along with her brother and sisters, More gave her a Renaissance education that was exceptional for girls of her class and era, covering Latin and Greek, classical literature, mathematics, science, history and music. Her husband, William Roper, who wrote a biography of More in the 1550s, described her upbringing in a culinary metaphor, as taking learning for its meat and play for its sauce. In the early 1520s, while she was still in her late teens, Margaret translated and published the Latin works and thoughts of Erasmus, pieces composed while the scholar was resident in the More family home. With levels of female literacy so low, publication by a woman was extremely rare at the time and had been, until then, exclusive to royalty. According to her husband, Margaret was also a prolific poet, writing in Latin and Greek, and composing a treaty called *The Four Last Things*.[2] She was her father's protegee, called his 'dearest Meg', and their relationship was remarkable for its warmth and closeness.

A few years earlier, it would have been impossible to believe that Thomas More would be condemned to death. A leading statesman, Lord High Chancellor, High Steward of Oxford and Cambridge, Secretary and advisor to Henry VIII, he used to walk arm in arm with the king in his garden, fulfilling the paternal role Henry had found difficult with his own father. A devout Catholic, loyal to Queen Catherine of Aragon, More had been a young law student witnessing her arrival in London in 1501, and the king's attempts to set her aside in favour of Anne Boleyn had troubled his conscience. He continued to support the Pope as head of the Church and refused to sign Henry's letter petitioning the papacy to grant his divorce and the Oath of Supremacy. He resigned his Chancellorship in 1532 and did not attend Anne's coronation, although he was not vocal in his criticism and sent her a letter expressing carefully worded encouragement. More's friendship with Henry protected him a little longer, but his luck ran out in April 1534 when he was arrested and refused to recognise the spiritual validity of the king's new marriage.

More had been in the Tower a little over a month when Margaret obtained permission by her 'earnest suit',[3] from Thomas Cromwell to visit him, in the hope that she would be able to change his mind and convince him to swear the controversial oath. However, as Roper reported, she found her father resolute:

> I believe (Meg) that they that have put me here, they have done me a high displeasure. But I assure you on my faith, mine own dear daughter, if it had not been for my wife and you that be my children, whom I account the chief part of my charge, I would not have failed, long ere this, to have closed myself in as strait a room and straiter too. But since I come hither without mine own desert, I trust that God of his goodness will discharge me of my care, and with his gracious help supply my want among you. I find no cause (I thank God, Meg) to reckon myself in worse case here, than in mine own house.[4]

Over the following year, Margaret visited frequently, as did her stepmother Alice, using every tactic they could to influence More's decision, but without success. Margaret's father was put on trial on 1 July 1535, and was repeatedly offered a pardon. His response that although he had not taken the oath, he had never spoken against it was not sufficient to save his life and he was sentenced to death. Upon his return from Westminster to the Tower by river, Margaret waited for him at the Tower wharf where he would disembark in order to receive his final blessing. As her husband recorded:

> As soon as she saw him, after his blessings on her knees reverently received, she, hasting towards, without consideration of care of herself, pressing in amongst the midst of the throng and the Company of the Guard, that with halbards and bills were round about him, hastily ran to him, and there openly in the sight of all them embraced and took him about the neck and kissed him, who well liking her most daughterly love and affection towards him, gave her his fatherly blessing, and many godly words of comfort besides, from whom after she was departed, she not satisfied with the former sight of her dear father, having respect neither to herself, nor to the press of the people and multitude that were about him, suddenly turned back again, and ran to him as before, took him about the neck, and divers times together most lovingly kissed him, and at last with a full heavy heart was fain to depart from him; the beholding whereof was to many of them that were present thereat so lamentable, that it made them for very sorrow to mourn and weep.[5]

The day before his execution, More sent to Margaret the hair shirt he had been accustomed to wear under his clothes as a sign of his faith, along with a letter he had written with a piece of coal. He hoped his sentence would not be delayed, to cause her more suffering, and that it was fitting that he died on St Thomas' Day, and longed to go to God. He added that he had 'never liked your manners better, than when you kissed me last. For I like when daughterly love, and dear charity, hath no leisure to look to worldly courtesy.'[6]

Thomas More was executed upon Tower Green on 6 July. As was customary, his head was displayed on a spike on London Bridge following his execution as a deterrent to others resisting Henry's changes. After a month, when it was due to be cast into the river, Margaret bribed the guard to release it to her, preserving it in spices, until it was buried in 1544, probably at the Church of St Dunstan, Canterbury, where the family retreated.

Holbein's portrait of More's family in happier times no longer exists, but a later copy shows Margaret in a gable bonnet and the chemise and kirtle of the day. Her expression is intense, dark eyes uplifted, her nose retrousse and her lips determinedly pressed together. Although she is not looking down, her fingers trace the words on the page of a book open in her lap. A second portrait, a miniature also by Holbein, dates from 1535–6, either during, or in the aftermath of, More's incarceration and death. Less than a decade has elapsed since the first painting, but Margaret is visibly older and thinner, almost gaunt, her heavy-lidded eyes and wide mouth marked by sorrow. According to William Roper, More had predicted Anne's downfall to Meg, asking after the new queen, and adding that it 'pitieth me to remember, in what misery she, poor soul, shall shortly come.'[7]

Margaret survived until 1544, devoting herself to gathering her father's letters and writings, in order to prove his innocence. She died at the age of 39, having witnessed Henry's repudiation of Anne Boleyn and her execution, less than a year after More's.

31

Maria de Salinas, Lady Willoughby

1 January 1536

Kimbolton Castle, Cambridgeshire, England

Finally, weary after hours on the road, the traveller was approaching her destination. Maria de Salinas pulled up her reins and paused a moment to look ahead. Even in the dark days of the new year, Kimbolton Castle looked imposing. Its red towers rose up from the moat, facing west, away from the fenlands, newly remodelled after falling into a state of disrepair. Darkness was falling. A few lights burned in the windows, especially in the south wing, where Maria knew from letters that her friend was lodged. The sight was a great relief. As she drew close, Maria realised how much her limbs ached, having fallen from her horse about a mile back on the road.[1] She had come in spite of being forbidden to do so, knowing she was disobeying a direct order from the king, but unable to stay away any longer. Inside, her dearest and oldest friend lay dying, if she was not already dead, and neither heaven nor earth would prevent Maria from being by her side.

At the age of 50, Catherine of Aragon's health was failing. Abandoned by Henry VIII at Windsor back in 1531, she had been moved between various remote country houses, finally arriving at Kimbolton in April 1534. Her daughter and friends were refused permission to visit or write to her. The lines of communication were kept open by the imperial ambassador, Eustace Chapuys, whose position allowed him access and whose concerns had reached Maria, explaining Catherine's deterioration. On 30 December, Maria wrote to Thomas Cromwell from her London home in the Barbican:

> When I sent my servant to you, he brought me word that you were in such importunate business that you could not despatch me or any other body. But now I must put you to pain, for I heard that my mistress is very sore sick again. I pray you remember me, for you promised to labour with the King to get me licence to go to her before God send for her, as there is no other likelihood. Unless the King will let me have a letter to show the officers of my mistress's house, my licence will be of no effect. No one can help me so well as yourself.[2]

There were no guards in place to prevent Maria's approach as she crossed the bridge and into the courtyard. She was conducted into the hall, where she met

Sir Edmund Bedingfield, custodian of the queen dowager and Catherine's chamberlain.[3] She told them she 'thought never to have seen the Princess again, by reason of such tidings as she had heard of her,' and the two men asked to see her license of permission to visit. Maria replied that it was 'ready to be shown', as she would 'not otherwise presume'. Although Bedingfield's letter to Cromwell describing these events is damaged, it appears Maria was admitted to Catherine's chambers and then disappeared, as 'since that time we never saw her, neither any letters of her license hither to repair.' Chapuys arrived two days later. Catherine's doctor observed that 'she hath somewhat taken comfort upon the coming of these folks, and somewhat falleth to more rest in the night.'[4]

Maria and Catherine's story had begun over thirty-five years ago in Spain. The daughter of high-ranking officials in the court of Isabella of Castile, Maria had initially served Catherine's mother as a girl, before joining her entourage to depart for England in 1501. Five years younger than her mistress, Maria was not yet in her teens when she turned her back on her homeland, never to return. The act was symbolic of the fates of any young women of rank, committed to new lives through service or marriage, and of the Anglo-Spanish union and the hopes it brought. Maria was with Catherine during her short-lived first marriage and through the years of penury, when the young widow could barely afford to feed and clothe her household. She had seen her mistress's fortunes change and celebrated her accession to the throne. After Catherine was settled and had been delivered of a daughter, Maria married an Englishman, William Willoughby, Baron d'Eresby on 5 June 1516. Catherine and Henry attended the wedding at Greenwich, with Henry making an offering of 6s 8d.[5] Then, Maria had watched as the Spaniard's fortunes turned. From her country seat of Grimsthorpe Castle, raising her daughter, Maria learned of her friend's rejection by her husband, her banishment from court and incarceration in the countryside. By 1534, she was petitioning the king to visit Catherine, but all her requests were denied. In spite of this, one of the sixteenth century's most devoted female friendships would not be repressed.

Maria must have set out on her journey almost as soon as she had dispatched her letter to Cromwell. Between writing it on 30 December and arriving at Kimbolton around 6.00 pm the following day, she covered the 65 miles between her and her friend. It is not clear whether Maria stayed with Catherine. No doubt she would have wished to, and some unverified accounts claim that the princess died in her friends' arms.[6] However, the sources are vague on this. Chapuys' letter to the emperor stated that she saw *'the principal officers of her household, such as her own chamberlain, who had not seen her for more than a year, and many others,'* but he does not mention Maria by name.[7] Nor does Catherine's final will bequeath anything to her close friend, although Maria's marriage had left her well provided for. Ambassador Chapuys remained at Kimbolton until Tuesday, satisfied that Catherine had regained a little strength, before beginning the ride south. However, messengers overtook him, bringing the news to Henry on Friday that she had died the previous afternoon, on Thursday, 7 January. Maria's whereabouts at the time are unknown, but perhaps she did remain at her mistress's side, bringing her comfort in her final hours and assisting with the arrangements for her interment that followed.

Maria survived her friend by three years, living with her daughter in the Barbican area of London. Her life had been dedicated to the Anglo-Spanish journey, from its initial negotiations and her departure from Spain, through Catherine's two marriages, and as witness to its failure and conclusion. She had integrated into English society but remained a Spaniard at heart, steadfastly loyal to her roots and her mistress, demonstrating her devotion at the end. She personified that which every Tudor monarch desired: the servant whose love transcended duty.

32

Women of the Devonshire Manuscript

1530s

The English court, London, England

A manuscript of closely written pages dating from the 1530s is securely stored away in the British Library.[1] It contains almost 200 poems[2], or fragments of poems, copied in anthology style for informal use. On first inspection, it looks plain, almost disappointing. It contains none of the illuminated letters, marginal decorations or illustrations that make many of its contemporary books remarkable. The pages are covered by a number of identifiable hands, some neat and tidy, some large and loose, with crossings out, the occasional doodle and comment, written on faintly scored lines, with some verses bracketed. Known as the Devonshire Manuscript, this modest-looking collection of poems offers an exciting insight into the nature of court life for elite women in the 1530s, who gathered, shared and transcribed the works of their friends and added poems of their own composition. It reveals that women were not just the passive consumers of male art that history has often supposed them to be, but equal creators and poets in their own right.

The court circle around Anne Boleyn was known for its vibrancy. For the young women attending upon the queen during her brief reign, it was a time of excitement and opportunity, when intellect, music and learning were prized as contributing to the witty interplay between the sexes, the playful flirtatiousness that was used against the queen in the spring of 1536 and contributed to her downfall. Among her ladies were those related to her, or the king, and those she had singled out for advancement. The Devonshire Manuscript was initially owned by her cousin, Mary Fitzroy, daughter of the Duke of Norfolk, whose marriage to Henry VIII's illegitimate son had been encouraged, if not proposed, by Anne. She was only 14 at the time of Anne's accession and lived at court apart from her young husband, waiting to come of age before the pair were allowed to consummate the match. Her handwriting dominates the text, including poems from her brother Henry, Earl of Surrey. Among Mary's close friends were the other contributors, Mary Shelton and Margaret Douglas. Mary Shelton was in her twenties, another Boleyn cousin on her father's side, whose sister may have been the king's mistress during his marriage to Anne. It is possible that confusion over the spellings of their names have mistaken her identity, and it was in fact Mary who shared Henry's bed.

Margaret was the daughter of the king's elder sister, Margaret Tudor, formerly Queen of Scots, who was being raised at the English court.

The poems in the Devonshire Manuscript include copies of famous historical works by Chaucer and Hoccleve, as well as the works of Thomas Wyatt, whose passion for Anne inspired many works but whose tone became more guarded after her marriage. The key themes of the works were courtly love and passion, particularly how women negotiated a path through societal expectations and male desire. In some works, Mary records the advances of admirers, and her marginal comments, and those of her friends, add additional context to her rejection of unwanted suitors. In a few cases, Margaret responds with an interplay between the women like a brief conversation in the margins.[3] However, the majority of the poems are transcribed by male hands, with those of Surrey, Wyatt and, later, Margaret's son, Henry, Lord Darnley, recognisable. An additional dozen scribes have been identified[4] by the differences in their written script, but their names are currently unverified: scholars have suggested they include Edmund Kynvett, Anthony Lee, Richard Hatfield and even Anne Boleyn.[5] The majority of entries date from the 1530s, but a few later entries show that the manuscript was still being used and expanded for three subsequent decades, commensurate with the lifespans of the three women involved. Men may have written and added to the works too, but the women were the curators and custodians of the books.

The Devonshire Manuscript also records the dramas and heartbreak of life for women at the Tudor court. The year 1536 proved particularly traumatic for their circle. Although it is not alluded to directly, Anne's fall that May was followed by the death of Mary Fitzroy's young husband, marking what some experts have identified as a change in the tone of the poems.[6] The following year, the 21-year-old Margaret became secretly engaged to Thomas Howard, with whom she had fallen in love the previous year, in the atmosphere of courtly love nurtured by the poems. The king was furious to discover this, given her proximity to the throne, and sent the pair into the Tower, although Margaret was soon released. The manuscript contains a number of poems from Thomas, adapted from Chaucer and others, with the pronouns and details changed in order to reflect his situation. After he died in captivity in 1537, Margaret composed an original piece in the form of her will, stating how she would rather be dead than live without him. Mary would also transcribe a further poem by her brother, who was executed for treason in 1547.

This rare surviving manuscript demonstrates the centrality of women to Tudor court culture, as its custodian and its creator. The poems they selected reflect the struggles of their world, from dealing with the trials of courtly love to the pain of loss, affording an insight into the lives of an elite whose voices are rarely heard. It is an unusual collaboration between the genders, revealing the changing tone of the court and the way in which oral culture was valued, shared and transcribed. As the manuscript was intended for circulation among a private elite – a very small, educated circle – it offers a confessional, diary feel for the elusive innermost thoughts and feelings of those women identifiable as its scribes.

33

Margaret Cheney

25 May 1537
Smithfield, London, England

She was the only woman to be made an example of. Dragged on a hurdle through the streets from the Tower to Newgate Prison and then on to Smithfield, Margaret would have been aware of this injustice. Blocking out the voices of the crowd, she tried to focus her mind upon God, knowing that her imminent death would be considered a martyrdom for the Catholic cause, although the forces that led to her condemnation were more to do with earthly morality. Somewhere nearby, her husband was undergoing a similar fate; the man to whom she had been united in affection, which had been her undoing. While he would be hanged before the crowd, she would suffer the slow agony of burning, caught up in a cause by association. Across the north, rebels were rising in indignation at Henry VIII's dissolution of the monasteries, and those who resisted his reforms were being quashed brutally.

Margaret Cheney's origins are obscure. Rumours emerging at the time of her arrest suggested that she was the illegitimate daughter of Edward Stafford, Duke of Buckingham, himself executed for treason in 1521. With four children by his wife, Stafford is credited with three others outside wedlock, one of whom is named Margaret in most sources, although she appears to have been married to the duke's ward, Thomas Fitzgerald of Leixlip.[1] Her identity was confused when Margaret's son reasserted his mother's noble paternity in 1584, although his motives for this are unclear and were potentially self-motivated. Margaret is listed as having been first wed to a Sir William Cheney[2] of London, so it is likely that these are two different women, although this did not prevent reports of her aristocratic origins turning a jury against her. Had she been Stafford's daughter, Margaret would have been a blood relation of the king, making her perceived rebellion all the more serious. Yet, there is a chance that she was not a rebel at all, only tainted by association.

Thomas Cromwell, Henry VIII's chief minister of the 1530s, rose to power on a promise that he would make his sovereign the richest king ever.[3] In 1535, he drew up the *Valor Ecclesiasticus*, a document recording the wealth of the English monasteries after his commissioners travelled the country recording the state of repair, goods and vices of each establishment. Centres of devotion, learning and knowledge were dismantled and sold to Henry's courtiers, who repurposed them for secular uses. Shrines to which pilgrims had made offerings for centuries were destroyed, images and icons burned, and anything of value absorbed into the royal coffers. Faced with the dismantling of the belief system and practices that had sustained generations, the conservative Catholic north went into rebellion twice. The 1536 Pilgrimage of Grace had apparently been resolved when its leader, Robert Aske, was granted an audience with the king and promised there would be no further trouble. However, the following January, Sir Robert Bigod raised troops in Yorkshire, despite Aske's best attempts to prevent him. Henry's plans to hold a session of parliament in York and crown his new wife, Jane Seymour, there further added to the indignation with which Henry responded to this new irritation.

At this point, Margaret was living at Wilton Castle, east of Middlesbrough, North Yorkshire, close to the estate of the Bigod family. Her marriage to Cheney had failed and she had attracted the attention of Sir John Bulmer, who was a member of the Duke of Stafford's household, which is potentially the source of confusion about her identity. Even Wriothesley's hostile chronicle described her a 'very fair creature and a beautiful',[4] and mutual affection arose between Margaret and Bulmer. In an unusual move, Cheney agreed to a wife sale[5], a way of ridding himself of Margaret and passing her on to Bulmer for a price, equivalent to a divorce. Freed from her first marriage, Margaret lived with Bulmer as his mistress, bearing his children until such time that both their spouses had died and the pair were married, the wedding taking place before 1536. Their closeness was such that people who knew them claimed John said he would rather be racked than parted from his wife.[6] When the north rose against the monastic reforms, John Bulmer was vocal in support of the rebels, becoming one of their leaders, but there is no list of Margaret's involvement. When they rose again the following January, he was arrested, while Margaret was at home at Wilton Castle, delivering their youngest son. Heavily pregnant, and then in confinement, she can hardly be accused of participation, yet the lone voice of a parish priest was sufficient to secure her arrest.

Despite there being no record of Margaret's involvement in treasonous activity in 1536–7, Parson John Watts of Esyngton Church[7] deposed that she had incited her husband to rebellion and maligned her influence. He reported having questioned a servant of the Bulmers, who swore loyalty to Margaret by saying 'pretty Peg, I will never forsake thee', for which he chided the man, saying 'take heede of your selfe, and ye are a wanton prest, beware ye falle not in love with her, for if ye do, ye wyll be maid as wise as yowr master and both wyll be hangyd thene.'[8] Margaret and John were already on their way to London, by their own volition, according to this same report. By the end of the month, they had been arrested and incarcerated in the Tower. The reports of John Bulmer's confession record that he 'concealed the treason of Margaret Cheyny (whom he calls his wife) ... the said Margaret counselled him rather to flee the realm (if the commons would not rise) than that he and she should be parted, and again, to take Bygod's part,' from which it is clear that Bulmer said nothing to implicate his wife, and that she would have rather gone into exile than be parted from him. The origin of her suggestion that he 'take Bygod's part' is not clarified.[9]

Margaret's own deposition survives in part. What is legible confirms her husband's comments, stating that she advised him 'to get a ship to carry him and her into Scotland' but it also contains a note of cynical recognition that 'the commons wanted but a head.'[10] Their son Ralph was also questioned and he tried to warn his parents that 'all was falsehood that they were dealt with.'[11] A memoranda in Cromwell's hand, written after the investigation, described 'John Bulmer and his pretended wife' as conspirators, introducing the element of moral judgement about the nature of their marriage. Their trial was conducted on 14 May, with Margaret as the only woman; none of the wives of the other dozen or so rebels appeared.[12] In the initial investigations, Margaret is listed as Lady Bulmer, but by this point, she is described in the court records as 'Margaret Cheyne, late wife of William Cheyne of London, esquire'. This was a significant shift in terms of how she was perceived by her male jurors, and how they would judge her as a woman of loose morals. For some reason, having initially pleaded innocent, John and Margaret changed their plea to guilty, while the jury were deliberating.[13] They were sentenced to death on 17 May. If she was related to the Staffords, Margaret's reputed half-brother Henry made no attempt to save her, appealing to Cromwell instead to help resolve a dispute over his house.[14]

Margaret suffered the horrific death of burning at Smithfield on 25 May 1537. Her involvement in the northern uprisings had not been conclusively proven, but her affection for her husband and the nature of their union turned the tide against her. Her story is remarkable in life and death. There is the extraordinary nature of her 'sale' to a man who adored her, and her sacrifice to Tudor justice, as a deterrent for religious rebels, but also as a warning to men to control their traitorous wives. At a time when women's reputations, or 'good fame', formed their characters in the eyes of the law and society, Margaret's beauty and love story contributed to her undoing.

34

Bona Sforza, Queen of Poland

1537

Lviv High Castle, Lviv, Poland

In 1537, England was not the only country facing rebellion. While Henry VIII was dealing with uprisings challenging his religious reforms, his Polish counterpart was facing dissent arising from his heavy taxation, property and agricultural reforms. However, much of the anger brought to the door of Lviv Castle was directed at King Sigismund's wife of almost twenty years, Queen Bona. The lower nobility rose in revolt, citing Bona's influence upon their king, and rampaging through the countryside. In order to survive, they ransacked the farms around the castle, stealing and eating all the poultry they could find, with the result that their actions gained notoriety under the comical name of 'The Chicken War'.

Bona was a member of the powerful Sforza family, born in Milan in 1494, and raised amid the turmoil and statecraft of the Italian wars. The sole surviving child of her parents, she was given a broad humanist education, and various important European husbands were suggested for her from Spain and among the Italian states. Sigismund of Poland was an outsider, ruling over a large kingdom combining Poland with Lithuania and Prussia, for the Jagiellon dynasty. Born in 1467, he had already been widowed by the time the Sforzas were seeking a husband for Bona, but they were keen to prevent the Pole from making a hostile alliance. With the emperor supporting her case and Bona's huge dowry of around 150,000 ducats, a treaty was swiftly concluded between the 24-year-old bride and her 50-year-old groom.

Bona brought a particular kind of queenship into Poland. Instead of the passive consorts who had preceded her, she engaged directly in politics, culture and childrearing, arousing suspicion from her people. Sigismund's first wife Barbara had remained in the domestic sphere, resisting attempts from her own family to influence her husband. Bona, though, introduced Renaissance art and architecture into Poland; oversaw the education of the heir; introduced new foods such as salad and green vegetables; and engaged in correspondence with other powerful women, such as Roxelana, wife of Suleiman I, to try and ease Polish-Turkish relations.[1] Recognising their common ground, Roxelana wrote to Bona 'we are both born of one mother Eve, made from the same dough, and serve similar men.'[2] She supported Sigismund in his new reforms and high taxes, which were intended to strengthen the country and fund an attack upon Moldovia.[3] A permanent conscription army was launched, former royal properties were reclaimed and agricultural land was purchased by the crown. When the middle and lower ranks of the nobility rose up in protest, they particularly directed their ire at the influence of the Italian Bona.

The chicken-eating rebels presented Sigismund with a list of demands. Among them was the creation of a permanent council to advise the king and the uncoupling of various titles that usually went together. They also insisted on a consolidation of nobles' rights, their exemption from taxes and that only men of their rank were appointed to the most important jobs. The rebels also wanted the treasury to be overhauled and for Bona to cease her acquisition of lands and her quest for influence. She was also accused of giving her son a 'bad upbringing' through her emphasis on Renaissance learning. Historically, Bona has been depicted as a bad counsellor, but recent scholarship has indicated that her efforts were only successful when they accorded with her husband's existing intentions. She bought land and appointed officers, but few documents testify to her direct influence upon Sigismund or his policies.[4] It may be that Bona was genuinely mistrusted, or that directing criticism at a foreign-born queen was safer than open criticism of the king. The age difference was a factor too, with Sigismund's advancing age proving problematic in contrast to a young, active woman. The imperial ambassador certainly believed that speaking to 'the old king is like talking to nobody... Bona holds everything in her hands, she alone rules the country.'[5] This perception did not necessarily match the reality, but it did contrast with the ideals of virtue and humility in the coronation oaths of the Polish queens.

An 1872 painting by Henryk Rodakowski depicts the differing perceptions of Sigismund and Bona during the rebellion. Entitled *The Chicken War*, it features the king and queen on the battlements of Lviv Castle while their minister addressees an unseen crowd beyond. Sigismund is seated, dressed in dark clothes, head in hand, defeated and overcast. By contrast, Bona stands behind him, looking upwards in a different direction, dressed in white and gold. Her youth and vigour stand in opposition to his age.

The rebels' demands of 1537 failed to achieve any lasting change in Poland, mainly because their leaders were divided. In the following parliament, Sigismund agreed to accept the nobles as consultants, but Bona's position remained unchallenged from the outside. However, it is clear as the years advanced that Bona's powers were limited. She bitterly opposed the marriage of her son to Elisabeth of Austria in 1543, but Sigismund insisted that the match go ahead. After Elisabeth's premature death, as the result of epileptic seizures, it was rumoured that Bona had poisoned her. In spite of their differences, Sigismund's death in 1548 caused his wife genuine grief. Her relationship with her son was difficult, and she eventually returned to Italy, dying in Naples in 1557. Her rule introduced a different style of culture and queenship into Poland and her influence upon her husband, although disputed, did not conform to gender expectations.

35

Queen Jane Seymour

12 October 1537
Hampton Court, Surrey, England

While Bona did not conform to expected gender roles in Poland, the new English queen was delivering the one thing that was desired of her: a son. Finally, after twenty-eight years on the throne, Henry VIII had his son. In her chamber at Hampton Court, on the eve of St Edward's Day, his third wife Jane Seymour had delivered a healthy boy after an ordeal lasting two days. Her body aching in pain, she knew just how pleased her husband would be as the heralds sent out their messages and the corridors clamoured with praise. Hugh Latimer, Bishop of Worcester, wrote that there was no less rejoicing than if John the Baptist had arrived. Three days later, the child was christened Edward in the palace chapel, although protocol dictated that his mother was not permitted to attend. She must remain in confinement, wrapped warmly in furs, until her churching. Yet within days, Jane had fallen ill, possibly with post-partum fever, or poor hygiene, or the retention of part of her placenta, and nine days later, she was dead.

Jane Seymour is best known to history for bearing a son and then dying. The significance of both those acts was huge in dynastic terms, for the Tudor dynasty was apparently secure with the arrival of a legitimate son, but her death also deprived Henry of a wife he is unlikely to have discarded, and who may have borne him other sons, and Edward of a mother to guide him through the years of his reign. It is no surprise that Jane's existence is frequently reduced to a biographical soundbite, a mere womb representative of dynastic need, a foil to her husband and son. She represented hope, both hopes fulfilled and lost, and one of the 'may have beens' of history. Quiet and demure, she has also been overshadowed by the huge characters around her, where the biographical lens has often focused upon the love triangle of Henry and his first two wives. Those October days in 1537 defined Jane, but she was more than her premature death, which was only the culmination of a life lived amid the turmoil of the Tudor court. In fact, she epitomises the brief but impactful roles experienced by many of her contemporaries, and the dangers that gendered expectations exposed them to, even if they managed to navigate a path through the many political intrigues and pitfalls inherent in being close to the king.

Like her predecessor, Anne Boleyn, Jane was never destined to be a queen. Born into a prominent gentry family around 1508 in Wiltshire, she was one of ten children raised in the Catholic faith, receiving the domestic education intended to secure her a local magnate as a husband. She was literate, but not scholarly, spending her time in learning how to run a household, devotion and embroidery. Yet in the 1520s, Jane and her younger sister Elizabeth were sent to court as maids of honour to Catherine of Aragon, to find husbands that matched their father's increasing aspirations. Loyal to Catherine's plight, Jane nevertheless made the transition into Anne's household where she drew the king's eye when his attentions began to wander. Seized upon as an instrument of the Catholic, anti-Boleyn faction, she secured Henry's affections by copying Anne's strategy, refusing to become his mistress but promising to deliver a son in matrimony. Jane was engaged to the king the day after Anne's execution on Tower Hill, and they married just ten days later.

Jane herself was a willing participant in this process. At 28, she understood the realpolitik of the Tudor court where individuals rose to power out of the failures and disgraces of their rivals, and she played the game just like all the others. Perhaps she genuinely believed in Anne's adultery, or at least that Anne had exerted an evil influence over Henry, diverting him from the true path of religion, and seeing her role as one of pacifying the king, repairing his family relationships and influencing his choices. Jane also reached out to Princess Mary, attempting to reconcile her with her father, and by example to guide Henry back to the Catholic faith. In her, Henry saw the opposite of his defiant, passionate former wives, a restful, pacific and, hopefully, fertile presence. Yet, unlike his former wives, Jane did not conceive swiftly after the wedding. Through the summer of 1536, the king was observed placing his hands upon her belly, murmuring 'Edward, Edward,' the name he had already selected for their son, especially after the loss of his illegitimate child, Henry Fitzroy.

It was January 1537 when Jane conceived. Her condition was made public that April, when it was mentioned in Parliament,[1] and soon found its way into public correspondence with Cromwell's associates writing that all men were 'rejoicing' with the 'greatest possible satisfaction'.[2] In May, Jane appeared in an open-laced gown to announce the child's quickening, indulging her craving for quails, which arrived at court the same month, having been dispatched from Calais. She remained at Hampton Court all summer to avoid the plague that had emerged again in London, while Holbein painted her into his Tudor family mural at Whitehall. She probably entered her confinement at the end of October, retreating into specially prepared chambers hung with tapestries and furnished with all necessary comforts for a month or more. During the time of waiting, Jane had everything to look forward to.

Most Tudor mothers did not die in childbirth. Large families were common. Jane's own mother, Margery, bore ten children, four of whom died in infancy or childhood. Her paternal grandmother bore eight and there were six on the maternal side, while her sister Elizabeth bore seven. Nor were sons scarce among the Seymour women, whose families typically comprised at least 50 per cent males. Academic studies have estimated that rates of maternal mortality varied between 1 and 2.5 per cent on individual births, and although these rose through the course of a woman's childbearing history, the risk was equal to that of dying from infection or disease, and lower than that of plague or the sweating sickness.[3] As Jane went into labour, with everything she could desire provided, there was every reason to believe that she and her child would both survive.

Yet, as the case of Henry's own mother proves, mortality was not predictable. A week had elapsed since her successful delivery, and Jane was recovering and writing letters. Plans were already being made for her churching ceremony when she suddenly began to decline. The usual all-female protocol of confinement was broken and six doctors were summoned to investigate, finding Jane in a very poor condition. On 23 October, a collection of doctors, including Henry's own physician William Butts, wrote to Cromwell that the queen had experienced a 'natural laxe' or blood loss, 'by reason of which she seemed to amend.' But with the approach of night, 'she has been very sick' and her confessor was summoned to administer the last rites.[4] At 8.00 pm, the Duke of Norfolk advised Cromwell to comfort Henry as 'there is no likelihood of her life, the more pity, and I fear she shall not be on lyve at the time ye shall read this.'[5] Jane died the following day.

Jane's premature death brought an abrupt end to her childbearing and queenship. Her path to power occurred at a unique moment in history, where rival factions sought opportunities and religious cultures struggled to facilitate a king's desires. Her rise was swift, as was her demise, as the Tudors were contending not just with the realpolitik of the moment but the unpredictable forces of nature.

In the twenty-first century, Jane feels somewhat distant and lacks champions. She suffers in comparison with the strong, colourful characters that preceded her, although this may be where her attraction for Henry lay. She was not Catherine nor Anne. Neither of those queens have any trouble inspiring devotees among modern historians and readers. Meek, gentle and submissive, Jane offered the form of ideal queenship modelled by Henry's own mother, Elizabeth of York, although she lacked her beauty and universal appeal. The rapidity of Jane's rise has also attracted criticism. Her speedy courtship, engagement and marriage in the shadow of Anne's demise feels distasteful to modern sensibilities, but this is unfair to Jane as a sixteenth-century woman in the Henrician court. She was as much a player on the Tudor political stage as her brothers, at a turbulent time when courtiers jostled for precedence and seized opportunities left vacant by death or disgrace. If Jane had not married Henry, some other woman would have. Most available noblewomen would have welcomed the king's favour, and Jane had not only a powerful, ambitious family behind her, but also the Catholic cause. Although she was fulfilling a personal role in the king's bed, Jane's rise must be divorced from the personal. It was a political move that happened to involve a marriage. As a woman, she should not be judged more harshly than the men who planned it. Jane's saving grace came with the birth of her son, but she still needs to find vocal champions to reassess her reputation.

36

Cecily Bodenham

25 March 1539
Wilton Abbey, Wiltshire, England

Her fight was over. Cecily was forced to admit defeat against the onslaught of the king's wishes. She had been abbess of the powerful Wilton Abbey for six years, set in a majestic Wiltshire location, sheltering women of royal blood and providing their final resting place. For centuries, people had flocked there on pilgrimage, praying at the shrine of St Edith, impressed by its imposing nave with two aisles, its illuminated manuscripts and quiet gardens. The responsibility for this place, and the thirty-three nuns resident in it, had been placed in Cecily's hands. Yet she would have the indignity of being the one to relinquish it.

Cecily is likely to have been destined for a religious life from an early age. Her birthdate is unclear, but it was probably in around 1510, the daughter of Roger Bodenham in Rotherwas, Herefordshire. Perhaps she was one of many daughters who needed providing for, or perhaps she had a genuine vocation. First, she joined the Priory of Kingston St Michael in Wiltshire, a twelfth-century establishment run by Dame Marie Denys, who had formerly been a nun at Lacock Abbey; Cecily later took over Kingston St Michael as prioress. According to one report[1], she was present as a child when the priory was raided and robbed, being briefly taken hostage before being returned to the nuns. Yet this incident is dated to 1511, when she was an infant, and has not been verified. Later, Cecily was known to Anne Boleyn, being appointed at Wilton in 1533, a year before the death of the former abbess, Isabel Jordayne. Jordayne had been a controversial choice, favoured over Anne's candidate Eleanor Carey, who was revealed to have borne illegitimate children. Cecily's appointment came from court circles, rather than the usual nomination by nuns. She arrived just as the most tumultuous period of English ecclesiastical history began.

Wilton had once been one of England's most significant abbeys. Set in Wiltshire, it was founded in the early tenth century, although a chantry chapel may have stood on the site as early as the year 800. King Alfred was reputed to have laid the foundation stone for an establishment for women in 890, and this was definitely functioning by 934 when King Athelstan approved a grant to the place. Perhaps its most famous resident was St Edith, daughter of King Edgar and the abbess, whose premature death was associated with numerous miracles. Her life was written by Goscelin, nearby churches were dedicated to her and a golden shrine was erected for her at Wilton by King Canute, who had prayed to her for delivery whilst on stormy seas. As the years passed, the abbey drew pilgrims, wanting to see or touch Edith's relics and leave their offerings and prayers. Although its popularity and prosperity had waned by the thirteenth century, Wilton was still one of the bastions of the English monastic network. Such establishments fulfilled a range of local roles, as major landlords and religious centres, but also visiting the poor, treating the sick, feeding the hungry, brewing ale, producing manuscripts for their libraries, growing medicinal herbs, employing the vulnerable and giving the location its defining character. Pilgrimage boosted the local businesses too. Their closure threatened centuries-old habits, traditions and ways of life, impacting on their community within and outside the walls.

Cecily knew what was coming. The Reformation had spread across Europe with little major impact on England until Henry VIII seized upon monastic closure as a means of taking control of the church. He ordered a series of investigations into the state of the country's religious houses, dispatching his men to every far-flung community, large and small, to assess their material worth and comment on the conduct of those housed there, recorded in the document *Valor Ecclesiasticus*. In September 1535, Cecily had had no choice but to host royal commissioner Sir Thomas Legh, who was conducting his inspection of the West Country. Reports had reached them of his visits that summer, creeping ever closer: Worcester, Malvern, Lacock Abbey and then Bruton, just 30 miles to the west. Eleven days later, he had arrived at Wilton. With an annual income of £674 6s and 2d,[2] it was the fourth richest abbey in the country, and the king had its wealth in his sights.

Legh's visit had prompted Cecily to write to the architect of the change, Thomas Cromwell, secretary and indispensable all-round servant to Henry VIII. Legh had tried to keep Cecily and her fellow nuns under closer confinement, and prevent visits outside the abbey walls, or even those of family visiting the community. She complained on 5 September 1535:

> Dr Legh, the King's visitor and your deputy, on visiting my house, has given injunctions that not only all my sisters but that I should keep continually within the precincts. For myself personally I am content; but as the house is in great debt, and is not likely to improve without good husbandry, which cannot be exercised so well by any other as by myself, I beg you will allow me, in company with two or three of the sad and discreet sisters of the house, to supervise such things abroad as shall be for its profit. I do not propose to lodge any night abroad, except by inevitable necessity I cannot return. I beg also, that whenever any father, mother, brother, sister, or nigh kinsfolk of my sisters come unto them, they may have licence to speak with them in the hall in my presence.[3]

Yet her requests were denied and the visitations continued. Through the late 1530s, she heard of the closures of other leading houses: Battle and Beaulieu, the London Charterhouse and Tintern, Lewes and Lindisfarne, even Walsingham, where the shrine of Our Lady drew so many pilgrims, as well as St Augustine's of Canterbury, guardians of the bones of Thomas Becket. Her former community at Kington had been disbanded in 1536. It was only a matter of time before the commissioners returned to claim Wilton. As Cecily took her last look about the place, she recalled its long history: the miracles recorded there, the respect afforded it by King Cnut, and the Conqueror William I, the way King Stephen used it as his headquarters during the Anarchy. Perhaps, like others in her position, she had the opportunity to remove some of the decoration and offerings on the golden shrine of St Edith, and place them in a secure location. She would have known all about the closure of Canterbury Cathedral in March 1539, the dismantling of the shrine of St Thomas Becket and heard the rumours about the destruction of his bones. Maybe Cecily took the opportunity to hide the relics of St Edith in order to preserve them for the future.

On 25 March 1539, Cecily surrendered the keys of Wilton Abbey to the king's commissioner, Sir Richard Rich, 'and all its possessions in cos. Wilts, Soms, Hants, and elsewhere in England and the marches thereof.'[4] Before the Gregorian reformed calendar was introduced in 1582, 25 March, or Lady Day, was considered the start of the new year, the day of new beginnings. It was a life-changing event for herself and the other thirty-two resident nuns, who were catered for with varying degrees of pensions, ranging between 7 marks 6s and 8d to just 2 marks, depending upon age and the duration of their service. Cecily herself was provided for with a much larger pension of 100 marks, some of which she received into her hands that very day: 'one quarter's pension to be paid at Lady Day, and afterwards half yearly.'[5] She was granted a house at Fovant, formerly leased to her kinsfolk, 'with the orchards, gardens and three acres of pasture and meadow belonging to the same,' and the right to one weekly load of wood taken from Fovant Woods. Protected by her position, Cecily was fortunate to be provided for as she was 'without father, brother or any assured friends',[6] but those offered a mere 2 marks must have struggled. All across the country, former monks and nuns were being turned out onto the streets, needing to find a new place in the world. Their sheer numbers drove up competition for work, housing and food, especially among the old and infirm, of whom many ended up on the streets. The community served by the abbey would have felt its loss keenly.

Within three days of Cecily being granted Fovant, she wrote to Cromwell that she had sequestered the tenants formerly living there but had leased the property of Wassherne to her friend Sir Philip Hoby. His tenants could not pay the rent as they were now prevented from sowing their crop of barley, presumably because it was sown on monastic land. She appealed for them to be allowed to do so, 'seeing she has only done what is lawful and just.'[7]

Little is known about the remainder of Cecily's life. A portrait reputed to be of her, produced in these later years by an unknown author, shows a prim, serious woman dressed in black and brown, with blackwork embroidery on her collar and cuffs, and a tiny book held between her fingers. Her reddish hair is pulled back under one of the new bonnets and her narrow eyes look forward, above an equally narrow mouth. She appears to be in her thirties. However, the identity of the sitter remains unverified. Cecily lived on at Fovant, taking in ten of her former sisters, and contributing to the cost of rebuilding the south aisle of nearby St George's Church. The remains of Wilton Abbey were handed to Sir William Herbert, Earl of Pembroke, who reused its stone to build Wilton House. Cecily drew up her will in 1543 but the exact date of her death, and the location of her final resting site, are unknown. Although she had chosen to dedicate her life to the church, and had risen to the position of Prioress, she was powerless to resist the will of a king who was determined to press through his reforms.

Cecily represents the thousands of women whose quiet, sheltered, regimented existences were suddenly and dramatically altered, finding themselves cast out upon the world, thrown upon the mercy of family, friends or community. This must have been a difficult, even terrifying life change for a generation of women, faced with difficult choices about whether to retreat or attempt to integrate into the world. Some sought marriage, others lived with relatives, found employment or else walked the streets, contemplating why either God, or their king, had forsaken them. The closure of the abbey also impacted local women, who had been accustomed to visit the golden shrine in times of need, found comfort and shelter in the infirmary, or in retreat, employment in the kitchens, dairy or gardens, were educated by the nuns and whose lives were structured around the daily, seasonal and annual rituals of the Catholic church. The Reformation, especially the dissolution of the monasteries, is often considered in terms of male existence, but it was definitive for women too.

37

Anne of Cleves

1 January 1540

Rochester Castle, Kent, England

The bride-to-be was thankful for the sight of the castle. Its solid square keep and thick walls offered a safe resting place after her long journey. It had been weeks since she set out from her family home in Germany, knowing she would never see her parents or siblings again. They had ridden through the emperor's lands in terrible weather, through hostile territory and strange cities, and the long days waiting at Calais for a suitable wind.[1]

England. It had once been just a word, distant, imagined, inaccessible. The white cliffs had loomed up beyond the waves before they landed at Dover, dominated by its cliff-top castle. She was to be queen of this land: the green fields, woods and orchards she had seen in their ride across Kent. And this place on the river, they told her, was Rochester, a mere short ride away from London. Soon, she would come face to face with her betrothed, Henry VIII, this notorious king about whom she had heard so much. She had tried to learn card games to please him and a few words in the English tongue, but for now, it was all new, and exciting, and tiring. Yet their meeting would happen sooner than Anne predicted.

The previous summer, in June 1539, Henry's ambassadors headed to Düren, in North Germany, midway between Aachen and Cologne. Their task was to seek an audience with the Duke and Duchess of Cleves to examine the appearance of both their daughters; Anne and her younger sister Amalia, and assess their personal charms. However, they were to be disappointed as the customs of Cleves only permitted the ladies to appear heavily veiled. Afterwards, Holbein was dispatched to capture their likeness, creating a miniature of Anne with a placid, symmetrical face that had made a suitable impression. The ambassadors from Cleves arrived in London on 16 September and by early October, the marriage contract had been drawn up. It did not matter that Anne had formerly been betrothed to the Duke of Lorraine as a child, for that union had been cancelled in 1535, and the ambassadors were satisfied. The 24-year-old Anne of Cleves, who had led a sheltered Lutheran upbringing and only spoke German, was set to become Henry's fourth wife.

Anne arrived in Calais on 11 December, where she was welcomed and entertained by Lord Lisle and his wife Honor.[2] Lady Lisle wrote her impressions that the Princess of Cleves 'was good and gentle to serve and please,'[3] to her daughter, Anne Bassett, who was then at York Place awaiting the arrival of the new queen.

It was not until 27 December that the fleet was able to set sail, landing at Deal the same afternoon and progressing on to Dover and Canterbury. On New Year's Eve, Anne had passed through Sittingbourne and reached the city of Rochester, where she stayed at the Bishop's Palace.

The following day, Anne was watching a bull-baiting through her window when a party of nine disguised men entered the room. They all wore hooded cloaks and the effect must have been quite sinister in comparison with the other welcomes she had received. Completely reliant upon her translators and still uncertain of courtly protocol, let alone Henry's penchant for disguise, she was taken by surprise when one of the men approached her, took her in his arms and attempted to kiss her.[4] In fact, considering the close closeting of her childhood and the strict way in which she had been covered up for the viewing of the ambassadors, this behaviour was probably scandalous to her. On her way to be married to the king, she had been as good as assaulted by a stranger, whose familiarity showed disrespect to her rank and threatened her reputation. No wonder she did not respond and turned away coldly. The court of Cleves, with its heavily moral tone, had not encouraged the sort of merrymaking, masques and lavish celebrations that had set the tone of Henry's court since his succession. In Henry's insensitivity and conviction of his own personal charm, he had overlooked Anne's possible feelings. If she really had swooned in the arms of a romantic stranger, without knowing it was her intended, surely it would not have been a good sign regarding her future fidelity.

Abashed at the failure of his romantic gesture, Henry retired and changed into regal purple before returning and declaring his true identity. Recognising her mistake, Anne bowed low and, according to Wriothesley, the pair 'talked lovingly together,'[5] although Lord Russell reported that he 'never saw His Highness so marvellously astonished… as on that occasion.'[6] Hall related how 'she with most gracious and loving countenance and behaviour, him received and welcomed on her knees, whom he gently took up and kissed,' after which they dined together.[7] Anne's reaction had disappointed the king, but her appearance had been an even greater surprise. In his opinion, she was not as attractive or as young-looking as he had been led to believe, although other observers praised her looks, including the French ambassador de Marillac, who described her face as lovely, of 'middling beauty and of very assured and resolute countenance.'[8] Edward Hall wrote in his chronicle of her long, yellow hair and that her French hood 'so set forth her beauty and good visage that every creature rejoiced to see her.'[9]

Every creature save one. While Henry afforded Anne the respect her position demanded, his growing anger seethed behind his diplomatic mask. The disguise he had adopted in the hope of sparking romance necessitated him retreating behind another to conceal his dislike. Riding back to Greenwich, he informed Cromwell in no uncertain terms that he did not like Anne. They were ominous words indeed to the man who had invested so much in arranging the marriage. Investigations were made into the Lorraine betrothal, but this had been satisfactorily dealt with in Germany. Rejecting Anne at this late stage would have resulted in a diplomatic scandal and potential hostilities with Cleves. There was no way out.

The wedding took place on 6 January in the Queen's closet at Greenwich. Anne was dressed in the round-skirted Dutch fashion again, this time in a gown of rich cloth of gold, ornamented with large flowers and pearls, and her fair, long, yellow hair hanging loose. On her head, she wore a coronet of gold set with jewels and decorated with sprigs of rosemary, a common medieval wedding custom that signified love and loyalty. With the most 'demure countenance'[10] she passed through the King's chamber into the gallery, and closet, where she greeted her future spouse with three curtseys. His heart might not have been in it, but Henry had at least dressed the part. His gown of cloth of gold, with raised silver flowers and black fur, a coat of crimson satin tied with diamonds and rich collar, were part of the mask of royalty that he hid behind on that day. Cranmer officiated and the Earl of Overstein gave Anne away. Henry placed a ring on her finger that bore the legend 'God send me well to keep.' From there, they walked hand in hand back into Henry's chamber to hear Mass and take wine and spices.[11]

Soon after, at nine in the morning, Henry changed into a gown of tissue lined with red velvet, and collected Anne from her chamber where she had been waiting, then they dined together. Then, it was the queen's turn to change again, with her choices yet again prompting criticism; this time, it was 'a gowne like a man's gown', and a cap she had previously worn at Blackheath, although chronicler Hall conceded that her apparel was 'rich and very costly'.[12] The hours between then and supper, probably served mid-afternoon in winter, are unaccounted for, but Anne and Henry emerge at that point to attend Evensong, eat together again and enjoy the banquets, masques and 'diverse disports' until 'the time came that it pleased the King and her to take their rest.'[13] It probably pleased Anne considerably more than it pleased Henry, but if he was displeased with his bride, things were about to get much worse. They retired to their chambers and were ceremonially undressed for the wedding night. It would prove a disaster.

Six months later, Henry had the marriage annulled with Anne afforded the title of King's Sister and given a generous settlement of properties and income. An investigation was conducted into their relations with evidence given by members of the court. Anne's ladies testified to her innocence while Henry's gentlemen spoke of the king's dislike of her person and mistrust of her virginity. Henry was keen to add that he was still able to perform sexually and had experienced several 'night-time emissions' during the period of his marriage. He then immediately married one of her young ladies-in-waiting, Catherine Howard, and ordered the execution of Thomas Cromwell, the architect of the marriage. Anne initially wept, but then accepted the situation with pragmatism, attending court at Christmas and dancing with the new queen. As the King's Sister, Anne lived out her days in comfort at Richmond Palace until 1557. Her role in Henry's life highlights the realities of gender relations and illustrates her own wisdom in accepting his decision. Like an elaborate, intimate waltz, women had to follow the male lead, or at least give the illusion of following, accepting their decisions in the interests of self-preservation. Anne was unable to forge any emotional connection with Henry, so she was able to extricate herself when the opportunity presented itself and avoid the tragic fate of her namesake queen.

38

Honor Grenville, Lady Lisle

May 1540

The Staple, Calais, English territory in France

By 1540, Honor Grenville had become a Tudor success story. Born into a wealthy family, daughter of the Sheriff of Devon and Cornwall, she had survived one husband and captured the affections of Arthur Plantagenet, Lord Lisle, illegitimate uncle of Henry VIII. They were married at some point before October 1532[1], moving soon after to Calais after Arthur was appointed Lord Deputy, living in the prestigious Staple Hall, where Anne Boleyn had once danced for Francis I. Honor and Arthur's surviving letters reveal the depths of their affection and intimacy, with loving wishes, pet names and longing during their periods of absence. Petite, pretty and with a love of fine clothes, beads and animals, she was twenty years his junior and much shorter,[2] but this was a perfect case of opposites attracting. Together, they set about ruling Calais and raising their combined family, some of whom were found places at the English court. It had all the appearances of a charmed existence. In the autumn of 1539, Arthur and Honor hosted Anne of Cleves on her journey to England. Yet, within months, everything went tragically wrong for the pair.

The problem was partly religious. As with all of her generation, Honor had been raised a Catholic, but she had been unable to embrace the tide of reforms advocated by some of her peers. One of their family chaplains, a Sir Gregory Botolf, was granted permission by Lisle to visit England, but instead went to Rome, from which Henry had broken and was now considered hostile. This move was then coupled with rumours of sexual immorality. First, the chaplain, also known as Gregory Sweetlips, was reputed to be Honor's lover, but Honor's daughter, Mary Basset, was also being courted by a French Catholic, who wrote her a number of love letters. When Botolf's trip to Rome was discovered, Mary panicked and threw these letters into a cesspit, which added to the suspicion that the Lisles were engaged in a plot to betray Calais and return it to the French.[3] A well-known Catholic, it would have been easy for Honor's enemies to imply that she had sanctioned Botolf's secret trip to Rome, or that she was plotting an unsuitable marriage for Mary, or even scheming with France, but no evidence supports this. Calais was an extremely Protestant town, and the Lisles' religious practices, against the changing reformation climate, singled them out as targets.

It is no coincidence that the next Deputy, the Earl of Arundel, was a committed Protestant.

An enquiry was launched in February, led by the Duke of Norfolk, with the result that Arthur was recalled to England to explain himself. Unsure of the exact charges against them, Honor must have watched her husband's ship depart for England with trepidation. Given her extensive correspondence, she was aware of the dangers posed by suspicion and rumour. Nor could she have escaped observing the changing nature of Henry VIII's state of mind, even from across the Channel. Her efforts to place her daughter Anne into the household of Anne Boleyn had failed, but Anne witnessed the aftermath of the queen's downfall, after being accepted as a lady-in-waiting by Jane Seymour. Honor's daughter lived through the following years at court, and is reputed to have become the king's mistress after Jane's death, supplying her mother with the latest news. Increasingly, Henry's mind became paranoid and after the 1536 Boleyn scandal, he had launched another purge in 1538 against his closest former friends – Henry Courtenay, Marquess of Exeter and Sir Nicholas Carew – who were both sent to the block on the flimsiest pretexts of treason; Henry also ordered the destruction of the Pole family, his rivals to the Yorkist claim. Aware of this context, Honor could only wait and pray that any misunderstanding would quickly be cleared up.

Arthur had been gone a few weeks when Honor received a visit at her imposing home of The Staple from a delegation of Henry's council. They brought bad news. Upon his arrival in England, Arthur was arrested and sent to the Tower. Now, Honor and her daughters were to be confined under house arrest, Honor initially in their home and the girls at other locations around the town. Then, on 1 June, Honor was taken to the Calais property of Francis Hall where she remained locked up for two years. The couple's home was stripped of all their worldly goods, which were confiscated by the treasury. The hostile John Foxe claimed that Honor became 'distraught of mind' as a result, and remained so for years as a result of this treatment.[4] If she did, it would be no surprise. Removed from her home and family, far from king and court where decisions about her life were made, missing her husband and fearing for his future, this time must have been intensely painful and traumatic for Honor.

Two agonising years passed. Locked away in captivity, they must have seemed unending for Honor as she daily awaited the arrival of letters. Finally, in March 1542, the news she had been longing to hear was brought to her. All involved were to be released, Arthur from the Tower and Honor and her daughters in Calais, although the town can hardly have felt like home to them. No charges had been proven against them. Perhaps Honor was permitted to return and attempt to make some order out of the ransacked home she had left behind. She may have tried to prepare it for her family's return, anticipating the reunion with her husband. By this point, though, Arthur was in his late sixties or early seventies[5] and his imprisonment had taken its toll. Even though he was a free man, he died in the Tower before he was able to leave. The nature of his illness is unknown. Broken-hearted, Honor left Calais for good after learning the news, and retreated into the

West Country where she had been raised. She lived out another twenty-four years, never remarrying, and died at Tehidy in 1566. Her desperately sad story, often overlooked by Tudor scholars, illustrates just how rapidly fate might turn against the successful, mirroring the lives of many of her contemporaries. The love story of Honor and Arthur, with its fond letters, happy home and mutual affection was blown apart by the Tudor realpolitik of the post-Boleyn years. The Lisles were victims of religious change, the plots of their enemies, and the suspicious mind of a paranoid king.

39

Sayyida al Hurra

1540

Tétouaen, Morocco, North Africa

The ancient city of Tétouaen in northern Morocco is designated a World Heritage Site. With its tumble of white-painted houses down the hillside, framed by the mountains, it has remained unchanged for centuries. Just a few miles south of the Straits of Gibraltar, it provided a refuge for Muslims fleeing from Spain after Ferdinand and Isabella's Conquest of Granada in 1492. Finding safety and tolerance in which to practise their faith, many renamed the city 'Little Granada' and kept the keys to their former houses as symbols, knowing that they were unable to return. Once such family who were forced to flee Spain were the Rashids, the daughter of which would become governor, or queen, of Tétouaen, and raise it to prosperity through her acts of piracy, allied with the great Barbarossa.

Aisha[1] Rashid was born around 1485 into a prominent Andalusian Muslim family, reputed to be descended from Mohammed himself. After the last remaining Islamic territories fell to the Catholics, a semblance of toleration was observed, although in reality, a programme of forced conversion took place and Muslim books were burned in the streets. Aisha was only a little girl when her parents followed the example of Granada's last king, Boabdil, who fled to Morocco to live and practise his faith freely. Her father founded a fort at Chefchaouen, which attracted Spanish refugees and expanded into a village. Aisha was raised here, taught by influential tutors and learning to speak several different languages, before a marriage was arranged for her at the age of 16 to Ali al-Mandri, the governor of nearby Tétouaen. She assisted him so ably, acting as deputy during his absences, that upon his death in 1515, the city accepted her as its sole ruler. From this point onwards, she was known as Sayyida al Hurro or Sovereign Lady.

By 1540, Tétouaen was flourishing and prosperous, largely due to an unexpected alliance Aisha made and her desire to avenge the loss of her homeland upon the Spanish Catholics. Knowing that her people would never receive an apology, or amends, from the current ruler, Emperor Charles V, she resorted to that common sixteenth-century tactic of piracy, assisted by the legendary Hayreddin Barbarossa, or 'Red Beard'. He had already reclaimed Algiers from the Spanish and was appointed by Suleiman I as Grand Admiral of his fleet; he then conquered Tunisia and defeated Charles at the sea battle of Preveza. With his assistance, Aisha's ships plundered those of Spain when they encountered them at sea, returning home with their wealthy spoils. Some writers go as far as to suggest she did not simply occupy an organisational role, but actually sailed with her men, as a corsair, participating in the raids herself.[2] In 1540, she allegedly took part in raids upon Gibraltar, taking 'much booty and many prisoners'[3] and has been described as 'the undisputed leader of the pirates in the western Mediterranean.'[4] She is recorded in official documents as the main person with whom Spain and Portugal would record trade deals or negotiate the release of captives.[5] It was unprecedented for a woman to exercise power in this way and, ironically, atypical for the Muslim world. Where women like Roxelana achieved influence through their intimate relations, Aisha's independence was facilitated by her inheritance. With the majority of Tétouaen's citizens originating from Spain, they were used to the rule of a powerful woman, even if this stemmed from one like Isabella, who had been their oppressor.

In 1541, when she was in her fifties, Aisha accepted the marriage proposal of the Sultan of Morocco, Ahmed al-Wattasi. However, she refused to give up her status and insisted that he travel from Fez to wed her in her hometown. She briefly juggled her governorship with her marriage, before being deposed by her son the following year. Aisha did not retaliate, but was sanguine in the face of him replacing her. She returned to Chefchaouen and lived out her final years, probably dying in the 1560s. As a Muslim queen, she had ridden the powerful wave of independence as well as those of piracy, making her truly remarkable for her times.

Anne, Duchess of Brittany, who was Queen of France twice over, having married two cousins. Her second marriage treaty allowed her to retain considerable power over the lands she had inherited. Picture taken from an illustration in her prayer book. (*Public domain*)

Caterina Sforza, the 'Tiger of Forlì', who fought by hand to defend her domain from Cesare Borgia in 1501. Painted by Florentine artist Lorenzo di Credi, this work is also known as *The Lady of the Jasmine*. (*Public domain*)

Catherine of Aragon, daughter of the influential Isabella of Castile, who had been raised to be England's queen since the age of 3. Portrait by Michael Sittow, possibly painted whilst Catherine was a young widow in England after the death of Prince Arthur in 1502. (*Public domain*)

One of the surviving ivory masks of Queen Idia of Nigeria, a ceremonial item for display, likely to have been commissioned by her son after her death. Currently held in the British Museum. (*Public domain*)

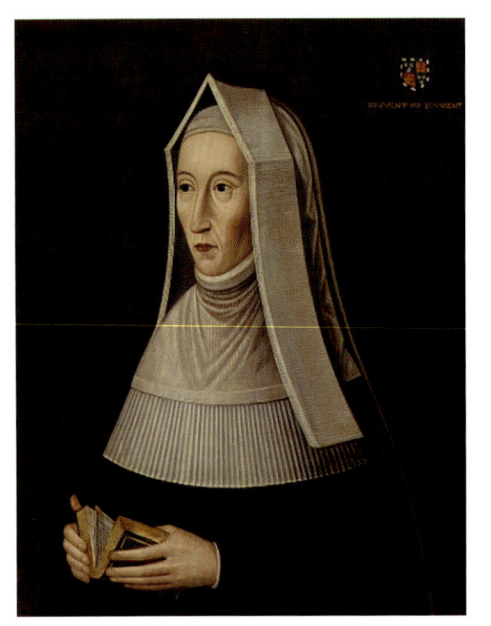

Margaret Beaufort, mother of Henry VII. This portrait, commissioned after her death in 1509, bears the motto of the Oxford College she founded, and two Cambridge colleges, 'souvent me souvient', or 'think often of me'. (*Public domain*)

Margaret Tudor, Queen of Scotland, daughter, sister, wife and mother of kings, married to James IV in 1503, and widowed a decade later. This seventeenth-century painting by Daniel Mitjens was probably based on a contemporary work. (*Public domain*)

The Money Lender and his Wife, Quentin Matsys, Antwerp 1514, depicting a married couple at work together. (*Public domain*)

Claude, Queen of France, taken from a book of hours. Her Paris coronation was delayed until May 1517 because of pregnancy. (*Public domain*)

A street in Strasbourg, in the old region of Alsace, the town in which Frau Troffea danced uncontrollably for days in 1518. Having been claimed by France and Germany throughout its history, Strasbourg is now on the French side of the border. (*Amy Licence*)

La Malinche and Hernán Cortés, in what may be a contemporary illustration, or the closest we have to it. She remains a controversial individual for having welcomed the conquistadors and assisted their progress in the New World in the 1510s. (*Biblioteca Nacional de España, Madrid, Spain*)

Roxelana, favourite wife of Sultan Suleiman, probably a copy of an earlier work by Titian, made in around 1550. (*Public domain*)

Former nun Katharina von Bora, in 1526, the year after she married Martin Luther, painted by their friend Lucas Cranach. A partner portrait of Luther, against the same background, also survives. (*Public domain*)

Lady with a Squirrel and a Starling, by Hans Holbein, dating to around 1527, thought to depict Anne Lovell of Harling. (*Public domain*)

Joseph and Potiphar, a carved frieze by Properzia de Rossi, sculptress from Bologna, dating from the 1520s. (*Public domain*)

Margaret Roper, educated and erudite daughter of Thomas More, who visited him in the Tower before his execution in 1535. (*Public domain*)

Mary Fitzroy, née Howard, Duchess of Richmond and Somerset, who was married young to Henry VIII's illegitimate son, Henry, and outlived him. She was also one of a group of women who curated, and contributed to, the Devonshire Manuscript. (*Public domain*)

The Chicken War, painted by Henryk Rodakowski in 1872, depicting Bona Sforza, Queen of Poland, faced with rebellion in 1537. (*Public domain*)

Cecily Bodenham, last Abbess of Wilton, forced to surrender her role and abbey in 1538 and enter retirement. (*Public domain*)

Catherine de' Medici, wife of Henri II from the age of 14, who had to wait until she was widowed before exercising any real power. She is depicted here in her widows' weeds, in the style of Francois Clouet. (*Public domain*)

Tétouaen, Morocco, formerly governed by Sayyida al Hurra, an imposing Muslim piratess, whose pact with Barbarossa benefited the town. (*S. Reid, Creative Commons*)

Woodcut depicting the murder of Arden of Faversham. Alice Arden looks on while her husband Thomas, mayor of the town, is murdered by her lover. The real crime was committed in 1551, and Alice was burned in nearby Canterbury. Woodcut taken from a 1622 edition. (*Creative Commons*)

Arden's house as it appeared in the 1950s; it remains standing today, in Abbey Street, Faversham. (*The Faversham Society*)

Mary I, in her betrothal portrait by Anthonis Mor in 1554, a picture of passion and restraint, a symbol of national beauty triumphing over the personal. (*Public domain*)

The Chess Game by the Milanese artist Sofonisba Anguissola in 1555, depicting her vivacious younger sisters and a maid. (*Public domain*)

A list of names on the Martyrs' Memorial, including the final women, Alice Snoth and Katherine Knight. (*Amy Licence*)

JOAN CATMER
WILLIAM WATERER
STEPHEN KEMPE
WILLIAM HAY
THOMAS HUDSON
WILLIAM LOWICK
WILLIAM PROWTING
JOHN FISHCOCK
NICHOLAS WHITE
NICHOLAS PARDUE
BARBARA FINAL
BRADBRIDGE'S WIDOW
WILSON'S WIFE
ALICE BENDEN
JOHN CORNEFORD
CHRISTOPHER BROWNE
JOHN HERST
ALICE SNOTH
KATHERINE KNIGHT

The Martyrs' Memorial, Wincheap, Canterbury, recording the spot outside the city walls where the final Protestant heretics were burned in the last days of Mary I's reign, in November 1558. (*Amy Licence*)

Elizabeth I in 1565, by Flemish miniaturist Levina Teerlinc, although the sitter has also been identified as her cousin, Catherine Grey. (*Public domain*)

A woman, possibly Amye Dudley, née Robsart, painted by Lucas Horenbout. She is in her eighteenth year, the time when Amye married Robert Dudley. (*Public domain*)

Coroner's report into the death of Amye Dudley. Recently discovered by historian Chris Skidmore, this report of 1560 concluded that Amye's death after falling down a staircase was not suicide, but a tragic accident. (*The National Archives*)

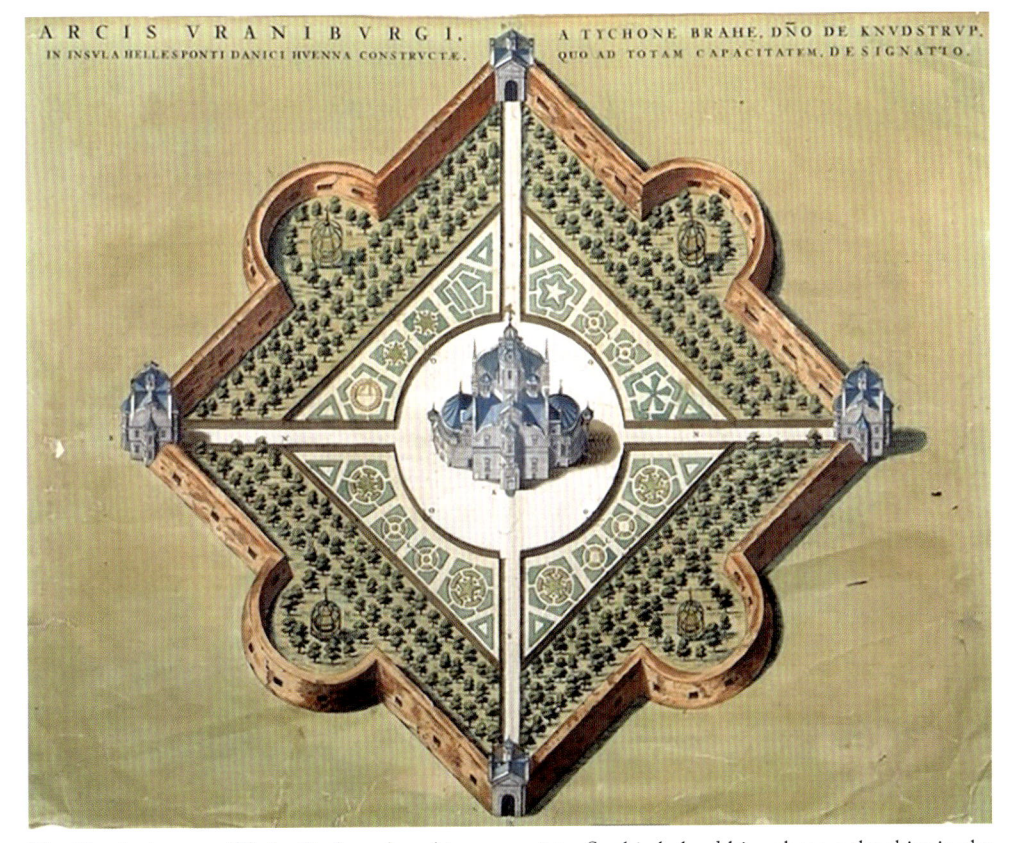

The Uranienbourg of Tycho Brahe, where his young sister Sophie helped him observe the skies in the 1570s. (*Public domain*)

Recent excavations taking place at the site of the original Theatre in Shoreditch, which Margaret Brayne helped her husband build in 1576. (*Archaeology South East/UCL*)

Lettice Knollys, who risked the inevitable wrath of Elizabeth I by marrying her favourite, Robert Dudley, in September 1578. (*Public domain*)

Anne Hathaway's Cottage in Shottery, near Stratford-upon-Avon. She married William Shakespeare in 1582. (*Public domain*)

A 1585 map of Roanoke Island in the New World, where English settlers, including Eleanor Dare, founded a colony; Eleanor bore her daughter Virginia there before disappearing. What happened to the colony remains a mystery. (*Public domain*)

The hirsute Tognina Gonzales, born in around 1588 to a family that included members with Ambras syndrome. She was treated as a pet, or animal, but became a favourite at the French court. (*Public domain*)

Tognina's parents, Peter and Catherine, whose marriage was arranged by Catherine de' Medici. (*Public domain*)

Red-haired courtier Elizabeth 'Bess' Throckmorton, who secretly married Walter Raleigh after falling pregnant with his child in 1591. Both were sent to the Tower and denied royal favour, although Walter was recalled to lead an expedition overseas. Bess retired to the country. (*Public domain*)

Medusa, a painting by Italian artist Caravaggio in 1597, depicting a terrifying female creature from Greek mythology, upon which the artist bestowed his own face. (*Public domain*)

Elizabeth Bathory, the 'blood countess', who stood accused of murdering hundreds of women at her Slovakian castle, although the charges may have been financially motivated. (*Public domain*)

Mary Frith, or 'Cut Purse Moll', the lively, colourful 'roaring girl' of the Jacobean stage, who was arrested for picking pockets in 1600. (*Public domain*)

40

Margaret Pole, Countess of Salisbury

27 May 1541
Tower of London, England

As the defiant Aisha sailed the waves, exacting her revenge, an elderly Englishwoman of noble blood awaited death after an exemplary life. Once upon a time Margaret Pole would never have believed this possible. A woman like herself, niece of Edward IV, aunt to Henry VIII, who had taught and nursed his daughter, was imprisoned in the Tower, awaiting dawn, on the day of her execution.

The charge against her were barely credible, aimed more at her name and heritage than her actions. She had never had a treasonous thought in her entire life, even when her sons were critical of the king when she advised loyalty and silence. She understood this was down to her Yorkist blood. Even after all these years, more than five decades since the overthrow of the previous regime, and peace in the land; even when she thought she was free, this terrible fate had come for her. She had seen her sons accused, imprisoned, exiled, and executed for their outspokenness or for trusting the wrong friends. Then she, herself, was arrested. She had hoped her nephew, the king, had forgotten about her, content to let her languish in this dark room, or better still had come to his senses. But then the men of Yorkshire had risen in rebellion, and Henry was reminded of her claim to the throne. A claim she had never sought, never encouraged and always dreaded. But her final hour was approaching. She continued her prayers.

They had all met with untimely ends, those Yorkist relatives. Her grandfather Richard, the Duke, betrayed and cut down in battle during the civil wars; her mother Isabel dying two months after childbed, although it was rumoured to be poison; her father George, Duke of Clarence, drowned in wine for his treason; and her brother Edward, Earl of Warwick, executed on Tower Green after a life of captivity. Then there were her cousins, the princes, who disappeared in this same vast grey edifice, and her uncle, Richard III, slaughtered in the field at Bosworth. They belonged to a time so long ago; few people remembered their faces now. She had been one of the survivors, along with her cousin, Elizabeth of York, who had borne the present king, giving Margaret every chance to hope that their futures might now be secure.

Margaret had been married to Henry VII's cousin, Richard Pole, and borne him five children. He had died in 1505, but she remained in favour as a lady-in-waiting to Catherine of Aragon, appointed governess to Princess Mary and was allowed to inherit some of the Salisbury lands that had belonged to her brother. Yet her sons had courted controversy. They had allied with outspoken men, whose words verged on treason, conscious of their own claim. Abroad, Reginald was critical of the king's marriage to Anne Boleyn; at home, Henry and Geoffrey were caught up in the 1538 Exeter conspiracy. Henry was executed and although Geoffrey was pardoned, he attempted suicide and the balance of his mind was destroyed. Margaret was arrested along with them in 1538. She had been examined for hours by Cromwell's agents, Southampton and Ely, who were forced to 'conclude that either her sons had not made her a sharer in their "treason", or else she was the most arrant traitress that ever lived.'[1] Then they had produced a white tunic, supposedly found among her possessions which they claimed linked her with the northern rebels. Margaret continued to protest her innocence.

On 27 May 1541, Margaret was informed that she would die within the hour. Two and a half years after her initial arrest, her end came very swiftly. It had been a miserable, undignified imprisonment. A woman of noble blood, at the age of 57, she had not been provided with sufficient clothing and had shivered and suffered terribly from the extremes of cold and damp, against which her cell had offered little protection. The one small comfort had been the presence of her grandson, Henry, but now she feared for his future under this tyrant king. They came for her about 7, as they had promised. She repeated that she had committed no crime, but now it was too late. She followed them from her cell to the place where a low wooden block had been set up, without a scaffold. If she had been expecting crowds for her final speech, Margaret was disappointed. It was unusually quiet. Chapuys estimated there were 150 present, but he was not among them to count.[2] As French ambassador Marillac commented, it took place 'in presence of so few people that until evening the truth was still doubted,' and he speculated that the manner of her death 'seems to argue that those here are afraid to put to death publicly those whom they execute in secret.'[3]

Margaret's death has become renowned for its brutality. An inept or 'novice'[4] executioner failed to kill her on the first stroke and was forced to hack away at her shoulders until she died. Later rumours that she attempted to escape are exaggerated, but if her death was not unnecessary enough, this made it even more painful and undignified as a result. Chapuys described how she 'commended her soul to God, and desired those present to pray for the King, Queen, Prince, and Princess. The ordinary executioner being absent, a blundering garonneau was chosen, who hacked her head and shoulders to pieces.'[5] Formerly described by her nephew Henry VIII as 'the most saintly woman in England',[6] he had subjected Margaret to unspeakable brutality and made a martyr of her. Margaret's only real 'crime' was her aristocratic blood. Her York heritage reveals how an accident of birth could be as dangerous as it could be ennobling.

41

Jane Boleyn, Lady Rochford

13 February 1542

Tower Green, Tower of London, London

Margaret Pole was one of several aristocratic women executed by Henry VIII in his later years. As if the death of Anne Boleyn had opened a floodgate and normalised such brutality, the king did not flinch from this new low and by 1542, Jane Boleyn should really have known better. She had escaped death once before, during the fall of Anne and George, but now the king was determined that she should die. So determined that he was prepared to change the law for her, to allow her to be brought out from her cell in the Tower, to kneel over a block stained with the fresh blood of a queen. If, by the morning of 13 February 1542, Jane regretted the part she had played in the intrigues of Catherine Howard, Henry VIII's fifth wife, it was too late to repent.

History has not been kind to Jane Boleyn. Her name has become synonymous with betrayal, jealousy and the embitterment of a wife excluded from a close family, resentful about her treatment by a 'playboy' husband. It is a trope repeated frequently in fiction, film and even documentaries, where Jane is cast as a foil to the popular Anne Boleyn, the villainess who helped bring her down. Yet the sources do not support this. If anything, they point towards a close relationship between Anne and Jane, and a harmonious, if childless, marriage with Anne's brother George.

Jane was born in 1505, the daughter of Henry Parker, Baron Morley, of Norfolk, ambassador, scholar and courtier. She had joined the household of Catherine of Aragon before 1520, when she was included in those listed as participating in the Field of Cloth of Gold at the age of 15. At some point before January 1526, she married George Boleyn, a witty, popular courtier, the only son of the ambassador Thomas whose family was about to rise spectacularly at court. The king granted the couple Grimston Manor in Norfolk and, later, Beaulieu Palace in Essex, and, from 1529, when her husband became Viscount Rochford, Jane was a Viscountess, known as 'Lady Rochford' at court.

When the Boleyns fell dramatically from favour in 1536, Jane was arrested and questioned, along with the rest of her circle, but any evidence she gave was only mentioned once in the trial. Even this was indirect, as George was asked if Anne had spoken to his wife about the king's sexual difficulties. George admitted she had, and was indiscreet or foolish enough to repeat this information before the court. Jane did not speak against her husband, or condemn his relations with Anne, or state that they had committed incest, or anything else that fiction has later attributed to her. Instead, Anne was condemned by the words of Elizabeth Somerset, Countess of Worcester, who testified to the 'many adulterous acts' that history now considers her to be innocent of. A conflation of Elizabeth and Jane appears to have occurred in the popular imagination, cemented by hostile sources such as George Wyatt, who called her a 'wicked wife, accuser of her own husband', and perhaps arising from Jane's survival and return to court with a pension of £100 and a position in Jane Seymour's household. She even helped in the divorce process of Anne of Cleves, testifying that the marriage had not been consummated.

Having already survived one of Henry VIII's bloody purges, Jane might have thought it wise to keep her head down, serving the queen, living devoutly and playing things safe. But just five years later, she was at the heart of another scandal when Catherine Howard's past and present activities were exposed. And this time, Jane was not innocent. Perhaps having been involved in the downfall of two queens, she thought she would not get caught, or that Henry would be lenient. But she was sadly mistaken. In the summer of 1541, Jane Boleyn crossed a line and her treasonous activities were sufficient to condemn her to death.

On 1 November 1541, Henry attended chapel at Hampton Court where he discovered a letter that had been left in his pew, outlining Catherine Howard's past sexual liaisons. The pair had been married fifteen months, and Henry had believed her to have come to his bed a virgin. The ensuing investigation uncovered that not only had she been precontracted to another, but that she had been visited at night that summer by one of Henry's favourites, Thomas Culpepper, a Gentleman of the Privy Chamber. They had been assisted by Jane, Lady Rochford. Not only had Jane known about these clandestine meetings, but she had kept watch and encouraged them. Even though it is unlikely that Catherine was foolish enough to consummate this relationship, she was certainly in love with the handsome Culpepper, as a letter written by her confirmed.

The first mention of Jane came on 13 November in the testimony of Katherine Tilney, who was:

> examined whether the Queen went out of her chamber any night late at Lincoln, where she went, and who went with her, says that the Queen went two nights to lady Rochford's chamber, which was up a little pair of stairs by the Queen's chamber... The second night the Queen sent the rest to bed and took examinate with her, but she was in a little place with Lady Rochford's woman and could not tell who came into Lady Rochford's chamber. Has been sent with such strange messages to Lady Rochford that she knew not how to utter them.[1]

Lady-in-waiting Margaret Morton added more details about Jane's involvement, including that 'at Pomfret, every night, the Queen, being alone with lady Rochford, locked and bolted her chamber door on the inside, and Mr. Dane, sent to the Queen from the King, one night found it bolted.'[2] The investigators concluded that during the 1541 summer progress to the north, 'the queen would, in every house, seek for the back doors and back stairs herself.' When they stayed at Pomfret Castle, 'she feared the King had set watch at the back door, and Lady Rochford made her servant watch in the court to see if that were so.' It was clear that many secret meetings had taken place, letters and gifts exchanged between Catherine and Culpepper, and that 'Lady Rochford contrived these interviews.'[3] When interrogated, Jane commented that 'she heard or saw nothing of what passed,' but was quite prepared to incriminate her mistress, saying 'since her trouble the Queen has daily asked for Culpeper, saying that if that matter came not out she feared not,' and finally, that 'she thinks Culpeper has known the Queen carnally.'[4] The queen Jane condemned to death was not Anne Boleyn, as is commonly believed, but Catherine Howard.

Jane was incarcerated in the Tower soon after where she is likely to have heard of the deaths of Culpepper and Catherine's former lover, Francis Dereham. According to witnesses, Jane's mental health completely deteriorated that autumn, which technically should have saved her. It was against the law for those of unsound mind to be condemned to death, but Henry was so determined that she must die, that he changed the law, allowing her to be condemned. She was executed on 13 February 1542, on a block fresh with the blood of Catherine Howard. Her personal effects, as confiscated upon her incarceration were listed as:

> A little steel casket with a purse and forty pounds in it
> A brooch with an agate
> A cross of diamonds with three pearls pendant
> A flower of rubies
> A flower with a ruby and a great emerald with a pearl pendant
> A tablet of gold with black, green, and white enamelled
> A pair of bracelets of red cornelians
> A pair of beads of gold and stones
> A broach of gold with an antique head and a white face[5]

These personal items of Jane's remind us of her humanity and her struggle for survival amid the tempestuous, ever-changing mood of Henry's court. She should also be remembered as a lesson for all subsequent historians and readers, revealing how far an individual's reputation can be distorted, and that distortion perpetuated, for future generations. When confronted with the kind of character attributed to Jane in fiction, film, TV adaptations and even in some documentaries, it is essential to return to the primary sources, verify such claims, and consider the motivations of those who perpetuated false information.

42

Lady Nata, or Otomo-Nata 'Jezebel'

1545
Bungo Province, Kyushu, Japan

Across Western Europe, the statues of saints were being torn down, wall paintings in churches washed over and monasteries dismantled. While England was in conflict about the way its people practised their faith, elsewhere, the spread of Christianity itself was being resisted. Nowhere more so than Japan. With the arrival of the first Jesuit missionaries in 1543, ancient Buddhist temples and Shinto shrines came under threat. One woman who strongly defended her faith, and her people's right to practise, was Lady Nata, even if this meant standing against her powerful magnate husband, and ultimately being rejected by him.

Lady Nata was born into a period of civil conflict following the collapse of the feudal system. Stretching from the 1460s through to 1615, it represented huge cultural and religious change on a scale that was also being experienced by the west, although differing in detail. Her family were devoted to their shrine which was dedicated to the war God Hachiman, who was also the divine protector of Japan and its people. Today, the Hachiman Nada shrine on the south-east coast of Lady Nata's Kunisaki peninsula stands in a pine forest overlooking a white sandy beach. Dating from the eighth century, it is similar to, if not directly associated with, Lady Nata's family, and representative of the practices they held dear.

Lady Nata's birthdate is unknown. In 1545, she married Otomo Sorin, who was then aged 15, so it is likely she was a similar age. He inherited his status as a daimyo, or head of the Otomo clan, in 1550 and their first two sons were born in 1558 and 1561, with other sons and daughters following. Sorin was still very young when he met with Jesuit co-founder Francis Xavier in 1551 and converted to Christianity, and many suspected this to be a strategic move as he hoped to secure trade with the Portuguese. Reading the Japanese character, Xavier cast off his austere asceticism and appeared elegantly dressed, with attendants, carrying images of the Virgin Mary upon cushions. By 1562, though, Sorin had become a Buddhist monk. Lady Nata continued to practise and encourage her people's beliefs in the Buddhist and Shinto faiths, becoming a Priestess of Hachiman with many followers. In 1578, Sorin had another change of heart. He reconverted to Christianity, this time taking the name Francisco. Influenced by the Jesuits, who called Lady Nata 'Jezebel', he divorced her and married a Christian woman.

This seems to signify the end of her strength as she was distraught at his actions, reputedly shaving her head and threatening suicide.[1] Sorin's response was to launch attacks against her shrine, burning it to the ground on more than one occasion. Lady Nata died in 1587, still steadfast in her faith. Her conviction, passion and refusal to renounce her lifelong beliefs finds parallels with many of the martyrs of the Tudor period, whether Catholic or Protestant.

43

Mildred Cooke

December 1545

Gidea Hall, Havering-atte-Bower, Essex, England

In the same year that Lady Nata married Otomo Sorin, a 19-year-old woman from Essex became the wife of William Cecil, one of the most influential statesmen of the era. Early in December 1545, with the assistance of her sisters at their Essex home, Mildred Cooke was preparing herself for her wedding, gathering together her trousseau, sewing linen and having her dresses fitted. In many ways, she had enjoyed the typical, privileged and sheltered upbringing of a girl of her class, but in others, her early life had been extraordinary. She was now on the verge of fulfilling society's expectations by making an excellent match, to a man who would become the most indispensable figure at court, but Margaret's talents were certainly equal to his. Erudite, scholarly and dedicated to her writing, nevertheless, there is very little paper trail surviving to record what her contemporaries recognised as her impressive achievements.

Mildred was the eldest of nine children of Sir Anthony Cooke, tutor to the young Edward VI. She was raised at Gidea Hall, near Havering in Essex, a crenellated manor house dating from the mid-thirteenth century, further developed in the 1460s. The family were descended from a former Lord Mayor of London, who was disgraced after offering financial assistance to exiled Lancastrian figures, but redeemed himself through the payment of a large fine. His great-grandson, Anthony, completed the house and raised his family there. Mildred received as good, if not better, an education than her peers, being instructed in French, Italian, Hebrew, Latin and Greek to a level that Roger Ascham thought equivalent to the famously erudite Jane Grey. Ascham claimed Mildred could speak Greek as fluently as she could English[1], placing her in a tiny, elite group, even among her class.

The Cooke household represented a similarly literary family to that in which Margaret Roper was raised by Thomas More. The skills Mildred acquired there would later be transferred into her teaching, during which she was made responsible for the education of royal wards. She also ensured her own children received a curriculum that included Classics, science, philosophy, music and poetry. While levels of female literacy were steadily improving as the century advanced, Mildred's education was a function of her class and her parents' enlightened views.

A month before the wedding, on 21 November 1545, Cecil's father Richard granted them the Manor of Essendine in Rutland and the surrounding lands.[2] The house had been associated with the Cecil family since 1509 and was built on the site of the old Norman motte and bailey castle, incorporating the church of St Mary Magdalene.[3]

Mildred became her husband's second wife in 1545 towards the end of Henry VIII's reign. William Cecil was then 25, and in the service of Edward Seymour, Duke of Somerset. It is possible that this was where the pair had first met. Mildred joined the household of Anne, Duchess of Somerset, in the early 1540s, and appeared to approve of her mistress as she later sought out Anne as a potential patron, dedicating to her a translation of St Basil's sermon.[4] Just over a year after the marriage, the accession of Edward VI propelled Seymour into a position of power as Lord Protector, and Cecil was favoured by him early, being one of two judges whom he selected to accompany him into Scotland. When Seymour fell in 1549, Cecil was able to transition successfully into the service of his replacement, John Dudley, and later, into the households of Mary and Elizabeth. The records relating to Margaret are quiet during these politically turbulent years. No surviving children were born to the couple for nine years, before the arrival of a short-lived daughter. Of Mildred's six known pregnancies, only three children reached adulthood.

Upon the accession of Elizabeth, William Cecil became principal secretary. Although he was dealing with matters of state, of national importance, he clearly respected and trusted Mildred enough to discuss these questions with her, with the result that Elizabeth sought her advice on Scottish matters.[5] Exactly how Mildred became such an expert in this field is unclear, but it may have been her skills of communication and empathy that appealed to the queen. During the 1560 Treaty of Edinburgh, Mildred corresponded with the Protestant leaders, and sensitive tasks were delegated to her by Elizabeth, such as consoling Margaret Douglas upon the loss of her son.[6] Mildred clearly had an imposing intellect, although the Spanish ambassador was intimidated by her talents, commenting that she was a 'tiresome blue-stocking' and a 'furious heretic' with 'great influence over her husband'.[7]

Along with her sisters, Anne Bacon and Elizabeth Hoby Russell, who were equally literary and able translators, Mildred represented the most cultured women of her era, second only to the queen. The poet Christopher Ocland, writing in the 1580s, described her as 'most famous, most learned, most skilled in Greek and Latin literature.' Recent critics have called the Cooke sisters 'the most politically significant women in Elizabethan England who were not of the royal blood.'[8] And yet, as some have rightly asked, where is her body of work? Her translations of St Basil and St Chrysotom are known, as are around five surviving letters; her library contained at least thirty-eight books that were hers alone,[10] in addition to many others she must have consulted. Yet Mildred barely left a literary footprint, for several reasons.

Paper does not always survive the ravages of centuries. It can only be assumed that a large number of Mildred's letters must have been lost. She was also very modest and self-deprecating, unwilling to publish, and avoiding publicity. When it came to her charitable giving, the extent of her philanthropy remained secret until after her death, even from her husband.[11] It is only fair to conclude that the absence of further surviving material by Mildred – letters, poems, translations – is indicative of her modesty and transience, rather than their lack of production. Thus, her life raises the frequent dilemma of the female artist, personified as Judith Shakespeare by Virginia Woolf in *A Room of One's Own*. Women had less access to literacy, books and paper, and bore the weight of expectations that their lives would be primarily maternal and domestic. Mildred's status enabled her to transcend many of these hurdles, but it could not guarantee the survival of her writings.

Cecil clearly loved his wife dearly, referring to her as a 'matchless mother' and 'dearest above all'. When she died in 1589, he wrote to the Dean of St Paul's of the 'harty love which I did bear her, with whom I lived in the state of matrimony forty and three years continually without any unkindness.'[12] She was buried in the cathedral, a remarkable woman of her age, of whom we can only yearn to know more.

44

Venus

1545

Florence, Italy

She is completely naked, hairless, white and plump: the epitome of a patriarchal male fantasy. Transported by joy, she sits with her knees to the left, upon a rippling fabric of light blue material. Her left arm hangs beside her, the hand against her thigh, fingers enclosing a golden apple given to her by Paris for being the most beautiful goddess of all. Her right arm snakes upwards, to encompass her son Cupid, from whose quiver she is stealing a golden arrow. At the same time, she turns, in a slightly awkward pose, to meet his lips, as he places one hand behind her head, dressed in pearls, while the other cups her breast. He tweaks her nipple as he attempts to steal her crown. A pair of masks sits at her feet, one old, bearded and turned towards the viewer, while the other is pinker, smoother, but facing away: coded symbols of deception. This mixed message of eroticism and the maternal creates an unexpected allegory, and is likely to have contained a political comment, commissioned as a gift for Francis I of France from Cosimo de' Medici.

Venus and Cupid are not alone. To their right, the little putti Folly is about to shower them with a handful of pink rose petals. Behind him, the winged, balding figure of Time holds up a darker blue backdrop, but an array of other figures is visible in the spaces between and behind, with their despairing or observant faces squeezed into the corners, disembodied amid fabric, creatures, foliage and drapes. Venus is oblivious to their emotions, though, engrossed in the moment.

Whichever model posed for the picture, whose name has been lost in the intervening centuries, Venus is the epitome of Renaissance beauty. Beside her ivory-white skin, the hair on her temples is golden and waving, with a single curl hanging down before her small ear. There is a faint blush of roses in her cheek, her eyebrow is plucked fine and the eye visible in profile appears blue-grey. Her nose is straight and roman with small, delicate nostrils. The pink lips are parted with a glimpse of white teeth and tongue. Her neck is solid, well-built, her chin rounded, her shoulders sloping. There is little that is ethereal about her; despite her allegorical context, she is a fleshy, erotic creature of the world, celebrating her sexuality, taking centre stage.

However, the darker aspects of sexuality are present in the work, with the figures of Folly, of foolish pleasure, having stepped upon a thorn; and Fraud, or Deceit, depicted as a pretty girl with a serpent's lower half, offering them honeycomb.

The suffering figure to the left, head in hand, may represent suffering, jealousy or syphilis. While art historians remain divided about its message, the parallels with Francis I's voracious sexuality, contracting syphilis around 1524, are likely to be more than incidental. Already well into the advanced stages by the time of the painting's composition, the disease was to kill him less than two years later. It was well suited to the French king too, in its rejection of the realistic style in favour of a polished mannerism, of intellectual artifice and sophistication.

Venus, Cupid, Folly and Time was painted by Angelo Bronzino, court painter to the Medicis, in his studio in Florence. It is smooth, glowing in bright colours, almost enamel-like, especially in the contrast between white and the blue. Venus appears sculpturesque, as if carved from marble, bright and precious, like a gem amid the scene. She is elegant, cold and detached, an object of veneration rather than a real woman to be touched, and in this she represents a sixteenth-century ideal, an abstract representation of love, with a quasi-religious feel. She is a symbol, not a woman, depicted by a man. Vasari referred to the painting as 'a picture of singular beauty', and as an international gift, between previously warring nations, it celebrated a shared love of culture and beauty. Venus remains an iconic figure, timeless in her inhumanity and the very human temptation she represents. Echoes of her are to be found throughout the sixteenth century in art and literature, in cultural perceptions of women and the real-life dramas that underpinned male-female relations all the way to the top of society.

45

Anne Askew

16 July 1546

Smithfield, London

The adjective 'askew' is defined in most dictionaries as at a slant, not aligned, not level or out of kilter. Its first appearance was in the mid-sixteenth century, and its origin is usually guessed at, as being derived from the Anglo-Saxon verb 'to skew', or skewer. However, there is another possible reason for the arrival of this word in the English language at this time. It might, alternatively, point to an act of Tudor brutality that shocked even the king. In 1546, a gentlewoman named Anne Askew, arrested for possible heresy, became the first woman to be racked and tortured in the Tower of London. By the time her interrogators had finished with her, she was unable to walk to the pyre, being carried there in a chair. With all her limbs broken, her bones making strange angles, Anne Askew was literally askew. It was technically illegal, as permission had not been sought from the king, and the council was outraged at her treatment. It was also a sight that Londoners would never forget.

Anne's fate was determined by her faith and zeal. Yet nothing about her origins could have predicted it. Born 1521, Anne was the daughter of Sir William Askew, an MP and knight who attended Henry VIII in France in 1520 and was a frequent visitor in the household of Princess Mary. This affiliation might suggest a Catholic bias in her father, as does their main home in Lincolnshire, the centre of the Pilgrimage of Grace in 1536. Anne was educated, but little is known about her syllabus, apart from the fact that she was taught to read. When her elder sister Martha died young, Anne was married to the man chosen as her husband, Thomas Kyme, a devout Catholic, and bore him two children. Exactly why Anne's path changed so dramatically is a mystery. From somewhere, Anne's faith wavered and developed into a deep, committed Protestantism. She began reading the Bible aloud to anyone who would listen, although her husband and brother forbade it. She was determined to travel to Lincoln Cathedral and see their Bible, but Kyme objected to the bishop, and her friends warned her that if she went, 'the priests would assault me and put me to great trouble.'[1] Eventually, Thomas had enough of her and threw her out.

Anne was not friendless. Her father had died in 1540 or 1541, but her brother, Edward, was cupbearer to Henry VIII, her half-brother Christopher was a Gentleman of the Privy Chamber and her sister Jane was married to George St

Poll, a lawyer in the service of Catherine Willoughby, Duchess of Suffolk. She also had at least one cousin nearby. With these connections in mind, Anne set out for London, aiming to attend the Court of Chancery and request a divorce. It was not exactly unprecedented, but very unusual, for a woman to do so at the time. When she arrived in the city, she met other Protestants, but also moved in court circles, meeting the Protestant Queen Catherine Parr. This did not prevent her from coming to the attention of the aldermen of London after she began to preach in the streets. On 10 March 1545, she was arrested and brought before Edmund Bonner, Bishop of London, to be interrogated.

On this occasion, Anne's friends came forward to support her. Four men, two of whom were gentlemen, were summoned to speak for her and ensure she 'was handled with no rigour.' Her cousin Brittain accompanied her, then went directly to the mayor to ask for Anne to be bailed. He asked the mayor to be a 'good lord' to Anne, who was 'a woman and he was nothing deceived in me... and not to set (her) weak woman's wit to his lordship's great wisdom.' Brittain was advised by the chancellor that 'if she said anything amiss', she could be reformed with godly counsel. The bishop told Anne he was 'very sorry for her trouble and wished to know her opinions,' assuring her that 'whatever she said in his house, no man should hurt her.'[2] Anne was accused of denying the Mass, but no witnesses came forward to speak against her. There was still considerable sympathy and support for her, especially as a woman judged to be misguided and open to correction. Anne was released without charge. The story could have ended there.

In the summer of 1546, conservative factions at court were gathering against Henry's sixth wife, Catherine Parr. Stephen Gardiner, Bishop of Winchester, attempted to halt the more extreme religious reforms being pushed through by Archbishop of Canterbury, Thomas Cranmer. Parr's belief in ideas like justification by faith and reading the Bible in English prompted a coup to prevent her from influencing the king further. A warrant was drawn up for her arrest, her rooms were searched and all her close friends questioned. Anne was rearrested in the hope that she would testify against the queen but she steadfastly refused. Both Anne and Thomas Kyme were summoned before the council at Greenwich, but as she denied being his wife, Kyme was sent away. The first interrogation lasted two days. In Anne's words, they charged her 'upon my obedience to show them if I knew any man or woman of my sect. Answered that I knew none. Then they asked me of my lady of Suffolk, my lady of Sussex, my lady of Hertford, my lady Denny and my lady Fitzwilliam.'[3] Questioning these women – Anne Seymour, Lady Hertford (see entry 54), wife of Edward Seymour; Joan, wife of Sir Anthony Denny; and Jane, wife of Sir William Fitzwilliam – was seen as a way of attacking leading reformists of the court.

It is clear from Anne's account that the focus had shifted from her own beliefs to her political connections. She was asked which ladies had sent her money, but she replied carefully that she could not be sure: 'I answered that there was a man in a blue coat who delivered me ten shillings and said that my lady of Hertford sent it me; and another in a violet coat gave me eight shillings, and said my lady Denny sent it me; whether it were true or no, I cannot tell, for I am not sure who sent it me, but as the maid did say.'[4]

Anne was then taken to the Guildhall, the central courts of justice in London. On 2 July 1546, an observer, Otwell Johnson, wrote to his brother that Anne received her judgement to be burned and sent to Newgate prison. However, because she refused to implicate anyone else, Anne was secretly removed to the Tower[5] and personally tortured by Thomas Wriothesley and Richard Rich, the leaders of the anti-reform group, 'taking pains to rack me with their own hands, till I was nigh dead.' She fainted 'and then they recovered me again.'[6] The keeper of the Tower, Sir William Kingston, objected, outraged at the violence against a woman, that had not been sanctioned by king or council. By the end of the process, Anne's limbs were all either broken or dislocated so that she was unable to stand.

On 16 July 1546, Anne was carried to the execution site upon a chair, with every movement causing her pain. Unable to walk, she was dragged to the pyre and tied to another chair against the stake. Offered a pardon if she recanted, she refused to compromise her beliefs and corrected the bishop, saying he spoke without the Book. According to onlookers, she died bravely. She was 25. Her first-hand account was published by John Bale and reprinted in Foxe's Book of Martyrs, securing her legacy. The two-part nature of her clash with authority reveals a misogynistic society initially concerned with Anne's plain speaking, her public position and her lack of a husband. As a lone, outspoken female, she was swept off the streets, but patriarchal figures attempted to protect her. A year later, she was the convenient scapegoat for a political coup that was struggling to find evidence, and she paid the ultimate price when that intrigue failed. Anne's religious conviction made her a public figure, but this proved to be her downfall. The horror of her treatment at the hands of leading figures of the Tudor court can be remembered in her name, which has passed into common use, more widely spread than the details of her short and tragic life. It is ironic, yet indicative, that Anne's suffering, rather than her bravery, has been enshrined in our language.

46

Ellen Sadler

1546

London, England

Perhaps Ellen received the news by letter. Her husband, Rafe, was then away on the king's business in Scotland, and wrote to her often as she awaited his return in their London home. Breaking the seal, she may have read the first lines with enthusiasm, before her mood changed upon reaching the main message. Perhaps she withdrew into a private room, away from the eyes of servants, or at least sat down, to process the confusing information it contained. All sorts of questions would have arisen in her mind, about her future, her identity, her children. Or perhaps Rafe, taking the news 'very heavily',[1] did not want to write, but waited until he had returned home and told his wife of eleven years in person.

Ellen was around 40 when the world she and Rafe had built was threatened with collapse. It had been a difficult path. She had been married before, when she was young, but her first husband had disappeared, presumed dead, leaving her with two small children. Fortunately, she found a place in the household of Thomas Cromwell, assisting his mother, and there she had met Rafe, Cromwell's secretary. The pair were married and were happy, and had seven children. But now a report surfaced that Ellen's first husband had been seen, alive and well in a London pub. Worse still, he was speaking of his wife as a bigamist.

Papal Registers of the late medieval and early Tudor period are full of uncertain marriages, conducted between individuals who were related by blood or undermined by previous vows made to others. Often one party speaks up after their spouse has contracted themselves to another, hoping for legal validation of their status, or the legitimacy of their children. The case of Ellen Sadler is unusual because of the high status of her second husband, which was the cause of her exposure, as her first husband was overheard in a tavern, claiming that he was married to a woman who lived with Sadler, almost boasting about this high-status connection. It would require a special act of Parliament to resolve.

Ellen was the daughter of John Mitchell of Much Hadham, Hertfordshire, and had probably been born around 1505 or 1506, based on the date of her first marriage in 1526. She became the wife of Matthew Barre in Dunmow, Essex, probably at St Mary's Church, and bore him two children. After this point, perhaps in around 1530–31, Barre disappeared. Ellen remained in the village for a year, making enquiries and travelling to visit his birthplace, seeking to discover his whereabouts. Some sources claimed he had gone to Ireland, but a member of his family assured Ellen that he was dead. Somehow, from this low point, Ellen found a patron in the Prioress of St Mary's, Clerkenwell, who recommended her to Mercy Pryor, Cromwell's mother-in-law who was then living under his roof, after her daughter, Cromwell's wife, had succumbed to the sweating sickness. Following his marriage to Ellen, Sadler survived the fall of Cromwell, being knighted, allying with Thomas Cranmer and undertaking more diplomatic missions to Scotland. By 1545, he had become Master of the Grand Wardrobe and owned a string of estates, including some confiscated after the closure of the monasteries.

Then Matthew Barre returned. A private man who was devoted to his wife, Rafe was, by contemporary accounts, devastated when reports reached him in October 1545. For Ellen, it must have raised mixed emotions. The man she had continued to seek, until she was persuaded of his death, had, in fact, deserted her. Now he returned to threaten her present happiness and the legitimacy of her children. She was fortunate in being married to such an influential man, that the matter was resolved with minimum scandal and even the law being reshaped to accommodate her.

Sadler was anxious to avoid a public scandal. He explained how when they first entered into an acquaintance, she told him she had been married and had two children 'and that her husband was dead, which she might easily think, for she had not heard of him in two or three years before, and even then it appeared that he was in Ireland.'[2] An investigation into Ellen's first marriage found that the union was still legal, meaning that her children by Rafe were illegitimate. However, it was also ruled that both had entered into their marriage in good faith, in the belief that Barre was genuinely dead, having made enquiries about his whereabouts and after an interval of several years. In 1546, a special act of Parliament was passed, predicated upon the Sadlers' good intentions, conceding that the children had been conceived in the belief of true and honest wedlock, thus they were considered to be legitimate. However, Sadler buried this deep, preventing the publication of the act or its appearance in any of the contemporary statues. It is only through a single reference in the Library of the Inner Temple that a transcript entitled 'The Unprecedented Case of Sir Ralph Sadleir' that the details of this case are still known.

The Sadlers' case has some similarities with another famous marital desertion story of the mid-sixteenth century: that of Martin Guerre's wife in France. Based in the Pyrenees village of Artigat, Martin and Bertrande de Rols had married in their teens and had a son, before Martin was accused of stealing grain from his father and disappeared in 1548. Because Martin was not declared dead, Bertrande was forbidden to remarry, so she could do little other than wait. Eight years later, a man returned to the village, claiming to have been away at war. He was accepted by most of the villagers, including Bertrande, with whom he lived for a further three years, before his true identity was revealed, as the real Martin had lost a leg in battle. The imposter was tried for fraud, initially supported, then rejected by Bertrande, and only convicted when the real Martin returned, minus one leg. The fake husband, a man named Arnaud du Tihl, was hanged in front of the Guerres' house in 1560.

The Sadlers' story had a less dramatic conclusion. Barre disappeared and the couple continued to live together quietly as man and wife for twenty-five more years, even though technically, Ellen was still married. The last reference to Ellen was in 1569 and Ralph died in 1587. Their story reveals the unstable nature by which marriages were brought to closure and the strength of their love, persisting in the face of public scandal and setbacks.

47

Levina Teerlinc

1546
London, England

The Tudors loved to be depicted in paint. From Henry VIII's imposing stance in the Whitehall mural, through to the more delicate depictions of his children as miniature adults in their jewels and furs, portraiture aided their projection of majesty. Before the 1540s, almost all of those who were allowed privileged access to sketch the royal family were male. There were two notable exceptions: Susannah Horenbout, who immigrated from Ghent with her artist father and brother, and Margaret Holewyther, who became Susannah's sister-in-law. As was often the case in professional spheres in Tudor England, both were able to achieve a degree of success through association with their male relatives. However, after the death of his court painter, Hans Holbein, in 1545, Henry VIII headhunted a prestigious female artist by sending an invitation across the sea to a small village in the Netherlands.

Levina Teerlinc was born as Levina Bening in the 1510s in the prosperous merchant city of Bruges. She was the descendant of men who had already made their name as miniaturists. Her grandfather, Alexander Bening, was an illuminator of manuscripts, especially Books of Hours, in which he painted the bucolic scenes of the Labours of the Months for wealthy patrons such as Emperor Charles V. His son, Simon, also painted miniatures and probably trained Levina and her four sisters in his Ghent studio. Levina was married by early 1545 to George Teerlinc, or Teerling, a burgher of Blankenberghe, and that February, they were listed as closing the estate of his father, which George presumably inherited. Although none of her work survives to prove it, Levina's abilities must have been considerable enough to establish her international reputation because the following year, she received a letter asking her to come to England. Some historians have seen the hand of William Cecil behind this move as he sought to establish an English school of miniaturists, but this cannot be proven. It is tempting to speculate why Levina, as a woman, was singled out, in comparison with her male peers, and even to wonder if Mildred Cecil had influenced her husband. The Teerlincs had arrived in England by March 1546 as the court accounts for the autumn contain the entry: 'Mrs. Levyna Terlyng, paintrix, to have a fee of £40 a year from the Annunciation of Our Lady last past during your Majesty's pleasure.'[1] The entry also states that she was 'preferred by Lady Harbert,' suggesting that she had found a friend or patron in Blanche Milbourne, Lady Herbert, who was about to retire as Lady Mistress to Princess Elizabeth.

Despite receiving her annual salary of a very impressive £40 a year for life, Levina never signed her work, so it is difficult to say exactly which are her paintings. She is recorded as giving a picture of the Trinity to Mary I in 1556, and of completing works of Elizabeth at regular intervals during her reign: 1559, 1562, 1563, 1564, a full-length work in 1567, 1568, 1575 and 1576. Matching these dates to the images is problematic, although a common style is identifiable. Teerlinc's delicate miniatures frequently have a bright, mid-blue background, small-bodied figures with thin arms shown to the waist, or just above, dressed in black clothing trimmed with white fur, often with ruffs and hats, or similar headdresses and styled red-gold hair. Her particular specialism was what the Elizabethans called the art of limning, or limming, of tiny paintings made on stretched vellum or the backs of playing cards.

Some of Levina's subjects can be tentatively identified, including a spindly image of frail Katherine Grey, called *The Beaufort Miniature*; perhaps another work depicting an older lady might be her mother Frances, while a third, draped in pearls, might be the beautiful Mary Dudley, prior to contracting smallpox as a result of nursing Elizabeth through the disease. Another portrait surviving from around 1550, featuring a young woman, has been identified as Princess Elizabeth; it includes the inscription 'Ano XVIII,' thus indicating the sitter was 18 years, as Elizabeth was in 1551. Yet, with its retrousse nose, the image does not look like the princess we recognise from most later portraits, leading some to speculate that this might be Jane Grey, although she was four years Elizabeth's junior. Teerlinc also produced a miniature of a crowded scene, with courtiers flocking around the queen on Maundy Thursday, in around 1560. It is an incredible feat, cramming the frame with dozens of figures and giving the impression of many more in such a tiny space.

It has been suggested by Roy Strong and V.J. Murrell,[2] and others[3] that Levina was responsible for training up her successor, miniaturist Nicholas Hilliard, whose first picture of Elizabeth was completed in 1572. There are stylistic similarities that might suggest this, but it cannot be verified. Levina bore one son and died in London 1576. Current scholarship continues to evaluate her artistic contribution, but because her work does not bear a signature, it is difficult to be certain about the extent of her production. This typical dilemma regarding sixteenth-century women in the arts excludes many who might otherwise be acknowledged for playing a more significant role.

48

Elizabeth 'Bess' Holland

14 December 1546
Kenninghall Place, Norfolk, England

It was early on a December morning. Dark and cold, as only the remote county of Norfolk could be, even with the fires being kindled by the servants. Bess knew she should be rising soon for chapel, but she was tempted to lie in bed longer and let the room warm a little. She doubted that the others in the house would be stirring yet. It was a house of women and children, anyway, with Bess herself; Mary Howard, daughter of the Duke of Norfolk; and Frances, wife of Norfolk's son Henry, Earl of Surrey, and her four children, with another on the way. The men were up in London, as they often were.

Bess had lived at Kenninghall for most of her life. Her father had been the steward there, serving the Dukes of Norfolk, and when she came of age, Bess was employed to do the laundry of Duchess Elizabeth. It had not been a happy marriage. As she wrung out the shirts and sheets, mixed the soap and water, Bess had heard them quarrelling. The duchess had been engaged to another, and apparently very much in love, until the duke stepped in and demanded her as his wife. Goodness knows why, as he often asked her since, as she had no liking for him, and his appetite quickly cooled before her sharp tongue. Perhaps it was the twenty-year age gap between them. And so, by 1527, Bess had found her way into his bed. He was in his mid-fifties then, her Thomas, and she had given him comfort through the turbulent years that followed. When his niece, Anne Boleyn, had been crowned queen, he had found Bess a place in her household. She, in turn, had comforted him when the marriage unravelled and Norfolk had to distance himself from Anne, and watch her go to her death. It had cost Bess the goodwill of the duchess, who had packed her bags and left by this time. But she knew what Elizabeth wrote about her in letters to those she thought would keep her secrets, calling Bess a whore, a drab, a bawd, the daughter of a churl and mocking her birth.

As day broke on Tuesday 14 December, while Bess was dressing, she heard a knocking at the gates. It was loud and persistent, rousing the servants to hurry down through the courtyard to see who was so impatient. There, they found three messengers from court – Sir Richard Southwell, John Gate and Wymond Carew – who strode inside, calling for the steward and almoner, and asking for all the doors in and out to be secured.[1] Bess and Mary were summoned to meet them, and were informed that Norfolk and Surrey had been arrested on charges of treason and sent to the Tower. The women were expected to cooperate while the messengers searched the house and made an inventory of the duke's belongings. Bess's lodgings were at the top of the house, above those of Norfolk on the second floor. They contained an outer chamber, bedchamber and maid's chamber, and a short gallery with a garret and turret. Bess herself was searched, and girdles, beads, buttons of gold, pearls and rings set with various stones were confiscated. Messengers were also sent to Bess's new house in Suffolk 'which they believed to be well furnished.'[2]

The arrest may not have come as a surprise to Bess. Norfolk had previously confided in her that he was mistrusted on the council because 'they were no noblemen themselves' and because he 'believed too truly in the Sacrament of the Altar.' He claimed that Henry disliked him too because he was popular, but would not court favour, following his own path instead, so he had been excluded from the king's inner council. As Bess confessed, Norfolk had told her 'that the King was much grown of his body' and that he could not go up and down the stairs, but was 'let up and down by a device'. And that his Majesty was 'sickly and could not long endure'; and the realm like 'to be in an ill case through diversity of opinions'. And 'that if he were a young man and the realm in quiet', he would ask leave to see the Vernacle; which, he said 'was the picture of Christ given to women by Himself' as He went to death. He was also aware that his son, Surrey, had used the arms of Edward the Confessor, which were intended only for royalty.[3]

On 24 December, the Duke of Norfolk confessed that he had 'concealed high treason, in keeping secret the false acts' of his son and offered his lands to the king by way of apology. At the trial, Duchess Elizabeth, Mary Howard and Bess all gave evidence against him. There was no love lost between Howard and his wife, but the actions of Mary and Bess are more difficult to understand, although they may have had no choice when faced with the threat to their lives. Surrey was condemned first and was beheaded on 19 January. Eight days later, Norfolk was attainted and Henry VIII consented to his execution. By a staggering twist of fate, though, the king died the following day, 28 January, and the duke was saved. However, his religious views ensured that he was kept in the Tower until the succession of the Catholic Mary in 1553.

Soon after Norfolk's arrest, Bess married Henry Reppes, a Justice of the Peace from Norfolk. She was, by then, in her late thirties, and this is likely to have been a pragmatic move as she realised the Howards were doomed and her relations with the duke were over. As his mistress, she was not entitled to any financial support; even the properties and gifts he gave her were forfeited to the crown, and she could hardly look to the duchess for help. Bess fell pregnant fairly swiftly, but died in childbirth at some point before April 1548. She has been judged harshly by some historians for the evidence she gave against Norfolk, singled out for censure even though all the women contributed. There may well still have been affection between them, but in Henry's final years, the shadow of the axe was forever looming over the aristocracy and, like so many of her female peers, she chose a pragmatic path. She chose survival. She did not live to enjoy it for long. The Duke of Norfolk outlived her by six years, dying a free man in August 1554.

49

Catherine de' Medici

31 March 1547
Paris, France

It had been worth the struggle. Catherine awaited the arrival of the messenger in her jewelled gown, rings upon the thin fingers that played with her rosary. Her time was coming at last. Today was her husband's birthday. The Dauphin of France, Henry of Valois, was 28. But as fate had decreed, the day would bring a different kind of rebirth for the old king was dying, and it was just a matter of time. The rumours had already been spreading, but the confirmation would come to them first. At the age of 52, Francis I lay dying at the Château de Rambouillet, complaining about the responsibilities of the crown. Henry would succeed and Catherine would become queen with all the power that brought, a triumph over her rivals, and, surely now, Henry would put aside his mistress and treat her with the respect she deserved.

Catherine was born into the notorious Medici family in Florence in 1519. Yet her parents' marriage had been a fairy tale celebration hosted by Francis himself at the Château d'Amboise. The pageantry had been devised by none other than Leonardo da Vinci himself, resident in the palace grounds in May 1518. The French king made a gift of 10,000 gold coins to the bride, Madeleine de la Tour d'Auvergne. The groom was Lorenzo de' Medici, Duke of Urbino, ruler of the elegant centre of Renaissance art, the city of Florence. Within weeks, Madeleine had conceived, delivering her baby daughter on 13 April 1519. However, Madeleine died fifteen days later, perhaps as the result of complications arising from the birth, or plague, or as some claimed, syphilis. Lorenzo died on 4 May, as the result of disease and his excessive lifestyle. Thus, the baby girl was orphaned at the age of three weeks. Catherine's great-uncle, Pope Leo, resisted the desire of Francis I to raise her at his court, sending her instead to her grandmother, before she was granted her own residence in the city and raised as a duchess.

It had been a cold, loveless marriage. She had walked into it at the age of 14 with no idea what to expect. Her husband, Henri, was just a boy, a second son, never intended for the throne. His early years had been difficult because his father Francis I escaped captivity with the emperor by offering his sons in his place. From the age of 7, Henri had spent over four years in various prisons in Spain, a process that had broken the health of his elder brother. It made Henri a reflective, melancholy boy who felt disconnected from the court upon his return. He found no connection either in his new wife, who he met shortly before their wedding ceremony, at the Eglise Saint-Ferréol les Augustins, in Marseille, on 28 October 1533. That night, King Francis remained in their bedchamber to observe that the match had been fully consummated, literally watching as they had sex. He was later joined by the Pope, telling him the pair had 'both shown valour in the joust.'[1] Whether the 14-year-old girl felt any embarrassment at being observed on this intimate, personal occasion was not recorded. The act of sex was an important part of legally binding the match, and with unions made for political reasons and bodily functions conducted with far less privacy, it may not have been such a sensitive question in the sixteenth century. Francis may also have borne in mind the very recent English difficulties over Arthur and Catherine of Aragon's wedding night, and aimed to prevent his son experiencing any similar subsequent problems with his Catherine. The French match was consummated but it was years before Catherine fell pregnant. She spent little time with her new husband, whose affections lay elsewhere. Then, unexpectedly, in 1536, the Dauphin Francis died and Henri was next in line to the throne. From that moment forward, Catherine was aware that she was likely to become queen of France.

Fourteen years later, Catherine had borne a son and daughter, and was pregnant with her third child. The hours were ticking past as the old king lay on his death bed. No doubt the devout Catherine passed part of the time in prayer for his soul, but her mind must have raced to the expected news and its implications. Francis had been ill for months, taking to his bed soon after the death of his English rival, Henry VIII, that January. Reputedly, Henry had sent the French king a message from his deathbed, reminding him of his mortality, which arrived after his death and the ageing Francis had been depressed since. He died on the last day of March, and news spread across the country with courtiers flocking to pay homage to the new king.

Catherine was now queen. That May, Francis I was given a magnificent funeral in the Basilica of St Denis in Paris, in conjunction with the reinterment of two of Henri's brothers, Dauphin Francis and Charles, who had died two years before, aged 23. The city was filled with pageantry and crowds lined the route. Henri himself, and probably the pregnant Catherine, watched the procession from a window in the Rue Saint-Jacques.[2] On 25 July, Henri and Catherine held their own magnificent joint coronation in Reims Cathedral. A contemporary book recording the event contains a poem in praise of Francis I, before describing their entry into the city under a triumphal archway, followed by the procession and the crowning, as they were anointed and sat side, by side, the picture of unity.[3]

However, in reality, this change did not bring Catherine any actual increase in power. For the last fourteen years she had been a neglected wife, then a mother, while the real influence lay in the hands of Henry's mistress, the older Diane de Poitiers. Catherine was still considered an outsider and untrustworthy, according to contemporary stereotypes about Italians. Her succession brought her a change in protocol but little more. She continued to bear Henri's children, delivering another daughter that November, followed by six more infants. It would not be until Henri's own death, twelve years later, that power would finally pass into Catherine's hands as the king's mother. By that point she was 44 and had spent thirty years waiting patiently, observing the French court, a paradoxical figure of status but little influence. Her time was still to come. For so many women of her time, life was a waiting game.

50

The Four Marys

7 August 1548
Dumbarton, Scotland

Dumbarton was built on the bank of the River Clyde, its imposing castle perched between rocks overlooking the water. Although it was August, the winds kept buffeting the waves and the skies were dark. Inside the grey and pink stone castle, the 6-year-old Queen of Scots was forced to wait before she could embark and leave behind the country of her birth, over which she now ruled. She watched the changeable weather outside, the tide rising and falling and the distant shores. Her mother's visit in May was just a memory and instead, for her companions, she had four little aristocratic girls of around the same age. This was not all they had in common: all the girls were named Mary. In fact, their names and this moment have come to define them, and history has recorded them as the Four Marys.

At 6, Mary Stuart was young for a queen. Yet there was never a time in her memory before she had been one. Her father, James V, son of Margaret Tudor, had been killed at the Battle of Solway Moss, fought against the English in 1542. Mary was the only surviving child born of his second marriage, to Mary of Guise, and inherited the Scottish throne at just six days old. The court was controlled by powerful magnates, some of whom favoured an alliance with England, while others favoured France. Mary of Guise removed her daughter to the safety of Stirling Castle and tried to replace the unpopular regent, the Earl of Arran, while fending off English attacks. On one occasion, Mary was nearly killed while attending a siege, when her party came in range of the English guns. This prompted her to seek a French alliance, and Parliament agreed that the infant queen should be betrothed to the dauphin and sent away to be raised at the Valois court. The departure date was set for 13 July, but the winds were so bad that the ships did not sail until 7 August. French naval commander Nicolas Durand, Sieur de Villegagnon, had been sent to pilot the ships, intending to take the longer route around the west coast of Ireland in order to avoid the English fleet.

As they sailed down the Clyde, the queen's young companions recognised the start of a new adventure. Mary Seton, Mary Beaton, Mary Fleming and Mary Livingston were all young daughters of Scottish nobility, perhaps not old enough to understand the implications and dangers of the journey ahead. They had been specially selected by Mary of Guise for the loyalty their family had demonstrated.

Mary Seton was born in 1542, so she was aged 6, the same as her mistress. Her French mother Marie Pieris had come to England in the entourage of Marie of Guise, as her lady-in-waiting, marrying Lord Seton the following year. Mary Beaton was the youngest at the age of 5, the daughter of another of the dowager queen's ladies-in-waiting. Janet Stewart, an illegitimate daughter of James IV, was the mother of 6-year-old Mary Fleming, making Mary the queen's cousin and a granddaughter of James IV. Her father had been captured at Solway Moss, then died at the Battle of Pinkie in 1547. Janet also sailed with the new queen to France in 1548. The eldest of the girls was Mary Livingston, aged 7, the daughter of the queen's guardian. Although they were very young to be taken away from their families, with the exception of Mary Fleming whose mother was with her, being chosen to accompany the queen was an honour. It would establish ties of loyalty and allegiance that could potentially be lifelong.

The voyage took about a week. For five small girls, leaving home for the unknown, crossing the stormy seas, it may have been a long week. Then, finally, land was sighted. The little fleet landed safely on the coast of Brittany, at or near Roscoff, and travelled to the Valois court. Over the next ten years, Mary received a wide education and grew into a young woman, as did her companions. Janet Stewart was initially appointed her governess, but following an affair with Henri II and bearing him a son, she returned to Scotland in 1551. In 1558, Mary married the dauphin, Francis, at the age 16. Her potential queenship seemed a long way off, but then Henri II was killed in a jousting accident, and her young husband suddenly succeeded to the French throne. Mary's tenure was brief, though, lasting only eighteen months, when Francis II died of an ear infection. The group of five Marys return to Scotland as grown women in 1561, ready for the adventures of marriage, motherhood and life that lay ahead.

Mary Seton was the only one of the three not to marry. As the queen's hairdresser, she accompanied Mary into exile in England until 1577, before returning to Scotland and becoming a nun. Mary Livingston was the first to wed in 1565 to John Sempill of Beltrees, amid rumours that she might already be pregnant and was 'lusty'. The queen gave her wedding gifts of cloth, silver thread and a velvet bed. Mary Beaton married Alexander Ogilvy of Boyne in 1566 and bore a son. She attended Mary during her confinement with the future James I the same year, and Mary remembered her at the end of her life, leaving books to her in her will, although Beaton did not receive them. Mary Fleming also married in 1566, to English-born Sir William Maitland at a ceremony held in Stirling Castle. Later, during James' minority she was forced to surrender her own castle and return a jewelled necklace given to her by Mary. Their lives were linked by the decision to bring them together in 1548, due to their status, connections and parity of age. Later, they would follow different paths, but the spectre of their queen remained with them.

51

Katherine 'Kat' Ashley

January 1549

Hatfield House, Hertfordshire, England

At first it was a footstep outside the door. Ever so quiet, even for that time of the morning, as he clearly did not want to wake the occupants in the bedchamber. All was silent in this wing of the old manor house in Chelsea. Then it would be the unseen hand, turning the key in the lock. It would creak slowly, open a yard, and he would appear. Bare-legged in his night shift and slippers, handsome as a devil, creeping across the floor to the bed, through the half-light. Then he would pull the curtains aside and surprise the sleeping girl with tickles and caresses, or a slap upon her thighs. The sound would wake her ladies, sleeping in the antechamber, who would blush and frown with concern. They were all afraid of him with his 'fiery passions' and his way of oppressing those under his roof.[1]

But one morning, in the spring of 1548, as Thomas Seymour headed for the bed of his wife's teenage stepdaughter, he received a nasty shock. Elizabeth was asleep with her red hair spilled across the pillow. As usual, he lifted the sheets and slipped in beside her, leaning forward to try and kiss her. Coming to, Elizabeth shrank away. And then, a stern voice from the room spoke aloud, breaking the spell. A woman's voice. 'Go away, for shame, go away.'[2] Seymour recognised Elizabeth's guardian, Kat Ashley, a woman in her mid-forties, sternly awaiting him, determined to prevent his actions. Over recent months, Kat had already seen quite enough, and been made aware of previous incidents by Elizabeth's maids, and by the girl herself. More than that, she had eyes and ears of her own, and she knew that all was not well in the house. Nor had she forgotten that before he was married to Catherine Parr, Henry VIII's sixth wife and surviving widow, Seymour had petitioned the council to be allowed to marry a princess, either Elizabeth or Mary would do. He had been denied, of course, as his status was nowhere near equal to that of their royal blood, but he was not a man who liked to be told no.

Kat Ashley had been in Elizabeth's household since she was four. Born in around 1502, as Katherine Champernowne, Kat's origins are uncertain but she had been well educated in a range of languages and had some knowledge of maths, history, geography and astronomy. In 1537, the birth of Prince Edward required a shift in the staff of the former princess. Declared illegitimate upon the fall of her mother, Elizabeth had been cared for by Lady Margaret Bryan, whose services were transferred to the nursery of the new baby. Kat remained with Elizabeth throughout her childhood, teaching her needlework, embroidery, dancing and singing, in addition to her formal lessons. The princess later stated that Kat had 'taken great labour and pain in bringing of me up in learning and honesty.'[3] When Elizabeth was ten, her father married his final wife, Catherine Parr, an educated reformist, whose attempts to reunite her husband's children brought Elizabeth increasingly back to court. In 1545, Kat married John Ashley, Elizabeth's senior gentleman attendant, and a cousin of Anne Boleyn. When Henry died, Elizabeth remained in her stepmother's care, going to live in her household, sometimes at Chelsea, sometimes at Hanworth. Her younger brother, son of Jane Seymour, became Edward VI.

The unmarried Thomas Seymour, approaching 40, was now uncle to the king. His elder brother and rival, Lord Somerset, was Protector, and in a position to block Thomas' marital ambitions. Thwarted in his plans for a princess, he married Catherine during her period of mourning, incurring censure from the court. It also served to intensify the existing rivalry between the brothers and their wives, after Catherine's new sister-in-law, Anne Somerset, saw the marriage as a demotion, lessening the status Catherine had formerly enjoyed as Henry's widow.

Initially, though, there was merriment at Chelsea. Seymour had arrived at the manor house in June 1547 and rapidly took over its management. Catherine joined in with her husband's high-spirited games, chasing them in the garden, and holding Elizabeth captive while Thomas slashed her dress. Even Kat had been charmed by the newcomer, looking on indulgently. But both she and the former queen had been unaware of the early morning visits, and soon the whispers of the maids reached Kat's ears, prompting her to keep a closer watch over her charge. She spoke to John Harington, Seymour's servant, to no avail, so took direct action herself by awaiting his presence in Elizabeth's bedchamber.

Catherine fell pregnant around Christmas 1547. It was probably her first pregnancy in four marriages, as she is not recorded as experiencing any previous stillbirths or miscarriages. At the age of 35 she was comparatively old for motherhood in contemporary terms, and early aristocratic marriages meant that many of her peers were soon to become grandparents. For a while, the idyll of the love nest at Chelsea continued with the impending arrival to look forward to. Then, in May 1548, Catherine came across Seymour and Elizabeth, locked in an embrace in the gardens. At once, Catherine packed up her household and decamped to Sudeley Castle in Gloucestershire, to await the birth of her child. Elizabeth and her governess were dispatched to the care of Sir Anthony Denny at Cheshunt. It was there, in September, that news reached them that Catherine had died in childbirth.

Kat must have retained some fondness for Seymour, or perhaps been aware that Elizabeth had feelings for him. In the weeks following Catherine's demise, she suggested that the princess write to him, in order to comfort him, but the shrewd 15-year-old already had an inkling of the danger posed by the situation, and replied that he had no need of her comfort. The autumn months passed quietly at Hatfield, but unable to accept his lot, or rein in his ambition, Seymour was plotting and planning and the clouds were shortly to break.

On 16 January, Seymour was arrested at Hampton Court. The circumstances are unclear, but it would seem that he believed he was being denied access to the king and attempted to break into his chambers in the middle of the night, perhaps with the intention of removing him. He gained access through the privy garden, but when one of the king's dogs began to bark, Seymour shot it to silence it. He was taken to the Tower; his behaviour was considered potentially treasonous, by which all his associations were tainted, even those with Elizabeth. His former dubious intentions towards her were recalled.

Five days later, the arrival of royal guards broke the peace at Hatfield. They were already too late, though, as news of the Hampton Court incident had already reached the princess's ears. The women had time to get their story straight. Kat and another gentlewoman, Blanche Parry, were taken to the Tower, without even being given time to dress, while Elizabeth was questioned at home. Sir Robert Tyrwhitt was convinced of her guilt, but found her careful and composed, answering with precision in a way that could not incriminate herself. All three women told a similar story about the limited extent of Elizabeth's involvement with Seymour, her ignorance regarding his plans and her loyalty to her brother. They admitted the details of his flirtatious behaviour but denied any collusion. After weeks of questioning, the council was forced to admit they had no evidence of Elizabeth's complicity.

Kat and Blanche were released from the Tower uncharged, returning to Hatfield on 7 March. Thomas Seymour was found guilty on thirty-three counts of treason and executed on 20 March. Elizabeth's comment upon Seymour's death was typically apt, both revealing of his character and unrevealing when it came to her feelings: 'this day died a man with much wit and very little judgement.'[4] It had been a narrow escape for the future queen and a harsh lesson she would never forget. The question of Seymour's attentions to Elizabeth, and their impact upon her, has attracted a range of responses, from her complicity and enjoyment, to Seymour as a predator, grooming an underage girl. The perspective of modern morality must not be allowed to cloud a sequence of events rooted in sixteenth-century ideals. Although beliefs about marriage, complicity, the age of consent and marital fidelity have changed, conclusions cannot be drawn from the outside. Elizabeth's true feelings cannot be known, although Kat's intervention and description indicate her disapproval. Yet her motives must be seen in context, as she later encouraged her charge to write to Seymour. Perhaps Kat's disapproval was based initially on Seymour's quasi-paternal role, and his marriage to Catherine Parr, concerns that were removed with Catherine's death. Alternatively, her experiences at the hands of Thomas may have convinced Elizabeth to avoid sexual relations, if her own father's history had not already done so. It is dangerous to speculate about the unknown emotions of people from the past, and even more so to apply modern standards to them. What can be stated is that the events of 1548–9 left an impact on the adolescent princess, and if anyone understood, it was Kat Ashley.

52

Beatriz de Luna, aka Gracia Mendes Nasi

1549

Ferrara, Northern Italy

The little girl from Portugal never forgot her Jewish roots. Anti-Semitism was one of the deep-rooted undercurrents of sixteenth-century life. England had banned Jews from its soil in 1290 after an active campaign of persecution and murder. Through the medieval period, France underwent a cycle of ejecting their communities, then inviting them to return. In Spain they were forbidden to practise, trade or mingle with Christians, taxed and oppressed with the intent of forcing them to convert, before they were expelled in 1492, given just four months to leave. Portugal followed suit in 1497. Some countries formally tolerated a Jewish presence, like in Germany, where they were forced to wear yellow badges, but they remained scapegoats, still subject to frequent assault and murder. One of the few areas where they were persecuted less were the Italian states and outside the Christian empire, among the Ottoman Turks.

Beatriz de Luna came from one such family, which had originated in Aragon, Spain, before her birth. Their surname may have originally been Nasi, with de Luna as an adopted Christian alternative. De Luna suggests a connection to Alvara de Luna, the controversial favourite of King John II, father of Queen Isabella. If so, this choice was a mixed blessing, associating them with a man who was a duke, Constable of Castile and Grand Master of the Order of Santiago, but who fell from favour and was executed, and who was demonstrably Catholic. Regardless of their descent, the de Luna family was established in Aragon when harsh laws were introduced to impoverish and restrict their lives in personal, cultural and business spheres. Forced into ghettos, they were forbidden from practising law or medicine or trading in certain substances, holding public office or hiring Catholic workers. Their appearance, including clothing, hair and facial hair was controlled, as were their personal relationships, with huge fines levied for those who broke the rules, and others who assisted them. The introduction of the Spanish Inquisition brought another level of persecution, where Jews, and even Conversos, were tortured and executed as heretics. It was under this climate that the de Luna family initially conceded to the authorities and converted, but after the Edict of 1492, they fled to Portugal. When that country followed suit, in 1497, they remained, with little choice but to conform to the new laws. It was there that Beatriz was born in 1510.

Little is known about Beatriz's Portuguese childhood, other than that she had one sister and a brother Samuel, who were likely to have been baptised in order to conform. In 1528, Beatriz married a wealthy Christian merchant from Lisbon, Francisco Mendes, who perhaps also bore the surname, Benveniste. The ceremony took place in Lisbon Cathedral, according to Catholic rites, although they also signed a Jewish contract. Her younger sister Brianda later married Francisco's brother Diogo. Some sources suggest that Francisco was Beatriz's uncle,[1] but this is not certain. The brothers were dealers in black pepper (probably imported from China or Madagascar), spices and silver, and owned banks and trading outlets across Europe. Beatriz bore one daughter, Ana, before her husband died in 1538, dividing his business between her and her brother.

Although she had lost Francisco, this new status as a woman in trade afforded Beatriz considerable status and freedom. It must have also taken a degree of bravery for her to leave Lisbon and relocate to Antwerp, which was the hub of the spice trade, to join Diogo and help run things there. Her decision may have also been prompted by the introduction of the Portuguese Inquisition. Within a few years she had proved herself a success, increasing their wealth, and also acting independently within the market and as a cultural influence. The family controlled the market with consignments between 600,000 and 12,000,000 ducats annually.[2] Using her influence, Beatriz established a network across Europe to assist Jews escaping from Spain and Portugal. With her help, hundreds fled on the Lisbon-Antwerp spice ships, across the Alps to Venice, and then by ship to the Ottoman Empire, where Jews were tolerated.

However, such wealth and success attracted hostility. In December 1540, Emperor Charles V, who was also King of Spain, ordered investigations into all the activities of Jews in Antwerp.[3] Posthumous charges of crypto-Judaism were brought against Francisco in an attempt by the local authorities to claim some of Beatriz's wealth. She was only able to escape after the payment of a considerable bribe to the emperor. Next, her rivals tried to access her finances by paying suit to her daughter Ana. These issues convinced her to relocate again, escaping to Venice in 1544, which angered the emperor, who placed an embargo on all her goods and properties left behind.[4] In Venice, the Jews were crowded into ghettos, but Beatriz and her family took a house on the Grand Canal, suggesting they were worshipping in private and outwardly presenting as Catholics. While the Venetians were usually tolerant, the family drew attention to themselves when conflict arose between Beatriz and Brianda over control of the business. As foreigners, their case was brought before the court, which ordered Beatriz to hand over half her fortune into the care of the Venetian authorities until her niece came of age. Instead, Beatriz moved to Ferrara, arriving in 1549 to a warm welcome by the Duke of Este, who was appreciative of the family's talents and assets. The move also brought personal freedom. For the first time, Beatriz was able to practise her faith openly and here, she put aside her Christian name and became known as Gracia Mendes Nasi. She settled into the intellectual community of exiled Jews from Spain and Portugal, and four years later, a translation of the *Ferrara Bible*, intended for Jewish use, was dedicated to her. Her role in repatriating Jewish refugees was described the same year in Samuel Usque's Portuguese book, *Consolation for the Tribulations of Israel*.[5]

Beatriz would not remain in Ferrara forever. She would return briefly to Venice and later achieve significant influence in Constantinople, continuing her fight for Jewish rights. In 1556, she organised a trade embargo against Papal ports in response to the execution of Conversos, and continued to build synagogues in the city.[6] She died in Constantinople in 1569, where she had come to be known as La Senora. Her name survives today for many reasons: her extraordinary business acumen and success; her resistance to attempts to claim her wealth; her agency in the world as an independent woman; her patience when forced to conceal her faith; her literary impact; but most of all, for her lifelong fight to protect her fellow Jews.

53

Alice Arden

14 February 1551
Canterbury, Kent, England

By the middle of the sixteenth century, the market town of Faversham in East Kent was thriving. Just 10 miles from the cathedral city of Canterbury and 40 miles from London, it was set on a winding creek that led out to the River Swale, enabling it to become an important seaport. Much of this fish and sea produce ended up at the thrice-weekly markets, which had been confirmed by Henry VIII in a charter of 1546, along with two annual fairs, in February and August. Faversham's wealth was also indicated by the fact that in 1549, it began to be paved, and it frequently entertained royal visitors.[1] The town had formerly been the site of an important abbey, founded by King Stephen in the twelfth century, which had been a major landowner and source of employment and comfort for local people. However, it had been dissolved in 1538, with Stephen and his family's bones reputedly thrown into the creek, and after the buildings were dismantled, the largest stones were shipped out to help fortify Calais. The land on which the monastery had stood, with some surviving structures, was given to the town mayor, Thomas Arden.

By this point, Thomas Arden was doing well. In his early forties, he was a self-made man who lived in a large, stone and timber-framed house on the corner of Abbey Street and Abbey Place, which was formerly the guest house of the abbey itself. It still stands today as a private residence, down the street from the market square. Thomas was also appointed the king's controller of imports and exports, and had his own coat of arms featuring an ermine with a chequered band across the middle, and the colours gold and azure.[2] He was married to a younger woman named Alice, née Brigantine, born in 1516, about whom little else is known prior to her wedding. They had one daughter, Margaret, born around 1538. Alice was reputed to be tall and good-looking.[3] Later, she began an affair with a local tailor called Richard Moseby, who was then in the service of Baron North and had a shop in London. Despite his commercial success, Arden frequently ridiculed Moseby for being in trade, although this may have been a response to his wife's affair, which was conducted in the Arden house with little secrecy. Something prompted Arden to make his will in December 1550. It may have been this which led Alice, tired of her husband, to plan his murder with the assistance of her lover and two other men, Black Will and Shakebag.

Alice's actions, and subsequent events, are known to us today through several sources, published in the aftermath of her death. First was Holinshed's *Chronicle* of 1577; and second, an anonymous play, entered into the Stationer's Register on 3 April 1592, sometimes attributed to Thomas Kyd, sometimes to Shakespeare or others, as well as broadsheet ballads. Also, the *Newgate Calendar* featured her tale among an improving collection of true crime stories from the eighteenth century. Most famous of all retellings, though, is the 1592 *The Tragedie of Arden of Feversham* [sic] *and Blackwall* that transformed the murder into popular culture, albeit with dramatic embellishments, but broadly following the narrative of events to which Holinshed's *Chronicle* dedicated five whole pages and a broadsheet ballad issued in the 1590s. In the play, Moseby's name is spelled Mosbie. From the start, when Arden is grieved by his wife's infidelity, her exchange of notes with Mosbie and her gift to him of her wedding ring, blame is rooted firmly in gender: 'it is not strange that women will be false and wavering.'[4]

It is fair to assume that the details of the killing, as outlined in the play, were taken from public knowledge, spread after Alice's trial. She resolved to murder her husband because of her lover's jealousy of her marital state, and mixed poison with his broth. However, the bitter taste put Arden off and he only ate a couple of spoonfuls, which were insufficient to kill him. When that failed, Alice's friends lay in wait for him in London and Rainham, with little success, as he evaded them again. Eventually, the hapless husband was stabbed whilst playing cards in his own home by Mosbie, Black Will, other servants and Alice herself. His body was hidden in the closet in the parlour, then dragged down the garden and placed outside the back gate, as if he had been attacked in the street on his way home. Alice alerted the town to his disappearance the following morning, but after he was discovered, bloodstains were found in the house and rushes from the parlour on the soles of his shoes. Thick snow had fallen a few days before, and the tracks through the garden were considered suspicious, as was the fact that Arden was dressed in his nightgown. Alice was charged with murder and she confessed, and her co-conspirators were arrested. After a brief trial, she was condemned to death and burned at the stake in Canterbury on 14 February 1551.

Subsequent literature continued to present the episode as an example of the vices of women. A 1592 pamphlet was entitled *The lamentable and true Tragedie of M. Arden of Feversham in Kent. Who was most wickedlye murdered, by the meanes of his disloyall and wanton wyfe, who for the love she bare to one Mosbie, hyred two desperat ruffins, Blackwill and Shakbag, to kill him. Wherin is shewed the great mallice and discimulation of a wicked woman, the unsatiable desire of filthie lust and the shamefull end of all murderers*. Another, published in 1693, attempted to present the event for the first time from Alice's point of view. However, its title *The complaint and lamentation of Mistresse Arden of Feversham in Kent, who for the loue of one Mosbie, hired certaine Ruffians and Villaines most cruelly to murder her Husband; with the fatall end of her and her Associates*[5] reveals that it merely uses Alice as a mouthpiece to confirm patriarchal judgements about her wickedness. The poem takes the form of a confession and repentance:

> Ay me, vile wretch, that ever I was borne,
> Making my selfe unto the world a scorne
> And to my friends and kindred all a shame
> Blotting their blood by my unhappy name.[6]

The narrative is concluded by another voice, who offers the grisly comment that 'his wife at Canterbury she was burnt, and all her flesh and blood to ashes turned.'[7]

For all the literary records of the death of Thomas Arden, Alice's actual voice is never heard. Her character and feelings are reimagined by men, after her death, in order to reassert the horror of her crime, The Tudors had a particular horror of the murder of a husband by a wife, designating it 'petty treason', as a man ruled over his spouse like a king ruled a country, and expected absolute loyalty. Alice's perspective and true motives are lost to history. We cannot truly know the full circumstances that drove her to such an extraordinary act, and she remains a significant historical figure for having committed the most notorious murder of the century. And the fact that she was a woman.

54

Anne Seymour, Duchess of Somerset

June 1552

Tower of London, England

The dinner hour was approaching. Anne was used to the routine now. This was her second stay in the Tower and she had no idea whether she was charged with any crime, or if she would be released, or even follow her late husband to the block. Under these circumstances it was difficult for the 42-year-old mother of nine to summon any appetite, but she was grateful to be provided for, and she needed to keep up her strength.

By June 1552, Anne Seymour had been in the Tower of London for eight months. Her husband of almost twenty years, Edward, who had been Lord Protector, and uncle to the young king, had been executed on charges of treason back in January. His rival, John Dudley, now Duke of Northumberland, had stepped into his shoes as Protector, but there was still no sign that Anne would be released. A surviving manuscript in the Lansdowne collection contains the daily allowance made for Anne's upkeep during her incarceration. Although she was a prisoner, she was still afforded a considerable diet, as befitted her position. It was a wholesome enough fare, typical of the times, although it contained little variety.

Details for Anne's breakfast are not listed, although this was typically a light meal consisting of bread and beer, so it is likely to have been covered by the daily allowance of those items. Having risen early, Anne would have prayed and then broken her fast with the dawn. She would have to wait for her first main meal of the day, dinner, until around ten or eleven in the morning. Her allowance consisted of mutton stewed with pottage, boiled beef, one leg of boiled mutton, roast veal, one roast capon, two coneys, bread, beer and wine. As expected, her diet was heavily comprised of meat, with few vegetables, although a few might be contained in the pottage, or stew. There was no fruit, or sweet dish, or treats.[1] This was probably more a guideline than exact requirements, and Anne may not have received all of these in one sitting, and her ladies may have shared them, or been expected to eat her leftovers. The custom was to have a range of dishes and eat a little from each.

This was not the lifestyle Anne was used to. Her incarceration was a humbling experience for a woman who had been her father's wealthy heiress since infancy, risen to the ranks of Lord Protector's wife and believed herself to take precedence over a former queen. Her peers considered her to be proud, quarrelsome and unpopular, with Antonio de Guaras, a Spanish merchant in London, calling her 'more presumptuous than Lucifer'.[2] Historian John Strype records that Anne took offence at an innocent comment made by the wife of Sir John Cheke, tutor to Edward VI, and that the duchess behaved in a very 'imperious' manner.[3]

Descended from Edward III, Anne had been born Anne Stanhope in 1510 and probably came to court as a maid of honour to Catherine of Aragon. Her mother's remarriage to Richard Paget, Privy Councillor to Henry VIII and vice chamberlain to Henry Fitzroy, would have strengthened her connections. At that point, her husband Edward was still married to his first wife, Catherine Fillol, but after it was discovered that she had been having an affair with Seymour's father, the former Lady Seymour was divorced and sent to a nunnery. Edward and Anne were married at some point before 9 March 1535. Their first child, Jane, was born on the same day as Edward VI, but she did not survive. Other children later arrived, nine of whom survived to adulthood.

Anne was a reformist. She maintained good relations with Henry VIII's final wife, Catherine Parr, when she was queen and was reputed to be part of her religious circle and friends with Anne Askew. When Askew was condemned, Anne reputedly sent a man in a blue coat with £10 to help her, perhaps to pay for the gunpowder about her body that mercifully hastened her death.[4] However, the dynamic at court changed after the death of Henry VIII in January 1547, when Catherine married Thomas Seymour. Anne was reputedly furious at the breach of etiquette. She believed Catherine had forfeited her rights of precedence, refusing to carry her train, and physically jostling with her in processions to enter and exit before her. Within a short time, fortunes had changed again; both Catherine and Thomas were dead and Anne's own hold on power was to be short-lived.

Just six months after Edward had sent Thomas to the block, unrest bubbled up again across England. The most famous uprising was led by Thomas Kett in Norwich against the enclosure of common land, and was brutally suppressed. Although these events were prompted by agricultural failures, ruined crops and rising prices, they were blamed on the failings of Protector Seymour, who had steadily been alienating his peers. The council moved against him, under charges of 'ambition, vainglory, entering into rash wars... negligent looking on Newhaven, enriching himself of the king's treasure, following his own opinion, and doing all by his own authority, etc'.[5] On 11 October 1549, Edward Seymour was arrested and sent to the Tower, leaving in Anne in limbo. In an attempt to reconcile with Dudley, the new leader of the council, she approached Dudley's wife and arranged a marriage between her daughter, also named Anne Seymour, and her enemy's son, John Dudley. Edward was released early in 1550 and even allowed to return to sit on the council. The Seymours breathed a momentary sigh of relief, believing they had survived the coup, but this was only a temporary reprieve. In October 1551, Edward was rearrested on charges of treason, accused of plotting against Dudley. This time, Anne was incarcerated too, helpless as the axe fell, making her a widow. She was kept company by her mother, two other gentlewomen and a manservant.

At four or five each afternoon, Anne would have heard footsteps outside her room again and the key turn in the lock. Supper was brought in by servants and set upon the table. There was more of the same fare she had been offered at dinner: mutton and pottage, roast mutton, sliced beef, two coneys, larks or other small birds one dozen, bread, beer and wine. In addition, the Lieutenant of the Tower was 'responsible for finding the Duchess all napery [table linen], plate, pewter vessels, spices, roasting of her meat, butter to baste meat, with vinegar, mustard, various, onions, salad etc.'[6] However, these items came at the Lieutenant's discretion, so were not guaranteed. Anne's diet cost 77s per week, with an additional 20s paid for wood, coals and candles. Meals, prayers and letter writing punctuated her days, spent in wondering whether she would ever be released.

Anne was finally granted her freedom on 30 May 1553, in the final days of Edward VI's reign. Mary Tudor returned to her a number of Seymour's former properties, including Hanworth, to which she retired. Later she married her husband's former steward, Francis Newdigate, and died in 1587. Anne was not popular among her peers, for the sake of her vanity and ambition, but her experiences of 1549–1553 must have been deeply humbling. Once again, the wheel of fortune turned swiftly, and irretrievably, leaving her brief position of power just a memory.

55

Jane Grey

10 July 1553

Tower of London, England

In an inner chamber of the Tower, a 16-year-old girl paused. Caught her breath. They were coming. The clatter of feet on stone and the hushed urgency of their voices confirmed it: this really was happening. She had lived quietly at Bradgate, Chelsea and Sudeley, studied her lessons, turned her mind to God. Yet now it seemed she must accept the crown. She must become Queen Jane.

On 6 July 1553, Edward IV had died after a lingering illness that left him in agony for those final summer weeks. He was 15. Once, there had been talk of a marriage between him and his cousin Jane, given their closeness in age, but his deteriorating condition put an end to those hopes. They'd been friends, too, and it was hard to hear of his decline, he of whom they had all expected so much from. But he had grown ill, weakened, and the handwriting in his letters to her was shaky, almost unrecognisable. There had been much discussion behind closed doors and visitors to the house.

Two weeks before Edward's death, she had been married, much against her wishes, but her protests counted for nothing. Her husband was Guildford Dudley, son of the second Protector, John Dudley, Duke of Northumberland. It was the duke who was now urging her to become queen, as Edward's death left the fragile new religious changes exposed to reversal and counter-reformation. In recent years, the Catholic paintings and texts on church walls had been whitewashed over; the statues destroyed, shrines dismantled, monasteries dissolved and the Bible translated into English. A new, simpler, reformed religion had been allowed to spread. Disgruntled Catholics looked to Henry VIII's eldest daughter Mary, hoping she would champion their cause. But Mary was miles away in the depths of Suffolk, and laws were made in London.

There was little time for Jane to mourn her cousin, with everything moving so quickly. On 6 July, she had heard the news at Syon House, but her father had quickly conveyed her downriver to the security of the Tower, where she was greeted by solemn-faced members of the council. Although she could scarcely believe it, they removed their caps and knelt before her, presented her with the crown and explained it was her cousin's dying wish. St Edmund's crown, placed upon the head of kings for 300 years, with the weight of history and the authority of God. Its gold wirework and little bells caught the light. 'Long live Queen Jane,' they chorused. 'Long live Queen Jane.' And yet she could not help thinking of her cousin Mary, more than twice her age, who had patiently waited her turn for years. It was her duty to her faith, they told Jane. Only she could prevent the country from falling back into the old ways.

Jane Grey never set out to go to war against her cousin, or steal Mary's birthright or her place in the succession. That was an unfortunate consequence of the belief that she was acting in the interests of religious reform. As the granddaughter of Henry VIII's younger sister Mary Brandon, Duchess of Suffolk, Jane had been raised as minor royalty, certainly not in the expectation of a crown. However, her main advantage in the eyes of the council was that she was a devout and committed Protestant. In the summer of 1553, the reformists feared their cause would be derailed, and in the eyes of the law, both Mary and Elizabeth had previously been declared illegitimate. The council saw Jane as a figure of continuity for the new faith, which they hoped Mary would not contest, but they underestimated the eldest daughter of Henry VIII. It was the ambition of men, which placed these queen-cousins in opposition, who were otherwise inclined to be merciful, even amicable, towards each other.

On 9 July, urged on by her parents, Jane accepted the crown with reluctance. The following day, she was proclaimed queen in the streets of London. Her future had been dramatically altered beyond her wildest expectations and, despite her youth, Jane was educated and intelligent enough to understand this was something more than mere power play. Her religious and political significance is often stated, but her position as England's first female monarch is often overlooked, due to the brevity of her reign. It is remarkable that the council elevated her to queenship, indicative of a mind shift in gender expectations brought about by a lack of choice. The Tudor dynasty simply had no mature male heirs. Therefore, they had no choice but to turn to a woman.

It was Tudor gender expectations that created the first dilemma of Jane's reign. When the crown was conveyed to Jane's apartments from the jewel house for her to try on, councillor William Paulet suggested she 'could take it without fear and that another also should be made, to crown (her) husband.'[1] Jane had not expected this, and immediately replied that Guildford was not automatically to become king. The royal bloodline was hers, not his. Their marriage had been made to secure Northumberland's position, to create a stronger alliance at the top, but Jane had clear ideas about the power balance between her and her new husband. She informed Guildford that if he was to become king, it would only be by an act of Parliament; in the interim, she offered him the Duchy of Clarence.

Yet the tide had already turned. Outside the walls of the Tower, popular support was rising in favour of Mary, who was rumoured to be marching to London to claim the throne. Bishop Ridley was shouted down when he attempted to preach about her illegitimacy. Northumberland rode out to Suffolk in an attempt to intercept her, and in his absence from the capital, his support base collapsed. On 20 July, barely ten days after they had offered the crown to Jane, the council declared in Mary's favour. Her rule was then pronounced from St Paul's Cross.

Their motivation appears to have been the straightforward belief in Mary's right of succession over that of Jane, but also the conviction that Northumberland had acted out of self-interest. No doubt there was an element of self-preservation.

The worst was still to come. As soon as Jane's father, Suffolk, heard of the council's defection, he too declared in favour of Queen Mary. Then he entered his daughter's chamber while she was at dinner, sitting under a canopy of state, and dramatically tore the hangings down around her. Jane went from queen to prisoner, removed from the royal apartments to the Gentlemen Gaoler's lodgings. It must have been difficult for her to avoid the angry conclusion that she had been betrayed by her father, that he had made her the instrument of his ambition, only to turn on her with the tide. After all, she had overcome her own doubts to carry out his wishes. Her mother and ladies-in-waiting were permitted to return home, which they did at once, but Suffolk found himself confined under lock and key.

At the age of 16, Jane's contribution to the Tudor dynasty was cut short before it had the opportunity to flourish. Undoubtedly, she was an intelligent, devout and astute girl for her years, proud and conscious of her duty, and could have made a model Tudor queen. Had she been allowed to reign, she could have steered the country through the continuity reform, and created a family with Guildford, including sons who would have reigned after her. The Tudor dynasty might even have lasted much longer than its remaining fifty years.

It would be wrong to dismiss Jane Grey as merely the pawn of ambitious men. Although her value for them lay primarily in her birth, personal ambition was not the only motivation of those members of Edward's council who sought to preserve his legacy. Jane was selected because of her Protestant sympathies, a cause which she felt deeply, and considered a question not just of life and death, but of the afterlife and the salvation of souls. As such, she overcame her initial scruples about the succession, in the belief that it was necessary for the good of her country. She placed duty and faith above personal inclination, troubled by the expectation that Edward's reforms would be undone and committed reformers would suffer, a fear that proved to be justified in Mary's later reign. Briefly, Jane was a figurehead of hope, a Tudor queen in the making, driven by an ideology that ultimately was not strong enough to counter the laws of succession. Her contribution was that she responded to the call, when it summoned her, and sacrificed her person, her freedom and her life for the sake of her beliefs. Her inclusion in John Foxe's polemic *The Book of Martyrs* reflects her position in the history of the reformed faith. Her nominal reign, of nine days, also exposes the nature of Tudor society, inheritance and government. As a girl of 16, her life exposes the dangers of being born with royal blood, especially at a time of crisis. Her nomination to the throne shows, though, that the Tudors were finally prepared to accept a queen regnant, and like her cousin Elizabeth, she was unwilling to share that right with a man.

56

Mary I

27 September 1553
Streets of London, England

Hers had been a life of two halves. First, the eleven or twelve years as the cherished princess, the only surviving daughter of Henry VIII and Catherine of Aragon, dressed in cloths of gold and silver, playing the clavichord for ambassadors. Then there had been the two decades as an outcast, separated from her mother, forced to serve her new half-sister, denied access to court. Mary Tudor's secure future had been destroyed by her father's infatuation with Anne Boleyn. His later wives had tried to be kind, but the ordeal had quite destroyed her fragile health; headaches, toothaches and the pains of womanhood added to her sorrows, and the religious reforms pushed through under her brother's reign attempted to limit her Catholic practices. Even the comfort of her mother's religion had been denied to her.

Yet Mary had waited patiently. She'd had little choice but to ride the waves of change. The succession had been discussed so many times, and both she and Elizabeth had been excluded from the line in 1536 and then returned in 1543, behind the younger Edward. Recent events had moved so quickly. The boy had died, and Jane Grey was proclaimed queen, but the news had barely reached Suffolk before it was all over. Mary's approximate 6,000[1] supporters braced themselves inside Framlingham Castle while the politicians gradually deserted the Protector, and waited for Northumberland and an attack that never came. Finally, official confirmation arrived that, at the age of 37, the Catholic, disinherited, bastardised daughter of divorce had been accepted by the council as England's queen regnant. It was unprecedented in terms of the law, and a chance to revoke the religious reforms that had attacked the faith of her mother.

Mary's first act was to order the erection of a crucifix in the chapel at Framlingham. She saw these events as nothing less than a clear mandate from God, as her mission to return England to its former Catholic state and reverse the estrangement with Rome. On 24 July, she disbanded her army and headed for Ipswich, where she was received by the town bailiffs and given gifts of coins and gold hearts.[2] Whilst there, she received a visit from Mary Howard, widow of her half-brother, Henry Fitzroy. As part of the reformist, intelligent circle around Anne Boleyn in the 1530s, the widow had previously insulted Mary in a letter to the council, so she was kept waiting overnight[3] before what must have been an awkward encounter. For Mary, such moments were validation of the long years of fluctuating fortune and the many slights of those who believed they would never see her in power. Mary Howard was never fully welcomed at her namesake's court. She was more fortunate, though, than Jane Dudley, Duchess of Northumberland, who attempted to see Mary on the same occasion and was completely denied.

From Ipswich, Mary proceeded to Colchester over the border into Essex, where she stayed with an old servant of her mother's, Muriel Christmas. At Newhall (formerly Beaulieu) in Essex, she received the dignitaries of London, who pledged allegiance to her as their queen and presented her with a crimson purse containing £500 in half-sovereigns. She also granted an audience to Frances Grey, mother of Jane, who pleaded the case for her daughter, based on their blood ties. Her next stop was Ingatestone Hall, arriving on 31 July, followed by Pingoe, Havering and Wanstead, from where she co-ordinated her entry into the city.[4]

On the evening of 3 August, Mary was ready to claim her capital. The sense of exhilaration must have been palpable, at the very start of a new reign with the opportunities that lay ahead. It must also have been balanced by the tension of being received in a city that had proclaimed the rule of another, just weeks before. By that point, all support for Jane had been quashed but as a woman, a Catholic and a recent exile, Mary brought a complex legacy. Accompanied by her gentlemen in green and white, 700 supporters and 1,000 armed horsemen, she rode triumphantly towards London. With the Tudor eye for symbolic appearances, Mary had chosen a gown of regal purple velvet for when she entered the city at around 7 on the evening. She received the sceptre from the mayor at Aldgate, where streamers had been hung and the length of the street from Leadenhall to the Tower was laid with fresh gravel. The city guilds displayed their banners in prominent support, trumpets sounded and the guns of the Tower were fired. She paused at the gateway of the Tower, to be greeted by its officials and meet with the council.[5] Riding behind her, the 20-year-old Elizabeth witnessed at first hand the welcome given to a woman who had succeeded in her own right, legitimised after being dismissed as a bastard and, while filled with trepidation, might also have taken heart at her own future.

Mary's coronation was planned for 28 September 1553. It was the confirmation of all her hopes and the vindication of her mother's marriage and her own legitimacy. The day before, she followed the custom of riding through the streets of the capital, from the Tower to Westminster, buoyed on a wave of popular support. Dressed in purple velvet furred with powdered ermine, she had her head covered with a cloth of tinsel, set with pearls and gems, topped with a gold circlet, and seated in a gold chariot under a canopy. Courtly and civic dignitaries rode before and after her, draped in colourful finery, with the Mayor of London, Sir Thomas White, freshly knighted by Mary, bearing the gold sceptre. After her, in another chariot made of white cloth of gold, came Princess Elizabeth and Anne of Cleves, drawn by six horses, and then ladies and gentlemen of the court, in red velvet, with their horses decked out to match. Pageants awaited her at Fenchurch Street and Gracechurch Street, made by the city guilds, with angels and trumpets, and the conduits ran with wine. The city waits, a band of musicians, played at Cheap and the cross there had been freshly gilded.[6] By another pageant outside St Paul's, the aldermen greeted her with a speech and purse of gold. Inside the churchyard, an acrobat climbed to the top of the steeple, waving a 5-foot-long streamer and holding a torch that would not burn due to the wind. London had accepted Mary as its queen.[7] The following day, 28 September, she was crowned inside St Paul's Cathedral.

Mary's unchallenged entry to London, followed by her ride through the city to her coronation, were significant milestones in the story of Tudor queenship. As the resolution of years of doubt, they were focused entirely upon a lone queen regnant, rather than a bride or consort, and marked the city's belief in Mary as the rightful successor of Henry VIII. Mary had acted decisively, refusing to accept the usurpation of the line to the throne, and, as a result, her position had attracted support from a wide base, not just the expected Catholics. Contemporary ideas about gender doubted the ability of women to rule justly and intelligently, detached from emotion and vice, as would be expressed in the writings of John Knox, and those who opposed the Spanish marriage she arranged the following year, but for the moment, in September 1553, Mary's future path was clear. It was the most important day of her life so far.

57

Louise Labé

13 March 1555

Lyon, France

In the sixteenth century, the city of Lyon, based slightly to the east of the centre of France, was flourishing with poetry and trade. The first printing press had been set up in 1472, turning out books by Erasmus, Rabelais and More, in a range of different languages. The humanist circle, centred around poet Clement Marot, met to discuss their muses, producing sonnets in the Italian style and celebrating the beauty of the expanding city, with its new cathedral, its silk industry, colleges and hospitals making Lyon simultaneously a centre of arts and industry. Amid this artistic circle, the poets singled out the woman they named the 'tenth muse', the 'daughter of Venus', aligning her with the city's two rivers, the Rhône and the Saône, the 'leading attraction of the city'. Punning on their location, they even named her Louise Labé Lionnoize.

Louise was the daughter of a wealthy ropemaker who rose to a position of authority in his home city. She was born at some point between her parents' marriage in 1516 and her mother's death seven years later. It was a second marriage for her father, Pierre Charly, whose first wife, Guillemette Labé died young and childless. Interestingly, in later life, Louise would elect to use the surname of this young woman, rather than that of her father or mother. Pierre Charly never learned to read, but he ensured his daughter was educated with Louise being schooled in Greek, Latin, Italian and Spanish beside her native French, and studying music, playing the lute. She was also an excellent archer and horse rider, and her friends would describe her as 'la belle Amazone', who reputedly rode in jousts and fought alongside the Dauphin at the Siege of Perpignan. By the terms of her father's will, she married another local ropemaker, Ennemond Perrin, between 1543 and 1545, and they bought a large property in the city in 1551.[1]

By this point, Louise was writing poetry and hosting her own literary salon, giving rise to the effusive praise of her friends and the moral condemnation of her enemies. Suggestions that she took lovers may, or may not, be true, although she was the composer and subject of many love poems. A scandalous poem about the behaviour of La Cordière (the ropemaker), published in Lyon in 1557, appears to have been inspired by her. Louise's reputation was further complicated in sixteenth-century eyes by her habit of dressing as a man, blurring the gender lines, which was seen as an indication of loose standards and a challenge to the patriarchy. She was also likened to Sappho, the ancient Greek poetess, with the associations of lesbianism that usually connotes. Louise's first volume, *Oeuvres*, included a feminist preface encouraging women to write, dedicated to a young aspiring poetess, Clemence de Bourges. It was published by Jean de Tournes, soon to become printer to the king, and, in addition to her own work, it included twenty-four poems by her friends in Louise's honour from the humanist circle, the Sodalitatum Lugdunense. Royal recognition came from King Henri II on 13 March 1555, when he granted Louise the unusual privilege of owning and publishing the exclusive rights to her work for five years. This was unprecedented recognition for a female poet and an acknowledgement of her contribution from the highest power in the land.

Sonnet 24 of *Oeuvres* is representative of Louise's themes of love and passion, loss and grief. In this work, though, she uses her experiences as a warning, an example for her own gender, who might condemn her but should learn from her:

> Do not reproach me, Ladies, if I've loved
> And felt a thousand torches burn my veins,
> A thousand griefs, a thousand biting pains
> And all my days to bitter tears dissolved.
>
> Thus, Ladies, do not denigrate my name.
> If I did wrong, the pain and punishment
> Are now. Don't file their daggers to a point.
> You must know, Love is master of the game:
>
> No need of Vulcan to explain your fire,
> Nor of Adonis to excuse your desire,
> But with less cause and far less occasion,
>
> As the whim takes her, idly she can curse
> You with a stronger and stranger passion.
> But take care your suffering is not worse!

Louise's husband died in the mid-1550s, and she bought a country estate outside Lyon, retiring there in 1564 when plague ravaged through the city. It was the end of an era, with many friends succumbing to the disease, and Louise herself suffering from ill health. A year after making her will in 1565, she died, probably in her mid-forties. Louise was a remarkable woman for the contemporary recognition her poetry brought her, and as a literary figure, but also in the way that she became identified with the spirit of the city in which she lived, as fluid and beautiful as its rivers, vibrant and full of life, and inspiring works of art and admiration in others. She truly was the spirit of Lyon in the mid-sixteenth century.

58

Susan Clarencieux

July 1555

Hampton Court, Surrey, England

Susan watched her mistress. The queen walked about the gardens at Hampton Court slowly, but lightly, too lightly for one supposed to be in her condition. Mary wanted so much to be a mother, to bear her Spanish husband's child, to secure an heir for England. And yet, Susan could not be sure. Each pregnancy was different, but some things about Mary's symptoms and behaviour made her uneasy. The summer months were advancing and she had never once spoken of feeling the child kick or turn. There had been no quickening. The shape of her belly was not quite right either, more in line with a swelling than a child. Not that she would ever dare voice this to the queen herself; despite their long-standing friendship, she could not be the one to break her heart. No, when Susan spoke of her doubts, she did so to Philip of Spain, in his wife's absence.

Susan was a little older than her mistress. She was born in 1510, right at the start of Henry VIII's reign, although some sources list her arrival as late as 1514. It is likely she was just old enough to remember the celebrations upon the safe arrival of the princess in 1516. Susan was one of the three children of Richard White and Maud Tyrrell, of Hutton in Brentwood, Essex. Through her father William, Maud may, potentially, have been the granddaughter of James Tyrell of Gipping in Suffolk, a close ally of Richard III, who later confessed to the murder of the Princes in the Tower, and was executed in 1502. If so, Susan's line was tainted with treason on two counts, as James' father also went to the block for his involvement in a plot against Edward IV.

Growing up in Hutton, Susan would have been familiar with the medieval All Saints' Church, set a little apart from the village, walking to worship in its fourteenth-century chancel, nave and aisles, and known its timber bell turret. A brass on the west wall of the south chapel depicts an unnamed local family, a knight and lady with their eight sons and eight daughters, and although it was erected in 1525 after Susan had left, there is no doubt she would have known this other prominent local family. It has been reported that the Whites were likely to have been born at Hutton Hall, the medieval moated house owned until the Reformation by Battle Abbey, but this did not pass into their hands until the 1570s. Perhaps the occupiers during her lifetime were the large family of the memorial.

The connection that brought the young Susan to court is unknown. By 1525, she had joined the household of Princess Mary, perhaps recruited due to her age, and when Mary was established as Princess of Wales in Ludlow Castle, Susan went with her to the chilly town on the Welsh border where her uncle Arthur had died. For seven years, Susan was part of Mary's household, seeing her undergo the trauma of her parents' separation, her father's remarriage and Mary's subsequent loss of status. Mary's ladies were disbanded when she was recalled to join the household of her new half-sister, Elizabeth. For the first time since her teens, Susan had to find her own way.

On 2 June 1534, Susan White married Thomas Tonge, a Clarencieux King of Arms and officer at the College of Arms in London. Yet the union was short-lived. Thomas died in 1536, but Susan retained the name of his role as her surname all his life, being known as Clarencieux, not Tonge, afterwards. In 1536, after the fall of Anne Boleyn, Mary was allowed to re-establish her household and requested that Susan return to her. From that point, Susan remained at Mary's side, until the princess's succession in 1553, when she appointed her old friend Mistress of the Robes. She was also granted the Essex manors of Loverdown, Thundersley and Thamberley Hall, a sum that was added to in 1555, so that she was in receipt of around £200 in annual rents alone.[1]

When Mary was keen to marry Philip of Spain, against the wishes of most of her council, Susan supported her mistress and spoke in his favour. In the spring of 1554, she met several times with the Spanish ambassador, Diego de Mendoza, in the house of a London alderman, which may have been her relative Humphrey White, and carried a letter in Latin back to Mary. The 'letter spoke of and advocated the Spanish match.'[2] When Philip came to England in July 1554, Susan attended the wedding and was included in 'a list of persons to be rewarded.' When Mary believed herself to be pregnant that autumn, Susan reassured that she was with child. At 38, she was old for a first-time mother in Tudor terms, when some of her contemporaries were already grandparents.

The suspected pregnancy was confirmed in October. Ruy Gomez de Silva wrote 'the Queen is with child. May it please God to grant her the issue that is so sorely needed to set affairs here to rights and make everything smooth' and 'this pregnancy will put a stop to every difficulty.'[3] Late in November, Mary was observed in her presence chamber at Whitehall, where she 'sat highest, richly apparelled, and her belly laid out, that all men might see that she was with child.'[4] She believed that she felt the child move on the last day of the month, suggesting she had conceived in the weeks following the wedding. In January, Parliament passed an act making Philip regent in the event of Mary's death in childbirth, and for the provision of education for any such children. However, for some reason, Philip was not entirely convinced that his wife had conceived, according to letters he wrote to his brother, but he still signed the circulars that had been produced in advance to spread the news.

The following April, which must have been approaching the time the queen expected to deliver, the bells of St Paul's were rung and a day of public celebration announced. She had prepared a suite of rooms at Hampton Court, where she retired in anticipation of the arrival. Susan waited with her, but she had her doubts and expressed them to the French ambassador.[5] Weeks later, Mary was observed in the garden, 'stepping' so well that her delivery date was rapidly revised. May and June passed and then her swollen abdomen began to go down, probably as the result of an infection or pseudocyesis: a phantom pregnancy.

By June, no child had appeared. Simon Renard wrote 'they say that the calculations got mixed up ... All this makes me doubt whether she is with child at all, greatly as I desire to see the thing happily over.' Even the brutally honest Ruy Gomez was fooled, thinking Mary 'seems to be in as good health as could be desired, so much so that one cannot doubt that she is with child', however by the end of July, Gomez 'doubted whether she is really with child, although outward signs are good and she asserts that she is pregnant'.[6] Within the gilded cage of Hampton Court, Mary had to come to terms with the fact that she had been mistaken and quietly left the palace. Susan was at her side, witnessing the painful journey and consoling her mistress as best she could. To compound her pain, Philip left England.

Abroad, the news took a while to spread. On 13 August, Philip Nigri, Chancellor of the Order of the Golden Fleece, wrote: 'we still have hopes that a child will be born to England by the end of this month'. But after Philip's arrival in the Netherlands, the emperor confessed in a letter dated 14 September: 'There is no longer any hope of her being with child.'[7] Mary underwent a second phantom pregnancy in 1557, after her husband's brief return, but this time there were no announcements or arrangements, and upon realisation of the mistake, Philip departed again. It would be the last time he set foot in England. Mary died in November 1558. Very soon afterwards, Susan Clarencieux left England for Spain with Jane Dormer, an English lady-in-waiting who married the Duke of Feria. No record exists for her after 1564. Her role at Mary's side had been one of close companion since their childhood and the queen's bitter disappointment and early death, apart from the husband she adored, must have been difficult to witness. Biographer Linda Porter's assessment of Susan is that 'her judgement was not always good' and raised her hopes; she was 'an overprotective servant rather than a trustworthy and objective advisor.'[8] However, this is indicative of the love and care she demonstrated towards Mary, of which the neglected queen was much in need.

59

Sofonisba Anguissola

1555

Cremona, Lombardy, Italy

The three sisters are seated around a chess board which has been set up under a tree overlooking a blue-grey view of a lake and town. On the left is Lucia, the eldest, in salmon-pink and grey, depicted in the act of capturing one of her opponent's pieces. One hand hovers on the board, the other rests at the side encircling another piece, and her eyes look towards the viewer. She appears to be in her early teens. Opposite her is the younger Minerva, perhaps 10 or 12, staring intently at her sister, one hand in its golden sleeve raised in protest. Between them, watching rather than participating in the game, is the youngest child Europa, directly in front of a tree trunk. She stands closer to Lucia with one hand resting on the carpeted table, and a cheeky smile directed towards Minerva. An older woman, a nanny or maid, in black and white, looks on from the side. The work is remarkable for the delicate colouring and the life and emotions on the girls' faces. Missing from the portrait, known as *The Chess Game*, is its 23-year-old artist, their elder sister Sofonisba.

Sofonisba Anguissola was born into a noble family in Cremona in 1532. She was one of seven children, of whom six were girls, and all studied art, writing or music. Her father, Amilcare, was inspired by the writing of Castiglione, in which he wrote that children should be pushed to cultivate and perfect their talents. In keeping with this idea, at the age of 14, Sofonisba was sent to study with local artist Bernardino Campi and, later, with Bernardino Gatti, who had worked with Correggio. She was the first woman locally, and more widely, to be apprenticed in this way, at a time when marriage was still the most desirable option and the pursuit of a practical career was dismissed as vulgar and lower class. Yet her talent and dedication set a precedent for other female artists and when Sofonisba was 18, she produced a double portrait of the artist composing a picture of herself. In 1554, she travelled to Rome and received tutoring and encouragement from Michelangelo. He set her the task of drawing a laughing child, to which she responded by sketching a crying one, saying it was more of a challenge. This impressed him so much that he offered her informal tuition. It was during this time, in 1555, that she completed *The Chess Game*.

A definitive early work by an emerging talent, *The Chess Game* features a delicate palette of green, grey, salmon-pink, gold and black. It shows the women as accomplished and strategic with a natural nobility, able to master what was considered to be an intellectual, chivalric game. Their clothing, with its gold embroidery, pearls and other adornments, speaks of their status, as does the Turkey carpet on the table. The landscape behind them, with its hills, bay and patches of light, is idealised, only suggested, as if it is mythical or aspirational. It is intense, energetic and alive, whilst also being subtle. The girls' game, at the moment of one sister triumphing over another, draws the viewer in. There is no concession made to Minerva's youth; it is a question of skill and strategy, at which the best player wins. The biographer Vasari saw this work hanging on the wall of Sofonisba's home in 1566, describing it as 'rare and very beautiful'. This is a female artist reclaiming the traditional tropes of the southern Renaissance and depicting them from within the feminine experience, rather than as an observer. The previous year, Sofonisba had painted a self-portrait and signed her name as 'Virgo', an unmarried young woman, independent of a man. It was a bold statement for a female artist of the era. The inscription on *The Chess Game* echoes this: 'By the maiden Sophonisba Anguissola, daughter of Amilcare, painted from the true effigies of three of her sisters and of her maid servant.'

Sofonisba travelled to Milan in 1558 and Spain in 1559, where she was tutor to Queen Elisabeth, herself a keen artist. Her work inspired Van Dyke, Rubens, Caravaggio and later female artists, Lavinia Fontana and Artemisia Gentileschi. She married twice, in later life, secure with a pension from Philip II of Spain, dying at the age of 93 in 1625. As one of the most remarkable leading female artists of her day, Sofonisba's work remains fresh and accessible, despite portraying daily life in the sixteenth century. She was one of the first to present her artistic identity as an independent woman.

60

Florence Wadham

1556

St Decuman's Church, Watchet, Somerset, England

She had been fast asleep. Deeply dreaming, perhaps even catatonic, so that the outside world felt very far away. Her limbs were heavy and closed, eyes tight shut. But then there came a scratching at her fingers. A strange kind of tugging and scraping. Someone was trying to steal her rings. Florence was wide awake at once. She sat up. But she was not in the comfortable bedroom she shared with the husband she had married a year earlier, at their home in Kentsford. She was lying in a hard wooden box in the cold church where they worshipped. Standing over her, the sexton's face was a picture of terror. He dropped his lantern and ran. Florence climbed out of her coffin.

Florence Wadham is mostly remembered by history for a single incident in her life: a most remarkable escape from death. Born in 1538, she was the daughter of Sir John Wadham and his wife Joan, who lived at the medieval manor house in Merryfield, Somerset, built by the Wadham family. Her grandfather had accompanied Henry VIII to France in 1520, for the Field of Cloth of Gold and sat on his Reformation Parliament of 1529. Florence had a traditional upbringing and was destined for marriage, as were all girls of her class. At the age of 18, in 1556, she married a local Somersetshire gentleman, Sir John Wyndham. The couple probably lived at Kentsford farmhouse in Watchet, which has had much later architectural work done to it, but inside the rear bedroom remains a plaster ceiling of Tudor roses and thistles, perhaps dating from the Anglo-French marriage of 1503, and therefore familiar to Florence. It might have been the ceiling she lay beneath, and closed her eyes upon, as she slipped into a deep sleep, one night shortly after the ceremony.

When Florence's husband discovered her, cold and motionless, he called for the doctor. No pulse or signs of life could be found and the young wife was pronounced dead from unknown causes. She was carried from the house to the nearby church, high on the hill overlooking the seaside town of Watchet, and placed in a wooden coffin, overseen by the local sexton, or verger.[1] No process of embalming or preservation had yet been undertaken. Florence's body lay waiting for burial in the Wyndham chapel, in the north-east portion of the church. The sexton was charged to prepare the family vault for her imminent interment. Had it not been for his own personal greed, Florence is likely to have been buried alive, perhaps never waking, or coming round only to die inside the tomb.

Having previously noted the rings adorning Florence's fingers, the sexton returned to the church later that evening. Taking a knife, he prised open the coffin lid and attempted to remove the jewellery from her hand. As one of the rings was too tight, he began trying to slice off the woman's finger instead. The pain jolted Florence out of her stupor, groaning at the unexpected injury and sitting up, to the horror of the sexton, who fled. In his haste, he abandoned his lantern, which lit the church, allowing the confused woman to work out what must have happened. By its shaky light, she found her way home from the church, to the great surprise of her husband. It must have been terrifying and confusing for Florence.

Florence and John enjoyed forty years of marriage. Their only son, named John after his father, was conceived in the months following their reunion and born in 1558. A late eighteenth-century version of the story claims that the incident took place later, in 1562, after Florence had borne her son. Little more is known about her life. She was widowed in 1578 and continued to live in Somerset until her own death in 1596. Her brother Nicholas founded Wadham College, Oxford. Had she not undergone such a strange experience, no doubt her name would be lost to history.

Over the years, the story of the Somerset woman awakening from the dead has become embellished and evolved into legend. Exactly what happened to Florence, and whether she did experience such a narrow escape, is difficult now to prove. However, if the details are accurate, her ability to cheat death was little short of a miracle, tapping into the fragility of contemporary life and fears about the afterlife. No wonder her story continues to be retold into the present.

61

Marian Martyrs

10 November[1] 1558

Wincheap, Canterbury, Kent, England

The land was slightly raised at this point. They could see the outer wall of the city of Canterbury, which encircled the old donjon, the square castle and further off, the twin spires of the cathedral. But there was no help to be anticipated from that quarter, especially since the late archbishop, Thomas Cranmer, had met with the same fiery fate the martyrs now anticipated. They had been brought out beyond the walls, past the inns and scattered houses, past the wine market, the win chepe, to the pyre that had become notorious in the last three years. A crowd was gathering about the grassy space, drawn by mixed emotions, preparing to witness the barbaric justice imposed by the Catholic Queen Mary I. Yet times were on the verge of change. It was already public knowledge that she was ill, and her death was anticipated, but Canterbury's archdeacon, the zealous Nicholas Harpsfield, hurried the process along to ensure the final Protestant martyrs met their end. Recording these events in his *Book of Martyrs*, John Foxe described him as 'the sorest and least compassionate' of all those in his role.[2]

Harpsfield had visited the diocese of Canterbury in early 1557. In an attempt to stamp out heresy, he investigated church attendance in the belief that people were drinking in taverns instead and neglecting to use the re-introduced rosaries. He ordered that people attend services and make regular confession. That April, the London heresy commission[3] began a programme of intense questioning, by which individual beliefs and levels of commitment were explored, which resulted in an escalation of the burnings. Across Kent, those with suspect convictions were weeded out, interrogated and sent to Canterbury gaol. Some had already sickened and died inside its walls whilst waiting for justice. One-third of the prisoners present in 1557 had starved to death.[4]

There were five of them. Three men and two women. Tried collectively, just days earlier, they had been condemned by Archbishop Reginald Pole for their views on the scriptures and their rejection of the worship of images and icons. John Corneford came from Wrotham, a tiny village 40 miles to the west, Christopher Brown from Maidstone and John Herst from nearby Ashford. Katherine Knight, aka Tylney of Thurnham, was described as an 'aged woman', a mother and widow, but Alice Snoth, a maid from Biddenden, was young. She summoned her grandmother and godfather to explain her faith to them, and called upon the spectators to witness that she was a true Christian and 'suffered joyfully for the testimony of Christ's Gospel.'[5] It is possible that Alice was the daughter of the widow Annes Snoth of Smarden, 3 miles north-east of Biddenden, who was burned at the same location on 31 January 1556.

In sight of Canterbury Cathedral, Katherine and Alice were tied to the stake and wood was piled up around them. A single word of repentance would have saved them, but neither were prepared to compromise their beliefs and forego salvation. They died bravely before the crowd. It was a slow, agonising death, sometimes hurried by the inclusion of gunpowder, strapped to the body in bags. They joined the men in praying that their blood would be the last to be shed. They were, indeed, the last of the Marian martyrs.

Mary herself died a week later. Archbishop Pole had predeceased her by mere hours. A total of forty-one people were burned in Canterbury during Mary's reign, one in seven of all those martyred across the country for their beliefs.[6] In 1899, a memorial was erected in Martyrs' Field Road, Wincheap, bearing the names of those who had died there. Along with Katherine and Alice, a significant number of women lost their lives at the site, some identified by name, some known only as the wife or widow of a named man, like Mistress Wilson, Benson's wife and Bradbridge's widow, who were burned there in June 1557. The act of burning was barbaric, exacerbated by its public dimension, but gender politics of the age particularly condemned women who broke the rules. Nor were such instances confined to the reign of Mary, although the 1550s did see a greater concentration of numbers. There were many more Katherines and Alices who suffered and died publicly due to the religious changes that formed a backdrop to their lives, called to martyrdom by a regime too inflexible not to make windows into their souls.

62

Elizabeth Tudor

17 November 1558

Hatfield House, Hertfordshire, England

Tradition places her under a great oak in Hatfield Park on this particular day in the autumn of 1558. A young woman with the red hair characteristic of the Tudors was passing the hours on a country estate, waiting for the moment to arrive: either to elevate her to power or return her to the Tower. For the 25-year-old Elizabeth, pronounced illegitimate at the age of 2, fearful of her sister's displeasure, the world was about to change forever.

The daughter of Anne Boleyn had endured two difficult decades. Following her mother's execution, she had spent her early years watching her fortunes fluctuate under a string of stepmothers, until she found a warmer welcome and a role model in Catherine Parr. Under her calming influence, Elizabeth had studied and translated classical works, as well as Catherine's own religious writings, and lived with her after Henry's death until Thomas Seymour's attentions broke up the family. Elizabeth found her brother Edward a sympathetic ruler in religious terms, and often went to court, but upon the advent of their half-sister Mary, her situation became more precarious. In 1554, rebels led by Thomas Wyatt rose up in protest against Mary's Spanish marriage and rumour suggested Elizabeth was involved, perhaps for religious reasons. She was summoned, interrogated and shut away, while Mary's officials argued over whether she should be put on trial. Spending almost a year in the Tower, she was close to her childhood friend, Robert Dudley, still imprisoned in the wake of Jane Grey's deposition, and they remained close after they were discharged. Elizabeth lived initially under close supervision, while Mary continued to urge her to follow Catholic rites. The princess was deferential but procrastinated when it came to compromising her reformed faith, and lived in constant fear of being rearrested, even executed. Ironically, it was Mary's husband Philip who pleaded for her life. In 1555, she was summoned to be with Mary during her false confinement, because if anything should happen to the queen, Elizabeth would succeed her.

Once it was clear that Mary was not going to bear a child, attention turned to Elizabeth as her heir. She lived at Hatfield House, north of the city in Hertfordshire, virtually under house arrest. The last time she saw Mary was in February 1558, when it was clear her health was beginning to fail, and it was to Hatfield that Philip sent the Duke of Feria to speak with Elizabeth. By October, she was beginning to plan whom she would choose to sit on her council, and in the first week of November, Mary formally acknowledged her sister as her heir. Two days later, her Comptroller and Master of the Rolls hurried to Hatfield to inform Elizabeth of her new status.

It was no great surprise, then, that the messengers came hurrying across the grass on the morning of 17 November. Elizabeth was perhaps sitting, perhaps walking, in the grounds of Hatfield Palace, when she spotted the Earls of Pembroke and Arundel hastening towards her, and must have guessed at their news. If anything, she may have been surprised that it followed so soon after the former announcement. They knelt and proclaimed her queen. She dropped to her knees and thanked God. The years of fear were over. At 25, an unmarried Protestant, Elizabeth was to become England's second queen regnant, succeeding unopposed. At once she summoned her chosen councillors and held her first meeting in the banqueting hall at Hatfield. A week later, on 23 November, she left her childhood home for the Charterhouse, cheered by the public. After five days there, she proceeded to the Tower. The poet John Hayward witnessed her arrival and recorded her words:

> Some have fallen from being Princes of this Land to be prisoners in this place. I am raised from being a prisoner in this place to a Prince of this Land; that dejection was a work of God's justice, this advancement is a work of his mercy.[1]

That November day was one of seismic change for Elizabeth. Years of danger and uncertainty were swept away in a moment. She did not have the benefit of hindsight to see that she would reign for the next forty-five years, or the cultural flourishing that would occur in her country. All that lay ahead. Yet, in November 1558, the illegitimized, rejected, imprisoned, third choice of Henry VIII's children had the crown.

63

Anastasia Romanova

7 August 1560

Kolomenskoye, near Moscow, Russia

The Tsar of Russia had chosen a traditional way of selecting his wife. Ensconced in the new Italian-style Kremlin, in one of the largest cities in the world, Ivan IV was the first Prince of Moscow to declare himself ruler of the entire country. After losing both parents young, he was crowned at the age of 17 and then prepared himself for marriage. Ivan did not initially have a specific woman in mind, but he did want a wife, so just like in a fairy tale, he sent out invitations to all the noble families, asking them to present their daughters at court. Such a method was considered akin to a cattle market in Europe, as Henry VIII discovered when he asked Francis I to parade the beauties of France before him, but such bride shows were common in Russia and Asia.

Anastasia Zakharina came from a minor branch of the Romanov family. Her father, Roman Yurievich Zakharyin-Yuriev, had been a boyar in service to the Grand Prince Vasily III, but his early death saw Anastasia and her siblings raised by their mother Uliana in the Orthodox tradition. In addition, one of her uncles, Mikhail Zakharin, had acted as Ivan's guardian during his minority. Potentially, the bride show could have attracted hundreds of applicants from all across the vast territory, but Ivan selected Anastasia, who was 16 or 17, the same as him. The wedding ceremony took place on 3 February 1547 at the Cathedral of the Annunciation, following ritual bathing, ceremonies and bowls of kasha. Bells rang, days of festivities followed in the city, and the bride and groom were depicted in the *Tsarstvennaya Kniga*, the Book of the Tsar, being crowned and toasted at the feast. Afterwards, they went on pilgrimage on foot to a nearby monastery. Ivan was already passionately in love with his young bride and it was widely believed that she would exert a calming influence on his more extreme characteristics. The English envoy, Sir Jeremy Horsey, wrote that she was 'wise, and of such holiness, virtue and government, as she was honoured, beloved and feared by all her subjects.' When it came to Ivan, 'he being young and riotous, she ruled him with admirable affability and wisdom.'[1] Her gentle, unassuming character and piety drew widespread affection, but as it transpired, she was unable to keep her husband entirely in check. The couple had six children.

In 1560, Anastasia fell ill. Serious fires had broken out in Moscow, leading to lawlessness, and Ivan sent his wife out to the royal estate of Kolomenskoe, a few miles to the south-east, while he remained in the city. It was a timely move. On 2 August, Moscow was invaded by forces from the Crimea. Although Ivan had dispatched a nurse to his wife, Anastasia's lingering illness did not improve and she died on 7 August, at the age of 30. Ivan was plunged into a state of grief, weeping and howling during her funeral, needing to be held up by his attendants.[2] There was little time for a tsar to indulge his personal feelings, though. Later the same month, Ivan was petitioned by the boyars and bishops to cease grieving, put his faith in God and remarry.[3]

Convinced that Anastasia had been murdered by his enemies, Ivan arrested two of his closest advisors, Adashev and Sylvester, who were found guilty of witchcraft and banished. Ivan may have had grounds for suspicion, though. Later forensic studies conducted upon a lock of Anastasia's hair indicated high levels of mercury, consistent with poisoning. It was after this point that the worst elements of Ivan's character were unleashed, as he turned against the boyars, torturing and executing their leaders and establishing the Oprichniki, a select secret army dressed in black robes. Ivan became paranoid, flew into rages and indulged in affairs. His policies became increasingly draconian. Anastasia's death unleashed the murderous character known to history as 'Ivan the Terrible.'

Ivan went on to marry at least five, possibly seven, more wives, although some were not recognised by the church. His second wife died young, and his third, just sixteen days after marriage, reputedly poisoned by a potion intended to increase her fertility. This only increased his paranoia. Two other wives were repudiated by Ivan and sent to monasteries. Ivan also beat to death his son by Anastasia, in a fit of rage, after possibly causing his daughter-in-law to miscarry. The number of Ivan's victims is unknown. One contemporary source suggests that in the 1570 Sack of Novgorod, lasting five weeks, 60,000 Russians were killed on suspicion of treason. Anastasia was a respected Tsarina, and her presence had been invaluable in calming her volatile husband. But her early death, probably by poisoning, unleashed the worst of his excesses.

64

Amye Robsart

8 September 1560
Cumnor Place, Oxfordshire, England

It was a Sunday in early September when the warmth of summer still lingered, but autumn was beckoning. A month after the death of Anastasia in distant Russia, another young wife was about to die, in equally mysterious circumstances. At Cumnor Place in Oxfordshire, home to the Blount family, the servants were preparing to visit the local fair. Some gossiped excitedly about what they would see, and purchases they might make, while others resented being forced to attend. In her chamber, a young woman of 28 stood and listened to the sounds of the house, but she was going nowhere.

Amye Dudley, née Robsart, was a guest in the home of her husband's steward. Since her marriage to Robert, she had moved from one country estate to another, an awkward, peripatetic existence, without children and few visits from her husband. It was no secret that Robert was the favourite of Queen Elizabeth and that she disliked him being far from her side. Some whispered that she was in love with him, and occasionally, those whispers reached Amye's ears. She was no fool. Her Robert was a handsome man and the queen rewarded him well, so that Amye never lacked for anything, save for his company. They had met and fallen in love when they were only 17, marrying at Richmond with Edward VI and the Princess Elizabeth in attendance. Now the boy-king lay in his grave and his sister ruled. Much had changed in a decade.

Amye Robsart was born in Norfolk in June 1532, not too far from the Dudley family's local estates. Her father, Sir John Robsart, was a gentleman farmer with a considerable sum to leave to his only surviving child, a fact that may have influenced Robert's ambitious father to allow his son to marry a girl of her status. She had been raised in Stanfield Hall, the house owned by her mother Elizabeth, a moated medieval manor, in an extended family unit with the Appleyards, sons from Elizabeth's first marriage. The household was strictly Protestant and Amye was educated and literate, although not as much as her sister-in-law Jane Grey. She probably met Robert in the summer of 1549 when he and his father called at the house, whilst helping suppress the uprising under Robert Kett, who had based himself in Norwich. It would have been a love match, based on their attraction at this meeting, and, as Robert was merely a younger son, Dudley agreed to let it proceed. They were married on 4 June 1550, three days before her eighteenth birthday, at Greenwich, with Edward VI attending. It was a good match for Amye, propelling her into court circles, although she would not remain there long.

It is likely that Robert and Amye were guests at Jane Grey's wedding to Robert's brother Guildford in 1553 at Durham Place in London, and grieved at her subsequent fall and the ruin of the Dudley family fortunes. In such a short space of time, Robert had restored their fortunes and Amye had cause to hope for a positive future. Yet increasingly he remained in London, and she was based in the country with no children to occupy and comfort her. She had lost count of the letters she had written, of the broken promises and hours spent watching the road. Accounts of her behaviour suggest she may have been depressed and had developed a malady in her breast. If she was not already upset about the amount of time he spent at court, the rumours must have reached her of his intimate friendship with Elizabeth and how she would not permit him to leave her side.

On that September day, Amye's household were angry with her when she asked to be left alone. Her companion, Mrs Odingsells, and her maid, Mrs Pirto, had insisted that they remain at Cumnor with her, saying Sunday was not a suitable day for them to attend the fair, especially not with the other servants. But Amye had been firm. At the upstairs window, she watched them walk away through the gentle September sunshine. Finally, the house was empty. At last, Amye was quite alone. It was all the time she needed.

When the servants returned to the house later, on the afternoon of Sunday, 8 September, they found Amye lying at the bottom of the staircase. Her neck was broken, and she had wounds consistent with such a fall. A message was immediately dispatched to Robert who was with the queen at Windsor. He appeared shocked, made every sign of grief, retired from court, ordered an inquiry and paid £2,000 for her funeral, an immense sum for the times. But the question that remains, haunting subsequent generations, is whether Amye's death was accident, suicide or murder. Within days, there were rumours circulating at court that Amye had been an inconvenience, dispatched to allow the queen to marry her favourite. Yet, if anything, her death made such a match impossibly dangerous, forever tainting Dudley with scandal. William Cecil, Elizabeth's minister and Dudley's political rival, appears to have already known of a plan to poison Amye well before her death, although this may have been designed to discredit Robert and prevent what Cecil perceived as a fatal error if the queen and Robert wed. Later, Jesuit propaganda and the novelist Walter Scott would also present the death as murder, embedding this interpretation in the popular imagination since.

Amye Robsart has come to represent the unwanted wife, the obstacle in the path of true love, the inconvenience that power sought to remove. The reality of her situation was more nuanced, though, and her demise had the opposite effect from that which some had predicted. It was fairly unusual among the upper classes to marry for love. The Dudleys' 'carnal marriage', as described by Cecil, plus their parity in age, was atypical of their peers, who usually allied for financial gain. Perhaps their youthful passion had burned out or time and distance had kept them apart. Dudley's star had risen to unpredictable heights, leaving Amye behind in a peripatetic existence, moving between the estates of friends. Such a dynamic was not unusual, as the Dudleys settled into a more typical arrangement, yet Robert's proximity to the throne made them national news. Had Dudley's relations with Elizabeth been less controversial, Amye's existence and death would have been a mere footnote in history. The mysterious nature of her demise, though, consistent with suicide and murder, propelled her to attention. Modern historians have considered factors including a potential diagnosis of breast cancer, given Amye's 'malady' and theorised that she may have been depressed, or suffering unbearable pain. Her maid, Mrs Pirto, reported that she had been praying to God to 'deliver her from desperation'.[1] Equally, the Elizabethans considered suicide to be a sin deserving of damnation and were unlikely to risk their salvation. Amye had placed orders for a new gown and other such items, which might suggest a lack of intent to die, but we can never know the circumstances, how hard she fought her pain or how her mood changed.

A significant breakthrough occurred in 2008 when royal biographer Chris Skidmore discovered the original coroner's report, considered lost for years, and the voices of Amye's contemporaries were heard. Declaring a case of death by 'misadventure', the inquest was closed without accusations. Dudley was a free man, but not free enough to marry the queen. Most modern thinking exonerates him, considering the resulting scandal and his reactions to her loss. Amye was buried in St Mary's Church, Oxford, four years after the martyr Thomas Cranmer was burned outside it. She continues to spark our imagination and theorising.

65

Isabella Cortese

1561

Venice, Italy

Sixteenth-century women wanted to look beautiful. And wealthy. To demonstrate their high status, they painted their faces with a mixture of ingredients that might include eggs, herbs, talc, tree sap, ass's milk, sulphur, lead and mercury. This gave them a white complexion, showing that they never had to work, but it also corroded the skin and turned it grey. When a new layer was required, it was simply applied over the old one and set with an egg-white glaze. Cheeks and lips were painted with ceruse, eyes were outlined with pencil, ground pearls made eyes shimmer and fake eyebrows were made out of mouse fur. Such techniques are familiar from portraits of Elizabeth I, but at the start of her reign, it was an Italian woman who perfected the art and published her book of cosmetic secrets. *The Secrets of Lady Isabella Cortese* was first printed in Venice in 1561 and, by 1599, it had gone through seven editions.

Isabella's book appeared amid a fashion for such scientific manuals that contained accessible recipes for medicinal and beauty purposes. The majority of medical texts were almost exclusively authored by men, so the supposed authorship by a woman, and the dedication of the text to 'every noble lady' was in line with rising female literacy among the upper classes. Among the rare few books produced by women in the contemporary field was that of Isabella Sforza, who died in Rome in 1561, and Anna Zieglerin, who worked as an assistant alchemist at the court of Duke Julius of Braunschweig and focused on remedies for childbirth and fertility.[1]

Yet the actual existence of an historical figure called Isabella Cortese herself is uncertain. No details are known about her life, although the 'autobiographical' elements of the text claims she lives in Olmütz in Moravia,[2] and that she learned alchemy by travelling through Europe, dismissing comparative works as 'only fiction and riddles'. However, this is a common literary device to engage the reader, by inventing an accessible figure to narrate the journey through the text, placing the recipes in the context of real experimentation. Additionally, the name 'Cortese' is an anagram of 'Secreto'. There may have been no Isabella Cortese at all. Some of her contemporaries questioned whether this really was a book written by a woman, or simply a man cynically trying to optimise sales, even naming the author Girolamo Ruscelli as a likely candidate.[3] Another indicator of the commercial focus is the book's instruction to keep the recipes secret, not to share them, but to burn the volume after use. Ruscelli was based in Venice from 1548 until his death in 1566 and earned his living by plagiarising the work of others, writing a book on alchemy under a pseudonym in 1555, *De Secreti Del Alessimo Piemontese*. The adoption of a female identity for the creation of a book of cosmetic secrets would seem a likely next move. Alternatively, Isabella may have been a real woman whose biographical details have been lost to time.

The Secrets contains a range of remedies and advice aimed at women of a certain class. They are instructed how to run a household; make glue, soap and toothpaste; and are given an exclusive but futile method for turning base metals into gold. Cortese's recipe for making face colouring requires a woman to 'obtain a few birds with white feathers' and feed them only pine nuts for two weeks before butchering them. Liquid obtained from the birds should be mixed with their meat, sweetbreads, white bread and goat's milk, and then heated. The final solution should be distilled, then applied to the face. Another way to clean the face involved lemon beans, wine, honey, eggs and goat's milk. To enhance her husband's prowess in the bedroom, Cortese's readers needed musk, amber, winged ants, oil from the elder tree and quail testicles.[4]

Whoever the author of *The Secrets* was, and however successful or not the recipes were, the book represents the increase in female literacy and the constant sixteenth-century preoccupation with physical appearance and beauty. Isabella Cortese captured the mood of her era, which was soon to be personified in the stylised persona of the English queen.

66

Aura Soltana

13 July 1561

London, England

On 13 July 1561, Elizabeth I dressed in her finery to attend a baptism. She was standing as godmother to an exotic child, brought to her court as a curiosity by an agent of the Muscovy Company. The girl had been purchased by Anthony Jenkinson for around the price of a loaf of bread, somewhere near Astrakhan in southern Russia. Her original faith may well have been Islam, but her entry into the Church of England was symbolic of her acceptance of her new life, or her lack of choice thereof. They called her Aura Soltana, or Ipolita the Tartarin. To celebrate the occasion, Elizabeth made her the gift of a chain of gold and a gold tablet, which was recorded in her expense accounts.

In 1558, Jenkinson was travelling in eastern Europe, seeking out an overland route to China through Russia and Uzbekistan. The Muscovy Company was still in its infancy, founded in 1551, receiving its charter four years later and trading furs and luxury items with Ivan the Terrible in Moscow. Jenkinson had reached that city on 18 September 1559, when he wrote home to a fellow agent, Henry Lane, that he had acquired a 'wench' called Aura Soltana in Astrakhan, where it was 'possible to buy a boy or wench for a loaf of bread.'[1] Other sources suggest she came from the Persian Shah Tahmasp I's court. It is not known how old Aura was at the time. In the middle of what would be a difficult journey, it is unlikely that Jenkinson was prepared to take on a very young child, whose needs he may not have been able to meet. More than likely she was old enough to dress and care for herself, but not so old as to be of marriageable age or considered a woman, which would suggest she was under 14, but likely to be older than 7. Both ages were considered significant milestones for childhood development. A later gift to her of a pewter doll confirms her youth. Her parentage is not referred to, so she may have been a slave or an orphan.

Jenkinson had an eventful journey after taking on Aura. He crossed the Caspian Sea and travelled with a caravan of traders across the Caspian Steppe, where they were frequently forced to fight off bandits. He was detained in Moscow during 1559 and had to wait for the following spring to thaw the ports, to allow him to sail for England. They probably did not arrive until late 1560 or early 1561. It must have been an eventful trip for the young girl, who may have been conscious of just how dramatically her life was changing. None of her words survive, either if she was literate or those recorded by others, and her feelings can only be surmised. When she reached England, though, Aura's reception at Elizabeth's court and the gifts made to her of clothing, showed her she was something of a curiosity. If she was in any way typical of her time, Aura would have seen her new status as an opportunity, potentially lifting her out of poverty, even slavery, and offering her luxury and protection. Described as Elizabeth's 'dear and well-beloved servant', she was swiftly equipped with two loose gowns of black taffeta, a French kirtle of russet satin, and another French kirtle of black satin.

Aura's subsequent life remains a mystery. The few glimpses of her after 1561 come through the wardrobe accounts: she had a biography constructed entirely of dresses. Three years after her christening, a swathe of new clothes was provided for her, probably because she had grown. She had a gown and kirtle of damask lined with velvet, another two sets made of grosgrain, a farthingale, a red petticoat, six canvas smocks, gold and silk thread to embroider the sleeves, a scarf, hat and gold and silver cauls. The last court record to relate to Aura was for fur to line her cloak in 1569. After that, the trail goes cold. Searches by several scholars have yielded no further results. Aura was probably in her twenties by that point, so it is likely that she married and perhaps left court.

One final clue remains. A painting entitled *The Persian Lady* was produced by Marcus Gheeraerts in the 1590s. It shows a woman in elaborate foreign-looking masque costume, set against an English park landscape, where she rests her hand upon the head of a deer. True to the fashion of the day, her skin is very pale, her eyes and hair dark, with nothing to suggest ethnic origins beyond the English court. This work has been traditionally associated with Aura, who would have been in her forties or early fifties at that point, but it equally may have attracted its title due to a court entertainment. The identity of the sitter is unlikely to ever be resolved, but it provides a tantalising possible glimpse of Aura later in life. The story of a Muslim Tartar girl, plucked from her native Russia and transported to the English court, has the feel of a romance, or a Disney biopic, but the feelings and experiences of Aura Soltana, and her final resting place, have been lost to history. She was not the first Russian at the English court, but she was the first woman and she grew to maturity there. Her status as 'other' or 'alien' made her an attraction among the largely homogenous court.

67

Isabelle de Limeuil

1562

Paris, France

She was one of the most beautiful women at the French court. There was no question about that. The poet Pierre de Rosnard enthused about wanting to kiss her rose-pink complexion and blonde hair, praising her blue eyes and sparkling wit. She knew all the tricks to accentuate her beauty that writers like her namesake, Isabella Cortese, described in their works.

Born in Limeuil in the Dordogne region in 1535, Isabelle was the daughter of a baron, Giles de la Tour, and was raised in the chateau overlooking the river. She was related to Catherine de' Medici, whose mother Madeleine had also been from the de la Tour family, and it was perhaps this connection that initially brought her to Paris, to serve in the widowed Catherine's household as a maid of honour. Soon, her charms had attracted so much attention that Catherine saw the opportunity to recruit her into a small band of women she employed to conduct her secret business.

In recent years, historians have questioned the existence of Catherine de' Medici's Secret Band of seductresses, referred to after 1695 as the Flying Squadron. Traditionally, it has been considered a network of women recruited for their charms in order to seduce leading men to gain information or influence them in certain directions. They were used at parties, pageants and feasts, and also behind the scenes, reporting their conquests and discoveries back to Catherine.

Pierre de Brantôme, born in 1540, extolled the beauty of the women of Catherine's court:

There are so many other ladies and maids that I beg them to excuse me if I pass them by with my pen, not that I do not greatly value and esteem them, but I should dream over them and amuse myself too much. To make an end, nothing to find fault with in their day; beauty abounded all majesty, all charm, all grace; happy was he who could touch with love such ladies, and happy those who could that love escape. I swear to you that I have named only those ladies and damoiselles who were beautiful, agreeable, very accomplished, and well sufficient to set fire to the whole world. Indeed, in their best days they burned up a good part of it, as much as gentlemen of the Court as others who approached the flame; to some of whom they were gentle, amiable, favourable and courteous. I speak of none here, hoping to make good tales about them in this book before I finish it, and of others whose names are not comprised here; but the whole told so discreetly, without scandal, that nothing will be known, for the curtain of silence will cover their names; so that if by chance they should any of them read tales of themselves they will not be annoyed. Besides, though the pleasures of love cannot last forever, by reason of many inconveniences, hindrances, and changes, the memories of the past are always pleasing.[1]

According to Brantôme, Catherine de' Medici controlled their movements and love affairs, with the women commanded to always 'appear in grand and superb apparel'.[2] In addition to the dresses they could afford out of their huge salaries, the women were gifted 'splendid liveries'[3] by the king and queen mother. In contrast with Brantôme's more celebratory view, Jeanne d'Albret, admittedly an austere Huguenot, despised the French court as a bed of iniquity, where women made the first move, not men, amid a hotbed of sexual depravity.

Isabelle probably arrived at court in the 1550s as a teenager. Initially, she would have been trained by Catherine and observed the behaviours of other women in seducing and gathering information from rivals to the dynasty. Her first lover was one of Catherine's enemies, Claude, Duke of Aumale, son of the Duke of Guise, brother to Marie, former Queen of Scots. In 1562, Catherine asked her to seduce another prominent enemy, the Huguenot Louis, Prince of Condé, who fell deeply in love with her. However, the queen's code of conduct insisted upon discretion and secrecy, and, in the autumn of 1563, Isabelle fell pregnant by Condé. After concealing her condition for as long as possible, she delivered his child the following May in the queen's chamber at Dijon. Isabelle appealed to Condé for assistance, but he rejected her, married someone else and Catherine dismissed her from court. Isabelle was forced to temporarily enter a convent and rumours were spread that she had attempted to poison one of her suitors. A backlash against Catherine's women saw male courtiers urged not to share political secrets with their lovers, but to keep the public and private spheres secret as a way of diminishing female power.[4] In 1567, Isabelle left the convent and married wealthy Tuscan banker Scipion Sardini, lived in Paris and bore him four children. She died in 1609.

The existence of this band of elite sexual predators, the Flying Squadron, has been questioned by later historians. The women of Catherine's court may well have exercised their feminine wiles to seduce leading men, and potentially carry that information back to the queen, but the degree of organisation and depravity suggested by her enemies may have depicted a far more organised system than existed in reality. Certainly, Catherine was clever and saw her ladies as valuable assets. Affairs and marriages had always occurred for the sake of political alliance as much as affection, just as Catherine's own had, and she was known for the streak of ruthlessness that ensured she retained her power. Another key member, arriving later on the scene, was Charlotte de Sauve, who became the mistress of Henri of Navarre, Catherine's future son-in-law. In line with Catherine's methods of exercising power in secretive, indirect means, the existence of the elite Flying Squadron is certainly possible. It was the ultimate kiss-and-tell.

68

Cecilia of Sweden

8 September 1565
Dover, England

Finally, the white cliffs of Dover appeared through the mist. The ship lurched and plunged with the swell of the waves, but Cecilia and her ladies were filled with hope at their first sight of England after such a long and arduous journey. Far from home, Princess Cecilia had an additional reason to be grateful for their imminent arrival. Her stays had already been loosened and her dress unlaced, as she was now in the ninth month of her pregnancy. Her first child would be born soon, in a foreign land, with six of her ladies to attend her. She was arriving at the invitation of Queen Elizabeth, with whom she had been in a lengthy correspondence, but Cecilia hoped to persuade her new ally to become an even closer relation through a proposed marriage to her brother, Prince Eric of Sweden. Yet Cecilia brought controversy with her, having survived a significant scandal in her youth.

Born in Stockholm in 1540, Cecilia was already renowned for her beauty, having had her portrait painted and her looks immortalised in verse. She was one of ten children born to Gustav I, King of Sweden and his second wife, Margaret, a talented and dedicated mother who died when Cecilia was 11. She was raised by nurses and aunts until her father remarried. When she was 16, Gustav launched Cecilia and his eldest daughter, Catherine, aged 17, on the marriage market. They sat for their portraits, had their beauty described in poetry and were each given a dowry of 100,000 daler. Edzard Cirksena, heir to East Frisia, an important trading ally, was invited to visit and select which of the sisters he wished to marry. He arrived in 1558, chose Catherine and married her the following October in Stockholm.

As the newlywed couple travelled through Sweden, they were accompanied by Cecilia and Edzard's brother John. They were staying at the newly rebuilt Vasteras Castle when a strange scandal erupted, known as The Vadstena Thunder, when John was found without his hose in Cecilia's chambers. Reputedly, the guards had observed a man climbing in through Cecilia's window four nights in a row and it was feared this would disrupt negotiations for her marriage. Catherine had to intercede for John and Cecilia to be allowed to leave. Cecilia was sent back to Stockholm, where she claimed her father beat her and tore her hair out. John was imprisoned until summer 1560, when he was forced to make a public statement that nothing of a sexual nature had passed between him and Cecilia. Her brothers created a coin depicting her as Susanna, implying she shared the innocence of the Biblical figure. However, her suitor Georg John chose to wed her younger sister Anna instead. Cecilia was inclined to accept the English Earl of Arundel, Henry FitzAlan's proposal, or that of a Polish count, but these came to nothing. Further scandal followed in 1563 when Cecilia was discovered by her brother Eric to be entertaining friends in her rooms at night, resulting in her being more closely observed.

In June 1564 Cecilia married Christopher II, Margrave of Baden-Rodemachern. Soon afterwards they accepted an invitation from Elizabeth I to visit England and departed on a year-long journey across Europe. Cecilia had been corresponding with the queen for years, but her intention in visiting was to try and convince Elizabeth to marry her brother Eric; her brother also asked her to enlist Elizabeth on their side to negotiate peace with Denmark. Three months after their departure, Cecilia fell pregnant with her first child. The journey was much longer than anticipated, taking them 400 miles over water and 750 across ice and snow in order to avoid Norwegian and Danish enemy territory. Among her company was a 16-year-old Swedish noblewoman called Helena Snakenbourg.

The Swedish party were met at Dover by William Parr on 8 September. They did not know at the time, but this handsome man in his fifties, brother to a former queen, would become Helena's husband. He conducted them to London where they made a state entry three days later and were lodged at Bedford House on the Strand. Cecilia wore black velvet with silver edging and her six ladies were dressed in red. Their arrival was only just in time. Mere days later, Cecilia went into labour and delivered her son on 17 September. Elizabeth named him Edward, carried him to his christening and later moved his family to Hampton Court. Afterwards, Cecilia was frequently in the queen's company, attending entertainments and weddings with her and taking communion together. Living extravagantly, Cecilia ran up a number of debts, so that Christopher was obliged to depart for Germany in November to try and borrow money. He returned the following March and tried to help his wife escape her creditors, for which he was put in gaol. Eventually, Cecilia was obliged to sell her jewels and clothes, but when they reached Dover in May 1566, much of their luggage was seized by officials. It was an ignominious way to leave.

Cecilia also left with one fewer lady-in-waiting. Helena became a maid of honour to Elizabeth, and William Parr married her in May 1571. Their happiness was short-lived though, as he died that October. Helena remained in England for the rest of her life, remarried and bore children. Arriving in Sweden, Cecilia had been pursued by her main creditor, but her authority there allowed her to order his arrest. Later, after being widowed, she converted to Catholicism in order to be accepted as her underage son's regent. At this time, in the mid-1570s, Elizabeth offered Cecilia the hand in marriage of her favourite, Robert Dudley, which Cecilia wisely declined. Instead, she bore an illegitimate daughter, fathered by the Spanish ambassador; the child was named Charitas and was placed in a nunnery.

Cecilia's life was never really free of controversy as she engaged in disputes with her family and creditors. She died in 1627 at the age of 86.

A portrait currently held at Gripsholm Castle, west of Stockholm, has been recently identified as Cecilia, dressed in a similar style to Elizabeth I, with the delicate fairy-wing ruff and rows of pearls, wearing a complicated gown of woven gold bands. Her grey hair is dressed high and smooth with ringlets around her forehead, topped with red feathery decoration, and her eyes large and brown, very much in the Stuart style of beauty.

Helena was a chief mourner at the funeral of Elizabeth I and lived on until 1635. A surviving portrait of her in ermine and scarlet coronation robes reminds us of her beauty and her heritage in an inscription painted at the side.

Cecilia herself was a fascinating character: beautiful, brave and attracting scandal throughout her life. Her royal blood gave her the platform from which to petition Elizabeth and opened many doors for her, both literally and financially. Yet it also meant that she had a certain image to maintain, above criticism in any form, which she sometimes struggled to maintain. Her long life demonstrates adaptability but also the human face of royalty.

69

Weyn Ockers

23 August 1566

Oude Kerk, Amsterdam

In the summer of 1566, a wave of iconoclastic attacks, or Beeldenstorm, spread through the Netherlands. Directed against Catholic images and symbols associated with their long-distance ruler Philip II of Spain, they saw the decimation of church interiors and clerical properties in key cities like Antwerp, Louvain, Maastricht and Ghent. Statues were smashed, images defaced and altars desecrated. Over 400 churches in the Netherlands suffered attacks in the space of a few weeks.

English Catholic exile Nicholas Sander witnessed the destruction at Louvain, where the rioters 'threw down the graven [engraved or sculpted] and defaced the painted images, not only of Our Lady, but of all others in the town.' He saw curtains torn, and brass and stone dashed into pieces; chalices and vestments stolen; grave brasses pulled up and pews broken; books, manuscripts and maps torn; and the sacrament of the bread trodden under foot and urinated upon.[1]

On 23 August, the rioting reached Amsterdam. The news came to the ears of a local woman from a wealthy family, Weyn Ockers, who was known among her circle for being tall. Her history contained a precedent for the riots, as her grandmother had been executed for taking part in an Anabaptist uprising in the city in 1534–5. Little more is known about Weyn. She was the daughter of Adriaen Ockersz and lived with her husband Jurriaen ter Meulen in Zeedijk, one of the old, narrow streets, then a very respectable neighbourhood. That day, she put on her outdoor shoes, and perhaps a coat for modesty, although the season would have been warm, and set out with her maid Trijn Hendricks. Perhaps she went out with intent to participate, perhaps she merely wanted to watch, or else she had business in town and got caught up in the activity. At some point, the two women ended up at the Oude Kerk, on one side of the square called the Oudekerksplein, in the city centre. Founded in the early thirteenth century, it featured painted panels by Renaissance artists Jan van Scorel and Maarten van Heemskerck, as well as a decorated ceiling. When Weyn and Trijn arrived, the looters were already defacing these images and attacking the fixtures. Weyn saw the statue of St Roch being pulled down, and picked up the little stone-carved dog that became detached from it. The priest, Simon Slecht, was shouting encouragement.

An account compiled from several sources by the historian G. Brandt in 1720 relates how the event began at nine in the morning, when several merchants gathered at the Exchange to describe what they had just seen in Antwerp. They brought fragments of stone and marble, broken pieces of church interiors, identifying them as belonging to certain well-known shrines. Immediately the word went out in the city that valuable items should be concealed, although this process appears to have attracted more attention and great numbers started to assemble. The Oude Kerk was quiet at first, with baptisms and exorcisms taking place, until a local corn porter threw down some verses on the floor and boys started throwing stones. Brandt has Slecht attempting to protect the statue of Mary which Weyn threw her slipper at. He claims it was the symbol of a guild of spinsters who used to gather about it in the church.[2]

After the excitement, Weyn and Trijn returned home. The regent of the Netherlands, Margaret of Parma, illegitimate daughter of Charles V, dispatched troops across the country to quell the riots. She had been appointed by her half-brother, Philip II, who had departed for Spain, leaving her little assistance, but eventually the cities were quietened and the clean-up process could begin. Time passed. Life continued in Amsterdam.

Not quite two years later, in March 1568, there came a knock on the door of the house in the Zeedijk. Somehow, questions had been asked, and information uncovered behind the scenes. Soldiers had come to arrest the two women for their involvement in the riots. A hearing was held on 13 March, at which Weyn and Trijn both admitted they had been present in the church for a short time, but the testimony of a witness under torture described Weyn throwing her slipper at the statue of the Virgin Mary, breaking statues and a glass section of the altar. Weyn was tortured and, on 21 March, admitted that she had been complicit in the attack upon the church. She added that her maid Trijn had broken several statues. Trijn made no confession beyond admitting her presence in the church. Nevertheless, both women were found guilty and condemned to death for heresy.

Their sentences were carried out that June. Both were drowned in a water-filled wine barrel in the city's central Dam Square. Margaret of Parma needed to ensure that heretics were visibly punished and that there would be no more attacks upon the country's churches. Weyn's act of throwing a slipper was a minor infringement, irreverent but small in comparison with many of her contemporaries' savage acts of destruction, but it was a symbolic rejection of the national faith which Parma could not allow. Equally, it could not be tolerated that a woman expressed heretical views or behaved in an unruly way in public. Controlled and defined by their menfolk, an anarchic woman spoke of a rottenness at the core of the family unit, the basic social fabric, which threatened the entire structure of civic life. Weyn and Trijn were singled out as wayward females, Weyn's protest of a thrown slipper quintessentially feminine, and thus even more dangerous.

70

Elizabeth Talbot, 'Bess' of Hardwick

2 February 1569
Tutbury Castle, Staffordshire, England

Tutbury Castle in Staffordshire had been empty for a long time. Set on a slight hill, overlooking the park, it was at the mercy of all the winds blowing across the plains. The inside was damp and the sparse furnishings were tattered and worn. Its glory days had been celebrated two centuries earlier, when it had been rebuilt by John of Gaunt, and admirers had compared it to Windsor Castle in feel. It was certainly large and rambling, in the same way, but lacked the charms and comforts of its southern counterpart.

Standing in the inner court overlooking the gate, she watched as the carts trundled in. Bess was not happy with this latest move. She and her husband had been happy at Sheffield Manor, beginning their life together, but the royal council had decreed that they make Tutbury habitable, taking down their hangings, rolling up their carpets and folding their linen. The carts drew to a halt and servants came forward to unload the velvets and brocades and carry them inside. Bess watched them warily. Her life was being disrupted for the sake of a fugitive. A fugitive who happened to be a queen. Bess motioned for the men to work more quickly. Mary, Queen of Scots was due to arrive before nightfall and her chambers must be ready, hung with tapestries and fires burning in every grate.

Elizabeth, or Bess, as she was known, had recently married her fourth husband, George Talbot, sixth Earl of Shrewsbury. In 1569, she was aged around 42, with six surviving children, aged between 13 and 21. Born into the minor gentry in Derbyshire, her series of marriages elevated her status until she finally became a countess through marriage to George, and she had also been a Lady of the Bedchamber to Elizabeth I. Now the queen had a different kind of role in mind for her. Their royal guest was to be entertained and kept in the manner her rank demanded, but she was also to be closely guarded and not permitted to leave. Mary was unaware of it, as she rode closer, but Bess and George were effectively to become her gaolers for eighteen years. Equally, Bess was unaware that the strain exerted upon her marriage by the presence of the beautiful fugitive would drive a wedge between herself and her husband.

Bess was fifteen years older than Mary. Before the Scottish queen was born, Bess had been raised in the Derbyshire manor of Slingsby, before possibly joining the household of Anne Gainsford, Lady Zouche, at nearby Codnor Castle. Her first marriage, to Robert Barley, a neighbouring landowner's heir, took place when they were both aged around 13. It was not consummated, and Robert died the following year. Had he not, Bess could potentially have fallen pregnant in around 1542, when she reached the age of 15, and had a child of the same age as Mary, who was born in December that year. Her second husband was William Cavendish, treasurer of the king's chamber, whom she wed in 1547 in the home of their friends, Henry Grey, Duke of Suffolk and his wife Frances, niece of Henry VIII. It was with William that she began to build Chatsworth House. Shortly after this wedding, Mary fled to Scotland at the age of 6, with her four companions, being raised in the Valois household as a future bride for the dauphin.

After Cavendish died in 1557, Bess took as her third husband, Sir William St Loe, Captain of the Guard and chief butler to Elizabeth I. In France, Mary was married to Francis, at the age of 16, and the pair became king and queen the following year when Henri II was killed in a joust. Six months later, Francis was dead too, so Mary returned to her native Scotland. St Loe died in 1565, in a case of suspected poisoning after cutting his siblings out of his will and leaving Bess wealthy. In the same year, Mary married her cousin Henry, Lord Darnley, son of Margaret Douglas, the daughter of Margaret Tudor, Queen of Scots. Mary bore a son, James, but her unravelling marriage resulted in Darnley's murder, Mary being forced to abdicate and her defeat at the Battle of Langside. After this, she fled to England in the hope of finding sanctuary with her cousin Elizabeth. Instead, she was sent to Carlisle, Bolton and then Tutbury. The castle was considered far enough south that it would prevent Scottish lords from attempting to rescue her.

In early 1569, furniture, bedding and tapestries were ordered to be sent from the royal wardrobe at the Tower of London to furnish Tutbury. Terrible weather caused them to be delayed, so Bess's home at Sheffield was emptied instead. Mary came with her own staff of sixteen, including her personal chefs, and her personal effects required thirty carts to transport them.[1] The young queen was 26 when she arrived at Tutbury, twice widowed and exiled from home, and was lifted down from her horse and carried inside the castle. She would describe it as being like a hunting lodge, draughty and damp, with its fitting loose. Within days she fell ill with a fever and rheumatic pain. After a couple of months, she was relocated to Wingfield Manor in Derbyshire, and from there to Chatsworth.[2]

1569 marked the beginning of Bess and Mary's association. In the coming years, they would be forced to accommodate each other, with the highs and lows that brought. At their best, the women worked together on items that became part of the Hardwick collection, but at their worst, Bess voiced concerns, real or imagined, that her husband was having relations with Mary. Ten years after their marriage, he had gone from referring to her as his 'jewel' to his 'wicked and malicious wife' and refusing to spend the night under the same roof as her.[3]

To describe Bess's and Mary's relationship as a friendship is too simplistic; the ties of nationality, duty and the conflicts these generated, coupled with the dynamic of trust and power imbalance, made for an uneasy balance between women. The Talbots' marriage broke down, despite efforts made by Queen Elizabeth to intervene, and Mary's tenure with them was finally ended in January 1585. She was handed over to Sir Amyas Paulet at Chartley Castle, whose approach to her was to prove far less sympathetic. Bess would bury George in 1590, promote the claim of her granddaughter Arbella Stuart and live on until 1608. Her will proved her to be one of the wealthiest women in the country, and the houses she built, especially Hardwick Hall which gives her the name she is commonly known by, stand as her memorial. She was formidable and iconic, one of the women who survived through difficulties, advanced her career by profitable marriages and rose higher than she could have imagined, but not at personal cost.

71

Unknown Woman

8 February 1570
Concepcion City, Chile

February was traditionally a dry, warm month. By 9.00 am, many women of the city had already been awake for a good few hours, tending to their families, fetching fresh water and gathering on the shore. Their language was Spanish, their words buzzing in the marketplace, reminders of the Old World. The city sat on a little piece of land jutting into the Bay of Concepcion on the western coast of Chile. The sun shone down upon the roofs of the houses, all built within recent years. The city was approaching the twentieth year of its foundation, but it had been rebuilt several times since then, razed by the local Mapuche tribe, only to rise slowly again, brick by brick.

She might be young, suckling a baby, or chasing after a toddler; she might be arranging her daughter's wedding, picking out fabrics and sewing a trousseau; she might be old, shelling peas in the sunlight or kneading dough. Perhaps she was wringing out clothes in a bucket or stream, or chasing away stray dogs, or arguing, laughing or crying. It started suddenly, without warning, all around her. A trembling and shaking, which she thought was inside her own head at first. She was too tired, she had not eaten and her old sickness was returning. But the shaking grew, the windows rattled and things fell off shelves and toppled from tables. She staggered, putting out her hand to the wall, only to find it unstable. Knowing what this was at last, she called to her loved ones, and whoever else was close, to run away, to head for the hills and avoid the town. Within seconds, though, the world was shaken by an earthquake of 8.3 magnitude, one of the most severe ever to hit the coastline.

At around 9.00 am on the morning of 8 February 1570, normal life in the city of Concepcion came to a sudden halt. She understood this at once, heading out into the sunlight as the walls began to crumble about her. Familiar buildings were crumbling, chimneys and roof tiles glancing down to the street and there were already strange gaps, through which the clear sky shone through, where windows once framed the view. Voices were already raised, in panic and pain, as the citizens emerged, some dusty, some bleeding, looking about them in disbelief.

Then the rumbling stopped. A great moment of stillness followed. She could hear her own heartbeat, the sound of her breath. Children ran up to her. But amid this all, something caught her eye, far out on the shimmering blue horizon. There, the strange ripple was rising, the ominous line of white getting higher.

She stood, shielding her eyes against the sun. Perhaps her basket fell the ground, but it mattered little, because she had seen what was coming next. She shouted, pointing out to sea. A giant wave was coming, a tsunami caused by the earthquake, still many miles away, but inevitable in its destination. Now the voices were rising in panic, urging people to run to the hills, to the high ground. She sought out her family, taking the hands of children, urging the old to rise, harnessing horses to a cart and loading up whatever she could find. The wave was a little closer, but still distant. Riding down the main street, leaving the crumbled houses behind, she realised that she might make it.

The woman of Concepcion and her family were lucky. Comparatively. Enough of their house had withstood the earthquake that they survived, and there was sufficient time before the tsunami struck for them to get to higher ground. Some other citizens were less fortunate. Once the wave hit, later that day, every house was destroyed. Around 2,000 lives were lost. What was then the capital of Chile represented a fragile presence of the Spanish conquistadors. Ravaged by locals, then by the earth and sea, it stands as a metaphor for the struggles of those trying to forge a new life in an environment that was new to them. For the surviving women, losing their homes, crops, possessions and, perhaps, family members, such an act of God required an extraordinary resilience to allow them to pick up the pieces and start again.

Concepcion stood on the site of the present-day city of Penco. In the two and a half centuries following the destruction of 1570, it suffered five more catastrophic events, until the capital was relocated to the Valle de la Mocha. There, women married, bore children, lived and died, expanding the population in spite of the dangers. Earthquakes, tsunamis and local tribes notwithstanding, life in the New World continued. Yet those who had witnessed the events of 1570 that destroyed their homes would never forget that day.

72

Suphankanlaya

1571

Pegu, Burma

A golden statue stands, hand on hip, in the Naresuan Army Camp in the Phitsanulok province of Thailand. It represents a young woman on a plinth, radiant in the daylight, with her hair dressed high upon her head and her chin lifted to convey a sense of nobility. She is dressed traditionally, with jewellery and decorated robes, looking out into the middle distance. The statue was erected in 1999 to commemorate Suphankanlaya, a Thai princess who became Queen of Burma. Yet it is an embodiment of an ideal, an imagined representation, the capturing of what a woman has come to represent: gold, bold and beautiful. In reality, there is no surviving image of Suphankanlaya. She has become a mythic figure, long neglected, whose reputation enjoyed a renewal of interest at the end of the twentieth century. Her popularity has meant the queen has achieved the status of a deity, but very little is known about the actual details of her life.

Born around 1554, Amyoyon, known as Suphankanlaya, was the daughter of the king of Ayutthaya, who took the throne of Thailand through a coup. In 1563, the kingdom was invaded by Bayinnaug of Burma, forcing her father into submission, leaving the family in a desolate situation. Suphankanlaya was presented at the Burmese court on 22 January 1567.

Four years later, when Suphankanlaya was 17, she was offered as a junior wife to Bayinnaug, in the hope of establishing connections of loyalty and ensuring peace. Her two exiled brothers were also able to return home as a result of the move. Born in 1516, her husband was almost forty years her senior, but she was one of many and it is unlikely she spent much time in his company. It was common for Burmese kings to have a number of wives and the young girl had to take her place in a complex social hierarchy behind several established women, who were the mothers of Bayinnaug's children. The arrangement was similar to something like that experienced by Roxelana, but they were at the opposite ends of the pecking order; while Roxelana was the favourite wife of Suleiman, and engaged in international diplomacy on his behalf, Suphankanlaya had to wait in line behind chief queens, senior queens and junior queens before receiving her husband's attention. Despite this, she managed to conceive and bear two children in the following decade.

In 1581, Bayinnaug died at the age of 65 and Suphankanlaya married his son and successor, Nanda, in addition to his five principal queens. However, this was not enough to guarantee a continuing peace and three years later, her father led a rebellion, which was suppressed. The family was not content to sit and endure this dynamic for long, though, and her brothers began plotting to regain control. In 1593, they killed Nanda's son. When news reached Nanda, he was so angry that he attacked and killed Suphankanlaya, who was then eight months pregnant with his child. Little other material survives regarding her life and death. The chronicles contain few references to her existence and especially her end. The brief duration of her influence was initiated and remained under the control of men; her father and two husbands. She was given in marriage and brutally murdered, along with her unborn child, because of her husband's uncontrollable anger. Nanda experienced no consequences for his attack and continued to rule until his death in 1600.

Suphankanlaya's story entered Thai legend, due largely to the nature of her death. In the late twentieth century, something in her life chimed with the mood of financial anxiety, and people increasingly turned to her as a deity for support. A golden statue was erected in her memory and her name was revived as a talisman for good fortune, drawing a positive element out of her enigmatic life and tragic demise. She was one of many women, worldwide, who experienced domestic violence, from the commonplace beatings through to loss of life, which the sixteenth century permitted on a daily basis, and explained away when it became fatal. A man's authority was sacrosanct and rarely challenged. Legal murders by a royal husband, such as that experienced by Suphankanlaya, Anne Boleyn and Catherine Howard, were indicative of many more untried, buried cases lower down the social scale. Attacks upon women were considered scandalous if perpetrated by a stranger or associate, but received little justice if the violence was carried out by a relative.

73

Marguerite of Valois

23–24 August 1572
Paris, France

For the 19-year-old Catholic princess of France, her wedding was a personal disaster. Decked out in ermine robes, diamonds and a crown upon her head, she was taken into the Cathedral of Notre Dame by her brother, Charles IX and mother, Catherine de' Medici, towards a husband she did not want to marry. Marguerite had protested loudly but it was a question of duty, not choice. In her memoirs, she wrote of her mother: 'I have no will but her own.'[1]

At the cathedral doorway, the equally reluctant groom, Henri of Navarre, had been forbidden entry and was forced to wait outside. Personally, he did not want the marriage to go ahead either, nor did his Huguenot family and friends, who saw it as a betrayal of his faith and the Valois royal family as unscrupulous and dangerous. Even the Pope had refused to issue a dispensation. Still protesting, Marguerite was marched up to the altar where another of her brothers stood in as proxy for the reluctant Henri and spoke his words of agreement. When it came to the moment that the princess was obliged to give her consent, Charles was ready and waiting, pushing her head forward so that she appeared to nod. There was no escape now. She and Henri were man and wife. As if this was not bad enough, five days later, tensions in the city of Paris were about to erupt into unimagined scenes of violence. Overnight on 23–24 August 1572, on the eve of the Catholic feast of St Bartholomew, thousands of French citizens were slaughtered in the streets with estimates varying wildly between 2,000 and 70,000 deaths.

As a Valois princess, Marguerite had always known to expect an arranged marriage, but she could not have predicted her family's choice of husband. Born in 1553, she was the seventh of Catherine de' Medici and Henri II's ten children, raised in the chateaus along the Loire. When Marguerite was only 9, the Catholic faction reacted against the growing Huguenot population, attacking them at Vassy, prompting a massacre that served as a catalyst for religious wars that raged for the next thirty-six years. Her marriage was seen as an opportunity to bring the strife to an end, with her mother making overtures to Jeanne d'Albret, whose son Henri was an eligible Huguenot bachelor, and son of the king of Navarre. Initially, Jeanne resisted, but having previously been an advocate of peace, she relented and assisted with the arrangements. Arriving in Paris ahead of the wedding, she proceeded to prepare her clothes for the ceremony, only to fall ill and die on 9 June, at the age of 43. Detractors of Catherine de' Medici claimed she had brought about Jeanne's death through a pair of poisoned gloves. For Marguerite, it was an inauspicious start to the festivities, only confirming her belief that the marriage was wrong.

The wedding festivities were short, lasting for only three days after the ceremony. Henri was in mourning for his mother and had brought 800 Huguenots with him for support. According to Marguerite, the weather was stifling hot. Then, in her own words, 'fortune, which is ever changing, did not fail soon to disturb the felicity of this union.'[2] On the day after the celebrations ended, on 21 August, an anonymous assassin attacked Gaspard de Coligny, a leading Huguenot and former friend of Charles IX. Shots were fired at him from a house owned by the Catholic Guise family, perhaps at the instigation of Catherine de' Medici, keen to remove his influence upon her son. Others suggested it was arranged by agents working for Philip II of Spain. Coligny's hand was injured, but he survived the night. The following evening, tensions were high; the Catholics decided to pre-empt any retaliation by the Protestant faction in the city with their own attack upon the remaining wedding guests, visitors and residents. Reputedly it was the young king Charles who gave the order, although Catherine has also been credited with the decision. One of the first targets was Coligny, who was stabbed, defenestrated and beheaded on the pavement outside his lodgings. After that, the massacre spread through the streets until they ran with blood.

Marguerite could not deny later that her brother was responsible, but she claimed to have been 'perfectly ignorant of what was going forward.' Her new marital status put her in the position that no one completely trusted her: 'the Huguenots were suspicious of me because I was a Catholic and the Catholics because I was married to the King of Navarre' so that 'no one spoke a syllable of the matter to me.' Her mother ordered her to go to bed and her sister warned her not to leave her room, in case she 'be the first victim of their revenge.' Catherine replied that 'if it pleased God, I should receive no hurt, but it was necessary I should go, to prevent the suspicion that might arise from my staying.'[3]

Terrified, Marguerite was unable to sleep. In the morning, a wounded man came banging on her door and ran in to throw himself upon her mercy, literally upon her bed, pursued by four archers. She rescued him from danger and allowed him to remain until his wounds had been dressed. As she was leaving the chamber, another man being pursued by pikemen was stabbed and fell dead at her feet, so that she fainted from terror.

Marguerite believed that the ultimate aim of the massacre was to kill her husband. News of it had spread through France to the point that Huguenots also came under attack in other major cities. Yet it was the marriage that saved him, as 'no attempt could be made on my husband whilst I continued to be his wife.'[4] Although she had initially disliked the match, and the man, Marguerite now saw this was the only way to save his life. Catherine asked her daughter 'to declare to her, upon my oath, whether I believed my husband to be like other men,' implying that she could divorce him through the suggestion that the match had not been physically consummated. Marguerite replied that she was 'content to remain as I am.'5 She resisted further calls to have the vows annulled and encouraged Henri to convert to Catholicism, which he did so in public, whilst intending to renounce the change as soon as he had fled to safety.

As the bodies were being cleared from the streets, one Catholic suggested that 2,000 had been killed, while a Huguenot put the number closer to 70,000! It is difficult to account for this wild discrepancy, save for the difference in sides and perspective between the initiators and their victims. Modern historians place their estimates at between 10,000 and 20,000. One record from the morning after is a payment made for workmen gathering dead bodies from out of the River Seine alone, which numbered 1,100. An additional 3,000 to 7,000 are thought to have perished in the provinces. Among those who escaped was the English ambassador to France, Francis Walsingham, his pregnant wife Ursula and their 4-year-old daughter, who opened their home as a refuge to Huguenots that night. Ursula and little Frances escaped to England soon afterwards, where Francis joined them the following April. European Protestants professed horror at the occurrence, as did the emperor but the Pope congratulated Charles for preventing an imminent Huguenot coup. No evidence suggests a coup was being planned. Writers commemorated the event, such as Christopher Marlowe's 1593 *The Massacre at Paris*.

In 1576, Henri escaped to Navarre, renounced his conversion and embraced the Protestant faith. He invited Marguerite to join him but Catherine and Charles refused to let her go, keeping her virtually under arrest in her rooms. Eventually, they were reunited but no children were born to the couple. Relations were strained, they both took lovers and Henri believed Marguerite may have conceived a child by another man. In 1585, she took the controversial step of leaving him and embraced the Catholic cause espoused by his enemies. After the assassination of her brother, Henri became king of France, as Henri IV, and they were briefly reconciled, only to divorce in 1599. Marguerite did not remarry. Henri took Marie de' Medici as his second wife, who bore him six children including the future Louis XIII and Henrietta Maria, future queen of England. Henri was killed in a jousting accident in 1610 and Marguerite outlived him by five years. Due to her birth, her marriage was seen as the pivot around which the wars of religion might turn. Yet her union with Henri exacerbated the tensions, and served to divide Marguerite's loyalties between husband and family. Sixteenth-century ideals of gender and wifehood insisted that a woman prioritise her husband, but Marguerite was a Valois and her mother would not let her forget it.

74

Sophie Brahe

11 November 1572

Herrevad Abbey, Scania, Denmark (Modern Sweden)

She followed where he pointed, squinting her eyes up into the darkness. It was just as her brother had said, something unrecorded in the night sky, dazzling, unexpected. It had appeared in the constellation Cassiopeia, with its scattered brightness, tilted on the side.

'And no one has ever observed it before?'

'No, it has just appeared. It doesn't change its position relative to the fixed stars, so it can't be a planet.' His blue eyes shone with excitement. 'It has to be a new star, a Stella Nova.'

'A Stella Nova,' she repeated.

He pointed again. 'See Venus over there? This is brighter.'

The comparison was clear. This new star was bright, very bright, visible even with the naked eye. Which was a good thing because Tycho Brahe did not yet own a telescope.

It was very dark at Herrevad Abbey. The solid 400-year-old edifice sat in the middle of nowhere, and although the monks had been dismissed only seven years ago, services were still held in the church and the school continued to receive pupils. After the Lutheran dissolution, the main abbey had been given to their uncle, a generous man who invited her brother to stay there and paid for a laboratory to be built in the old monastic buildings. So Tycho Brahe moved in and began work on a new paper mill and a glassworks, but then his attention had turned to the wide skies above. One night, he had seen it there among the constellations, and built his own sextant, an instrument used for measuring astrological distance, to observe it. Visiting him at Herrevad, his sister Sophie, aged perhaps as young as 13, had the chance to see it too. It would later be known as SN 1572, one of only eight supernovas visible from Earth without scientific instruments, despite being 7,500 light years away.

Sophie and Tycho were full siblings but had not been raised together. He was at least ten years older than her, perhaps as many as thirteen years, both born to an influential Danish couple: Otto Brahe, a chief advisor to King Frederick, and Beate, a leading lady in Queen Sophie's household. Both children were born at Knutstorp Castle, a medieval red brick manor in Scania, which had been in the Brahe family for decades. Tycho arrived in December 1546 and Sophie in

August 1559, although some sources claim 1556. At the age of 2, Tycho was sent to live with Otto's childless brother and his wife, while the Brahes' subsequent children were all raised at Knutstorp. Tycho studied medicine at the University of Rostock from 1566, but soon after his arrival, he was drawn into a dispute with his cousin, which resulted in a duel. Losing a portion of his nose from a sword blow, he was forced to wear a prosthetic replacement, made from brass, fixed in place with glue or paste, for the remainder of his life. After he graduated, when he began to influence Sophie and steer her reading, she would have known him with this distinctive appearance.

Tycho must have been an exciting older brother for Sophie, teaching her what he knew in the fields of alchemy, or chemistry, and horticulture. However, due to patriarchal beliefs or a lack of faith in her, he tried to dissuade her from studying astronomy, claiming it was too complex for a woman to understand. Sophie persisted, however, taking her education into her own hands, and reading whatever books she could find. Nor did she let any language barriers prevent her, frequently reading in German or using her own money to pay for Latin works to be translated. She was later described as 'a very gifted woman, possessing unique talents and an even more unique refinement of these talents.'[1]

Sophie's determination impressed her brother, changing his mind, and by 1572, she was observing the stars with him at Heerevad Abbey, and a lunar eclipse the following year. Acting as his assistant, she helped record his observations, using the instruments he had made, in order to note distances. It is Sophie's measurements that underpin Tycho's theories. Recognising her abilities, he praised her for her 'determined mind' and allowed her to complete many of the fashionable astrological charts requested by their paying customers. In the later 1570s, she visited him at his self-built observatory, the Uranienbourg, on the island of Hveen. Set in gardens and grounds of a geometric design, with an underground section, it was located on an island between Zealand and Scania. Dedicated to Urania, the muse of astronomy, it included rooms for visiting scientists, royalty and scholars, as well as housing Tycho and his family, laboratories and a printing press. James VI of Scotland visited in 1590.

Sophie followed the traditional path for women. In 1579 she married Otto Thott, a nobleman from Eriksholm, and bore one surviving child, a son named Tage. She was widowed upon Otto's death in March 1588, but continued to run the estate until Tage reached the age of maturity. Continuing to visit Tycho at Hveen, Sophie met one of his students, a young nobleman named Erik Lange, who had spent most of his family's fortune on futile attempts to turn base metals into gold. They became engaged in 1590, despite the strong objections of all her family to his lack of prospects, with the exception of her brother.[2] Often separated from Erik by circumstances, Sophie composed a long verse letter dedicated to him, a love poem from Urania to Titan. They were finally married in 1602, living together in Germany often in difficult circumstances, until Erik's death in 1613. Sophie returned to Sweden in 1616, where she continued her astrological work until 1643, when she died at the age of 87. She outlived her brother by decades as

Tycho had died in 1601. Other letters written by Sophie to her sisters survive, full of learning, astrology and her personal views about life and love.

Less well known to history than the more famous Tycho, Sophie Brahe was, nevertheless, at his side, assisting with some of his key discoveries and carrying out his work in his absence. Her involvement in astrological discoveries was facilitated by her brother, but she had to prove herself capable in spite of his doubts. Like a handful of other women of her time, she wanted to enter a traditionally masculine sphere; when excluded from the normal paths of study, she found her own way forward by convincing a male relative of her worth. Such women had to work doubly hard to pursue their ambitions as a result of the circumstances they found themselves in. Had a woman of Sophie's talents and inclinations been born in an era of greater equality, she is likely to have reached the top of her field. Hers is also a love story, of persistence against all odds, and the triumph of romantic love over material need.

75

Margaret Brayne

1576

The Theatre, Holywell Street, Shoreditch, London

They came streaming out through the gate. Apprentices, gentlemen in smart clothes, women with curious eyes, foreign visitors and Londoners with a few pence to spend, seeking pleasure outside the city walls. Just before 2.00 pm on a summer's afternoon, a bell tolled and a flag could be seen fluttering in the breeze, high above the jumble of rooftops and spires, the wisps of smoke rising to the sky. When Londoners wanted to play, they left the city and went into the suburbs where the new theatres were being built, outside the jurisdiction of officialdom. They came laughing, warm with drink, keen to see the latest play. Waiting at the door, ready to collect their entrance fees, was a woman in her thirties. Margaret Brayne received their coins and directed them towards their seats. Nor was this her only job. Alongside her husband, Margaret had helped build the first theatre with her own hands. It was quite an unusual career for an Elizabethan woman of her status.

Margaret's origins are lost. She first appears in the records in January 1565 when she married John Brayne, and her name is given as Margaret Stowers of the parish of St Dionis Backchurch, in Langbourn, London, along the stretch of modern Fenchurch Street. Brayne was the son of a tailor. After their marriage, the couple lived in the parish of St Stephen Walbrook, in the adjoining street of Bucklersbury, where their four children were baptised. The Braynes ran an early theatre in Whitechapel called the Red Lion, outside the city walls as it was a cheaper place to live. A few years earlier, John's sister Ellen Brayne had married James Burbage, a joiner-turned-actor and they had four children. By 1576 they were living in Shoreditch, raising their sons Cuthbert and Richard, who were to become leading theatrical figures, and daughters Ellen and Alice.

The futures of the Braynes and Burbages were to rise with the growth of Elizabethan drama. Developed from medieval pageantry, morality plays and Tudor interludes, the new style of plays were performed by troupes of actors employed by leading nobles in stately homes, at court and in the yards of coaching inns. Outbreaks of plague in the 1570s had halted the industry, with all plays banned in 1572 and actors prohibited from within the city walls in 1575 as a means of preventing the spread of the disease. As a result, players moved just outside the jurisdiction of these rules, and, in 1576, Brayne and Burbage joined forces in an ambitious plan to build a new theatre. By this point, John Brayne was a wealthy man and offered to provide the £200 funding required.

The location they chose was close to home. The Burbages were resident in Holywell Street, the site of the former dissolved Holywell Priory, an 8-acre stretch that had passed into secular hands. Here, they leased a piece of former monastic land in Burbage's name. Although he promised to add the Braynes to the official paperwork, this never happened. In 1576 they started to build on Curtain Road, abutting Finsbury Fields, standing just a few hundred yards from the city walls, allowing for easy access. Brayne's former skills as a joiner proved invaluable as timber by timber, the Theatre began to rise, the first of the traditional octagonal-shaped designs. An early sketched map shows its entrance was to the east, facing the city, aligned with a space in a long brick wall that flanked the ditch that ran along the field. Above it was Alice Daridoe's house and garden, one of three houses facing a courtyard; to the right was the great horse pond, larger in size than the theatre, and below was a barn that contained a cattle pen and slaughterhouse. The surroundings were less than salubrious.

The construction costs quickly began to rise. John and Margaret pitched in, helping to build the theatre with their own hands to reduce the price of labour. Yet their initial £200 became closer to £700, driving them to the verge of bankruptcy. It was necessary that they made the venture a success. Together, they cut, sawed, drove nails home, swept, painted, recruited actors and gathered props and costumes. Yet there was one area from which Margaret was excluded. As a woman, she was prohibited from acting. It was considered scandalous, inappropriate and would have damaged her reputation, had she not been booed off stage. There would be no official female actors for almost a century. When it was time for the first performance, Margaret was on the door collecting money as a gatherer, working behind the scenes, perhaps even selling refreshments, instead of performing.

Margaret had avoided the scandal of acting as a woman, as her position in the completed theatre was one of organisation and catering. Over the coming years, the stage was occupied by the Lord Leicester's Men, then the Admiral's Men and soon, with James' son Richard as its leading actor, the Lord Chamberlain's Men. Also among the cast was the young William Shakespeare. However, a different scandal arose to cloud Margaret's success. Having invested so much money and been left off the lease, John contested the sole ownership claimed by Burbage. When he died in 1586, the situation was unresolved. Initially, Margaret believed that her husband had been killed by their business associate Robert Miles, and pursued him in court. Later though, they became friends and Margaret was no longer able to conceal that she was pregnant. The timing of this is unclear. She claimed the child was posthumously John's, but the Burbages believed she had conspired with Miles to kill John as they were engaged in an affair. By 1588 she was being financially supported by Miles. Burbage tried to sue her to prevent further counterclaims made on the theatre and in response, Margaret counter-sued. It must have been a frustrating situation, having invested so much time and work, for her to be excluded and unacknowledged. Seeking a male protector to assist her through the legal process was a logical move for a woman in Margaret's situation, regardless of any personal relationship between them.

Margaret did not live to see the dispute resolved. She died in 1593 of the plague, leaving everything she owned, including the care of her infant daughter, to Miles. The child, Katherine, died three months later, also of the plague. The Theatre remained in the hands of the Burbage family until it was dismantled in December 1598 and ferried over the water to the Southbank. There, the individual timbers crafted and built by John and Margaret were used to rebuild the most famous of Elizabethan theatres, the Globe. Margaret's name may be forgotten now in theatrical history, but her legacy lives on.

76

Lettice Knollys

21 September 1578
Wanstead Hall, Essex, England

One crisp September morning, just before 7.00 am, a small group of friends gathered at Wanstead Hall in Essex. A smallish but beautiful property, it had been used as a hunting lodge by Henry VII and Henry VIII, and had now come into the hands of Robert Dudley, Earl of Leicester. Semi-rural, it lay just 10 miles to the north-east of Whitehall Palace, surrounded by parkland. And it was there, with just six guests to witness his actions, that Queen Elizabeth's favourite planned to get married in secret.

The bride knew exactly what she was doing. Lettice Knollys was 35 years old, a widow and the mother of six children. On her mother's side, she was closely related to the queen, as Catherine Carey was the firstborn child of Mary Boleyn, sister of the ill-fated Anne, who died seven years before Lettice arrived. Some said, though, that she was even more closely tied into the Tudor bloodline, and that Catherine had been fathered by Henry VIII himself. Whatever the truth of her descent, Lettice had inherited the striking red hair and looks that gave her an uncanny resemblance to the queen, although she was a whole decade younger. When she was painted by George Gower in 1588, Lettice was depicted very much in Elizabeth's style, with her dark red curls dressed up high under a small black hat, ornate with jewels and feather, and a stiff, cartwheel ruff. Like Elizabeth in her Armada portrait, completed in the same year, Lettice wears a drop-pearl in the centre of her forehead, making a further visual connection with the queen. Lettice's string of pearls and her black, white and gold clothing further echo the royal composition, in a deliberate act of comparison, stating her affinity with, and relation to, a queen who by that point had not spoken to her for a decade. As she went to marry Dudley that morning, dressed in the loose-fitting gown that was fashionable at the time, Lettice knew she was taking a terrible risk. By marrying a man the queen had loved for two decades, and believed to belong exclusively to her, Lettice was not breaking the law. However, by breaking the queen's heart, she knew there would ultimately be repercussions.

Lettice and Leicester would have met when she first attended court, as a 17-year-old maid of the Privy Chamber in 1559. She was well placed to observe the closeness between monarch and favourite, who were close in age, and spent so much time together that rumours arose. Elizabeth's council had been urging her to wed since her accession, but she only had eyes for Robert. After his wife Amye was found dead at the bottom of a staircase, the taint of scandal made their union impossible, even though an inquest exonerated Dudley. Later that year, Lettice married Walter Devereux, Viscount Hereford, subsequently Earl of Essex, and bore him six children. On one occasion when she returned to court, she attracted the attention of the increasingly frustrated Dudley, whose attempts to flirt with her provoked jealousy in the queen. Essex also resented the connection and, during his absence in Ireland, rumours arose about the pair, from visits made by Lettice to Dudley's castle at Kenilworth, to the unlikely suggestion that she bore him illegitimate children. By the time of Essex's death in 1576, Dudley had come to recognise that Elizabeth, then in her mid-forties, would never become his wife. He turned to Lettice instead.

Gathered at Wanstead Hall on the morning of 21 September 1578 were the close family and companions of the couple: Lettice's brothers Francis and Richard, Dudley's brother Ambrose and two trusted friends, Henry Herbert, Earl of Pembroke, who was newly married to Dudley's niece Mary Sidney, and Roger, Lord North. They were married by chaplain Humphrey Tyndall, whose observation that Lettice wore a loose gown gave rise to later rumours of a pregnancy, although this was simply the fashion and no child materialised at this point. The marriage had been planned for over a year, so it was not a question of necessity. The Dudleys' period of unchallenged happiness was brief. Only a few months elapsed before Elizabeth was informed about the match and, in her fury, banned both Robert and Lettice from court. She soon found herself unable to do without her favourite, though, and Robert was invited back, but Lettice would never be forgiven and was excluded from court for the duration of Elizabeth's life.

Lettice lived mostly in the country, at Wanstead or with her family at Rotherfield Greys in Oxfordshire. She was resident at Leicester House on the Strand when she bore a son in 1581, named Robert after his father, or the 'noble imp'. At last, Dudley had a legitimate male heir, but the child's unexpected death three years later left his parents devastated. Dudley himself died in 1588, with Lettice at his side, on their way to take the spa waters at Buxton. Even after his death, the queen barely relented, agreeing to see her cousin just once more. Lettice's crime had been to fall in love with the wrong man, and Elizabeth would never let her forget it.

77

St Teresa of Avila

1579

Convent of St Joseph, Toledo, Central Spain

It was forty-four years since she had first entered a convent. Now, as she contemplated her life, the elderly nun was reminded of how it had been a calling from her earliest years. Yet Catholicism did not go back many generations in her family; her grandfather had been a Converso, a Jew forced to convert to Christianity by Ferdinand of Aragon and Isabella of Castile. The alternative was to face harsh punishments or exile. Teresa was born in Avila in 1515, twenty-three years after all remaining Jews were commanded to leave the country. Raised as a Catholic in a noble family, she was convinced of her role by the age of 7, running away in a bid to fight against the Moors and become a martyr. After her mother died, when she was 11, Teresa was sent to be educated at an Augustinian nunnery, before entering a convent at the age of 20.

Teresa quickly established herself as a mystical figure. She experienced a year-long period of religious ecstasy and illness, only recovering after an appeal to the saints. Later, she began inflicting mortifications upon her the flesh, an extreme practise of self-harm by which religious figures reminded themselves of the limitations and temptations of the flesh, as well as Christ's bodily suffering. She is recorded as having visions, instances described as levitation, and fits, which some later historians have questioned as potential elements of undiagnosed frontal lobe epilepsy.[1] These episodes terrified the young Teresa, who documented them all, afraid that her experiences and the spiritual knowledge she believed she derived from them might actually come from the Devil, rather than divine inspiration. In a further attempt to regain control over her life and soul, she renounced ownership of all property and lived in conditions of extreme poverty. Her notoriety spread. She would dispense wisdom to the community from behind the metal grille at the convent. The Pope judged that she was attracting attention for the wrong reasons and issued her with a sanction.

Judging that the traditional monastic life needed reform, Teresa founded a string of new Carmelite priories in the late 1560s and early 1570s. Her beliefs dictated such a life of privation, though, that more conservative members of the order began to turn against her and worked to halt the founding of further new establishments. Teresa was pressured to retreat and retired to St Joseph's at Toledo, which she had founded in 1562. At the same time, she founded the order of Discalced Carmelites, who dedicated their life strictly to prayer and austerity, contemplation and remaining in the cloister. As with many sixteenth-century women who challenged existing mores, Teresa's gender was given as a reason for her radicalism, and she was seen a 'restless wanderer, disobedient, and stubborn *femina* who, under the title of devotion, invented bad doctrines, moving outside the cloister against the rules… teaching as a master against St Paul's orders that women should not teach.'[2]

By 1576, her friends and supporters were targeted, then she was arrested and taken to be examined by the Inquisition. Whilst there, she began to write her famous tracts *The Way of Perfection* and *The Interior Castle*. She was initially doubtful about writing, but God appeared to her in a vision:

> …a most beautiful crystal globe, made in the shape of a castle, and containing seven mansions, in the seventh and innermost of which was the King of Glory, in the greatest splendour, illumining and beautifying them all. The nearer one got to the centre, the stronger was the light; outside the palace limits everything was foul, dark and infested with toads, vipers and other venomous creatures.[3]

Teresa's castle contained seven mansions, each describing a step closer in the journey to God. It could be entered through prayer and meditation, proceeding through various stages of asceticism, as the soul seeks humility and rejects sin. Next, the penitent advances through daily prayer and recognition of God's work into the final stages of an exemplary life, before finally achieving spiritual marriage with God. Her autobiography described a similar journey towards God in four stages, culminating in a lack of awareness of the physical body and spiritual absorption into the divine.

Eventually, Teresa's many appeals to Philip II of Spain bore fruit. In 1579, the case against her was dropped and she was freed. Vindicated, she spent her final years founding more monasteries before dying in 1582. Teresa's remains were buried in Alba de Tormes, but after a year, she was exhumed and a number of various body parts were removed and interred elsewhere; her right foot and jaw reside in Rome, a hand is in Lisbon, another hand and an eye are in Ronda in Spain, and fingers are elsewhere, including Paris. She was canonised in 1622 and remains a key figure of inspiration in the Catholic church.

78

Jury of Matrons

3 July 1581
Rochester, Kent, England

There were fourteen women assembled in the hall. Mature, honest matrons of good fame, above reproach, dressed modestly as befitted their station as the wives of local businessmen. Rochester was an important port in north Kent, situated on the Thames within the London Basin, with a cathedral, Norman castle and regular markets and courts. Traditionally, the peripatetic assize court was held in the city in Lent or summer and may have been held in the original guildhall or the castle's great hall. In advance, a number of women were summoned to do their duty, chosen by association with their menfolk. It was a traditionally female task using the practical knowledge of birthing practices they had learned through personal experience and observation. These were the jury of matrons, charged to carry out intimate, hands-on examinations, seeking bodily changes, swellings and foetal movement, in order to satisfy the judge that a woman's sentence should be delayed.

As the matrons awaited their instructions, on the morning of 3 July 1581, another group of women were also gathered nearby. These were the prisoners, held for crimes ranging from theft to murder, many with the sentence of death hanging over them. When it came to women of childbearing age, this was complicated by the possibility of pregnancy. Any female prisoner carrying a child would automatically have her sentence reprieved until after the birth, so many were tempted to fake their condition or even to try and fall pregnant inside gaol itself. Before the invention of reliable pregnancy tests, the courts had to rely upon physical examination to determine whether or not a woman's body showed signs of having conceived. This was the job of the jury of matrons.

The names of the matrons assembled at the Rochester Assize courts on 3 July 1581, were recorded by the clerk:

Joan Fryer, Margaret Bisto, Elizabeth Tomson, Alice Borowes, Anne Davies, Christine Ward, Dorothy Rowe, Elizabeth Clercke, Emma Wyat, Agnes Browne, Milicent Yeomanson, Elen Tottonton, Isabelle Jarman and Joan Thorneton. Some of them had possibly been employed in this capacity before, with an Agnes Browne serving at Maidstone in 1571, Elizabeth Clarke at Maidstone in February 1573 and Rochester in July 1576, and both women again at Rochester in February 1590, although these are both common names.[1]

On 3 July, the matrons were tasked to examine Elen Handmore, then in Maidstone gaol, and Margery Browne and Alice More, who had been remanded in custody in Canterbury gaol, and brought to Rochester. No details survive about the crimes of which they were accused, although the typical charges brought against women in the courts were theft, witchcraft and infanticide. Presumably, the intimate examination of the women's bodies took place in a private room, away from prying male eyes, but it cannot have been a pleasant or dignified process. The female prisoners would have had to strip and submit to the exploration of other women's hands, in order to determine their condition. The attitude of the matrons would have been decisive in setting the tone too, whether they were sympathetic or business-like towards these prisoners suspected of crimes. Assuming all were local, the women may well have been known to each other: members of the same community, potentially with history or previous knowledge of the women's good fame, or lack of it. The dynamic of women examining women within the legal framework may have highlighted existing tensions and played on contemporary expectations of femininity, motherhood and the law.

Following their examinations, the matrons concluded that Handmore and More were pregnant but that Browne was not. Browne's sentence was presumably carried out swiftly, as she disappears from the records. Handmore and More were still in custody eight months later when the assizes were held at Rochester again on 15 March 1582. Presumably, both had given birth during this time and were now preparing to receive their punishment. Neither appear in the records for July 1582 or March 1583 and are likely to have suffered capital punishment. The fates of their children were not recorded. It is likely that Elen and Alice delivered their infants in gaol and if the babies survived this process, they might either have been given to family, or raised by the parish. The practise of using a jury of matrons continued. Mostly they are anonymous beyond their names, but their sanctioned, invasive role is a brutal reminder of the harsh justice of the era. The attitudes of the female prisoners towards them is difficult to recapture; whether they represented the 'enemy' of patriarchal authority, or if they offered the opportunity for a brief reprieve. Equally, there may have been varying degrees of zeal by which the matrons went about their duties, and with varying degrees of empathy. With such high stakes at play, the interaction between the matrons and the female prisoners may well have been fraught, accentuating the loss of liberty of the captives over their freedom and bodies. The physical invasion of their person by these elected officials was a significant step on the road to their loss of life. At the end of the examination, the condemned women were returned to the cells, while the matrons were absorbed back into civic life, having performed their duty.

79

Ursula Kemp

February/March 1582

St Osyth, Essex, England

St Osyth is an ancient village overlooking the mudflats of the River Blackwater in Essex. Set between Clacton and Mersea Island, for centuries its main draw was an early medieval priory, with the village growing up between its quiet grounds and the river, where fishermen propelled small craft through its winding, salty channels. The sound of the bells across the marshes was punctuated with the cries of wading birds.

When Ursula Kemp was born in the village in around 1525, the priory was still the heart of her community, offering shelter, salvation, medicine and employment as one of the largest religious establishments in Essex. It sustained sixteen monks under the rule of its prior. When Ursula was 14, though, the priory was dissolved and passed into private hands, creating upheaval and uncertainty in the village. Ursula eked out a living as a local midwife and wise woman, using herbs and charms to assist her neighbours when they were unwell. By 1582 she was living with her illegitimate son, Thomas Rabbett, who was then aged 8. This would place his birth around the year 1574, when Ursula was approaching 50, which is not impossible by modern standards but less likely by those of the sixteenth century. It may suggest her actual birthdate was later than 1525.

Before the regulation of midwifery, and while doctors were expensive, male and often distant, many women drew upon a vast oral tradition of medical knowledge that was passed down the generations in rural villages. The overlap between such cures, which often had accompanying rituals or chants, and magic, or witchcraft, could be great. Women in Ursula's position frequently exaggerated their special powers – their sympathetic or positive magical abilities – in order to attract customers, and. equally, this could turn against them if their methods failed to work or further harm was incurred by their patients. Thus, the women, rather than science or poor hygiene, were considered the ones to blame. No doubt there were instances when their advice or potions did more harm than good, but questions of timing were crucial, and women who had negative social encounters, or fell out with their patients, could be blamed for placing a curse upon them in the days, weeks, months or even years after the event. Some even manipulated the concept of cures and curses in order to bring the client back, begging for assistance, or for the lifting of the supposed curse. Such was the case with Ursula Kemp, when circumstances in 1582 spiralled out of control. Ursula's adult life also coincided with a period of increasing persecution of women perceived to be witches, and her activities in St Osyth led to her gaining a reputation for such practices.

When local woman Grace Thurlow's son Davy fell ill, a number of women visited him at home, including Ursula. Taking him by the hand, she muttered some mysterious words and he immediately began to improve. Impressed by Ursula's abilities, Grace invited her to attend her new-born baby girl Joan, but in an accident shortly afterwards, the child fell from its cradle and died. Grace blamed this on Ursula, although it is unclear what her motivation might have been, having already cured one of Grace's children. Ursula retaliated, threatening Grace with lameness, and when Grace retorted that Ursula should 'take heed' as she had a 'naughty name', she found herself crippled and unable to walk. Later, Grace asked Ursula to cure her lameness, which she did for the fee of 12 pence. Five weeks later, Ursula called to collect her money, but Grace said she did not have it, and also rejected Ursula's request for payment in cheese. Ursula said she would be revenged, and Grace was lame again the following day.[1]

It is difficult in modern times to understand this result in terms other than the logical; either Grace experienced a psychological reaction, or she was tricking Ursula, or perhaps Ursula somehow injured her or secretly dosed her with a concoction that could induce muscle cramps. Perhaps Grace had already experienced lameness, in arthritis, or some other form, and it was just a matter of time before her pain emerged again, allowing Ursula to hold this knowledge over her. It is unclear how much time elapsed between the threat and Grace's pain. Whatever happened, it was unwise of Ursula to make such a threat, and she would suffer for it.

Grace complained to the local sheriff, Justice Brian Darcy, and her son Thomas was questioned. Other local women came forward to testify against Ursula, perhaps after bad experiences of her magic, or who disliked her, or as the result of the bad name, or reputation alluded to by Grace. The questioning focused upon Ursula's activities as the leader of a circle of women, who suggested she was skilled in the art of poison, and her ownership of four familiars, usually domestic pets, whom she would suckle from her thigh and involve in her spells. Thomas named them as Tyffin, a grey cat; Jack, a black cat; Tyttey, a white lamb; and Pygine, a black toad, who his mother fed beer and cake and suckled them with her blood. It is likely that the 8-year-old boy was led by his interrogators. Ursula was accused of the deaths of Joan Thurlow, another child named Elizabeth Letherdale whom she had 'bewitched to death' and a woman, Edna Stratton, as well as killing cattle and preventing beer from brewing. Darcy claimed that she had made a full confession to him in private and revealed the recipe that had cured her own lameness, which she had used for others, including charnel, sage, pig dung and St John's wort. Apparently, she told him that 'though she could unwitch, she could not witch.'[2] Her close friend Alice Newman was also arrested and questioned by Darcy, who found that 'shee could bee brought to confesse nothing', so broke down her resistance by threatening he would 'sever and part her and her spirites a sunder'.[3] Twelve other women were named. Many made a full confession, perhaps under pressure, or out of genuine belief in their own powers, or because they had either been promised leniency or threatened with violence. Darcy promised Ursula that 'if shee woulde deal plainly and confesse the trueth, that she should have favour, and so by giving her faire speeches, soe confesseth.'[4]

The investigations and trial took place in February and March 1582. Ursula Kemp was hanged in Chelmsford shortly afterwards. Accounts suggest that between six and twelve other women were hanged with her for witchcraft. Their case, known as the St Osyth witch trials, is one of the most famous of similar cases in the dying years of the sixteenth century and beyond, where reputation, gossip and gender collided with superstition, fear and a lack of understanding of cause and effect. What is also clear, from the account of the event, is the shameless abuse of power from those keen to secure a conviction. What happened to Ursula's son Thomas Rabbett is unknown.

80

Anne Hathaway

November 1582

Stratford-upon-Avon, Warwickshire, England

Anne Hathaway has become famous for being the wife to whom Shakespeare left his 'second best bed' in his will of 1616. When he died, in their family home of New Place in central Stratford, his choice regarding her bequest has been interpreted and dissected, as has her possible character and role in his life. Anne has occupied the imagination of many writers since, mentioned in Woolf's *Night and Day* (1919), and being the subject of Carol Ann Duffy's poem 'The Second Best Bed' (1999), Maggie O'Farrell's prizewinning novel *Hamnet* (2020) and the film *All is True* (2018). Given the continuing fascination with Shakespeare and his life, it is not surprising that the woman he married as a youth of 18 should excite such interest, especially as so little is known about her.

Anne, or Agnes, was 26 when she fell pregnant by a young local man, the son of a glover in Stratford. She was born in 1566 and had grown up in Shottery, a village a mile to the west of Stratford, where a house still stands in which she is reputed to have lived. Her father was a yeoman farmer who left her a small inheritance when he died in 1581, to be paid upon her marriage. Anne had probably already met William by this time, falling pregnant the following August. The age of 26 was relatively old for a first marriage at the time, so Anne may have stayed at home to look after younger siblings before her condition made the wedding necessary. However, this does not mean it was a forced marriage or there was any lack of affection or choice between the two.

Anne bore their first child, Susanna, in May 1583 and then twins, Judith and Hamnet, in February 1585. Soon afterwards, Shakespeare embarked for his career in London as a playwright, but according to seventeenth-century biographer John Aubrey, he returned regularly and sent home money for his family. As far as is known, Anne remained in Stratford raising the children, with just the two girls after Hamnet died of plague in 1596. The purchase of New Place in 1602, the second largest house in Stratford, marked Shakespeare's success in the wider world and raised Anne's profile in the town. Perhaps he wrote to her about his plays, the crowds they drew and problems he encountered, preserving a level of intimacy between them. It is not even certain whether the playwright's wife could read and write, and their daughter Judith signed legal documents with a mark, an 'x', rather than her name. If not, she would need any letters read aloud to her and to have her responses dictated, perhaps to a friend, clerk or scribe. Perhaps this is the greatest unanswered question about Anne, the issue that leads people to scrutinise her life and search for more. When we ask what was special about Shakespeare's wife that elicited the love of a literary genius, the answer might be that she was, in fact, a normal woman. What if there are no more secrets to uncover, no surprises, no 'special' qualities, beyond love?

It was to Anne at New Place that Shakespeare returned upon his retirement in 1613, as the famous figure who included her in his will with the notorious detail. The second-best bed does not imply that she was second-best in his eyes; it might be so-named for a number of reasons, perhaps as the less new, more comfortable bed in which she had slept, or delivered their children. There may have been personal associations that have been long lost. 'Best' at the time meant pristine, not nicest, or most familiar, or softest. Shakespeare died three years later in 1616 and Anne outlived him, dying in 1623. Both were buried in the Church of the Holy Trinity in Stratford-upon-Avon.

Anne's life, or lack of the life and opportunities enjoyed by her husband, represents the eternal female dilemma of conformity and motherhood versus the quest for individuality and personal freedom. She followed the traditional path of many women, static and nurturing, to enable their menfolk the freedom of travel and expression. Many men who pursued a career at court maintained a family in the countryside, living a peripatetic existence, not unlike that of Shakespeare in London. They would attend court, or business, for weeks at a time, then sojourn in the country before returning to the city. Anne is also one of the earliest figures to present the dynamic of the woman married to a famous artist or writer, and the sacrifices required to support their art. The familiar trope of the woman in the background, maintaining a household to support the artistic or cerebral existence of their man, prey to all the loneliness and hard work this can bring, is personified in the life of Anne Hathaway.

81

Penelope Rich

1583

The Elizabethan Court, London, England.

She looked down at the paper. A single sheet, rolled and sealed with wax. Red and shining, barely dry, bulbing up around the seal impressed upon it. She recognised the device at once.

The handwriting was familiar, too: well-controlled, clean without smudges, neat with the tails of letters trailing. It contained another sonnet: fourteen lines of imagery and rhyming flattery, in praise of her beauty. Once again, she unscrolled his words and read his barely-contained passion. There, in black ink, was the special name he had coined for her: Stella, his star, his beloved, dazzling and beautiful. It filled her with mixed emotions.

By the 1580s, the Elizabethan court was nurturing an unprecedented number of literary and artistic talents. Following the tone set by the queen, it was a place where flirtations deepened into love affairs during passionate dancing, banquets and the witty exchanges between her gentlewomen and leading men. With Elizabeth reaching her fiftieth year, she had finally relinquished all pretence of marriage, refusing her final suitor, and mourning the secret marriage of her favourite, Robert Dudley. Yet her court thronged with young men and women, and an increasing tension between patriarchal expectations of marriage for advancement and the heady atmosphere of romance, encouraged by the poets and playwrights.

Penelope was the daughter of the woman who had stolen Dudley from under the queen's nose. She was born in 1563, in Staffordshire, the eldest daughter of Lettice Knollys and her first husband, Walter Devereux, Earl of Essex. It was her father's intention that she be married to a young courtier from Kent, nine years her senior, accomplished and handsome. But her father had died when she was 13, and Penelope was sent to live under the austere guardianship of her Hastings uncle and aunt, before her mother Lettice remarried. It was only later, when Catherine Hastings took her to court as a teenager, that she encountered her former intended, but it was too late as a match had been arranged for her with Sir Richard Rich. Penelope protested, claiming she could not marry Rich, no matter what his wealth and status might be. Her wishes went unheeded. She was married to Rich in January 1581, around the time of her eighteenth birthday. All Philip Sidney could do about it was to write her sonnets.

The sonnet sequence *Astrophil and Stella* was composed in the early 1580s, portraying the 'lover of stars' Astrophil, and his inspiration, the Star, Stella. Modern criticism has questioned just how far these poems are autobiographical, suggesting that these are mere poetic personae required to tell the story, but Sidney goes to some lengths to identify Penelope and disparage her husband, punning upon his surname. The suffix 'phil', Greek for 'to love', is also a direct link with Sidney's given name of Philip. Sonnet 35 contains the line 'long needie Fame/ Doth even grow rich, meaning my Stellas name,' implying an existing, or pre-existing love connection between the pair, with the pronoun of ownership, 'my', and the pun of 'rich' setting the poet in opposition to the wealth of her husband. Sonnet 37 goes further, praising Stella's innate riches in comparison with the temporary advantages of material wealth. The last line can hardly be more explicit in condemning her marriage:

> Rich in all beauties which man's eye can see;
> Beauties so farre from reach of words that we
> Abase her praise saying she doth excell;
> Rich in the treasure of deserved renowne,
> Rich in the riches of a royall heart,
> Rich in those gifts which give the eternall crowne;
> Who, though most rich in these and every part
> Which make the patents of true worldy blisse,
> Hath no misfortune but that Rich she is.[1]

Her husband is later criticised as being rich in folly with a 'base and filthy heart', and growing wretched from longing for more money. In comparison, Astrophil argues, love is a sacred thing:

> But that rich foole, who by blind Fortunes lot
> The richest gem of love and life enjoys,
> And can with foule abuse such beauties blot;
> Let him, deprived of sweet but unfelt joys,
> Exiled for all from those high treasures which
> He knowes not, grow in only folly rich![2]

Sonnet five confirms the sense that Astrophil and Stella, or Sidney and Penelope, were intended for each other and that Rich stole the prize, in the line 'but thou, rich in all joys, dost rob my joys from me.'[3]

The sonnet sequence *Astrophil and Stella* was one of many poems written and circulated among a courtly elite. In manuscript form, it was entrusted only to that audience the author chose, and thus likely to have excluded Rich and his associates, making Sidney bold in his expression. Married women of the court were selected as muses by poets and artists, at a respectful distance, but the history of the couple and references in this sequence is more personal. While the queen maintained a chilly distance from those who immortalised her in verse, Penelope and Sidney may have been closer, if not physically, then at least emotionally.

The couple's passion, whatever form it took, was to be short-lived, though. Sidney died in 1586 after being injured at the Battle of Zutphen. The following year, Penelope bore her first of seven children by Rich. The first printed edition of *Astrophil and Stella* was published in 1591 and set to music in 1597. At least three other later poets dedicated their work to Penelope on account of her beauty. Unhappily married, she engaged in a love affair with Charles Blount and bore him several children. She was denounced by Rich as a traitor after the unsuccessful rebellion of her brother, Robert Devereux, Earl of Essex in 1601, but was restored to favour after the death of Elizabeth, travelling to Scotland to welcome Anne of Denmark and serving in her household. The Richs were divorced after she admitted adultery, and Penelope was finally married to Blount in 1605. Again, her happiness was short-lived as Blount only lived for a further year, and Penelope died in 1607 at the age of 44.

Penelope was not typical of her era in being immortalised in verse, but she did typify what the Elizabethan poets aspired to in a woman. As their muse, she combined beauty, breeding, intelligence and grace with the expected courtly accomplishments. Attracting so much poetic attention from her generation, she transcends the reality of her existence as a lady-in-waiting and a wife into an Elizabethan icon. Taken out of biographical context, Sidney's puns might line up with other comparative poems, but they take on greater significance given the derailment of his engagement to Penelope and her objections in 1581 to Rich as a suitor. The real woman amid the imagery is glimpsed more closely in her admission of guilt and remarriage to Blount.

82

Mary Fillis

1583

Smithfield, London, England

Black faces have been notoriously absent from Tudor portraits, artwork and designs, leading many scholars and historians to assume there were no people of African descent present in sixteenth-century England beyond the lone figure of royal trumpeter John Blanke. The recent work of Miranda Kaufmann,[1] though, has uncovered many more living and working quietly, mostly in the south of England, in trade or service. Among them was Mary Fillis, about whom little is known, but those details of her life are typical of many others.

Mary was the daughter of a shovel-maker and basket weaver from Morocco named Fillis. She was born in 1577 and came to England in 1583 or 1584, at the age of 6 or 7. Why she came, how, and with whom is unclear, but she entered service in the household of John Barker, a merchant of Mark Lane, near the Tower. Barker was an agent for John Dudley, importing items like sugar and saltpetre, used in fireworks and gunpowder, so it is possible that he brought Mary back with him after one of his voyages. Mary grew up in Barker's wealthy household, in service rather than as a slave, an important distinction at the time, allowing her freedom of movement. Nor was she the only servant of African descent there, joining Leying Mouea, aged 20, and 'George, a blackamoor'.[2] Mary had left Barker's employ by 1597, when she was aged around 20, although he appears in literature relating to mercantile activities in London and Bristol into the early1620s.

In 1597, Mary was working as a seamstress and living in the house of her employer, Millicent Porter, in East Smithfield. By that year, she had converted to Christianity, a common move among immigrants who wished to assimilate more easily into Elizabethan society. Mary was baptised in the church of St Botolph's Aldgate, where the record states that she was a 'black moor' from 'Morisco'. The occasion was well-attended and she gave her answers in a graceful, Christian manner and was able to recite the Lord's Prayer.

> She was of late servant with one Mistress Barker in Marke Lane, a widow. She said her father's name was Fillis of Morisco, a black more, being both a basket maker and also a shovell maker.
>
> This Marie Fillis being about the age of xx yeares and having been in England for the space of xiii or xiiii years, and as yet was not Christened,

and now being become servant with one Millicent Porter a seamster dwelling in the liberty of Eastsmithfield, and now taking some hold of faith in Jesus Chryst, was desirous to become a Christian.

Wherefore she made suite by her said mistress to have some conference with the Curate of this the parish of St Buttolphees without Aldgate London...

So that I do say that the said Mary Fillis a black more at this tyme dwelling with Millicent Porter a seamester of the liberty of Eastsmithfield was christened on Fryday being the third day of June, in the presents of the under named and divers others, viz William Benton, Margerie Barrick, Millicent Porter, M(ist)res Magdalyne Threlkeld, Mathew Pearson, Mistress Young, Gertrud Ponder, Thomas Harrydance, being the parish Clarke, Thomas Ponder, being the sexton, and divers others.[3]

Mary is likely to have continued working for Porter up until her mistress' death in June 1599, after which the trail goes cold. Mary might have died, married, or continued to ply her trade in the city that she now called home. Equally, she may have left England, although it seems her baptism would be a move intended to help her stay.

If Mary remained in the parish, she might have been one of the two Marys buried there in 1623 or 1631, but equally, she may have moved on. The details of her life are lost in time, but the fact of her existence as an independent black woman with a profession is remarkable. She was one of sixty individuals of African descent baptised in London during this period,[4] and was accepted by her community, becoming a familiar face. Being an outsider in Tudor England was never an easy position to be in; the fact that Mary persisted, and achieved success, is a testament to her character.

83

Jane Dee

1584

Cracow, Poland

Jane Fromond was married to one of the most infamous and controversial men of the sixteenth century. The details of her life survive because her husband was John Dee, Elizabeth I's astrologer, and he kept diaries throughout his life, relating to his work, their marriage, domestic arrangements, the arrival of their children, arguments, travels and milestones. Reading what Dee recorded on a daily basis gives a glimpse into the life of his much younger wife, including the times that he led her into controversial territory.

Jane was born in Cheyham, or Cheam, Surrey, in 1555, to Bartholomew Fromond and his wife. As a young woman, she found a place in the household of Elizabeth FitzGerald, Countess of Lincoln, a lady-in-waiting and friend to Elizabeth I. Jane might have accompanied her to court on many occasions, which could be when she had opportunities to see Dee as he read the queen's astrological charts or gave her medical advice. The pair were also living comparatively close, so they might have met that way. They were married in the first half of 1578 when she was 23 and he was 51. On 14 July, he recorded a visit to his 'sister Fromond' and in August, visited his 'father-in-law at Cheyham'. Dee had been married twice before, but had no children.[1] Jane moved into his house at Mortlake High Street, close to the river, not far from Richmond Palace. That October, Dee records that his wife attended Elizabeth's court, which was then in residence.

Jane's new husband was described by biographer John Aubrey as having 'a very cleare rosie complexion, a long beard as white as milke. A very handsome man, he was tall and slender. He wore a gowne like an artists gowne, with hanging sleeves, and a slit. A mighty good man he was.'[2] No corresponding description or portrait survives of Jane. Within months of the wedding, she was pregnant, giving birth to Arthur on 13 July. Jane was still recovering when her son was christened three days later. Elizabeth's closest companion Blanche Parry was his godmother, and is also listed as Dee's 'cousin', although this was a fairly catch-all term to signify a close connection. Jane was churched on 9 August, probably at St Mary the Virgin, which had stood opposite Dee's house on the High Street since 1543.

Dee's diaries continue with details of Jane and their children. In January 1580, Arthur was suffering with a 'cold phlegm' which prevented him from sleeping, eating and drinking.[3] That August he was weaned and Nurse Darant was discharged with a modest reward. Two months later, Jane was pregnant again, delivering Katherine in June 1581. The baby was sent out to nurse, but illness necessitated a swift change, so a new wet nurse was found. Dee recorded when Arthur fell down the length of the Water Gate Stairs, the steps leading down to the river, cutting his forehead and right eyebrow, and when Jane visited the nurse by boat, taking her candles and soap. Later that night, his wife was troubled by cramp and colic, vomiting in church the next day and growing 'stiff in the soul'.[4] Katherine was also ill and was brought home to be weaned. In late January 1583, Jane bore Rowland who was baptised on 2 February and sent out to be nursed nine days later. The middle-class practise of mothers not breastfeeding their own children was common, to allow them to resume family life and their fertility with the resumption of their menstrual cycles.

Family life was interrupted, though, when Jane's husband made two new controversial friends. In 1582, Dee met Edward Kelley and began working with him more exclusively on supernatural and spiritual matters, such as the practise of meditating and conferring with angels who would dictate books using Kelley as a medium. The following year, Dee met Polish nobleman Albert Laski at court, who invited the doctor to return to Poland with him when his debts mounted up and he had outstayed his welcome. On 21 September, Dee and Jane left Mortlake with their children and joined Kelley and Laski at Gravesend, where two ships were waiting to transport them to Poland. Once there, they lived a fairly peripatetic existence, moving between key locations, as Dee and Kelley practised their spiritualism, even meeting the emperor. At some point, Jane miscarried a child, which may have been in Cracow in 1584. In either late 1585 or early 1586, she bore Michael, who was weaned that November. The following January, Dee recorded that Jane was given the gift of a chain and jewel estimated at 300 ducats by his patron, Lord Rosenberg.[5]

Jane was unhappy about the way things were about to change, though. In 1587, Kelley said the angels wished him and Dee to share all their possessions, including their wives. Kelley's young wife was unhappy and neglected, and Jane had sided with her, distrusting Kelley from the start. Yet Dee suggested they follow the advice and swap. Her husband's suggestion outraged and upset Jane. According to his diary, she 'fell a weeping and trembling for a quarter of an hour,'[6] but given the rules of the time, Jane was Dee's possession to dispose of as he wished. Pressure was brought to bear upon her, and she was obliged to sign an agreement and go through with the swap. Without choices and dependent on her husband in a foreign country, Jane's personal autonomy, her rights over her own body and her privacy were violated with the permission of the man she trusted most. The child Jane bore nine months later, Theodore, may well have been conceived by Kelley. It makes for horrific reading today and illustrates the nature of married women's lives, prey to the whims of their husbands.

The Dees returned to England in 1589, only to find their Mortlake home had been burgled and most of the library and scientific instruments stolen or destroyed. Later, three more daughters were born to the couple and Dee accepted a position at Christ' College, Manchester, moving the family north. Jane died there of the plague in 1605. She was buried in Manchester Cathedral.

84

Mary, Queen of Scots

8 February 1587

Fotheringhay Castle, Northamptonshire, England

Fotheringhay Castle had seen better days. Since it had been the seat of the York dynasty, over a century before, the medieval moated castle with its defensive walls and river views had been long neglected. Once, a family had lived within these austere rooms, and future kings had prayed in the chapel and learned to ride and shoot in the surrounding parkland. Important guests had been entertained before roaring fires in the great hall and women had waited, patiently, to hear about the safety of those they loved.

A century had passed since then, and the castle had fallen into a state of poor repair. Instead of entertaining queens, its thick walls held them hostage while their fate was being decided. Early in 1587, a woman in her forties watched the winter days passing, conscious of her impending sentence. Mary, Queen of Scots was a queen displaced from her own country, who was now at the mercy of another. Almost eighteen years had passed since she had arrived at Tutbury Castle under the guardianship of Bess of Hardwick. Her youth had slipped away before her eyes, in endless days of confinement, spent in prayer and embroidery. Her frustration growing, Mary had begun to despair of ever regaining her freedom, or being able to return to Scotland, or seeing her young son again, in whose favour she had been forced to abdicate. She became increasingly desperate, and increasingly willing to take a risk.

Mary had waded into treasonous waters in 1586 when she allowed herself to be pulled into a plot against the life of her cousin, Elizabeth I. After almost two decades of being a prisoner in England, moved between different properties and closely guarded, she finally made a bid for her freedom, allowing herself to trust those involved in the Babington Plot to assassinate the cousin she had never met and replace her with Mary, as a Catholic queen of England. But Elizabeth's spy networks were too strong, and her intelligence networks too far-reaching, so that even the most secure means of smuggling letters under the noses of Mary's gaolers had been infiltrated. Mary's words had been read by Elizabeth's spymaster general himself, Sir Francis Walsingham, and her complicity was enough to condemn her. She was arrested and taken to Fotheringhay in September 1586.

Three weeks later, Mary was put on trial in the castle's great hall. A contemporary sketch shows the layout of a central table, flanked by seated men, with additional figures on benches on three sides, facing the dais where a chair of estate stood alone, awaiting the queen. Mary herself is being conducted into the room, in black velvet, with a guard on each side. Initially, she had refused to attend, but was informed that the proceedings would go ahead, with or without her presence. Additional figures stand at the back in significant numbers. A total of thirty-six noblemen listened as she defended herself against the charges of treason. Mary's first line of defence was to deny the validity of the court: she was a queen and not an English subject, so they had no right to try her. She had not been permitted any form of defence, any support or witnesses to speak on her behalf. Neither was she allowed to see any of the charges against her, nor examine any letters or documents that were to be used in the trial. Mary denied that she knew the ringleader of the plot, the double agent Anthony Babington, or that she had received any letters from him. The letters had been written in code and sent inside a beer barrel cork. The prosecution presented her with the deciphered letters she had written ad a confession from Babington, upon which she broke into tears, but continued to assert her innocence. She claimed she would 'never make a shipwreck of my soul by conspiring the destruction of my dearest sister' and insisted the evidence had been tampered with, demanding to be tried before the queen or Parliament. The court found her guilty of treason on 25 October. Only one voice, Lord Zouche, opposed the verdict. The problem now was what to do with her.

Four days later, Parliament met to discuss the verdict. Elizabeth was reluctant to sign the death warrant of her cousin and fellow queen, conscious of the dangerous precedent it would set and the potential reaction on the European stage. Mary was, after all, a former queen of France and a Catholic supported by countries such as Spain. During her defence, she had appealed to the court to consider the wider perspective, not just England. Parliament decided to make Mary's guilt public on 4 December and petitioned Elizabeth to sanction her execution. Elizabeth procrastinated for weeks. Eventually, on 17 January, Elizabeth put her signature to the paper but then asked Sir Amyas Paulet privately to kill Mary, so that she would not feel responsible. Horrified, Paulet refused. Sir William Cecil quickly sent the signed warrant up to Fotheringhay, with instructions to carry out the order as soon as possible, and not to inform Elizabeth until after it was done.

On 7 February, Mary was informed that her execution would take place in the morning. That night, she prayed, rested and composed her final letter, to Henri III of France, her brother-in-law. Preparations were being made in the great hall. Perhaps the sounds of the activity reached Mary in her solitude, watching as the hours passed by. A platform and scaffold were being erected, draped with black cloth and equipped with a cushion for her knees, as well as benches and chairs carried in for the jury and the onlookers. This was to be no ordinary execution. It was the death of one queen, ordered by another.

Soon after the arrival of dawn, they came for her. The hall was full, the air heavy with expectation. She was brought forward to the scaffold, where her ladies helped her undress, revealing red petticoats, traditionally the sixteenth-century colour for courage. After forgiving her executioner and making a short speech,

Mary, Queen of Scots knelt and placed her head upon the block. 300 witnesses had gathered in the hall to witness her demise. Among them was George Talbot, Earl of Shrewsbury, husband of Bess of Hardwick, with whom Mary had gone to live in 1569. They had become close, sharing meals, evenings and journeys, with Bess and Mary often sitting and embroidering together. But this was not enough to save her. Talbot had his orders. He had participated in her trial and was now here to watch as she met her end. His was a familiar face but she could take little comfort in his presence. He would have seen the bungled first blow to her neck, followed by the decisive one, and the executioner holding up Mary's head, from which her long red wig fell away. Reputedly, Talbot wept after her death. Everything relating to the execution was burned and Mary's body was not buried in France, as she had wished, but in Peterborough Cathedral.

Upon hearing the news, Elizabeth was furious. She ordered the arrest of her secretary, who remained in the Tower for nineteen months. Mary's death served as a catalyst for the Anglo-Spanish war that resulted in the Armada of 1588. In 1603, her son, James I, succeeded Elizabeth on the English throne and, nine years later, ordered his mother's body to be exhumed and reinterred in Westminster Abbey. Mary now rests opposite her nemesis and cousin, Elizabeth I. Her reputation over the intervening years has varied, but modern historians tend to view her as a figure who was manipulated by those around her, or overwhelmed by the demands of her role, rather than the scheming murderess viewed by previous generations. Her level of involvement in the Babington Plot remains controversial, exacerbated by the unjust process of her trial and her protested innocence. It may be that she conspired against her cousin, but her words concerning her soul have the ring of truth about them. Perhaps Mary was too dangerous an individual to remain in Elizabeth's realm, and through various methods of entrapment, was led into the most convenient solution for England.

85

Eleanor Dare

18 August 1587

Roanoke Colony, Roanoke Island, Dare County,
North Carolina, US

By the 1580s, European travel routes to the New World had been long established. From Christopher Columbus' expeditions paving the way for the Spanish conquistadors who traded with La Malinche and her people, to the travellers who brought back tobacco and parrots, guinea pigs and potatoes, the New World had become well established in the popular imagination.

Queen Elizabeth's main explorer in the west, Sir Francis Drake, travelled to the East Coast and, in 1584, chose the location of Roanoke Island, off the coast of North Carolina, as the ideal setting for an English colony. He named the settlement Virginia in honour of the queen, and the first ship arrived in 1585, bringing 107 men, including artists and scientists, who were charged with investigating and recording indigenous life. This settlement lasted little more than a year, due to a lack of supplies and inclement weather, but the travellers returned home with significant amounts of data. Using this information, the second colony was planned. They sailed from England in April 1587.[1]

In July, new governor John White arrived at Roanoke Island, accompanied by 150 men, women and children. Among them was White's daughter, Eleanor, aged around 20, and heavily pregnant, and her husband Ananias Dare, a bricklayer and tiler from London. They had been married in St Bride's Church, on modern-day Fleet Street. White and Dare had both been part of the first expedition, while Eleanor awaited them in London, before accompanying them across the Atlantic to settle permanently. What prompted her to leave England, five months pregnant, with few supplies, is a matter for speculation. It may simply have been her desire to join her male relatives in the New World, to be a pioneer in a new land, or, as some historians have suggested, they may have been religious radicals, seeking to escape Elizabeth's more Protestant-leaning regime. The Atlantic crossing cannot have been comfortable for Eleanor, having to endure twelve weeks at sea in her condition, but the sight of land must have consoled her as she gave thanks for her safe arrival and looked ahead to her delivery.

Eleanor bore her child in the city of Ralegh on 18 August 1587. It was a daughter who was christened Virginia six days later. She was not the only mother to deliver, as a son arrived soon afterwards to Margery and Dyonis Harvey.[2] His name is unknown. The celebrations, though, were marred by a murder which took place the previous day, when the settlers had waded out to catch crabs. George Howe, the father of a son who was also at Roanoke, was attacked and killed by the local tribespeople, necessitating an envoy being sent to the Croatoans in an attempt to negotiate peace.

The settlers had arrived too late to plant crops, so White set out for England to bring back more supplies on 27 August. During his absence, war broke out between England and Spain, to which all shipping and resources were diverted. When White finally returned in 1590, he discovered the colony abandoned with no sign of the inhabitants. The only clues they left were the word 'Croatoan' carved into a gatepost and 'Cro' on a tree.[3] Theories about their fates have included starvation, crop failure, a storm, murder by Native Americans, or integration into those tribal groups. The Roanoke stones, reputedly discovered in the 1930s, purported to record the deaths of Eleanor and Ananias at the hands of locals, and while they have been largely discredited, some historians believe the first stone to be genuine.

Eleanor Dare was one of a small group of pioneers, daring to voyage to a new world and try to carve out a life among alien surroundings. Whether her motivation was personal or religious, she was brave enough to take a leap of faith, endure a difficult voyage and settle in the New World, surviving the delivery of her child. Her disappearance, and that of her companions, remains a mystery, but is suggestive of suffering and privation. Although the Roanoke colony ultimately did not succeed, the spirit represented by Eleanor was that which pushed boundaries and enabled the era to advance.

86

Lady Nene, aka Kodai-in

1588
Osaka Castle, Osaka, Japan

The building work was progressing well. Lady Nene looked around Osaka Castle at the wide, deep moat, the turrets and tower covered with gold leaf. The gifts were ready and waiting, the castle kitchens were busy cooking up a banquet, and the guests would be arriving soon. As the wife of Japan's most important samurai, intent upon unifying the country, she would be the gracious hostess for the visit of Emperor Go-Yozei that day.

The future emperor's wife was born Kita no Mandokoro in the 1540s, in the Owari province of Japan. She has also been known as Nene, One and Nei. Her parents were the samurai Sugihara Sadatishi and Ashai-doni, and although her father was a descendant of a former emperor, she was adopted by an uncle at a young age, for reasons that are unclear. She was originally arranged to marry another, but in 1561, became the wife of Toyotomi, or Hashiba, Hideyoshi, despite her mother's protests because he was lower in status. Hashiba did not remain low for long, though. After starting life as a peasant, he rose to being governor and then chancellor and imperial regent, or Sessho, in 1565. Nene was given the title of Kita no mandokoro and became Hashiba's trusted confidant and most favourite wife of his harem. She advised him in many contexts, especially to show mercy in cases where his subjects might be exempt from tax. Many of her relatives also joined his government. When Japan invaded Korea, she assisted with the practical arrangements and methods of supplying the army. When Hashiba successfully unified Japan, it was with the assistance that Nene had given him.

In 1583, Hashiba began the building of Osaka Castle, which was to be a key residence and defensive structure sitting on a kilometre square plot of land in the middle of Osaka city. Built on the site of an ancient temple, it was constructed upon rock foundations and surrounded by two moats, with the buildings standing five storeys tall. Picturesque pleasure gardens were also contained within its walls. Five years later, Hashiba and Nene hosted Emperor Go-Yozei, where she excelled in the role of hostess and distributed gifts amongst their guests. In return, Go-Yozei bestowed upon her the title of Juichii, or junior first rank.

Although Nene was a political success, her personal relationship with Hashiba was not always smooth. She bore no children and he expressed frustration with her and spent time with other women, having at least fifteen wives. She inspired great loyalty from her retainers and servants, who held her more highly in their affection that Hashiba. When he died in 1598, she moved out of Osaka Castle and became a nun, under the name Kodai-in Kogetsuni. She spent much of her time giving assistance to women who had been made homeless through contact or association with the army after the Battle of Sekigahara in 1600.

In 1606, she founded the Buddhist temple of Kodai-in, in Kyoto, which became her final residence. The temple contains a bronze bell with an inscription dating from its foundation and a portrait of Nene, seated on a rug in the garden, wearing nun's robes in pale shades of grey. She died in 1624 and was buried in the grounds of the temple. Like many women who rose to power by marriage during the sixteenth century, Lady Nene provided inspiration to many and guided her husband through difficult times.

87

Elena/Eleno de Céspedes

1588

Toledo, Spain

The people of Toledo were confused by the gender of their surgeon. In the 1580s, men and women were usually easy to identify: they conformed to obvious visual identities and their forms of behaviour were determined by social convention. Men wore breeches and women wore dresses; men were active and women were passive; men entered certain professions while women remained in the domestic sphere; men fathered children while women carried and bore them. On the whole, people tended to conform. When exceptions occurred, it was usually in relation to one aspect of a long list of stereotypical features, such as clothing, behaviour or sexual activity. However, the activities of one individual challenged almost every aspect of gender beliefs, leading to their investigation and conviction, and the removal from society of a talented but controversial figure. The biological and elective gender of Elena or Eleno de Céspedes continues to be uncertain, so shall be referred to throughout by the pronouns they, them and their. Whether they were transgender, intersex or lesbian, Elena/Eleno's story illustrates just how far sensibilities regarding personal freedom have changed over time. On 23 February 1589, Céspedes disappeared from sight. What happened to them afterwards remains a mystery.

A baby was born in 1545 in Alhama de Granada, designated female by the local doctor and named Elena. They were illegitimate and of mixed race, described at the time as a Mulatto. Their father was Pero Hernandez, a white Christian peasant and their mother was a slave, a black Muslim woman named Francisca de Medina.[1] Being born into slavery, the child was branded upon both cheeks as a sign of ownership and took the surname of their owner's wife. At the age of 15 or 16, Elena married a man, a local stonemason called Cristobal Lombardo. They fell pregnant and delivered a male child, but the marriage was an unhappy one and Lombardo left, dying a short while later.[2] Presuming this is correct, it initially suggests a female identity, with the presence of menstruation, vagina, womb and everything necessary for conception. Later, when questioned about their life, Elena/Eleno claimed that an intersex condition became apparent as the result of giving birth. It is possible that Elena suffered a severely prolapsed uterus, which can have the appearance of a penis.

This was a turning point in Céspedes' life. They left their child with a friend, adopted the name Eleno and travelled around Spain, wearing 'masculine' clothes and having relations with women, who apparently accepted them as a male.[3] At various points, Eleno was a farmhand, a tailor, a soldier and a shepherd, but became embroiled in a fight which resulted in a man being stabbed. Coming to the attention of the authorities, Eleno's appearance aroused suspicion as they wore earrings but had no facial hair. Considered to be a woman in men's clothing, they were ordered to resume a female identity and appearance. Eleno escaped and ran away again.

At some point, Céspedes had learned to read and write, and now purchased medical textbooks and studied independently to become a surgeon, with the help of Madrid-based friends already working in the field.[4] Soon, they were employed in local hospitals and acquiring a reputation for the quality of their work. This alone is an extraordinary feat for a figure outside social convention, rising in such a male-dominated profession after having been exclusively self-taught. Eleno was clearly an individual of exceptional talent. For a brief time, this was recognised in their community. As things were going well, Eleno hoped to marry and settle down, conforming to social expectations about the sanctity of the family unit. They had met a local woman, Maria del Cano, the daughter of an artisan, and after she agreed to be their wife, Eleno applied in person for a license in December 1584.[5]

The application was met with suspicion. The vicar of Madrid was concerned by Eleno's appearance and asked whether they might be a eunuch, a male castrated for cultural reasons, such as being in service to royal women. Eleno submitted to a physical examination, the usual contemporary method of ascertaining gender, sexual activity and ability to perform. They were examined by four men including a doctor, from the front only, implying that the investigation was not particularly invasive. The doctor identified male genitals and a license was granted to the couple. The banns were then read aloud in church, but this prompted two members of their community to come forward and testify that Eleno possessed both male and female genitals. Whether they had acquired this knowledge through observation, rumour or intimate contact with Eleno is unclear, as are their motives, but, as a result, the priest refused to go through with the ceremony.

Eleno underwent a further, more thorough examination on 17 February 1586. It was reported that they had male genitals plus a 'crease and aperture' that could have been the entrance to a vagina.[6] As a result, the wedding was allowed to proceed. Eleno and Maria became man and wife in the eyes of the church and lived quietly in Yepes, near Toledo, for a year.[7] During this time, Eleno was working as a surgeon. Then, unexpectedly, they were arrested on suspicion of sodomy based upon the accusation of a neighbour and sent to the city jail at Ocana. There, they were forced to submit to a third physical examination, where no male organ was observed. On 4 July, Céspedes was formally charged with sodomy, transvestitism, impersonating a man, using witchcraft to deceive previous doctors and mocking the sanctity of marriage. In their defence, Eleno argued that the marriage was legitimate because he had male genitals at the time he married Maria, although this only confuses modern attempts to fully understand his physical condition. At the time, the punishment for lesbianism was death, but due to the inclusion of witchcraft charges, the case was referred to the Spanish Inquisition. Eleno and Maria were both sent to prison in Toledo.

Under oath, Eleno spoke further to clarify their physical condition, yet this may only serve to confuse modern understanding further. They described a penis-like organ which first emerged as the result of childbirth, which became engorged when aroused, and retracted inside their body.[8] The organ had originally curved downwards, held by a fold of skin, but a surgeon was able to successfully sever this skin and free it. Eleno stated they were able to regularly urinate and ejaculate through the organ, and named a number of former female lovers who could testify to this. However, when midwives studied Eleno in 1589, they saw no male genitals but instead what appeared to be a tight, impenetrable vagina.[9] Eleno also claimed to experience irregular menstruation, explaining this to Maria as the result of haemorrhoids.[10] Dr Diaz, physician to Philip II, who had previously identified male genitals on Eleno was then no longer able to find them. Eleno claimed his penis had been injured and amputated from a riding injury, shortly before his arrest.[11] They continued to identify as a male throughout the proceedings.[12]

The conclusion reached by the Toledo medical authorities was that Céspedes had always been female. They imposed the charge of bigamy due to Eleno's failure to report the death of Lombardo, for which they were sentenced to 200 lashes and a prison sentence of ten years.[13] The lashes were inflicted publicly, in the central square in Toledo, where Eleno was paraded in the penitential mitre and robes of the Inquisition. The prison sentence was commuted, though, to service in Toledo's Hospital del Rey, which allowed for Céspedes to continue using their medical skills. Yet Eleno's reputation spread, and patients flocked to be treated by them, causing what the authorities referred to as an 'annoyance and embarrassment.' As a result, Céspedes was transferred to a more remote location on 23 February 1589, after which nothing further was heard of them.

Remarkably, it was Céspedes who gave the clearest medical defence of their condition. Drawing on their expertise, Eleno provided 'behavioural and psychological features of masculinity and gave precedents from the writing of Cicero, Pliny, Aristotle and Augustine, to prove that intersexuality was not unnatural or unprecedented.'[14] Sadly, for all their erudition and learning, Céspedes disappeared without trace. It is likely they were intersex in an era that did not understand or accept such conditions. The intrusion into their life, the indignity of physical examination and the imposition of unwelcome identity were all experiences familiar to those who did not fit the sixteenth-century mould.

88

Tognina Gonsalvus

1588

Fontainebleau, France

Their eyes stare back disconcertingly from portraits. Black, questioning eyes, set amid faces covered with fur, sometimes cat-like, or with the appearance of monkeys, or occasionally avian in aspect. They are perfectly dressed, in the style of their contemporaries. They wear ruffs and robes, adorned with buttons, pearls and fur, clasp papers, pets and lean upon rocks. In the second half of the sixteenth century, the Gonsalvus, or Gonzales, family was renowned across Europe as 'monkey-people', kept at the French and Italian courts as oddities, covered in hair from head to toe, the earliest known example of hypertrichosis universalis, or Ambras syndrome. In around 1588, a new child arrived into the family, a hair-covered girl named Antonia, or Tognina. Just like Eleno de Céspedes, she would know what it felt like to be outside society's narrow definitions.

The first recorded member of the Gonsalvus family is Tognina's father, Peter, who was born in Tenerife. Some sources say this was in 1537, others, 1556. Nothing is known of his parentage or whether he came from a line of hirsute individuals, which was likely as hypertrichosis universalis is a congenital condition. At the age of 10, he was sent by the Venetian ambassador to the court of Henri II in France, at which point he was unable to speak a language, was fed raw meat and kept in a cage.[1] After an examination by doctors, he was judged to be harmless and kept by the king as a pet. He was given an education, mastered several languages and proved himself intelligent, being called upon to display his learning to visitors. Peter became something of a favourite of Queen Catherine de' Medici, who arranged his marriage to a non-hairy woman, Catherine Raffelin, the daughter of her servant. She bore him seven children, four of whom were covered in hair, and three who took after their mother.

Tognina was born around 1588 in the royal Château of Fontainebleau. She was raised as a noblewoman, dressed, fed and educated, but was still considered to be a possession of the royal family. The Gonsalvuses were classified as animals, or slaves, lacking in souls, so the details of their lives; births, marriages and deaths went unrecorded. Henri II granted them part of the park at Fontainebleau so they could live in their 'natural habitat', and this contrast of wildness and civilisation is captured in a later portrait of Peter in a cave, who stands in red and black robes, his hand upon a rock, 'petrus' in Latin, also symbolic of his 'animal' roots. A double portrait of the Gonsalvus parents was painted by Lavinia Fontana and Joris Hoefnagel, where the 'miracle of God', Peter, faces the viewer in ruff and robes, his wiry gold-brown hair brushed away from his face and Catherine stands beside him, one hand upon his shoulder, looking to the side. Other images survive of Madelina, looking serious in a jewel-encrusted dress adorned with a cross, young Enrico in a red hat and outfit, looking intense, and Tognina herself, by Fontana, in embroidered silk, holding up a letter with a quizzical air. It gives the known details of her life:

> Don Pietro, a wild man discovered in the Canary Islands, was conveyed to his most serene highness Henry the king of France, and from there came to his excellancy the Duke of Parma. From whom [came] I, Antonietta, and now I can be found nearby at the court of the Lady Isabella Pallavicina, the honorable Marchesa of Soragna.[2]

No portraits were painted of the three non-hairy children. They were permitted to remain with their parents, attracting little attention, but the hirsute Francesca, Antonia, Madelina and Enrico were sent away as gifts to other European rulers. As her portrait states, when Tognina was young, the family travelled to visit Margaret of Parma, regent of the Netherlands and were fêted at her court. They also went to Basel, where they were examined by anatomist Felix Platter and their portraits were painted. Later, Tognina was sent to live with Isabella Pallavicina, Marchioness of Soragna, near Bologna in Italy, a cultured and educated woman who loved poetry and writing. Isabella was born in 1549 and her household already contained two children, Giampaolo and Camilla, but she had been widowed in 1571. Tognina lived with them as something of a curiosity, where she was observed in 1594 by visiting Italian scientist Ulisse Aldrovandi, who recorded that:

> The girl's face was entirely hairy on the front, except for the nostrils and her lips around the mouth. The hairs on her forehead were longer and rougher in comparison with those which covered her cheeks, although these are softer to touch than the rest of her body, and she was hairy on the foremost part of her back, and bristling with yellow hair up to the beginning of her loins.[3]

He also created a sketch of her in a long, embroidered gown with leaves in her hair.

Tognina is fascinating for what she represented to her peers. With a status somewhere between animal and slave, denied the existence of a soul, kept as a pet, she occupied a position on the margins, enjoyed and enabled by the wealthy, exhibited like a trophy. She was considered to be a warning from God, the influence of the exotic, or the manifestation of her mother's imagination. Her identity was not too dissimilar to those of disabled people at court, especially dwarves, taking on the catch-all role of 'fools'. She was present, yet not present, significant yet insignificant, with human characteristics but considered an animal. So far as can be ascertained, Tognina differed physically from her peers only due to the presence of hair, caused by an abnormal eighth chromosome. She had the ability to think, speak, learn and express herself, yet had no choice but to accept her position.

Perhaps her condition even gave her an advantage. Although she lacked personal freedom, the majority of individuals in the late sixteenth century were bound in service of some form, and Tognina's unique appearance meant she would never have lacked for patrons, ensuring she lived a life of luxury among the courts of Europe. Perhaps she considered her hairiness a blessing, not a curse.

Tognina's story peters out. Her trail is not recorded after 1594. Her father was last mentioned attending the christening of one of his grandchildren in 1617 and died the following year at Capodimonte near Rome. No grave has ever been found, as he is unlikely to have been given a Christian burial. What became of his wife and children is unknown, but his story has been cited as both the inspiration behind the fairy tale *Beauty and the Beast*, and the legend of the werewolf. Portraits of the family painted by Joris Hoefnagel and Lavinia Fontana were kept at Ambras Castle in Innsbruck, and following their rediscovery in 1933, the condition they had was named Ambras syndrome.

89

'Fair Em, the Miller's Daughter'

1590

'Manchester' in London, England

London theatregoers in the 1590s had a vibrant and evolving scene to choose from, so long as they were prepared to leave the city jurisdictions. As a result of the plague, actors had been banned from within the walls, so they crossed the Thames and built their circular wooden playhouses on the Southbank, setting in motion a whole host of little craft, bobbing on the water, carrying Londoners to afternoon performances. Companies of actors found rich patrons and managers like Philip Henslowe and James and Richard Burbage, employing emerging stars like Edward Alleyn, Christopher Marlowe, Robert Greene and Thomas Kyd. At the Theatre, the Rose, the Swan, the Curtain and the Globe, they wrote to a fast pace, enacting scenes of love, betrayal, history and warfare as their two hours of traffic each afternoon. Among them was the young William Shakespeare, watching as the boy actors dressed up as women in their long gowns, and spoke their lines with falsetto tones.

One of the characters paraded on the London stage in around 1590 was Fair Em, the Miller's daughter from Manchester. Created by an anonymous playwright, the play proclaimed itself to have been 'sundry times publicly acted' by Lord Strange's Men, who are known to have been active in London from November 1589, staging works at the Cross Keys Inn, the Rose Theatre and at court. Their leading actors were William Kempe, who later played Falstaff, Thomas Pope and George Bryan, who later joined Shakespeare in the Chamberlain's Men. The character of Fair Em, and her 'pleasaunt commedie' was known to many hundreds of London theatregoers, if not more. Yet they would have found that she was neither a woman, nor fair, being played by a boy, nor was she from Manchester. As one of the early representations of a secular, non-royal heroine on the Elizabethan stage, Fair Em exposes how patriarchal the late sixteenth-century fictional constructs of womanhood could be.

Despite being the title character, Fair Em's story forms the subplot to a play about William the Conqueror. While William falls in love with a woman's image painted on a shield, and is deceived in his pursuit of her, the beautiful Em attempts to deal with three suitors: Manvile, Mountney and Valingford. She is advised by her father to conduct herself according to her status and not succumb to flattery or lust:

> Let not vehement sighs,
> Nor earnest vows importing fervent love,
> Render thee subject to the wrath of lust:
> For that, transformed to form of sweet delight,
> Will bring thy body and thy soul to shame.
> Chaste thoughts and modest conversations,
> Of proof to keep out all enchaunting vows.[1]

Em virtuously resists the advances of her father's servant but after choosing Manvile, she decides not to appear too willing, for fear of appearing forward:

> If touching love my Manvile charge me thus,
> Unkindly must I take it at his hands,
> For that my conscience clears me of offence.[2]

She feigns blindness and deafness to avoid the others, but Manvile is jealous of her other suitors. The Miller praises his daughter's response and virtue:

> As for those gentlemen, I never saw in them any evil intreaty.
> But should they have profered it, her chaste mind hath proof
> enough to prevent it.[3]

Yet, Em's virtue and beauty are not enough to reassure Manvile who betrays her, so she weds the devoted Valingford instead. At the end of the play, her father's true identity as a knight is revealed, of which the audience have been aware all along. Her story inspired William to restore his faith in women, and he relinquishes his idol and accepts the love of another, thus uniting the two plots.

Em's appearance would have not deceived anyone. Women were prohibited from the stage until 1660, so the role would have been played by one of the boy actors, possibly one trained up from Lord Strange's Company, although many attended the schools attached to churches, signing up at the age of around 8. At 12 or 13, they might make their debut, in wig, dress and make-up, inviting the audience to suspend their disbelief and enter into the character and its romances. Elizabethan drama contained so many examples of cross-dressing and disguise to allow the boys a brief respite from cumbersome female clothing.

Fair Em was not a real woman. She was a fictional, dramatic construct created as a plot device for the stage. As a symbol of femininity, she is not that different from the other female figures represented by men in art and literature that feature in this work. By allowing us to witness a construct of womanhood through the male gaze, Em helps the modern reader glimpse the patriarchal expectations and ideals which sixteenth-century women had to navigate. Tried and tested by impatient and false lovers, she remained virtuous and honest, and was ruled, above all, by her father. Written by a man, represented by a boy, obedient to a husband, in an imagined city, the concept of Em is femininity in the abstract, an expression of a masculine ideal, a foil for the real women watching her from the audience.

90

Mistress Minx

1592

Streets of London, England

In 1592, the satirist Thomas Nashe composed a popular pamphlet called *Pierce Penniless: His Supplication to the Devil*. It is the embittered rant of a man who has not enjoyed wealth or fame, and turns his critical, patriarchal eye upon those around him. Unsurprisingly, his targets include women, in whom he identifies sinners being rewarded, and hopes that they will end up in hell.

One particular woman who drew his wrath was a merchant's wife, whom he named Mistress Minx. His pen paints a harsh portrait of her foibles, reducing her to the level of a caricature, but it does little to endear him to the reader, instead drawing sympathy for the unknown woman due to his misogyny:

> Mistress Minx, a merchant's wife, that will eat no cherries, forsooth, but when they are at twenty shillings a pound, that looks at simperingly as if she were besmeared and jets [struts] it as gingerly as if she were dancing the Canaries [a Spanish dance]: she is so finical in her speech as though she spake nothing but what she had first sewed over before in her samplers, and the puling accent of her voice is like a feigned treble, or one's voice that interprets to the puppets.
>
> What should I tell how squeamish she is in her diet, what toil she puts her poor servants unto, to make her looking-glasses in the pavement? How she will not go into the fields, to cower on the green grass, but she must have a coach for her convoy, and spends half a day in pranking herself if she be invited to any strange place? Is not this the excess of pride, signior Satan? Go to, you are unwise, if you make her not a chief saint in your calendar.[1]

Nashe went on to publish more pamphlets and books, including his most famous *The Unfortunate Traveller*, which contain some less harsh portrayals of women. He was last recorded in 1599, and was definitely dead in 1601, although the cause and circumstances are unknown. Mistress Minx vanished into the crowd and, hopefully, lived happily ever after.

91

Elizabeth 'Bess' Throckmorton

May 1592

England

It was certain. The queen's trusted gentlewoman had married her favourite, in secret, and borne his child. After all the gifts she had showered upon them in recent months, Elizabeth found herself rewarded by this deceit, this treachery, this betrayal. The memories of Dudley and Lettice came flooding back from twenty years ago, and the heartbreak had not lessened. She was furious, incandescent. Those who had made a fool out of her with their secrets would not escape punishment.

'Send them to the Tower!' she ordered.

The servant hesitated, thinking of those involved, of how high they had risen and how close they had become to the queen.

'To the Tower!'

This time, no one dared hesitate but went at once to arrest Sir Walter Raleigh and his new wife, Bess Throckmorton, two of the brightest jewels of the Elizabethan court, and conducted them by river to the dark and foreboding Tower of London. No doubt Bess was scared, regretting having to leave her young son behind, and enter the keep where the ground had been stained by the blood of past queens.

Elizabeth, or 'Bess', Throckmorton was born in 1565 to Nicholas Throckmorton, a cousin of Catherine Parr and his wife, Anne Carew. She became a Gentlewoman of the Privy Chamber to Elizabeth in 1584, with the help of her brother Arthur, who was already at court. Whilst fulfilling her duties to the queen, Bess could not help but notice the dazzling figure of Sir Walter Raleigh, who had served in France and Ireland, and was newly returned from America. Eleven years her senior, he had been brought to court by his mother's aunt, Kat Ashley, who had served Elizabeth during the turbulent years before her succession. Raleigh was also handsome and witty, which attracted the attention of the queen. She rewarded him with gifts, lands and income from sources such as Durham House on the Strand, and the licensing of vintners and wine sales, both of which she granted him in 1583. In return, Raleigh spent much time in her company, talking, riding, dancing, card playing and indulging in poetry, during which he was also in the company of her gentlewomen. Often, he would be waiting at her chamber door, early in the morning, to greet her as she rose.[1] Yet a permanent distance existed between the queen and her favourites. At twenty years her junior, Raleigh could have been Elizabeth's own son. Soon his attention was caught by her namesake, Bess Throckmorton, and in July 1591, Bess found herself pregnant by the royal favourite.

Elizabeth's dramatic reactions to the marriages of her ladies-in-waiting was well known. Couples had been forced apart, banished from court, or even imprisoned, including the queen's own Grey cousins. So Bess and Walter made the decision to keep their wedding on 19 November a secret, and both remained at court, while Bess did her best to conceal her increasing belly under her vast skirts. When she was within a month of her due date, Bess made an excuse to go and stay with her brother Arthur in his home at Mile End, London. There, she gave birth to Damerei on 29 March, and another royal favourite, the Earl of Essex, son of Lettice, Duchess of Leicester, stood as the boy's godfather. After a few weeks spent in recovery, Bess returned to court and resumed her duties. However, rumours began to circulate about the couple, and Robert Cecil, son of Mildred and William, conducted an investigation. Initially, Raleigh denied everything but by June, the truth was out. In her fury, Elizabeth sent both him and Bess to the Tower. Bess was also dismissed from her position at court.

With its long history of torture and execution, the Tower was the most intimidating place for Elizabethan prisoners. Raleigh and Bess would have been lodged in separate rooms and the queen is unlikely to have allowed visits of any significant duration, given that previous couples held there had been able to beget children during their stay. Yet Walter did not remain incarcerated long. With the threat of invasion remaining in the wake of the Armada, Raleigh was required to lead an attack upon the Spanish coast, departing in August and returning in September. Bess remained in the Tower until December, when she was released and joined her husband at their estate in Sherborne, Devon.

The couple were finally reunited, but were devastated to learn that during their trials, their young son Damerei had died of the plague. A second child, Walter, arrived the following year. Elizabeth expected them to ask for her forgiveness, but neither Bess nor Walter felt they should apologise for their marriage, choosing instead to remain out of favour for around five or six years. Throughout their lives together, Bess often had to continue without Walter, as he was absent in service, on voyages to places like the Azores and in his role as Governor of Jersey. Accounts agree that she was a strong, determined character and adapted to her role with stoicism. She may have experienced more infant loss, or miscarriages, before another healthy child was born to them, in February 1605, whom they named Carew.

The Raleighs' peace was called into question after the death of Elizabeth in 1603. The attack was led by two men: Henry Howard, younger brother of the Duke of Norfolk, and Robert Cecil, who had long seen Walter as a rival. With the arrival of King James I, they took the opportunity to discredit him, calling him disloyal to the new regime, an atheist, incompetent and indiscreet. Walter was thrown out of Durham House, lost some of his titles and was detained in the Tower for questioning over a plot to replace James with another Stuart descendant,

Arbella. Learning that he was to be put on trial, Raleigh suffered a breakdown and may have attempted suicide. The trial was held in Winchester due to outbreaks of plague in London. Found guilty of treason, Raleigh was sentenced to be hanged, drawn and quartered, but this was commuted to a life sentence in the Tower. Bess took a house on Tower Hill so as to be able to visit, but Raleigh was deeply depressed, throwing himself into studying science as a way of distraction. He languished in jail until 1617, when James pardoned him so that he might lead an expedition to search for El Dorado, of the Cities of Gold, in Venezuela. Whilst there, Raleigh broke the terms of his orders, violating peace treaties with Spain in the aftermath of the shooting of his son, Walter. Upon his return to England, the Spanish ambassador insisted that his sentence be reinstated. Raleigh was given opportunities to escape but did not take them. He was executed on 29 October 1618 at Westminster Palace. Bess is reputed to have kept his head with her in a velvet bag until her death in 1647.

92

Margaret Winstar

August 1592
Dalkeith Castle, Midlothian, Scotland

Margaret Winstar, or Vinstarr, was a Danish noblewoman whose fate was bound up with that of her royal mistress. Whatever her early life may have been, its backdrop included the romantic beginning of the Stuart marriage. Anne was only 14 when she was betrothed to James VI of Scotland and convinced herself that she was in love with him, unaware that his personal tastes were for his male favourites. Anne had attempted to sail across the North Sea to marry James in the summer of 1589, only to be beaten back by the weather. However, James was keen to do his duty and, in an impulsive move, he sailed to her instead, braving the elements and landing safely in Denmark, where the pair underwent the ceremony and spent six months visiting her relations.

Margaret may even have witnessed the wedding in Oslo, at the Old City Hall, or seen the pair at Elsinore or Copenhagen. As a noblewoman, she may already have been part of Anne's entourage, wearing the matching costumes with velvet hats and feathers or the co-ordinating riding habits. Perhaps she was even aboard the *Gideon* and attended Anne's coronation at Holyrood. Or else she went across to Scotland later, to join the new queen's household, when two of her existing ladies, Sophia and Catharina, returned home. If so, Margaret would have accompanied the Flemish diplomat Dr Paul Knibbe, who arrived in Scotland on 10 July 1591. She would have had her first glimpse of the Stuart court a week later, at the Renaissance-modelled Falkland Palace in Fife, given by James as a gift to his bride. Margaret was soon a regular figure accompanying the queen out riding. Soon, she had fallen in love with a valet in James' bedchamber, John Wemyss of Logie, whose sister Euphemia was a gentlewoman in Anne's household. Margaret and John may have been betrothed or even secretly married.

Margaret's lover was of dubious reputation, though. Logie was previously reprimanded for fighting in public, near the king's person and possibly also for defying orders. In August 1592, he was arrested for plotting to capture the king and implicated Margaret in his scheme, claiming she had agreed to steal keys and let the rebels into the castle. Logie's confession was enough to condemn him, but the queen and Margaret pleaded for his life and he was imprisoned in Dalkeith Castle. Whilst he was there, Margaret helped him escape by leading him out through the bedchamber in which the king and queen slept, where he climbed out of the window using bedsheets, to where a horse was waiting for him below. This daring escape was told in the ballad of *The Laird o' Logie* and the narrative account of *The History and Life of King James the Sext*. Margaret was portrayed in both as a romantic, sympathetic character, motivated by love, and it was perhaps this reason that led James to step back from his demand that Anne should send Margaret back to Denmark, as well as Anne's refusal to do so.

The Laird of Logie describes the episode in early modern Scots, where Margaret's surname is given as Twynstone:

> Young Logie's laid in Edinburgh chapel;
> Carmichael's the keeper o' the key;
> And may Margaret's lamenting sair, [sore]
> A' for the love of young Logie.
>
> 'Lament, lament na, may Margaret,
> And of your weeping let me be;
> For ye maun [must go] to the King himsell,
> To seek the life of young Logie.
>
> May Margaret has kilted her green cleiding [clothing],
> And she has 'back her yellow hair –
> 'If I canna get young Logie's life,
> Farewell to Scotland for evermair.'
>
> When she came before the King,
> She knelit lowly on her knee –
> 'O what's the matter, may Margaret?
> And what needs a' this courtesie?' -
>
> 'A boon, [good deed] a boon, my noble liege,
> A boon, a boon, I beg o' thee!
> And the first boon that I come to crave,
> Is to grant me the life of young Logie.' -
>
> 'O na, O na, may Margaret,
> Forsooth, and so it manna be;
> For a' the gowd [gold] o' fair Scotland
> Shall not save the life of young Logie.'
>
> But she has stown the King's redding kaim, [comb]
> Likewise the Queen her wedding knife,
> And sent the tokens to Carmichael,
> To cause young Logie get his life.
>
> She sent him a purse o' the red gowd,
> Another o' the white monie;
> She sent him a pistol for each hand,
> And bade him shoot when he gat free.[1]

Margaret and Logie were married at some point between October 1593 and March 1594, after which she was known as Lady Logie. Queen Anne gave her gifts of a bed with rich curtains and blue velvet nightclothes. When she visited her family in Denmark in the summer of 1594, Logie created trouble again, turning up in London on a pretended diplomatic mission, although both James and Anne insisted there was not one. He was arrested and pardoned again, before leaving for the Netherlands claiming he was going to see his wife, whom he missed. At Veere, a town in Zeeland, he confessed to planning to capture a tower in the harbour and claim it for the Spanish. He was sentenced to death and executed on 7 January 1597. Logie's exploits and intentions, his impulsive travels, his constant trouble-making and drama raise a swathe of questions that cannot be answered. He appears to have been a dissatisfied man courting the disaster that finally caught up with him at Veere.

What became of Margaret is unknown. She may have remained in Denmark with her family or returned to serve Queen Anne, who lived until 1619. The manner, location and date of her death went unrecorded. She is remembered in history through the contemporary ballads and accounts as a heroine who freed her imprisoned lover. An ironic legacy, perhaps, which has eclipsed the rest of her existence.

93

Eleanor Bull

30 May 1593

Deptford Strand, Kent, England

She ran a quiet house. It might be situated in notorious Deptford, south of the river, but Eleanor's tavern was no common bawdy shop. She was a respectable woman, the widow of a gentleman, and it was frequented by those employed in business circles, at court, or merchants or supervisors at the docks. She described it more as a 'rooming house', where chambers were hired for meetings, and on 30 May 30 1593, out of the four men who paid the rent of a room, she recognised one or two as agents of the crown. They shared a common master, Sir Francis Walsingham, principal secretary to Queen Elizabeth I, more often referred to as her 'spymaster'. Yet on that May day, the occupants of her chamber were to bring Eleanor disrepute and notoriety.

Eleanor Whitney was born around 1550, probably in Herefordshire. Her family was reputable but not rich, with some court connections. In 1571, she married Richard Bull, who worked for the Clerk of the Green Cloth, at the Church of St Mary le Bow in London, and they took a house in Deptford. It was then, technically, located in Kent, a village of fields and scattered houses, used for shipbuilding. Eleanor may have been a witness when Elizabeth had knighted Sir Francis Drake there in 1581. She was related to Blanche Parry, a close friend and Privy Chamberer to the queen, who referred to Eleanor as her cousin, in an era when the term was more loosely defined and denoted many forms of kinship. When Blanche died in 1590, she left Eleanor the considerable legacy of £100. Eleanor also claimed cousinship with William Cecil, Elizabeth's secretary and her astrologer, John Dee. Richard also died in 1590, but Eleanor stayed on in their home, continuing to open it to the public, serving meals and renting out space. It is not known whether she had children, or if they or any other family members were resident in Deptford with her. It is probable that she hired local staff to help with the smooth running of the place; extra pairs of hands to help cook and clean, to wait upon the guests, or to step in if things ever became rowdy.

By the afternoon of 30 May 1593, the four men in the rented chamber had run up a considerable bill. They were mostly in their late twenties, chancers with dubious reputations, not quite the kind of clients Eleanor wanted, and the sound of their laughter and raised voices filled the building. There was Ingram Frizer, a business agent, moneylender and defrauder; Nicholas Skeres, a government agent and well-known con man; Robert Poley, a government messenger and double agent; and Christopher Marlowe, a playwright and spy, who had been arrested in Flushing the previous year for counterfeiting coins. These men usually existed in the underbelly of Elizabethan life, but their skills of subterfuge had uncovered the 1586 Babington Plot against the queen, so they retained her gratitude and some social standing. In recent weeks, Marlowe had been in trouble. Various libellous poems appeared in London, attributed to him, and when the rooms of his friend Thomas Kyd were searched, a heretical tract was discovered, the blame for which Kyd attributed to Marlowe. A warrant was issued for his arrest on 18 May and two days later, he attempted to present himself to the council, although they were not in session, so he was sent away.

It is unlikely that Eleanor was aware of this as she prepared the food for the four men in the rented chamber. Whatever they had met to discuss came to an end, and they called for the bill, or the 'reckoning'. Eleanor made up the receipt for all the food and drink consumed, and the rent of the room, and brought it to them, anticipating their exit and her task of cleaning up their mess. However, it proved to be a most costly bill. The sum swiftly provoked an argument between Frizer and Marlowe about who should pay which share. Reclining on a couch, Marlowe disagreed with Frizer, who was sitting at the table between the two other men. Most likely, Eleanor had already retreated when Frizer jumped up and plunged his dagger into Marlowe's right eye, but no doubt the commotion brought her swiftly back. Marlowe's wound would have bled profusely and it would have been immediately apparent that it was fatal. The playwright may even have already been dead by the time she arrived.

It was not the kind of publicity that Eleanor's establishment needed. No doubt she called for help to assist with the removal of the body, the clean-up of the blood and the involvement of the authorities. An official inquest was held two days later, on Friday 1 June, presided over by William Danby, Coroner of the Queen's Household, at which Skeres and Poley testified that there had been an argument over the reckoning, and that Frizer had acted in self-defence. Barely a month later, he was pardoned. This did not prevent subsequent speculation about the nature of the gathering that day, and Marlowe's spying activities and sexual orientation, which have exercised scholars since, even speculating that his death was faked and that he fled abroad, or wrote Shakespeare's plays. According to the inquest details, the body of Christopher Marlowe was laid to rest that same day, 1 June, in the Church of St Nicholas, Deptford, in an unmarked grave.[1]

For Elizabethan scholars, the death of Marlowe is a significant literary event that raises more questions than it answers. For Eleanor Bull, it was a mess and a nuisance, upsetting the order of her house and potentially damaging her reputation. After the body was cleared away and the men departed, presumably having paid her bill, she was left with a murder scene. She and her staff would have scrubbed the blood off the couch, swept up the mess, righted the chairs and carried away the plates. Eleanor's identity would otherwise not be known to us. She was a woman who happened to be in a particular place at a particular moment in history. Her property provided the location, and it was into her space that these men brought their dramatic quarrel, which redefined her rooming house. The event would have remained fresh in the minds of local people for the remaining three years of Eleanor's life. When she died in March 1596, she was buried in Deptford and it is likely that her rooming house closed, if it had not already done so.

Like so many women of her time, Eleanor's historical reputation was secured by a brief moment of interface between herself and a famous man. Marlowe's interaction with her was minimal, but the fact of his death in her property enshrined Eleanor's name in the records. Had the men attended another establishment that day, or had the fight not escalated, the entire existence of Eleanor, a whole forty-six years of life, is unlikely to have been illuminated by the processes of history. Information about her would have remained in the parish registers, and the wills of her cousins, but her life would have not been studied in its own right. She illustrates just how many women's lives remain unrecovered, and the discrepancy between the historiography of 'normal' individuals and that of the famous. Her partially-lit life reveals the patriarchal processes of recording history; how the illumination of men's activities can, of necessity, bring unknown females to the fore.

94

Grace O'Malley

September 1593

Greenwich Palace, Kent, England

The present-day tourist trail that hugs the Irish west coast from Derry to Cork, known as the Wild Atlantic Way, is just as wild as it is remote. Half-way around, ringed by the mountains of Mallaranny and Murrisk in County Mayo, sits Clew Bay, its swirling waters filled with tiny scattered islands, although not as many as the 365 of legend. At the mouth of the bay sits the largest of them all, Clare Island, maintaining a small, present-day population of around 150, with a village, lighthouse, tower house and semi-ruined abbey. Inside the abbey, dedicated to St Bridget, the walls are painted with images of mythological animals, wolves and dragons, fishermen and hunters, and the tombstones, dedicated to the O'Malley family, lords of the island, are carved with knotted ropes, ships, and bows and arrows. Their motto was *terra marique potens*: powerful on land and sea. One sepulchre claims to be the final resting place of the most famous female member of the family, Grace, or Grainne, whose childhood among the islands prepared her to become a notorious pirate queen. Typical of her era, though, women were not valued enough to be recorded in Irish records, nor to be captured in paint.

Grace O'Malley was born around 1530, somewhere in the environs of Clew Bay, possibly on Clare Island itself. She was the daughter of Eoghan Dubhara, the head of a fierce seafaring family who taxed those fishing in their waters and defended their territory by building tall, austere castles. Grace's native language would have been Irish, but she learned Latin and English, and on her travels, she would have picked up some Spanish and French.

The O'Malleys were established pirates and raiders, with one fifteenth-century poem calling them 'lions of the sea', acquainted with Spain, for whom a mile by sea was only a 'short distance'.[1] Legend has it that Grace was keen to travel with her father to Spain on a merchant trip, and when he told her that her long hair would get caught in the ropes, she cut it off, earning herself the nickname of Grainne, or the bald. With only one half-sibling, she was her father's sole heir, unusually for a woman of her times. She was married young and bore three children, but returned to Clare Island when her husband was killed in 1565. She took a lover, but after he was killed by the MacMahon family, she embarked on a personal feud against them, which lasted long after her second marriage.

Anglo-Irish relations at this time were notoriously difficult, but Grace tried to work with Lord Deputy Sir Henry Sidney in the 1570s, in a plan intended to bring the Irish chieftains into line with English policy. However, when Sidney was replaced by Sir Richard Bingham, things changed. The English occupied Irish castles, and Grace's own properties and lands had been confiscated, then she was arrested and condemned to be hanged for resistance before a last-minute reprieve arrived from Elizabeth I. Out of desperation and frustration, Grace began a correspondence with the queen, and, in 1594, when she was in her sixties, she made the trip from Ireland to Greenwich so that she might petition for her freedom in person.

Reputedly, Grace sailed to England in one of her own ships and appeared at court barefoot, in the clothes of an Irish queen. She would have been conducted to the opulent, ornate Greenwich Palace, with its ritual and protocol, its carvings and paintings, where the most influential and wealthy courtiers were gathered, a far cry from the shores of Clew Bay. Yet it is unlikely that Grace was intimidated. Elizabeth extended her hand in greeting, having to lift it in order to meet Grace's height as the Irish woman towered over her. Both women were powerful, charismatic and determined, prevailing in a man's world. Grace later described Elizabeth's 'clemency and favour' while the queen instructed Bingham to have pity on the 'poor old woman'.[2] After promising to consider her requests, Elizabeth made Grace wait until the end of the month, then set her sons free. Grace was to be given an income from her sons' estates and a guarantee that she could live out her years in peace, free from Bingham's intervention. Elizabeth noted that Grace departed 'with great thankfulness and with many more earnest promises that she will, as long as she lives, continue a dutiful subject and will employ all her power to offend and prosecute an offender against us.'[3] By 1599, Grace's name was so famous in England that it was included on an engraved map of Ireland, published in Suffolk by an Italian master.

Back home in Ireland, Grace rebuilt her fleet with three particularly large ships, totalling a capacity of 300 men. Bingham decided to ignore Elizabeth's instructions, imposing a troop of his own men upon her fleet in order to monitor her activities and forcing some of her household into his service. Grace took to the seas to avoid him, but Bingham encountered her grandson and killed many of his company. Grace returned to England in 1595, addressing her pleas to William Cecil. The following year, Bingham was replaced and charges were brought against him for his treatment of Grace and others of her countrymen. He was incarcerated in the Fleet prison, but was released on account of illness, although he was suspended from duties. It allowed Grace to enjoy a more peaceful existence at the end of her life. She died in 1603, possibly in Rockfleet Castle in Newport, and is traditionally claimed to be buried at the Clare Island Abbey.

Grace was a remarkable combination of queenliness and warrior. As fearless as a man captaining his own fleet, she commanded loyalty and led from the front, reputedly giving birth on board ship, then picking up a gun to successfully defend herself against Algerian corsairs. When Elizabeth I stood on the deck of a ship at Tilbury, after the main battle against the Armada was over, inspiring her men with her imagery of having the heart and stomach of a king, she was employing majestic imagery. It was her contemporary Grace O'Malley, though, who embodied the warrior identity that Elizabeth projected. Although there were many similarities between the women, the circumstances of their lives led those to be manifest in different arenas. Despite the lack of surviving material related to Grace, she emerges as a queenly figure, powerful, active and fearless, challenging patriarchal expectations well into her final years.

95

Mathurine de Vallois

27 December 1594
Louvre Palace, Paris, France

The thrilling, carnivalesque atmosphere of the French court could not quite mask the memories of violence and death that had underpinned it in recent years. As she whirled and danced about the room lit by hundreds of candles, dressed as an Amazonian warrior complete with wooden shield and sword, Mathurine's mind wandered to the death of the former king. She had always been considered amusing, quick to tell a story or make a smart remark, adept with her tumbling and tricks, so she had been summoned to court as a plaisante, to amuse the king and his family. That was why they called her Mathurine la Folle, the fool, instead of by her name, la Vallois. A jester was often given a new name like that. But the blade of a dagger had ended the life of Henri III, at the age of only 23, after a reign tainted by the bloodshed of Catholics fighting against Protestants. There had not been much call for a fool in such sombre times.

The Christmas celebrations continued. Music played and servants brought round plates of food. There was a new king now, Henri IV, a Huguenot king, a Bourbon, so that Mathurine and others had been forced to conceal their devout Catholicism, smile, bow and serve. She was philosophical about it: a king was a king, but the court had felt on edge ever since. Sometimes she tried to use her humour to convert people, sidling up to them, making them laugh, trying to jolt them out of their beliefs. It was as much an act of self-preservation, or solidarity among the jesters at court, who all understood that the Huguenots had no stomach for them, and would dismiss them all at a moment's notice. The contemporary anonymous author of *La Lunatique* asked the jesters 'where would all your pensions be if the reformers had the upper hand?'[1]

Then, in 1593, Henri had bowed to pressure and made a show of converting to Catholicism. The first assassination attempt took place soon afterwards, that very August, and the king stepped up his security in response. But he was still mortal, thought Mathurine, swaying in time to the music, as susceptible to a cold steel blade as any other. Now there were rumours flying around that the Spanish were training up an assassin, intent upon killing the tyrant, as they called him. It was hardly a good time to go away on progress, always moving between places, exposed along the road, so they were more vulnerable to the unfamiliar. But Henri had insisted. And so it happened, that on the evening of 27 December, when the king was relaxing in his chamber with Mathurine dancing to amuse him, an assassin somehow gained entry with a knife concealed about his person.

19-year-old Jean Châtel was a cloth merchant who had spent three years being trained by the Jesuits. His mission, in December 1594, was to dispatch the heretic king and help restore France to Catholicism. The court was always thronging with people hoping to see Henri, bringing gifts and asking for commissions, but the guards were still wary, watching the new faces at every new stop. In spite of this, Jean found his way inside. He chose a moment when two officials were just entering, slipped in with them and waited, as they knelt before the king. Henri stooped to help them rise and Châtel lunged forward with his knife, wounding the king upon the lip. Henri drew back, the guards rushed forward and the assassin desperately sought an escape route. It was at that point that Mathurine sprang to block the door, allowing the guards to take Châtel. He was tried and convicted, and the hand that wielded the knife was burned with wax, lead and sulphur, before he was disembowelled. There was some suggestion that perhaps Mathurine had been aware of the conspiracy, on account of her swift response, but she quickly cleared her name.

Investigations into Châtel's history uncovered a hotbed of treason in the Jesuit College de Clermont in central Paris. One of his former teachers was hanged and two others exiled, while the college itself was closed down. The Jesuits were briefly banned from France.

Mathurine later married a merchant named Fabien Juel, with whom she lived in St Malo, who predeceased her. In 1602, she remarried to Louis de Fleury. After Henri IV was assassinated in 1610, Mathurine remained in the household of his widow, Marie de' Medici, and was award a pension of 1,200 livres in 1622. Her final appearance in the records was in July 1628. Mathurine's life was at the heart of the French court, albeit in a minor role, but her status as jester meant that she was both overlooked and present, dismissed as a fool but in position to help save the king's life. Had she not been in the right place at the right time, though, her name may have only survived in the margins of history.

96

Medusa

1597

Rome, Italy

She stares out with devastating intensity. Painted against an olive-green background, set in a roundel, the expression on her face is frozen in the moment of death. Blood streams from her severed neck and her hair is a wild mass of vipers. Caravaggio's depiction of the goddess Medusa is shocking and direct, but even more surprising is that her features are those of the artist himself. By this replacement, the artist has created a strange hybrid of his own identity, and the traditional association of the goddess with the personification of female anger. It was a subject matter that had famous precedents: Caravaggio is likely to have known da Vinci's portrait of Medusa, now lost, and Cellini's sculpture of the 1550s has Perseus holding her severed head aloft, dripping with blood, but serene in expression.

This was the second time Caravaggio had depicted Medusa. The first had been a private commission but on this occasion, she was intended to feature on a ceremonial shield for the Medici family's agent in Rome, Cardinal Francesco Del Monte, who had been taken by the original image when visiting the artist's studio. The choice of a rampant, powerful female at the moment of death was a potent one for a cardinal. It was also a choice that represented female weakness as, according to the myth, Medusa's two sisters were immortal but she was not, and was slain by the cleverness of Perseus, who avoided her direct gaze by using a mirror. The image depicts her in the moment before death, still animate, conscious in pain and disbelief, but her eyes are turned away, depriving her of the ability to transfix the viewer. This means we are able to witness directly her moment of death and, no matter how terrifying she appears, the power resides in the eyes of the onlooker.

Caravaggio's *Medusa* is typical of late sixteenth-century attitudes towards women: a dual fascination and terror about the power and raw sexuality they exude. Here, her potency is awesome, yet it has been conquered and although not sanitised, it is safe to look upon. The female monster in its unleashed form tapped into contemporary misogyny such as that expressed in John Knox's *First Blast of the Trumpet Against the Monstrous Regiment of Women* and medical beliefs about female duplicity and lasciviousness. It was rarely depicted, though, in such alarming rawness as in Caravaggio's dying Medusa. The unusual decision to replace her traditional features with his own was an extraordinary act of association by the artist, transcending gender to make this terrifying female into a self-portrait. By using a convex mirror to capture his own face, the artist made the surface of the painting appear concave, so that Medusa's head appears to be thrusting forwards. It was Caravaggio who captured the true passion of Medusa, but in these misogynistic times, it was only allowed to be an animalistic, defeated passion, glimpsed through the features of a man.

It is highly unlikely that Caravaggio had Elizabeth I in mind as he worked. As a young impoverished man in his twenties, newly arrived in Rome and seeking patrons, she would have been far removed from his sphere of associations, known to him by reputation alone. And yet, in her dying years, as a new generation of English courtiers ceased creeping about her and barely concealed their impatience, the beheading of the deadly goddess finds symbolic echoes in the chambers of Greenwich. Having transfixed her people for so long, her favour representing life and death for them, Elizabeth was soon to be replaced by a triumphant young man, to whom many looked in hope. Her secretary, Robert Cecil, had been corresponding with James Stuart for years, smoothing the way for a transfer of power. It would only take place in 1603, after the woman who had held England in her gaze had finally succumbed.

97

Louise Boursier

1598

Paris, France

Giving birth in the sixteenth century was perilous and fraught with danger. If a woman survived the risks of pregnancy, she had the potential complications and inevitable pain of birth to endure, without the benefits of modern medicine, hygiene and gynaecological understanding. Although many women survived the process multiple times, and bore large families, surviving parish records[1] indicate the regularity of maternal and infant death. It was prevalent to the point that everyone would have known at least one woman who died during, or shortly after, giving birth. Research suggests a rate of maternal mortality between 1 and 2.35 per cent, rising to 6 or 7 across a woman's childbearing years.[2] There were no forceps, no antibiotics and little hand-washing.

Women typically gathered their female friends and family around them, as 'gossips' or 'good sisters', during the month of lying-in. They were responsible for keeping her spirits up, feeding her, cleaning and tidying the chamber, keeping it well stocked, changing and washing linen, undertaking housework and the care of other children, applying lotions, administering medicines, prayers and any other necessary tasks. This was a collective effort, based on generations of collective experience, passed down through an oral tradition. Male doctors and surgeons had been excluded from the process for generations, although they were the authors of most of the scientific manuals on the topics. It was women who had the 'hands-on' experience, but as the century advanced, they were increasingly allowed into the birthing chamber, especially when a mother experienced complications. The role of midwife was formalised in 1562, when Eleanor Pead swore an oath of office in Canterbury, making her accountable to the church and regulating her activities. One of the most trusted and prolific midwives of the period was Louise Boursier, who passed her medical examination in 1598 and later delivered the children of Marie de' Medici and her circle in Paris. Publishing five volumes of her midwifery manual, Boursier helped spread her knowledge to the next generation of women. One volume of her work was even addressed as 'advice to my daughter' because many of her children also went into medicine.

Louise was born in 1563 in Paris. Her father was a builder, working on houses in the nearby village of Bussy, although the family was of the bourgeois class and Louise was given a good education. In 1584, she married a professional surgeon,

Martin Boursier, in the church of St Suplice, and they moved out to the suburb of Faubourg St Germain. There, Louise quickly bore three children. Boursier had studied under the surgeon Ambrose Pare, whose extensive work and publications covered the area of pregnancy and childbirth, and served in the Valois court. Louise was different from other midwives and gossips because she did not learn her knowledge from the female oral network, but from observing her husband and reading Pare's writing. She began to practise and learn from within the male tradition and worked initially as a part-time midwife, building a reputation among upper Parisienne women.

In 1589, the Boursiers' comfortable life, and Louise's studies, were disrupted. When Henri III and the future Henri IV came into conflict, Martin served as an army surgeon, leaving his family for almost two years. When the Huguenots attacked Paris, Louise was forced to flee from their home and possessions with the children and take refuge within the city walls, where she earned money as an embroiderer, in addition to continuing to deliver babies. Martin returned in 1591, considerably poorer, and it may have been to assist their finances that Louise joined the Guild of Midwives, allowing her to practise as a regulated professional, and then worked in the charitable hospital, the Hotel Dieu. In 1598, before a panel consisting of a doctor, two surgeons and two midwives, Louise passed her examination and was awarded a license to practise. The Boursiers moved into a fashionable house on the left bank in the Rue Saint-Andre-des-Arts.

In 1600, Queen Marie de' Medici chose Louise as her midwife, rejecting her husband's preferred candidate, after which Louise assisted at each of her six deliveries. On each occasion, she was required for two months: for the lying-in, the birth and the period of recovery. She received 500 crowns for each royal son and 300 for each daughter born, and, in 1610, was awarded an annual pension of 300 crowns.[3] One of the children she delivered was a future king of France and two others became queens of Spain and England. This added to Louise's reputation and standing within the profession. In 1609, she published her work on obstetrics, calling herself 'the first woman practising my art to take up the pen,'[4] and writing in a self-aware, semi-autobiographical style. The work was enlarged and reproduced several times over the coming years and was translated into English, Dutch and German. According to her own account, Louise delivered over 2,000 babies in her career. When it came to normal births, she encouraged midwives to be patient and gentle, not to intervene and to let nature take its course. Her role was to comfort and support the mother and child. When the Duchess D'Orleans died as the result of post-partum infection whilst under her care, Louise's career suffered, and she defended herself in a written Apologie:

> I have practiced my profession now for fully thirty-four years, faithfully, diligently, and honourably, and acquired not only a good certificate, after various examinations, but have also written books treating on this subject, which have been printed and published in several editions and were translated into foreign languages, for which trouble many noted physicians have rendered me thanks and have gladly confessed that they were of great use to humanity.[5]

Louise died in 1636 at the age of 73, having served the French court for twenty-six years. Her career crossed the gender divide when it came to midwifery, uniting the typically female role of practical assistance with her entry into the world of publishing, being the first woman to commit her expertise to print. Some of her views and methods are archaic according to today's understanding, but much of it remains relevant and illuminative of sixteenth-century practices.

98

Rani Roopmati

1599

Madhya Pradesh, India

She was already dead by 1599, but the memory of her beauty and tragic end still haunted those who lived in and around the palace she had loved, with its views over the Narmanda River. Women of the court, and the shepherdesses and washerwomen of the forests around, still whispered about her love story, unable to forget how one of them had risen so high in favour and had fortune turn against her so dramatically. It was among the breathtaking views of the Nimar plains, that year, that an official in the service of a Mughal prince began to write her story, gathering together her poems, reviving the tale that had captured his imagination. Meticulously, Ahmad-ul-Umri Turkoman copied out twenty-six poems written by Rani Roopmati, the Queen of Malwa, later known to the western world as *The Lady of the Lotus*. His introduction compared her to the flower of perfection, full of poetry, who would be remembered long after her pavilions had crumbled into dust.[1]

The exact date of Roopmati's birth is unknown. Working backwards, it can be estimated to have taken place in the late 1520s or early 1530s, into a lower-class Hindu family. Tradition has her born on the river bank, working as a shepherdess and singing with a beautiful voice, which is what attracted the attention of the passing young Sultan, Baz Bahadur. As described in the 1926 English translation of Turkoman's work:

> In the silence of the forest he heard a voice, whereof
> the beauty and sweetness pierced him to the soul…
> through the leaves they espied the face of Rup Mati, excelling in
> beauty even the voice, which yet rang high and clear. Baz
> Bahadur's companions looked to him for an order, but
> beheld him in open amaze, staring at the maid as if he had
> never before seen woman.[2]

Roopmati became his wife, even though he was a Muslim, retaining her title of Rani, or Queen, rather than adopting the Muslim titles of Sultana or Begum. Her smitten husband built her a palace with a separate reservoir nearby, to preserve the view she loved of the river; both of these buildings still stand, as well as many of

Bahadur's other palaces, in reddish sandstone amid the fertile plains. The couple adored each other but Baz spent too much time on love and poetry, instead of defending his kingdom.

Seeing an opportunity, Mughal Emperor Muhammed Akbar the Great sent his stepbrother Adham Khan to conquer Mandu. Unprepared, the city was easily taken and Baz was defeated at the Battle of Sarangpur, fleeing to seek assistance. On occupying the city, Adham was struck by the beauty of Roopmati, desiring her for himself, but she took poison and died to avoid having to submit. The Sultanate of Malwa was abolished and his territories were absorbed into those of the Mughal dynasty. Adham Khan himself was killed the following May by Baz and his allies, allowing him to briefly regain control of the city. But, eventually, in 1570, Baz Bahadur bowed to the inevitable, surrendered to the Mughals and joined their service.

The 1926 translation of Roopmati's story comments that 'she died a martyr to faithfulness and an example to the sect of lovers. Verily women hold a rank in love whereto men cannot attain.'[3] In the intervening centuries, Roopmati has become a figure of Indian legend, largely due to the survival of the manuscript telling her story. Some consider her tale to be fictional, spun out of the existence of a real historical figure but embellished by the poets. Whether Roopmati's tragic fate was true or not, she represents the ideal of devoted love central to Mughal literature, and has become a cultural symbol still remembered today.

99

Elizabeth Bathory

1600

Cachtice Castle, Slovakia

In 1610, a widowed Hungarian noblewoman aged 50 was imprisoned within her own home, accused of being one of the most prolific serial killers of all time. Four of her servants were believed to have assisted her in the torture, mutilation and murder of an estimated 650 young girls, who were sent to the school she had established, over the course of twenty years. Locked away until she died four years later, Elizabeth Bathory has been attracting attention and spawning myths ever since. From burning girls with hot needles to bathing in their blood, she has entered the canon of figures of horror, inspiring writers in that genre to recreate her atrocities, drawing out reputed vampiric tendencies. In recent years, though, while some continue to cast her as a 'female psychopath',[1] revisionist thinkers have questioned whether she really was guilty of such extreme acts, or whether this was a targeted smear upon a powerful woman by her Hapsburg neighbours.

Elizabeth was born in 1560 into the upper aristocracy of Hungary, and was closely related to the king of Poland. She was educated and able to speak a number of languages. Her childhood has been retold in the light of her later crimes, with an emphasis on acts of cruelty perpetrated by family guards, with whom she was supposed to have witnessed executions and participated in satanic rituals. As a sufferer of epilepsy, she may have been subjected to a contemporary cure that required ingredients such as blood or pieces of skull to be rubbed upon her lips, but there is no evidence for this. Further rumours among local people at the time of her imprisonment suggested she bore a child at the age of 13, which either did not survive or was spirited away. She was married two years later to Count Ferenc Nadasdy, who took her surname as the Bathorys were more powerful, and they moved into the hilltop Cachtice Castle, which was among their wedding gifts. After a decade of childlessness, Elizabeth bore at least five children.

In the 1570s, the Hungarians were at war with the Ottoman Empire, having made their first attempt to sack the city back in 1529. In 1578, Ferenc was made captain of the Hungarian Army and was frequently absent, defending the city. Elizabeth was left to run the estates and administration for the seventeen surrounding villages they had inherited, dangerously situated on the main road between Vienna and Cracow. Elizabeth's time was mostly occupied with her social calendar, financial transactions, local elections and managing her household, including either growing or selling marijuana, which features in her surviving letters.[2] She lent considerable sums of money to the state, and negotiated for the return of Ferenc after he had been captured by the Turks. She also wrote in support of a young woman who had been raped, demanding that the man be punished.

Elizabeth was widowed 1604. As a lone woman in such a position, she was far more vulnerable than when she had the authority of her military husband behind her. According to some of her letters, she soon felt overwhelmed by dealing with constant infringements upon her status, including attempts to take over her lands or try and force her to sell her crops at a loss. Simultaneously, she was apparently luring young girls into a finishing school for daughters of the aristocracy, torturing and killing them, disposing of their bodies around the estate. The first rumours about her had already been spread during Ferenc's lifetime, with complaints being made by her enemies in Vienna, and investigations launched. They were pursued between 1602 and 1604, and again in 1610–11, when around 300 witness statements were collected,[3] although it is unclear under what circumstances or incentives they were made. Many of the accounts were exaggerated, based entirely upon hearsay or proven to be false, such as the assertion that she was found covered in blood in the process of torturing a victim, although she was actually arrested while she ate dinner. An irregular trial was held in 1610, during which Elizabeth was not allowed to speak in her defence. She was convicted, meaning that the state no longer had to pay back the huge sums it owed her. Four of her servants were found guilty of assisting her and were executed. Elizabeth spent the last four years of her life locked inside a chamber in Cachtice Castle. She died in 1614 and her final resting place is unknown.

Recent scholarship has revised the nightmarish story of a countess bathed in blood, suggesting that Elizabeth was the victim of a smear campaign by the Hapsburgs, intent upon reducing her power and eradicating their debts. However, the details of her supposed crimes chimed with the rise in popularity of the Gothic genre, perpetuating the countess's grotesque afterlife and giving rise to further speculation. If Elizabeth was entirely innocent of the charges against her, then hers must be one of the most extreme cases of legal injustice against a woman targeted purely for her position.

100

Mary Frith

26 August 1600
Middlesex, England

In the late summer of 1600, a girl of around 16 was brought before the judge of the local assize courts. Her accusers claimed that she had stolen a purse containing 2s and 11d, although the young woman protested her innocence. Fortunately for her, on that day, the judge was disposed to be lenient, a position he may have later come to regret. It was not the first time Mary had been in trouble, and it would not be the last. Within a few years, she would be notorious, finding her way into the works of playwrights, who celebrated her exploits as Moll Cutpurse or The Roaring Girl. Her life was told in a best-selling biography, published three years after her death, from which most of the details of her story survive, but are almost impossible to separate from the accompanying myths.

Mary came from humble roots, born to a shoemaker and his wife in the Barbican district of London. After her frequent arrests for theft, her family tried to reform her by sending her to the New World, but before the ship departed, she jumped overboard, disguised herself as a man, smoking, swearing and roaming the streets. Joining a band of pickpockets, she would cut people's purses from their clothing. Over the coming years she was continually in trouble for robbery, cross-dressing and was wrongly accused of being a prostitute; she was forced to do public penance and branded upon the hand as a sign that she was a thief.

Mary scandalised her contemporaries by breaking so many of the gender taboos. Not only did she regularly dress as a man, speak loudly and boldly, but she was the first woman to smoke a pipe in public, considered to be unladylike and defiant. Mary used male costume as a disguise, to enhance her performances in taverns with her lute, but probably also as her preference. She also appeared on stage at a time when women were excluded from the exclusively male world of the theatre, as the star attraction in plays written for her, such as Nathan Field's *Amends for Ladies: with the merry pranks of Moll-Cutpurse*. Her speech is indeed bold, and challenges stereotypes:

> Z'oones, (God's wounds) does not your husband know my name, if it had been somebody else, I would have called him Cuckoldy slave...
>
> ... I have seen a woman look as modestly as you, and speak as sincerely, and follow the friars as zealously, and she has been as ever found a jumbler as e'er paid for it.[1]

Other female characters in the play, ironically played by men, question her gender:

> I know not what to tear me thee man or woman, for Nature shaming to acknowledge thee either sex; some say thou art a woman, others a man, and many thou art both woman and man but I think rather neither.[2]

Moll also took elements of theatre outside into the streets, riding a performing horse named Maroco, owned by her friend William Banks, from one side of London to another for a bet, blowing a trumpet and waving a banner. Her ride attracted near-riotous attention with Londoners following her, shouting and some calling for her to be pulled from her horse. In 1610, playwright John Day composed *A Book called the Madde Pranckes of Merry Mall of the Bankside, with her Walks in Mans Apparel and to what Purpose*. Illuminating as this text would appear when it comes to understanding Moll's motives, the text unfortunately no longer survives. The following year, Moll acted again in an 'afterpiece' following Middleton and Dekker's *The Roaring Girl* at the Fortune Theatre, making 'lascivious' speeches. She was arrested shortly after because she sat 'upon the public stage in the full view of all the people there present in man's apparel and sang a song and played upon the lute,'[3] and was sent for a brief spell to Bridewell, which was intended to be a correctional centre, not just a prison. She would have spent her days engaged in hard labour like rock-breaking, or being whipped for disobedience.

Released the following winter, she was almost immediately rearrested in St Paul's Cathedral for tucking up her petticoats 'in the fashion of a man'. This time, she was forced to do penance at St Paul's Cross, a popular gathering place where news was spread. As an eyewitness recorded:

> Last Sonday Mall Cut Purse, a notorious baggage (that used to go about in man's apparel and challenged the field of divers gallants) was brought to St Paul's Cross, where she wept bitterly and seemed most penitent, but it is since doubted she was maudlin drunk, being discovered to have tippled three quarts before she came.[4]

Apparently, the crowd gathered to see Moll rather than listen to the sermon of the preacher.

In 1614, Moll sought a little legal protection by marrying Lewknor Markham, perhaps the son of author Gervase, so that she could present herself as a married woman when accused of indelicacy. The marriage is likely to have been one of convenience and no children were born to the couple. In the 1620s, she was apparently procuring male lovers for married women, as one upper-class woman confessed upon her deathbed, but Moll insisted she was not a prostitute and not interested in sex herself. By the early 1640s, in her fifties, she was again in Bridewell, perhaps as the result of having robbed General Fairfax, although this time she was described as having been 'cured' upon her release. Her cure and release may have owed more to the payment of a large fine than any real 'recovery'. Moll died of dropsy in 1659 in Fleet Street. The biography released after her death enshrined her reputation as a female celebrity, with a playful, proud narrative tone.

Moll was undoubtedly a colourful, theatrical character who rejected the law in favour of her own fun. A cross-dresser, whose own sexuality remains ambiguous, possibly an alcoholic, she sought out the limelight on stage and in the street, coming across as a true individual in an era that prescribed so many forms of acceptable behaviour. In many cases, she did break the law through theft, but in others she questioned moral and gender codes, specific to her time. She saw herself, as one critic has observed, not as a transgressor, but 'a mediator between the licit and illicit.'[5] Moll's life, with its emphasis on the roaring, theatrical, disguised individual who conceals criminal activity perfectly typifies the mood of the fin de siècle Elizabethan into Jacobean era, during which the identities of women would undergo further redefinition, perhaps even a step backwards from the recognitions of feminine achievement made under Elizabeth.

101

Women of the Sixteenth Century

So often, history is presented as a series of male events, with women as appendages necessary for the continuation of the dynasty. Sometimes an accident of birth throws them into the limelight as a martyr, a mother or a ruler. What this study of women of the sixteenth century reveals is just how many remarkable, talented, brave women there were, numbering many more than a hundred. The problem was not who to include, but how to justify the exclusion of so many women whose lives deserved to be told. Before I began the selection process, I was aware that it would be difficult to narrow the field down. I thought that limitations of time and space would necessitate hard decisions regarding the final list, but I had no idea of the vast quantities of women I would learn about and the scale of their contributions. It's a complete misnomer that information about women from the past does not survive. Scratch below the surface and there they are, in all their glory. I could easily have filled five volumes.

Even though more history books are, thankfully, focusing upon women's lives, it is still rare for them to look outside Europe for material. I was determined to do this, to explore the wider world outside the walls of Whitehall and Richmond. To help with my selection, I used the metaphor of a tree. The big personalities of the Tudor dynasty, Elizabeth of York, Henry VIII's wives, Mary I, Elizabeth I and other similar names form the trunk, providing a recognisable time-line and springboard into the unknown. From this spring the thick branches, drawing in Scottish, French, Italian, German, Netherlandish and Spanish women, Isabella of Castile, Louise of Savoy, Claude of France, Elizabeth van Culemborg and others, because these were the countries with which England traded, fought and married. All of these women had a direct connection with another positioned on the trunk of the tree. From these wide branches spring thinner ones featuring other fascinating women who contributed to the life of Europe without overlapping directly with Tudor women. It is possible that Elizabeth of York had heard of her Italian contemporary Caterina Sforza, or that Jane Seymour knew of Bona Sforza in Poland or that Elizabeth I knew of the poetry of the French Louise Labé, but they lay beyond those women's immediate orbit.

From these thinner branches spring many leaves. These come from the wider European context, from Russia, Sweden, Slovakia and Turkey, from the lives of women like Anastasia Romanova, Empress of Russia at the time of Elizabeth I's accession, and Roxelana, born in the modern Ukraine, who became mistress of the Sultan in Constantinople around the same time Henry VIII took Mary

Boleyn to his bed. These are European women from further afield, pursing their own lives, such as the Swedish scientist Sophie Brahe, pursuing love in the final decades of the century, and the Danish Margaret Winstar, embroiling herself in scandal at the Scottish court of Anne of Denmark. Among the leaves are bright, dazzling flowers: queens, mistresses, pirates, martyrs and cultural leaders from India and Burma, Chile and America, Africa and Japan. They are comparable with the Tudor women for many reasons. Margaret Beaufort and Queen Idia of Nigeria fought fiercely for their sons; Lady Nata in Japan refused to renounce her faith under pressure, like Mary I and the Native American La Malinche; and from her base in Morocco, Sayyida al Hurra engaged in piracy in the waters around Spain, just as the Irish Grace O'Malley did half a century later.

These hundred women represent the full range when it comes to power. Some were queens by birth, others by marriage; some ruled in the absence of their male relatives or assisted them with either direct advice or gentle suggestion. On the other hand, a number of them are powerless or anonymous. Many are women in a desperate situation, on the verge of death or defeat, or who disappeared without trace. Some were in the hands of the authorities as the result of their beliefs, like the martyrs Margaret Cheney and Elizabeth Barton, or because they had broken the law as Alice Arden and Mary Fitton had. In a few cases, perceptions of these laws have dramatically changed over time, such as with the intriguing Eleno de Céspedes, underlining the huge changes in our approach to personal freedom across five centuries.

A handful of women in the collection are without personal identity. They might represent a goodwife of London, glimpsed in the street by a passing man, or a prostitute hired for the night, or a maid working at the royal court, lacking in name and detail, but representing an almost 'everywoman' character, which could be anyone. Others are glimpsed indirectly, through the lens of art, such as the enigmatic Lisa del Giocondo, who inspired the Mona Lisa, or Penelope Rich, the muse of Elizabethan sonneteer Philip Sidney. Others represent depictions of women that might be disconnected from a specific individual, or else that link is no longer traceable, such as the Money Lender's Wife depicted by Matsys in Antwerp, whose position and expression speaks volumes about her dynamic with her husband. Was she based on a real woman? Did an anonymous Antwerpian model for the artist, or was she a figment of his imagination? Portrayals of iconic female characters like Venus and Medusa, and even of the dramatic character 'Fair Em', continue the dialogue about the male gaze in art and help us better understand sixteenth-century interactions between the genders.

These hundred women pursued a wide, and often unexpected, range of occupations. Some had no choice but to follow a path that unfolded before them, such as Jane Grey with her royal blood and Tognina Gonsalvus, whose hirsute appearance dictated her course. Others chose a path which then spiralled out of their control, as in the case of Cecily Bodenham, the last Abbess of Wilton, and Amye Robsart, who could not have foreseen how her marriage would become crowded when she accepted the hand of Robert Dudley. Fate and coincidence often played a decisive part in their lives. A number of women are included because they happened to be in a certain place at a certain time, and the combination of circumstances derailed an otherwise quiet life; Frau Troffeau dancing through the streets of Strasbourg or Weyn Ockers, caught up in the iconoclastic riots that spread across northern Europe. For many, it was impossible to avoid the seismic changes in religion and culture that straddled the century. Numbers of others pursued the most amazing lives, as innkeepers, midwives, thieves, witches, prophetesses, jesters, pirates, jury members, colonists, cosmeticians, astronomers, advisers and more. They illuminate their age in so many ways that their stories deserve to be researched and told in far greater detail than has been possible in this book. If I have introduced any reader to a new historical woman, or inspired them to go away and learn more, then my work has been a success.

What became clear from studying these women was just how far their gender dictated their treatment. Too frequently they were at the mercy of patriarchal desires, either in terms of lust or financial advantage, and their lack of equality could reduce them to an obstacle, a nuisance or an object of desire to be exploited by unscrupulous men. To be clear, though, not all sixteenth-century men were unscrupulous: many were respectful, loving and kind, but even they existed in a world where stereotypes defined female ability and intelligence. Thus, women were constantly in a position of having to sublimate ambitions and wishes. It was when they found the courage to pursue their desired paths, either on a personal, professional or spiritual level, that they often came into conflict with authority. Some of the luckier ones were supported in their careers by sympathetic male relations and friends, while others had no choice but to step into vacant male roles. Powerful women were characterised as unfeminine and unattractive, and their status could be dependent upon the goodwill of the men around them. Every woman was dependent on a male network of approval, from the church and law to personal relations, which carried great risks, from the dangers of violence, desertion and exposure experienced by mistresses and prostitutes, to the sanctioned murder of queens. Although women were bound by the collective experiences of misogyny and patriarchy, and sympathised with and supported each other's immediate predicaments, this did not translate into any active championing of women's rights. There was no sense of proto-feminism or sisterly solidarity generally. There was no campaigning on behalf of the gender. All too frequently, women's reactions re-enforced their patriarchal constraints, judging and shaming other women for breaking taboos or following their hearts. Nor has history treated them kindly, or even fairly, until recently. As late as the Victorian era, historical women were being judged against standards of acceptable female behaviour. Unfortunately, this judgement lingers in the work of some twenty-first-century historians, perhaps unaware of the connotations of their language or inappropriateness of their comments and assumptions. The battle continues.

Notes

Abbreviations: CSPS (*Calendar of State Papers, Spain*); SLP Henry VIII (*State Letters and Papers Henry VIII*)

1. Anne of Brittany
1. Sanborn, Helen, *Anne of Brittany* (CreateSpace, 2016)
2. Ibid
3. Ibid
4. Ibid
5. Warr, Constance de la, Countess, *A Twice Crowned Queen: Anne of Brittany* (Evelyn Nash, London, 1906)

2. Caterina Sforza
1. Lev, Elizabeth, *Tigress of Forli: The Life of Caterina Sforza* (Heads of Zeus, 2012)
2. Ibid
3. Frieda, Leonie, *The Deadly Sisterhood: A Story of Women, Power and Intrigue in the Italian Renaissance* (Weidenfeld & Nicolson, 2013)
4. Ibid
5. Lev
6. Ibid
7. Ibid
8. Fletcher, Catherine, *The Beauty and the Terror: An Alternative History of the Italian Renaissance* (Bodley Head, 2000)

3. Unnamed Prostitute
1. Burkardi, Johannis, *Liber Notarum*, Volume 2, (ed.) Louis Thuasne (Citta de Castello, 1900)
2. Ibid
3. Ibid
4. Sabatini, Rafael, *Life of Cesare Borgia* (Stanley Paul and Co., 1912)

4. Catherine of Aragon
1. Hall, Edward, *Chronicle* (J. Johnson, London, 1809)
2. Ibid
3. Kipling, Gordon (ed.), *The Receyt of the Ladie Kateryne* (Oxford University Press, 1990)
4. Brewer, J.S. (ed.) *State Letters and Papers Henry VIII*, Volume 4 (London, 1875) pp2572–2585, 5574

5. Margaret Drummond
1. Drummond, Peter R., *Perthshire in Bygone Days: A Hundred Biographical Essays* (London, W.B. Whittingham and Co., 1879)
2. Strickland, Agnes, *Lives of the Queens of Scotland*, Volume 1 (William Blackwood and Sons, 1850)

3. Ibid
4. Letter of Margaret Tudor/Stewart, Cottonian Collection, Caligula, British Library (24 November 1523)
5. Burke, Bernard, Sir, *A Genealogical History of the Peerages of the British Empire* (Harrison, London, 1866)
6. Drummond

6. Elizabeth of York, Queen of England
1. Nicolas N.H. (ed.), *The Privy Purse Expenses of Elizabeth of York* (London, Pickering 1830)
2. Ibid
3. Hall, Edward, *Chronicle* (1548; London, J. Johnson, 1809)

7. Lisa del Giocondo
1. Hales, Dianne, *Mona Lisa: A Life Discovered* (Simon and Schuster, 2014)
2. http://www.ub.uni-heidelberg.de/Englisch/news/monalisa.html
3. Vasari, Giorgio, *Lives of the Artists*, Volume 4 (1550; G.C. Sansoni, Florence, 1879)
4. Hales
5. Ibid

8. Isabella of Castile
1. CSPS, Nov 1504, pp337–342 413
2. Tremlett, Giles, *Isabella of Castile: Europe's First Great Queen* (Bloomsbury, 2017)
3. CSPS, Supplement to Vols 1 and 2, pp 63–9 5
4. Tremlett
5. CSPS, 413

9. Joanna, Queen of Naples
1. CSPS, Volume 1, pp353–361 June 1505 436
2. Ibid
3. Ibid
4. Ibid
5. Ibid

10. Queen Idia
1. www.britishmuseum.org/collection/search?agent=Queen%20Mother%20Idia
2. Ibid
3. Hodgkin, Thomas, *Nigerian Perspectives: An Historical Anthology* (Oxford University Press, 1960).

11. Margaret Beaufort, Countess of Richmond
1. www.cambridgeindependent.co.uk/news/500-year-old-art-mystery-solved-at-st-johns-college-9065909/
2. Hymers, J. (ed.), *Funeral Sermon of Margaret, Countess of Richmond and Derby* (Cambridge University Press, 1840)

12. Women of London
1. Brown, Rawdon (ed.), *Calendar of State Papers Relating to English Affairs in the Archives of Venice, Volume 2, 1509–1519* (London, 1867) pp. 88–94 219

13. Elisabeth van Culemborg, Countess of Hochstrate
1. Tremayne, Eleanor, *The First Governor of the Netherlands: Margaret of Austria* (Methuen, 1908)

2. Tremlett
3. Ibid
4. Tremayne
5. Ives, Eric, *Anne Boleyn* (Blackwell, 1986)
6. Hall

14. Margaret Tudor
1. Dunbar, William, *The Thistle and the Rose* (1503)
2. Strickland, Agnes, *Lives of the Queens of Scotland*, Volume 1 (William Blackwood and Sons, 1850)
3. SLP Henry VIII, Vol 1, pp1012–1023 2248
4. SLP Henry VIII, Vol 1, pp997–1012 2248
5. Strickland
6. Ibid

15. The Money Lender's Wife
1. Redondo, Manuel Santos, 'The Money Changer and His Wife: From Scholastics to Accounting' (University of Madrid e-prints, 2008)

16. Claude, Queen of France
1. Knecht, R.J., *Francis I* (Cambridge University Press, 1981)
2. Ibid
3. Ibid
4. Ibid
5. Ibid
6. Ibid
7. Ibid

17. Joanna, Queen of Castile and Aragon
1. CSPS, Volume 1, Introduction
2. Fox, Julia, *Sister Queens: Katherine of Aragon and Juana, Queen of Castile* (Weidenfeld and Nicolson, 2012)
3. CSPS, Vol 1, pp 141–153
4. CSPS, Vol 1, Intro vii-lxxx
5. Ibid
6. Ibid
7. Brandi, Karl, *The Emperor Charles V* (Germany, 1939; Jonathan Cape, 1968)
8. Ibid
9. CSPS, Vol 1, Supplement pp 153–156
10. CSPS, Vol 1, Intro

18. Frau Troffea
1. Waller, John, *A Time to Dance, A Time to Die* (Icon Books, 2009)
2. Ibid
3. Turner, Osie, *The Dance Manias of the Middle Ages* (The Forlorn Press, 2013)
4. Waller
5. Ibid
6. Turner
7. Shakespeare, William, *Hamlet*
8. Waller
9. www.//patient.info/doctor/sydenhams-chorea

19. La Malinche
1. Cypess, Sandra Messinger, *La Malinche in Mexican Literature: From History to Myth* (University of Texas Press, 2010)
2. Pedrick, Daniel Harvey, 'Reconciling a Myth: In Defence of Dona Marina' in Levesque, Rodrigue, *La Malinche* (Levesque Publications, 2007)
3. Cypess
4. Pedrick
5. Cypess
6. Ibid
7. Romero, Rolando and Harris, Amanda Nolacea, *Feminism, Nation and Myth: La Malinche* (Arte Publico Press, 2005)
8. Ibid

20. Elizabeth 'Bessie' Blount
1. SLP Henry VIII, Vol 2, pp1458–1463
2. Hall
3. Ibid
4. Ibid
5. SLP Henry VIII, Vol 2, pp1371–1383
6. Page, William and Round, J. Horace, *Victoria County History: Essex*, Volume 2 (London, 1907) pp 146–8

21. Roxelana, aka Hurrem Sultan
1. Peirce, Leslie P., *Empress of the East: How a Slave Girl Became Queen of the Ottoman Empire* (New York Basic Books, 2017)
2. Ibid
3. Adler, Philip and Pouwels, Randall L., *World Civilisations* (8th edition, Cengage Learning, 2012)

22. 'Kindness' (Mary Boleyn)
1. Hall
2. SLP Henry VIII, Vol 3, pp1539–1543

23. Louise of Savoy
1. Knecht, R. J., *Francis I* (Cambridge University Press, 1984)
2. Ibid
3. Ibid
4. Ibid
5. Ibid
6. Ibid
7. Ibid

24. Katharina von Bora
1. Recent scholarship has suggested Hirschfeld as an alternative location for Katharina's birth.
2. Roper, Lyndal, *Martin Luther* (Vintage, 2017)
3. Ibid

25. Maid of Honour
1. *A collection of ordinances and regulations for the government of the royal household, made in divers reigns: from King Edward III to King William and Queen Mary, also receipts in ancient cookery* (John Nichols, Society of Antiquities, 1790)

2. Ibid
3. SLP Henry VIII, Vol 4, pp852–878 1939
4. SLP Henry VIII, Vol 4, pp1672–1698, 3748
5. Nichols

26. *Lady with a Squirrel and a Starling*
1. Moyle, Franny, *The King's Painter: The Life and Times of Hans Holbein* (Heads of Zeus, 2021)

27. Properzia de Rossi
1. Vasari, Giorgio, *Lives of the Artists* Part 4 (1568)
2. www.Encyclopedia.com
3. Vasari
4. Ibid
5. Ibid
6. Castiglione, Balthasar, *The Book of the Courtier* (1528)
7. Vasari
8. Encyclopedia.com
9. Strozzi, Lorenzo de Filippo, *Description of the Plague at Florence in the Year 1527*

28. Anne Boleyn
1. SLP Henry VIII, Vol 6, 912
2. Hall
3. SLP, Henry VIII, Vol 6, 653
4. SLP, Henry VIII, Vol 6, 585
5. Ibid
6. Hall
7. Weir, Alison, *The Lady in the Tower* (Jonathan Cape, 2009)

29. Elizabeth Barton
1. Lambarde, William, *A Perambulation of Kent* (1576; reprinted from 1826 Chatham Edition, 1970)
2. Parkin, E.W., 'Cobb's Hall, Aldington and The Holy Maid of Kent' in *Archaeologia Cantiana*.86:15-34 (Kent Archaeology 086 LXXXVI.pdf)
3. SLP Henry VIII, Vol 6, pp613–626 1546
4. Ibid, Vol 6, pp 562–578 1419
5. Ibid, Vol 6, pp418–432 967
6. Ibid, Vol 6, pp578–591 1460
7. Ibid, 1464
8. Parkin

30. Margaret Roper
1. The Bell Tower is the most likely location for More's incarceration, but this has been disputed.
2. Roper, William, *The Life of Thomas More* (Early English Text Society, 1935)
3. Ibid
4. Ibid
5. Ibid
6. Ibid
7. Ibid

31. Maria de Salinas
1. SLP Henry VIII, Vol 10, pp1–12 28
2. SLP Henry VIII, Vol 9, pp350–367 1040
3. SLP Henry VIII, Vol 10, pp1–12 28
4. Ibid
5. SLP Henry VIII, Vol 2 p1471
6. This information is included in the Wikipedia page for Maria, but without a source.
7. CSPS, Vol 5, no 2, pp1–10

32. Women of the Devonshire Manuscript
1. www.bl.uk/collection-items/the-devonshire-manuscript#
2. Different scholarly studies quote between 185 and 191 items in total (Heale, Siemens).
3. bl.uk (as 1)
4. Heale, Elizabeth (ed.), *The Devonshire MS: A Women's Book of Courtly Poetry by Lady Margaret Douglas and Others* (The Toronto Series, 2012)
5. Siemens, Raymond G.; Armstrong, Karin; Crompton, Constance; *A Social Edition of the Devonshire Manuscript* (Arizona Centre for Medieval and Renaissance Studies, 2015)
6. bl.uk (as 1)

33. Margaret Cheney
1. Davies, C.S.L., 'Edward Stafford' in *Oxford Dictionary of National Biography* (2004)
2. SLP Henry VIII, Vol 12, no 1 pp539–557 1207. Of the famous Cheney family, Sir William died in 1487, with his heir Thomas born in 1485. It is impossible that this William was Margaret's husband, given that her reputed father Stafford was then only 9, but William may have fathered a second son named after him in 1486 or 1487.
3. Borman, Tracy, *Thomas Cromwell* (Hodder, 2014)
4. Wriothesley, Charles, *Wriothesley's Chronicle* (Camden, 1875)
5. This was unusual as wife sales were not common practice in England until the seventeenth century.
6. SLP Henry VIII, Vol 12, no 1 pp477–516 1084
7. Ibid
8. Ibid
9. Ibid
10. SLP Henry VIII, Vol 12, no 1 pp539–557 1199
11. Ibid
12. Ibid
13. SLP Henry VIII, Vol 12, no 1 pp557–574 1227
14. SLP Henry VIII, Vol 12, no 1 pp574–584 1270

34. Bona Sforza, Queen of Poland
1. Stone, Daniel Z., *The Polish-Lithuanian State 1386–1795* (University of Washington Press, 2014)
2. Kosior, Katarzyna. 'Bona Sforza and the Realpolitik of Courtly Counsel in Sixteenth-Century Poland-Lituania' in *Queenship and Counsel in Early Modern Europe* (2018)
3. Beem, Charles, *Queenship in Early Modern Europe* (Macmillan, 2018)
4. Kosior
5. Ibid

35. Queen Jane Seymour
1. SLP Henry VIII, Vol 12, Part 1 pp354–66 816
2. Ibid 839
3. See Licence, Amy, *In Bed with the Tudors* (Amberley, 2012) for more.

4. SLP Henry VIII, Vol 12, Part 2 pp 335–345 970
5. Ibid 871

36. Cecily Bodenham
1. Emerson, Kathy Lynn, 'A Who's Who of Tudor Women' (www.tudorwomen.com)
2. Pugh, R.B. and Crittall, Elizabeth (eds.) *Victoria County History: Wiltshire*, Volume 3 (London, 1956)
3. SLP Henry VIII, Vol 9, pp 81–96
4. SLP Henry VIII, Vol 14, no 1 pp 226–239
5. Ibid
6. Pugh et al
7. SLP Henry VIII Vol 14 Part 1 pp 239–264

37. Anne of Cleves
1. Hall
2. Ibid
3. Byrne
4. Hall
5. Wriothesley
6. Warnicke, Retha M., *The Marrying of Anne of Cleves* (Cambridge University Press, 2000)
7. Hall
8. Warnicke
9. Hall
10. Ibid
11. Ibid
12. Ibid
13. Ibid

38. Honor Grenville, Lady Lisle
1. Honor is first listed as Lady Lisle among the attendants upon Anne Boleyn to Calais in October 1532.
2. Byrne, Muriel St Clare, *The Lisle Letters* (Abridged version, Penguin, 1985)
3. Ibid
4. Ibid
5. Based on an estimate of his birth occurring in the late 1460s or early 1470s.

39. Sayyida al Hurra
1. Her first name is also given as Lalla. Aisha is the name used in Duncombe, Laura Sook, *Pirate Women* (Chicago Review Press, 2017)
2. Ibid
3. Ibid
4. Mernissi, Fatima, *The Forgotten Queens of Islam* (Polity Press, 1993)
5. Duncombe

40. Margaret Pole, Countess of Salisbury
1. Kelly, Blanche M., 'Blessed Margaret Pole' in *The Catholic Encyclopaedia* (1913)
2. SLP Henry VIII, Vol 16, pp429–437
3. Ibid pp409–429
4. Kelly
5. SLP Henry VIII, Vol 16, pp409–429
6. Kelly

41. Jane Boleyn, Lady Rochford
1. SLP Henry VIII, Vol 16, pp613–629 1337
2. Ibid 1338
3. Ibid 1339
4. Ibid
5. Ibid 1340

42. Lady Nata, or Otomo-Nata 'Jezebel'
1. https://historyofjapan.co.uk/2021/03/21/the-road-to-kyoto

43. Mildred Cooke
1. Allen, Gemma, *The Cooke Sisters: Education, Piety and Politics in Early Modern England* (Manchester University Press, 2013)
2. SLP Henry VIII, Vol 20, no 2, grants 910
3. Page, William, *Victoria County History: Rutland*, Volume 2 (London, 1908)
4. Allen
5. Lawrence-Mathers, Anne and Philippa Hardman, *Women and Writing c.1340–c.1650: The Domestication of Print Culture* (Woodbridge, Suffolk: Boydell and Brewer, 2010)
6. Ibid
7. Ibid
8. Beilin, Elaine V., *Ashgate Critical Essays on Women Writers in England 1550–1700 Vol 1: Early Tudor Women Writers* (Routledge, 2017)
9. Ibid
10. Ibid
11. Allen
12. Ibid

45. Anne Askew
1. Beilin, Elaine V. (ed.), *The Examinations of Anne Askew* (Oxford University Press, 1996)
2. SLP Henry VIII, Vol 2, no 1 pp165–179
3. Ibid
4. Ibid
5. SLP Henry VIII, Vol 21, no 1 pp582
6. Ibid

46. Ellen Sadler
1. SLP Henry VIII, Vol 20, no 2 pp301
2. Ibid 697

47. Levina Teerlinc
1. SLP Henry VIII, Vol 21, no 2 pp203–248
2. V & A exhibition, 1983
3. Coomb, Katherine and Derbyshire, Alan, 'Nicholas Hilliard's Workshop Practice Reconsidered' in T. Cooper et al (eds.), *Painting Britain 1500–1630: Production, Influences and Patronage* (Oxford, 2015), pp241–251

48. Elizabeth 'Bess' Holland
1. SLP Henry VIII Vol 21 no 2 Preface
2. Ibid
3. Ibid

49. Catherine de' Medici
1. Knecht, R.J., *Francis I*
2. Frieda, Leonie, *The Deadly Sisterhood: A Story of Women, Power and Intrigue in the Italian Renaissance* (Weidenfeld and Nicolson, 2013)
3. https://www.bl.uk/treasures/festivalbooks/BookDetails.aspx?strFest=0012

51. Katherine 'Kat' Ashley
1. Norton, Elizabeth, *The Temptation of Elizabeth Tudor* (Heads of Zeus, 2016)
2. Ibid
3. Ibid
4. Ibid

52. Beatriz de Luna, aka Gracia Mendes Nasi
1. Such as the Wikipedia entry!
2. Birnbaum, Marianna D., *The Long Journey of Gracia Mendes* (Central European Press 2003)
3. Ibid
4. Bodian, Miriam, *Dona Gracia Nasi The Shalvi/Hyman Encyclopaedia of Jewishness*: Jewish Women's Archive.
5. Published in 1553, Ferrara (unknown publisher).

53. Alice Arden
1. *The History and Topographical Survey of the County of Kent* Vol 6 (W. Bristow, Canterbury, 1798)
2. Ibid
3. Anonymous Play and Newgate Calendar
4. Anon, *The Tragedie of Arden of Faversham and Blackwall* (1592) Act 1, lines 20–21
5. English Broadside Ballad Archive, 30458
6. Ibid
7. Ibid

54. Anne Seymour, Duchess of Somerset
1. Lansdowne MS no 113 (32)
2. Multiple authors repeat this: Weir, Warnicke, Fraser
3. Matzat, Don, *Katherine Parr: Opportunist, Queen, Reformer: A Theological Perspective.* (Amberley, 2020)
4. Franklin-Harkrider, Melissa, *Women, Reformation and Community in Early Modern England* (Boydell, 2008)
5. North, Jonathan (ed.), *The Diary of Edward VI 1547–1553* (Ravenhall, 2005)
6. Lansdowne MS No 113 (32)

55. Jane Grey
1. Tallis, Nicola, *Crown of Blood: The Deadly Inheritance of Lady Jane Grey* (Michael O'Mara, 2016)

56. Mary I
1. Porter, Linda, *Mary Tudor: The First Queen* (Little Brown, 2010)
2. Ibid
3. Edwards, John, *Mary I: England's Catholic Queen* (Yale University Press, 2011)
4. Ibid
5. Nichols, John Gough, *London Pageants* (J.B. Nichols, 1831)
6. Ibid
7. Ibid

57. Louise Labé
1. James, Ann Rosalind, *The Currency of Eros: Women's Love Lyrics in Europe 1540–1620* (Indiana University Press, 1990)

58. Susan Clarencieux
1. Samson, Alexander, *Mary and Philip: The Marriage of Tudor England and Habsburg Spain* (Manchester University Press, 2020)
2. CSPS, Vol 12, pp179–180
3. CSPS, Vol 13, pp55–71
4. Samson
5. Whitelock, Anna, *Mary Tudor: England's First Queen* (Bloomsbury, 2010)
6. CSPS, Preface
7. Ibid
8. Porter, Linda, *Mary Tudor: The First Queen* (Little Brown, 2010)

60. Florence Wadham
1. Delderfield, Eric, *West Country Historic Houses and their Families* (Newton Abbot, 1968)

61. Marian Martyrs
1. Some sources claim the burnings took place on 15 November, but 10 November is widely accepted in many academic publications
2. Foxe, John, *Book of Martyrs*
3. Doran, Susan and Freeman, Thomas S. (eds.), *Old and New Perspectives* (Palgrave Macmillan, 2011)
4. Foxe
5. Ibid
6. Duffy, Eamon, *The Church of Mary Tudor* (Taylor and Francis, 2016)

62. Elizabeth Tudor
1. Hayward, John, *Annals Camden Society* (1840)

63. Anastasia Romanova
1. Payne, Robert and Romanoff, Nikita, *Ivan the Terrible* (Cooper Square Press, 1975)
2. Ibid
3. Madariga, Isabel de, *Ivan the Terrible* (Yale University Press, 2006)

64. Amye Robsart
1. Skidmore, Chris, *Death and the Virgin* (Weidenfeld and Nicolson, 2010)

65. Isabella Cortese
1. Robin, Diana, Larsen, Anne R. and Levin, Carole (eds.), *Encyclopaedia of Women in the Renaissance: Italy, France and England* (ABC-Chio Inc., 2007)
2. Ray, Meredith K., *Daughters of Alchemy: Women and Scientific Culture in Early Modern Italy* (Harvard University Press, 2015)
3. Ibid
4. Ibid

66. Aura Soltana
1. Andrea, Bernadette, 'The Tartar Girl, The Persian Princess, And Early Modern English Women's Authorship From Elizabeth I To Mary Wroth' in Gilleir, Anke; Montoya, Alicia; and van Dijk, Suzan (eds.), *Women Writing Back/Writing Women Back: Transnational Perspectives from the Late Middle Ages to the Dawn of the Modern Era* (Brill, 2010)

67. Isabelle de Limeuil
1. Brantôme, Pierre de, *The Book of Ladies* (Hardy, Pratt and Co., Boston, 1899)
2. Ibid
3. Ibid
4. Butterworth, Emily, *The Unbridled Tongue: Babble and Gossip in Renaissance France*. (Oxford University Press, 2016)

69. Weyn Ockers
1. Sanders, Nicolas, *On the Origin and Progression of the English Schism* (1571)
2. Brandt, Georg, *Collection* (London, 1720)

70. Elizabeth Talbot 'Bess' of Hardwick
1. Guy, John, *The Life of Mary, Queen of Scots* (Fourth Estate, 2004)
2. Ibid
3. Ibid

73. Marguerite of Valois
1. *Memoirs of Marguerite de Valois, Queen of Navarre, written by herself* (L.C. Page and Co., Boston, 1899)
2. Ibid
3. Ibid
4. Ibid
5. Ibid

74. Sophie Brahe
1. Heiberg, Johan Ludvig, *Sophie Brahe* (Kjobenhavn, 1861)
2. Ibid

77. St Teresa of Avila
1. Barton, Marcella B., 'Saint Teresa of Avila: Did she have Epilepsy?' in *Catholic Historical Review* LXVIII (4)
2. Hsia, R Po-Chia, *A Companion to the Reformation World* (Wiley, 2004)
3. Lewis, David (ed.), *The Life of St Teresa of Jesus* (Burns, Oates and Co., London, 1870)

78. Jury of Matrons
1. Cockburn, J.S. (ed.), *Calendar of Assize Records. Kent Indictments, Elizabeth I* (HMSO, 1979)

79. Ursula Kemp
1. Summers, Montague, *A Popular History of Witchcraft* Volume 8 (1937; Routledge, 2011)
2. Clark, Stuart, *Thinking with Demons: The Idea of Witchcraft in Early Modern Europe* (Oxford University Press, 1999)
3. Durston, Gregory, *Crimem Exceptum: The English Witch Prosecution in Context* (Waterside Press, 2019)
4. Ibid

81. Penelope Rich
1. Sidney, Philip, *On Defense of Poesie: Astrophil and Stella* (Orion, 1997)
2. Ibid
3. Ibid

82. Mary Fillis
1. Kauffman, Miranda, *Black Tudors* (Oneworld, 2017)
2. Ibid
3. Ibid
4. Ibid

83. Jane Dee
1. Dee, John, *The Diary of John Dee*, (ed.) James Orchard Halliwell (1842)
2. Aubrey, John, *Brief Lives*, (Clarendon, Oxford, 1898)
3. Dee
4. Ibid
5. Ibid
6. Ibid

85. Eleanor Dare
1. Miller, Lee, *Roanoke: Solving the Riddle of England's Lost Colony* (Random House, 2015)
2. Ibid
3. Ibid

87. Elena/Eleno de Céspedes
1. Velasco, Sherry Marie, *Lesbians in Early Modern Spain* (Vanderbilt University Press, 2011)
2. Ibid
3. Delgado, Maria Jose and Dyer, Abigail, *Lesbianism and Homosexuality in Early Modern Spain* (Vanderbilt, 2011)
4. Soyer, Francois, *Ambiguous Gender in Early Modern Spain* (Brill, 2012)
5. Ibid
6. Ibid
7. Ibid
8. Velasco
9. Soyer
10. Vollendorf, Lisa, *The Lives of Women: A New History of Inquisitional Spain* (Vanderbilt University Press, 2005)
11. Ibid
12. Soyer
13. Delgado
14. Soyer

88. Tognina Gonsalvus
1. 'The Real Beauty and the Beast.' Smithsonian Channel, 2014.
2. https://journals.openedition.org/apparences/1283
3. Ulissa Aldrovandi, *Monstrorum Historia*, (Bologna: Typic Nicolai Tebaldini, 1642; rpt. Paris: Belles lettres, 2002), p.18.

89. 'Fair 'Em' the Miller's daughter'
1. *Fair Em* (listed as by Shakespeare) Adam, Tony and Widger, David (ed.), Project Gutenberg (e-book no. 5137
2. Ibid
3. Ibid

90. Mistress Minx
1. Scott, A.F., *Everyone a Witness: The Tudor Age* (White Lion Publishers, 1975)

91. Elizabeth 'Bess' Throckmorton
1. Whitelock, Anna, *Elizabeth's Bedfellows: An Intimate History of the Queen's Court* (Bloomsbury, 2013)

92. Margaret Winstar
1. Lyle, Emily, *Scottish Ballads* (Canongate Books, 1994)

93. Eleanor Bull
1. Nicholl, Charles, *The Reckoning* (Jonathan Cape, 1992)

94. Grace O'Malley
1. Cook, Judith, *Pirate Queen: The Life of Grace O'Malley* (Mercier Press, 2004)
2. Chambers, Anne, *Grace O'Malley: The Biography of Ireland's Pirate Queen* (MJF Books, 2003)
3. Ibid

95. Mathurine de Vallois
1. Doran, John, *The History of Court Fools* (Bentley, London, 1858)

97. Louise Boursier
1. Licence, Amy, *In Bed with the Tudors* (Amberley, 2012)
2. Ibid
3. Dunn, P.M., 'Louise Bourgeois: Perinatal Lessons from the Past' in *BMJ Journals: ADC Fetal and Neonatal*, Vol 89, Issue 2
4. Bourgeois, Louise, *Diverse Observations*, trans. Stephanie O'Hara, (ed.) Alison Klairmont Lingo (Iter Press, Ontario, 2017)
5. Dunn

98. Rani Roopmati
1. Turkoman. trans. *The Lady of the Lotus* (1926)
2. Ibid
3. Ibid

99. Elizabeth Bathory
1. Penrose, Valentine, *The Bloody Countess* (Elektron, 2013)
2. Craft, Kimberley L., *The Private Letters of Countess Erszebet Bathory* (CreateSpace, 2011)
3. Ibid

100. Mary Frith
1. Field, Nathan, *Amends for Ladies* (John Okes, London, 1639)
2. Ibid
3. Drouet, Pascale, 'Appropriating a Famous Female Offender: Mary Frith 1584?–1659 alias Moll Cut-Purse' in Hillman, Richard and Ruberry-Blanc, Pauline (eds.), *Female Transgression in Early Modern Britain: Literary and Historical Explorations* (Routledge, 2016)
4. Ibid
5. Orgel, Stephen, *Impersonations: The Performance of Gender in Shakespeare's England* (Cambridge University Press, 1996)

Bibliography

A collection of ordinances and regulations for the government of the royal household, made in divers reigns: from King Edward III to King William and Queen Mary, also receipts in ancient cookery (John Nichols, Society of Antiquities, 1790)

Adler, Philip and Pouwels, Randall L., *World Civilisations* (8th edition, Cengage Learning, 2012)

Allen, Gemma, *The Cooke Sisters: Education, Piety and Politics in Early Modern England* (Manchester University Press, 2013)

Aubrey, John, *Brief Lives*, (ed.) Levy (1693; F.J Albion, 1984)

Beem, Charles, *Queenship in Early Modern Europe* (Macmillan, 2018)

Beilin, Elaine V., *Ashgate Critical Essays on Women Writers in England 1550–1700 Vol 1: Early Tudor Women Writers* (Routledge, 2017)

Bergenroth, G.A. (ed.), *Calendar of State Papers, Spain*, Volume 1 (London, 1862)

Beilin, Elaine V., (ed.), *The Examinations of Anne Askew* (Oxford University Press, 1996)

Birnbaum, Marianna D., *The Long Journey of Gracia Mendes* (Central European Press, 2003)

Borman, Tracy, *Thomas Cromwell* (Hodder, 2014)

Bourgeois, Louise, *Diverse Observations*, trans. Stephanie O'Hara, (Ed.) Alison Klairmont Lingo (Iter Press, Ontario, 2017)

Brandi, Karl, *The Emperor Charles V* (Germany, 1939; Jonathan Cape, 1968)

Brandt, Georg, *Collection* (London, 1720)

Brantôme, Pierre de, *The Book of Ladies* (Hardy, Pratt and Co., Boston, 1899)

Burkardi, Johannis, *Liber Notarum*, Volume 2, (ed.) Louis Thuasne (Citta de Castello, 1900)

Burke, Bernard, Sir, *A Genealogical History of the Peerages of the British Empire* (Harrison, London, 1866)

Butterworth, Emily, *The Unbridled Tongue: Babble and Gossip in Renaissance France* (Oxford University Press, 2016)

Byrne, Muriel St Clare, *The Lisle Letters* (Abridged version, Penguin, 1985)

Castiglione, Balthasar, *The Book of the Courtier* (1528)

Chambers, Anne, *Grace O'Malley: The Biography of Ireland's Pirate Queen* (MJF Books, 2003)

Clark, Stuart, *Thinking with Demons: The Idea of Witchcraft in Early Modern Europe* (Oxford University Press, 1999)

Cook, Judith, *Pirate Queen: The Life of Grace O'Malley* (Mercier Press, 2004)

Coomb, Katherine and Derbyshire, Alan, 'Nicholas Hilliard's Workshop Practice Reconsidered' in T. Cooper et al (eds.), *Painting Britain 1500–1630: Production, Influences and Patronage* (Oxford, 2015), pp241–251

Cypess, Sandra Messinger, *La Malinche in Mexican Literature: From History to Myth* (University of Texas Press, 2010)

Delderfield, Eric, *West Country Historic Houses and their Families* (Newton Abbot, 1968)

Delgado, Maria Jose and Dyer, Abigail, *Lesbianism and Homosexuality in Early Modern Spain* (Vanderbilt, 2011)

Doran, John Dr., *The History of Court Fools* (Bentley, London 1858)

Doran, Susan and Freeman, Thomas S. (eds.), *Old and New Perspectives* (Palgrave Macmillan, 2011)

Drummond, Peter R., *Perthshire in Bygone Days: A Hundred Biographical Essays* (London, W.B. Whittingham and Co., 1879)

Drummond, William, 'History of the Drummond Family Part xvii' in *Histories of Noble British Families* (William Pickering, London, 1846), p10

Drouet, Pascale, 'Appropriating a Famous Female Offender: Mary Frith 1584?–1659 alias Moll Cut-Purse' in Hillman, Richard and Ruberry-Blanc, Pauline (eds.), *Female Transgression in Early Modern Britain: Literary and Historical Explorations* (Routledge, 2016)

Duffy, Eamon, *The Church of Mary Tudor* (Taylor and Francis, 2016)

Duncombe, Laura Sook, *Pirate Women* (Chicago Review Press, 2017)

Dunn, P.M., 'Louise Bourgeois: Perinatal Lessons from the Past' in *BMJ Journals: ADC Fetal and Neonatal*, Vol 89, Issue 2

Durston, Gregory, *Crimem Exceptum: The English Witch Prosecution in Context* (Waterside Press, 2019)

Edwards, John, *Mary I: England's Catholic Queen* (Yale University Press, 2011)

Emerson, Kathy Lynn, 'A Who's Who of Tudor Women' (www.tudorwomen.com)

Fletcher, Catherine, *The Beauty and the Terror: An Alternative History of the Italian Renaissance* (Bodley Head, 2000)

Fox, Julia, *Sister Queens: Katherine of Aragon and Juana, Queen of Castile* (Weidenfeld & Nicolson, 2012)

Frieda, Leonie, *The Deadly Sisterhood: A Story of Women, Power and Intrigue in the Italian Renaissance* (Weidenfeld & Nicolson, 2013)

Guy, John, *The Life of Mary, Queen of Scots* (Fourth Estate, 2004)

Hales, Dianne, *Mona Lisa: A Life Discovered* (Simon and Schuster, 2014)

Hall, Edward, *Chronicle* (J. Johnson, London, 1809)

Heale, Elizabeth (ed.), *The Devonshire MS: A Women's Book of Courtly Poetry by Lady Margaret Douglas and Others* (The Toronto Series, 2012)

Heiberg, Johan Ludvig, *Sophie Brahe* (Kjobenhavn, 1861)

Hymers, J. (ed.), *Funeral Sermon of Margaret, Countess of Richmond and Derby* (Cambridge University Press, 1840)

Ives, Eric, *Anne Boleyn* (Blackwell, 1986)

James, Ann Rosalind, *The Currency of Eros: Women's Love Lyrics in Europe 1540–1620* (Indiana University Press, 1990)

Kauffman, Miranda, *Black Tudors* (Oneworld, 2017)

Kelly, Blanche M., 'Blessed Margaret Pole' in *The Catholic Encyclopaedia* (1913)

Kipling, Gordon (ed.), *The Receyt of the Ladie Kateryne* (Oxford University Press, 1990)

Knecht, R.J., *Francis I* (Cambridge University Press, 1981)

Kosior, Katarzyna, 'Bona Sforza and the Realpolitik of Courtly Counsel in Sixteenth-Century Poland-Lituania' in *Queenship and Counsel in Early Modern Europe* (2018)

Lambarde, William, *A Perambulation of Kent* (1576; reprinted from 1826 Chatham Edition, 1970)

Lawrence-Mathers, Anne and Philippa Hardman, *Women and Writing c.1340 – c.1650: The Domestication of Print Culture* (Woodbridge, Suffolk: Boydell and Brewer, 2010)

Letter of Margaret Tudor/Stewart, Cottonian Collection, Caligula, British Library (24 November 1523)

Lev, Elizabeth, *Tigress of Forli: The Life of Caterina Sforza* (Heads of Zeus, 2012)

Mernissi, Fatima, *The Forgotten Queens of Islam* (Polity Press, 1993)

Moyle, Franny, *The King's Painter: The Life and Times of Hans Holbein* (Heads of Zeus, 2021)

Nicholl, Charles, *The Reckoning* (Jonathan Cape, 1992)

Nicolas N.H. (ed.), *The Privy Purse Expenses of Elizabeth of York* (Pickering, London, 1830)

Nichols, John Gough, *London Pageants* (J.B. Nichols, 1831)

Norton, Elizabeth, *The Temptation of Elizabeth Tudor* (Heads of Zeus, 2016)

Page, William and Round, J. Horace (eds.), *Victoria County History: Essex*, Volume 2 (London, 1907) pp 146–8
Page, William, *Victoria County History: Rutland*, Volume 2 (London, 1908)
Pedrick, Daniel Harvey, 'Reconciling a Myth: In Defence of Dona Marina' in Levesque, Rodrigue, *La Malinche* (Levesque Publications, 2007)
Peirce, Leslie P., *Empress of the East: How a Slave Girl Became Queen of the Ottoman Empire* (New York Basic Books, 2017)
Pietikainen, Petteri, *Madness: A History* (Routledge, 2015)
Porter, Linda, *Mary Tudor: The First Queen* (Little Brown, 2010)
Pugh, R.B. and Crittall, Elizabeth (eds.), *Victoria County History: Wiltshire*, Volume 3 (London, 1956)
Ray, Meredith K., *Daughters of Alchemy: Women and Scientific Culture in Early Modern Italy* (Harvard University Press, 2015)
Redondo, Manuel Santos, 'The Money Changer and His Wife: From Scholastics to Accounting' (University of Madrid e-prints, 2008)
Robin, Diana, Larsen, Anne R., and Levin, Carole (eds.), *Encyclopaedia of Women in the Renaissance: Italy, France and England* (ABC-Chio Inc., 2007)
Romero, Rolando and Harris, Amanda Nolacea, *Feminism, Nation and Myth: La Malinche* (Arte Publico Press, 2005)
Roper, Lyndal, *Martin Luther* (Vintage, 2017)
Roper, William, *The Life of Thomas More* (Early English Text Society, 1935)
Rubin, Nancy, *Isabella of Castile: The First Renaissance Queen* (St Martin's Press, 1991)
Sabatini, Rafael, *Life of Cesare Borgia* (Stanley Paul and Co., 1912)
Samson, Alexander, *Mary and Philip: The Marriage of Tudor England and Habsburg Spain* (Manchester University Press, 2020)
Sanborn, Helen, *Anne of Brittany* (CreateSpace, 2016)
Sanders, Nicolas, *On the Origin and Progression of the English Schism* (Reims, 1585)
Scott, A.F., *Everyone a Witness: The Tudor Age* (White Lion Publishers, 1975)
Sidney, Philip, *On Defense of Poesie: Astrophil and Stella* (Orion, 1997)
Siemens, Raymond G.; Armstrong, Karin; Crompton, Constance; *A Social Edition of the Devonshire Manuscript* (Arizona Center for Medieval and Renaissance Studies, 2015)
Soyer, Francois, *Ambiguous Gender in Early Modern Spain* (Brill, 2012)
Stone, Daniel Z., *The Polish-Lithuanian State 1386–1795* (University of Washington Press, 2014)
Strickland, Agnes, *Lives of the Queens of Scotland*, Volume 1 (William Blackwood and Sons, 1850)
Summers, Montague, *A Popular History of Witchcraft*, Volume 8 (1937; Routledge, 2011)
Tallis, Nicola, *Crown of Blood: The Deadly Inheritance of Lady Jane Grey* (Michael O'Mara, 2016)
Tremlett, Giles, *Isabella of Castile: Europe's First Great Queen* (Bloomsbury, 2017)
Turner, Osie, *The Dance Manias of the Middle Ages* (The Forlorn Press, 2013)
Tyler, Royall (ed.), *Calendar of State Papers, Spain*, Volumes 12 and 13 (HMSO, 1949 and 1954)
Vasari, Giorgio, *Lives of the Artists*, Volume 4 (1550; G.C. Sansoni, Florence, 1879)
Velasco, Sherry Marie, *Lesbians in Early Modern Spain* (Vanderbilt University Press, 2011)
Vollendorf, Lisa, *The Lives of Women: A New History of Inquisitional Spain* (Vanderbilt University Press, 2005)
Waller, John, *A Time to Dance, A Time to Die* (Icon Books, 2009)
Warnicke, Retha M., *The Marrying of Anne of Cleves* (Cambridge University Press, 2000)
Warr, Constance de la, Countess, *A Twice Crowned Queen: Anne of Brittany* (Evelyn Nash, London, 1906)
Weir, Alison, *Mary, Queen of Scots* (Jonathan Cape, 2003)
Whitelock, Anna, *Mary Tudor: England's First Queen* (Bloomsbury, 2010)
Wriothesley, Charles, *Wriothesley's Chronicle* (Camden, 1875)

Acknowledgements

Many thanks go to Nicola, Lucy, Laura, Michelle and the team at Pen and Sword. Thanks also to my husband Tom and my wonderful sons, Rufus and Robin, to my mother Susan, my godmother, Lady Susan and my dear friend Anne Marie for their constant love and support. Thank you to all my friends, for their belief in me, their interest in my work and their kind encouragement. They know who they are. I am also very grateful to my colleagues and friends at work who have been so supportive, and to my amazing, inspiring pupils. Finally, a huge thank you to all my readers, whose kind words have reached me and been so very much appreciated.